DANGEROUS WIVES AND SACRED SISTERS

Dangerous Wives and Sacred Sisters

SOCIAL AND SYMBOLIC ROLES
OF HIGH-CASTE WOMEN IN NEPAL

Lynn Bennett

COLUMBIA UNIVERSITY PRESS
NEW YORK

The Andrew W. Mellon Foundation, through a special grant, has assisted the Press in publishing this volume.

Printed in the United States of America
Columbia University Press
New York   Oxford

Library of Congress Cataloging in Publication Data

Bennett, Lynn, 1945–
    Dangerous wives and sacred sisters.

    Bibliography: p.
    Includes index.
    1. Women—Nepal—Social conditions.   2. Women—
Nepal—Religious life.   3. Sex role—Nepal.
4. Kinship—Nepal.   5. Goddesses—Nepal.   I. Title.
HQ1735.9.B46   1983   305.4'2'095496   83-7528
ISBN 0-231-04664-2
ISBN 0-231-04665-0 (pbk.)
c 10 9 8 7 6 5 4 3 2

Contents

Preface   vii

  1. Village and Family: The Socioeconomic Context of
     Women's Lives   1

  2. Religion: Conceptual Framework and Some Central
     Oppositions   34

  3. Life-Cycle Rites for the Householder's Path   52

  4. Complementary Kinship Structures: The Dual Status
     of Women   124

  5. Status and Strategies: Patrifocal and Filiafocal Di-
     mensions in a Woman's Life   165

  6. Female Sexuality and the Patrifocal/Filiafocal Op-
     position   214

  7. The Goddess: Mythic Resolutions to the Problem
     of Women and Women's Problems   261

  8. Symbolic Mediation and Individual Choice   309

Glossary   319

Bibliography   339

Index   343

Preface

This study explores the ways in which the social and symbolic roles of high caste Nepali women combine to define their position in patrilineal Hindu society. Two ranges of analysis are included within the scope of my study. The first is an interpretation of the Hindu perception of women in general, as this is articulated in the social, mythic, and ritual structures of a particular Hindu community. The second concentrates on how individual women in this community interpret these structures and manipulate them in specific situations to achieve their own goals. I try to show how women's social roles in Hindu kinship and family structure are related to their symbolic roles in the ritual and mythic structures of Hinduism—in Geertz's (1965) terminology, the relationships between social phenomena and ideological structures.[1]

Hindu women cannot be understood in isolation from Hindu culture—that "system of meanings" which is so important in defining how women perceive the world and their proper place in it, and how they are perceived by others. In other words, the gender system which shapes the particular meanings which Hindus attach to male and female and to sexuality and reproduction is embedded deeply within the culture as a whole—its symbolic idiom, its value system, its social and economic structures (Ortner and Whitehead 1981). Thus, the first three chapters of this book and part of the fourth establish the social, ritual, and ideological framework of Hindu culture. These chapters introduce certain central and interrelated Hindu themes that recur throughout the book. In chapter 2, sets of mutually reinforcing oppositions—between purity and pollution, rebirth and release, and between the religious status of the householder and the ascetic—are presented as part of the conceptual framework of village Hinduism. Chapter 3 explores these oppositions as they are expressed in the major life-cycle rituals.

The Hindu view of woman grows out of what I call the "ideology of the patriline." The agnatic kin group, whose members accept the authority of the senior male and owe each other loyalty as well as economic and ritual support, is central to Hindu society. And a set of cultural ideas that attests to the strength and importance of the patriline is evident on many levels of analysis—economic, legal, political, and religious. But regardless of the form through which it is expressed, Hindu patrilineal ideology entails a deep ambivalence toward women.

Initial consideration of the patriline as a social institution begins in chapter 1. Chapters 2 and 3 develop the religious significance of patrilineal organization in the Hindu context. The reader particularly interested in learning about Hindu *women* may wish to pass over chapter 3, as the rituals it describes are predominantly focused on males and on articulating the key social relations and obligations entailed by the dominant patrilineal organization of society.

In chapter 4, where Brahman-Chetri kinship is discussed in some detail, the implications of Hindu patrilineal ideology for the position of women begin to emerge. An analysis of the differential status accorded women in their affinal and consanguineal roles gives strikingly clear expression to their ambiguous position: two opposed but complementary modes of kinship relation are revealed which I have called the patrifocal and the filiafocal models. Each model is based on a different cluster of values and concerns, and each posits a radically different view of women. In the dominant patrifocal system, the predominant theme is duty and obedience, and each individual is ranked according to the two principles of male superiority and respect for age. In this system affinal women rank beneath everyone else in their husband's home. But within the alternative structure of filiafocal relations, the sacredness of consanguineal women is stressed. Here, the patrifocal hierarchy is reversed: female ranks over male and youth over age.

The status of women in both patrifocal and filiafocal models is related to their relative ritual purity—i.e., their purity with respect to affinal and consanguineal men. Thus, the low status allotted affinal women in the patrifocal model is explained in terms of the inferior ritual purity of these women. This notion is reinforced by the Hindu view of sexuality, which sees in-volvement in procreation as polluting and celibacy as pure. The affinal woman, involved as she is in her reproductive roles, is linked with sexuality and pollution. Hence the strict rules governing her behavior in her family of marriage are justified as a means of controlling her sexuality.

By contrast, women enjoy high status in their filiafocal relationships because of their *superior* ritual purity within these relationships. Consanguineal women, through certain rituals which symbolically shield their sexuality from filiafocally related males, remain categorically "pure." As such, they are worthy of both the high status and the relative freedom they are allowed in their natal home. The greater concern with maintaining control over the sexuality of affinal women is clearly related to the fact that they become members of their husband's lineage and, more important, the producers of its next generation, while consanguineal women are transferred at marriage from their natal lineage and obviously have no part in its biological continuation.

Chapter 5 examines the opposing patrifocal and filiafocal roles of women and explores the ways in which this opposition affects their lives. It is here that I move from the consideration of Hindu kinship and family organization as abstract structures to the investigation of how individuals in particular situations adjust to and utilize these structures for their own ends.

With chapter 6 I take up the symbolic—or, one could say, religious—dimensions of the Hindu ambivalence toward women. Through a study of certain key mythic and ritual complexes involving female sexuality, I uncover some of the contradictory sentiments and religious ideas that surround women in Hindu culture. Finally, I attempt to show how these contradictory meanings are related to women's contrasting patrifocal and filiafocal social roles. Fundamental conceptual oppositions which were considered in chapter 2—e.g., purity versus pollution and asceticism versus fertility—are reconsidered as they are articulated in the symbolic conception of the female body and female reproductive processes.

In chapter 7 I approach the symbolic role of women from the perspective of mythic woman—the goddess. Through a structural analysis of two literary texts, the *Candi Path* and the *Swasthani Vrata Katha*, I explore the contradictory nature of the goddess (Devi) with her gentle and terrible aspects. I interpret

Devi as a core symbol that both expresses key oppositions within Hindu culture and reinforces the social roles of actual women. The fact that village men are more ritually involved with the terrible aspect of the goddess and women with the gentle aspect is also suggestive of a discrepancy between the way women are perceived by men and the way they perceive themselves within the shared conceptual matrix of Hindu culture.

Fieldwork

The major part of my fieldwork for this study was carried out in a community I call "Narikot," a single Brahman-Chetri settlement within a larger dispersed village. I am not, however, presenting this work as a village study. Instead, my unit of study is the family as it operates within the kinship network. This network extends through ties of blood and marriage, within the village and beyond, and sometimes several days' walk to other villages. My focus on the family unit was not planned but grew naturally as a reflection of the concerns of women, my central subjects.

The first nine months of my research were spent with my husband in a small, comfortable mud-and-thatch house in Narikot. Here we shared a courtyard with a Chetri farming family. I became a "daughter" of this family when, after six months, their eldest daughter asked me to become her *mitini*, or ritual friend. From this point on my relations with the family became much more intimate and, in addition, my presence in Narikot at large became much more comprehensible and acceptable to other villagers. After nine months, when my husband and I moved closer to Kathmandu, it was expected that my ritual sister's house would be my headquarters on my daily visits to the village and that I would stay with her family during festivals or when my husband left town on research of his own.

My increasing intimacy with my mitini's family and my increasing fluency in Nepali helped me to become more and more involved with the women in other Brahman and Chetri families in Narikot. As these relationships with women grew stronger, many married women invited me to accompany them to their natal villages when they returned for festivals, weddings or the "vacations" allowed them after the birth of a child. These visits not only expanded my observations well beyond Narikot; they also impressed on me the great difference between a woman's status as wife or daughter-in-law in her husband's house (*ghar*) and her status as daughter or sister in her parent's home (*maiti*).[2]

Besides participant observation, my work included other standard anthropological field activities. I collected genealogies, drew maps, gathered fertility histories, and conducted surveys on marriage patterns, ritual practices, and religious beliefs. I spent many hours with an eighty-two-year-old, Sanskrit-educated, village pandit who was an expert on matters of ritual and myth. I also gathered relevant texts on caste and religion and produced a working translation of the *Swasthani Vrata Katha*, a religious work found in the homes of most of the people I studied, and a text that is of particular importance to women.

Perhaps the most productive part of my research was the series of in-depth life history interviews I conducted with ten women over the course of my second year of fieldwork. To obtain a representative sample, I chose Brahman and Chetri women of different ages and marital, educational, and economic status from among the families I studied. Interviews were conducted in a rented village room and, except for the tape recorder (which to my surprise the women almost totally ignored) and sometimes a small nursing infant, my informants and I enjoyed a degree of privacy which is almost unknown in the village setting. To keep the interviews focused, I prepared a series of open-ended questions adapted from Levy's "Check Sheet of Topics for Psychodynamic Interviews" (Levy 1973). The subjects ranged from childhood and present family relations, puberty, illnesses, and friendships; through women's attitudes about sex, their status vis-à-vis men, marriage, and motherhood; to more abstract topics such as religion and the supernatural, death and moral controls. I, of course, was not attempting anything in the realm of psychodynamics. I wanted only to be able to enter as much as possible into the memories, hopes, values, and concerns of the women I was seeking to understand.

Including my initial nine months in Narikot and a year of fieldwork carried out several years later in a more distant village related to Narikot by marriage, I have now had ten years of steady contact with the families I studied. During this time babies have been born and have assumed distinct personalities, people have died, sons and daughters have married, husbands have taken second wives, joint families have separated, new quarrels have broken out and old ones have been reconciled. I have been able to observe the process of social relations as they are lived within—and sometimes around—the idealized structures of Hindu culture.

In researching and writing this book I have had the help and support of many people both here in Nepal and in the United States. I would like to take this opportunity to express my thanks.

First of all I would like to thank my husband and colleague Gabriel Campbell, who introduced me to the field of anthropology and shared all his years of experience in South Asia in helping me initially to fit into and begin to understand village Nepal.

I am also grateful to the Center for Nepal and Asian Studies (CNAS) with which I was affiliated during my fieldwork period.[3] I wish particularly to thank Dr. Prayag Raj Sharma, who in his capacity as Dean of the Institute at the time of my fieldwork and subsequently as a friend and senior colleague, has supported my work in numerous ways—even taking time from his busy schedule to read and comment on the entire manuscript.

I would also like to express my thanks to my adviser Theodore Riccardi for his guidance throughout. It was he who before I left for the field alerted me to the importance of the *Swasthani* text and even lent me his own copy of the work. There are a number of others who have read and made useful comments on the manuscript at various stages. Among them are David Rubin, Linda Stone, Conrad Arensberg, Ainslee Embree, James Martin, Jr., and Sherry Ortner. In particular I would like to thank Barbara Stoler Miller, whose combination of perceptive criticism and warm encouragement helped transform the raw manuscript into a book. For help in that process I also owe special thanks to Karen Mitchell, who took on the job of editing what must have been a very daunting manuscript.

I would also like to thank Narendra Basnet for his help with the graphics and to David Sasoon for his photographic eye in helping me to choose from among my slides and photographs. Thanks go also to Linda Stone, Alice Wygont, and Ane Haaland for their excellent photographs.

Above all I am grateful to the people and especially the women of Narikot, who welcomed me and my endless questions with a wonderful generosity and patience. Finally, I want to extend a special thanks to my mithini and her family whose warmth and acceptance transformed Narikot into my maiti.

Kathmandu, Nepal

Lynn Bennett

Notes

1. Geertz defines the anthropological study of religion as "first, an analysis of a system of meanings embodied in the symbols which make up the religion proper and second, the relating of these systems to social structural and psychological process."

2. *Maiti* refers to a woman's consanguineal relatives; *maita* refers to her natal home. However, the two seem to be largely interchangeable in Nepali usage.

3. This fieldwork was carried out as part of the USAID fund study on the Status of Women in Nepal.

FIGURE 1

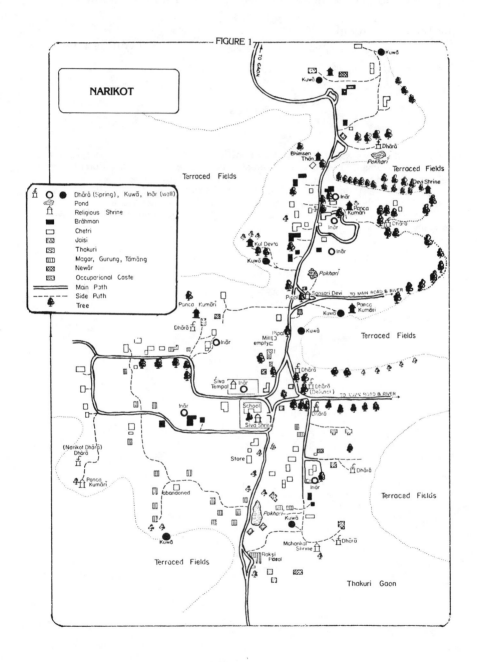

NARIKOT

CHAPTER 1

Village and Family:
The Socioeconomic Context
of Women's Lives

Narikot is built along the spine of a ridge that drops 200 feet to a large river on one side and slopes up over a series of plateaux and connecting ridges to the valley rim on the other. The village pictured on the map no longer exists as a political unit. Since the advent of panchayat democracy,[1] in the early 1960s, it has been divided up into wards and, along with adjoining areas, become part of a new village panchayat whose official center is beyond Narikot. But the residents, especially the women, still use the old village name to designate where they live.

As the map shows, the high castes have tended to cluster together around the central school, the teashop, and along the path to the northeast end of the village, while the middle-ranking castes are grouped mostly at the southwest corner of the village. It is also evident that there are very few (three) untouchable households within the village bounds—though several families of untouchable blacksmiths and leatherworkers who serve Narikot patrons live in adjoining villages.

Private Spaces

There is little neighborly visiting in the Brahman-Chetri hamlet. Relatives (unless they are having a dispute) may make casual visits to one another; but villagers are reluctant to go uninvited or without specific purpose into the courtyard of a nonkinsman. They do not want to appear to be idly loitering or expectantly waiting for something. Often, in fact, visiting neighbors do want something—a cup of milk to make tea for an important visiting relative, some cucumbers to make pickles—and are willing to humble themselves on such occasions to get it. The only adults in the village who move freely from house to house are the few poor old women whose prestige is already so low that they have nothing to lose by asking for vegetables or a few handfuls of corn from their better-off neighbors.

Casual conversation and exchange of news tends to take place during chance encounters in public spaces. If one enters another's private space, one is suspected of having a motive for doing so. Villagers worry about theft and about witchcraft from their uninvited visitors. For example, when an old woman from the village came upstairs in a neighbor's house to ask for a handful of spinach greens, her request was granted in a friendly manner. But as soon as she had turned to leave, the head woman of the house told her son in an urgent whisper to follow the old woman downstairs and see that she didn't steal any brass cooking vessels on her way out.

On another occasion, I was sitting in the courtyard enjoying tea with the women of one household when a neighbor woman entered and began to talk. Though the other women were friendly and chatted with her, they did not offer her tea, but casually covered the tops of their glasses with their hands and patiently waited until she left. When she had gone and I picked up my glass, they urged me in excited tones not to drink until I had touched the glass with my big toe. The woman was a witch, they said, and since I had neglected to cover my glass, I now had to remove any possible spells before drinking.

Both these encounters reveal not only the sense of distrust which pervades many village interactions, but also the habits of courtesy and politeness which often mask this distrust.

Since villagers are aware that uninvited visiting might inspire suspicion, they consider "dropping in" an undignified thing to do. Rather than be called a busybody (or worse) it is better to stay in one's own courtyard. This sentiment is particularly acute among women. Men, who are involved in village government, who must arrange the schedules for planting and harvesting and find buyers for cash crops, have more legitimate reasons for being out and about than women. Of course, women too have much legitimate work which takes them out of their court-yards. It is their job to fetch water from the village tap or spring. They should not linger, but if they have a heap of laundry or if they must wait in a long line to fill a water vessel, they will have a chance to exchange news with the other women there. And during the peak agricultural seasons, the women see more of their neighbors, since most of them participate in labor ex-change groups that plant, weed, and harvest the crop together. Nevertheless, the proper demeanor for women—especially those married into the village—is *laj manne,* "modest, shy, ashamed." This refers not only to reticent, self-effacing behavior in the presence of others but also to general shyness about going out in the village alone. A phrase often used to compliment a wom-an's behavior is that she "sits and says nothing" (*cup lagera basne*). The opposite is the contentious, noisy, immodest woman who "says what she likes and goes where she likes" (*je pani bhanchi, jaha pani hirchi*). There are strong overtones of sexual looseness attached to such bold behavior, especially in a young woman. Except when their work or religious activities take them outside, Brahman and Chetri women tend to spend most of their time in their own houses and courtyards.

Houses in Narikot vary greatly in size and construction. A few are just tiny, one-story mud-wattle huts, while others are four stories, built of baked bricks over cement foundations, with beautifully carved windows and tile roofs. Most, however, are two-story houses of mud brick with steep thatch or tile roofs. All the houses have courtyards where grain is dried, children play, weddings are performed, and people sit to warm them-selves in the cold sunny winters. Some courtyards are made of baked tile bricks, but most are dirt covered with a paste of cow-dung and mud (*gobar*). Courtyards are surrounded with low walls of brick or stone, or sometimes just a hedge. Always there should be a place for Visnu's sacred *tulsi* plant in one corner.

Usually there is a raised veranda in front of the house. This will be spread with a smooth coat of red mud paste and covered with mats when people sit there to work or talk. Often a basket will be hung from the eaves of the veranda where a small baby sleeps while its mother works. There may be a foot-mill, or a grinding stone which the women use for the unending task of husking and grinding grains.

Most houses have an animal shed attached to or near the

main house where whatever goats, cows, and buffaloes the family owns are kept. There is usually a kitchen garden too, where vegetables are grown and sometimes a few fruit trees are planted.

The floor plans of the houses differ. One of the most important variations is the placement of the kitchen. The kitchen is the purest part of the house, where the ritually significant staple food *dal-bhat* (lentil broth and boiled rice) is cooked and eaten. If their house is big enough, Brahman and Chetri families prefer to cook on a higher floor or the top floor of the house. Dogs, chickens, lower-caste workers, etc. are less likely to stray upstairs and pollute the cooking space. There is also better ventilation, since most houses have only very small latticed windows on the ground floor. Poorer families, however, must make do with a dark corner on the ground floor separated from the livestock by a low mud-brick wall. Wherever the cooking area is located, near it are squares outlined by ridges in the mud floor. Each adult male in the family usually has his own eating square, where his wife also eats after he has eaten. Small children may eat anywhere, but by the time a child can feed himself he usually has a regular place.

Twice a day, after the morning and evening rice meals, the women clean and purify the kitchen area, including the low mud stove and the eating squares. First, a moist ball of cowdung is rolled over the floor to pick up spilled food and bits of leftover rice, which are *jutho* or polluting to touch. Then the ball is thrown out into the garden or scrap pit. Next a paste of fresh mud and cowdung is spread over the entire area. Though a few houses have a cemented drain area for washing dishes indoors, most women must wash dishes outside—a cold dark task on a winter's evening—and then bring the dishes back to dry in the kitchen area where they are less likely to be defiled.

While rice meals must be cooked in the sacred hearth area, snacks and tea can be prepared outside it on a separate fire—sometimes over a three-legged metal stand in a portable clay basin. Larger houses may have a fire pit downstairs where mash for the animals is prepared as well as the afternoon snack of popped corn or roasted soybeans.

Every house has at least one storeroom where supplies of grain, spices, oil, and extra vessels are kept. The storeroom door is always locked, and the key kept with the head woman of the household. Nonvaluable items like old shoes, tin cans,

A Chetri woman prepares the family meal in her kitchen. *Photo by author*

broken vessels, pieces of window frame, or tool handles are stored in the eaves, or under the stairs.

Furniture is minimal, but almost every house has at least one wooden bed and a dowry chest, since brides must bring these articles when they are married. Standing wardrobes or cupboards, wall mirrors, tables, straight-back chairs, and radios are luxuries owned by a few. Most living is done on floors covered with straw mats or woven cotton carpets and perhaps spread with a thick rug or blanket of natural-colored wool (*radi*) or some thin cushions. Walls are painted with either a gray mud wash or distemper—sometimes in a garish metallic green or blue. The walls are full of niches and rough built-in shelves where dirty clothes, useful rags, and tattered school notebooks are stored. Valuable clothes, jewelry, and makeup are kept under lock and key in a chest or standing wardrobe. Holy books, wrapped carefully in cloth, are stored on the top of the wardrobe or on a high shelf where children can't tear or otherwise defile them. Around the walls are bright colored pictures of gods, a few formal family photographs, and possibly a family-planning poster or a Nebico Biscuit calendar featuring a plump young woman in a clinging sari.

The husband sleeps on the bed that his wife has brought

as dowry; and she—if she is the favored wife—sleeps on a mattress at the foot of his bed. The older wife, in cases of polygamous marriage, will be given a room of her own, usually containing the marriage bed she brought as a bride, which is visited less frequently now by her husband. The sleeping patterns of the children vary with the size and number of rooms in the house. Children from infancy until at least the age of six or seven sleep with their mother in her bed. If a new infant comes along, the older child may be sent to sleep with siblings in another room. But children in small houses sleep all in a line with their mother and siblings until they are twelve or older. Brahmans and Chetris think it unkind to make a child of any age sleep by itself in a room, and even adults prefer not to sleep alone.

Public Areas and Community Interaction

As I have noted, the isolation of the courtyard does not affect men and children as much as it does women. Men congregate at the tea stall near the schoolhouse and sometimes at the mill to smoke and talk. There is also the panchayat building—but since the panchayat is large and its headquarters more than a mile and a half away from Narikot, it has not become an active social center for Narikot men. Villagers do, however, participate in the panchayat cooperative, which purchases and advances fertilizer and improved seeds and also sells cooking oil, rice, and other basic household supplies at the low government rates. The panchayat also maintains a breeding buffalo and runs periodic innoculation campaigns for both humans and livestock. It was through a collective panchayat effort several years ago that Narikot and the surrounding villages got electricity.

But for most of the more immediate and localized needs like water supply (Bennett 1973), road repair, education, and even entertainment, there are various smaller groups of men—both formal and informal—which work to get things done. One of the formal groups is the five-member school committee that in the early fifties organized Narikot's first public school. In the beginning, school was taught on the green in front of the tea-shops under a great pipal tree, but later, a small two-room house with a straw roof was built. When that collapsed, the students were again out on the green until the late sixties when the school committee raised Rs. 4,200[2] and the necessary voluntary labor (*sramdan*) to build the two-story cement and brick schoolhouse which serves Narikot today.

Another formal group in Narikot is the Bandu Mandal, or youth organization. Led by an energetic and talented Brahman man, it was formed in 1972 and has about thirty members. This youth organization meets once a month—though attendance is irregular, since many of its members work or study in Kathmandu and return to the village only on holidays. It is divided into four special-interest committees: culture, sports, agriculture, and education/library. The sports committee recently raised money for a volleyball net and the education/library committee has managed to start a small library in one room of the school building. But the most active part of the Bandu Mandal is the cultural committee, which for several years in a row has produced well-rehearsed, well-attended plays in the schoolyard at the major fall festival of Dasai (see Bennett 1974).

The members of the Bandu Mandal raise money for its activities by singing from house to house in the traditional caroling (*deusi khelne*) during the festival of Tihar in November and by occasional fund drives for specific projects like the play. Fund drives are also organized by informal groups in Narikot for repairing roads, improving water supply, or perhaps putting doors and window frames in the school building, since there are no panchayat taxes to provide funds for such projects. Village families are expected to give according to their means—some giving two or three rupees, others ten and twenty.

The men who collect the funds and organize the voluntary work groups for such projects are for many purposes the effective village-level government. They are the village *thulo manche* (big men) whose age, wealth, and personalities make them the informal leaders of the Narikot "neighborhood" within the larger, somewhat unwieldly panchayat unit. Two of the thulo manche of Narikot are also ward representatives to the panchayat council, representing the two wards that fall within the old Narikot boundaries.

Such thulo manche increase their prestige by using their influence to benefit Narikot whenever they can. For example, one man was able to get tarpaper roofing for the school through his relative in the Electricity Department. The authority of Narikot's thulo manche is often sought in the mediation of quarrels and minor land disputes. One of the ward representatives, for example, was called on many occasions during my research period—once when two neighbor women had come to blows over their quarreling children; once when a widow claimed she was being beaten by her brother-in-law who wanted her land; and once when an untouchable man came for advice on how to get his wife (whom he had beaten) back from her parents' house. But, in turn, the representative had to call in a respected elderly Brahman to arbitrate when the representative's own son wanted to partition the family land and live separately with his wife. Neither son nor father was pleased with the property divisions, and the son at one point even threatened a lawsuit. But in the end both accepted the old Brahman's authority. Such internal solutions seem to be common—indeed, the older men in the village say they can't remember a single case (out of the many threats) where villagers actually went outside Narikot to the police or government courts.

Caste

The Nepali version of the Hindu caste system marks one important framework within which the people of Narikot relate to each other. Caste defines certain groups in a hierarchy of ritual purity and pollution and prescribes intergroup behavior in certain spheres, particularly marriage and commensality. The simple diagram of the caste hierarchy presented in figure 2 cannot be accurately characterized as *the* Nepali version of the caste system. For that the best source is Höfer's (1979) comprehensive analysis of the caste hierarchy as it was set forth in the National Legal Code of 1854.[3] The code encompassed and ranked not only the Nepali-speaking *Parbatiya* or hill Hindu castes which are our main concern here, but also the numerous Newari-speaking castes of all ranks, the many Tibeto-Burman or "tribal" ethnic groups such as the Gurung and Tamang, the Tibetan-speaking *Bhotia* groups from the high Mountain Regions, as well as the Muslim, Hindu, and indigenous populations of the Southern Terai belt. However, the citizens of Narikot, though diverse, do not encompass the full variety of Nepali peoples; hence the simpler scheme presented here is adequate for understanding the caste hierarchy as it functions in the village.

FIGURE 2

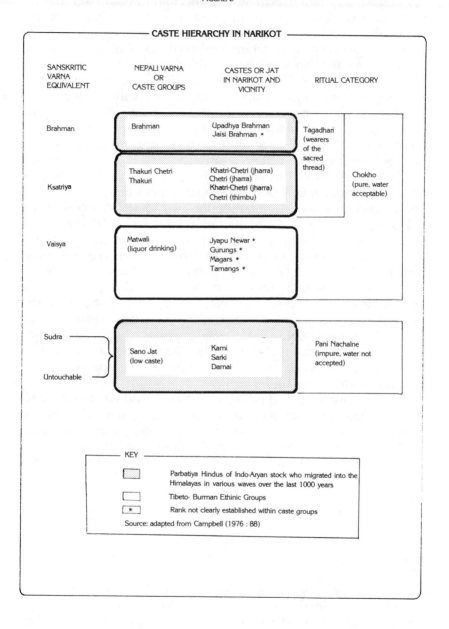

CASTE HIERARCHY IN NARIKOT

SANSKRITIC VARNA EQUIVALENT	NEPALI VARNA OR CASTE GROUPS	CASTES OR JAT IN NARIKOT AND VICINITY	RITUAL CATEGORY
Brahman	Brahman	Upadhya Brahman Jaisi Brahman *	Tagadhari (wearers of the sacred thread)
Ksatriya	Thakuri Chetri Thakuri	Khatri-Chetri (jharra) Chetri (jharra) Khatri-Chetri (jharra) Chetri (thimbu)	Chokho (pure, water acceptable)
Vaisya	Matwali (liquor drinking)	Jyapu Newar * Gurungs * Magars * Tamangs *	
Sudra Untouchable	Sano Jat (low caste)	Kami Sarki Damai	Pani Nachalne (impure, water not accepted)

KEY

Parbatiya Hindus of Indo-Aryan stock who migrated into the Himalayas in various waves over the last 1000 years

Tibeto- Burman Ethinic Groups

* Rank not clearly established within caste groups

Source: adapted from Campbell (1976 : 88)

Like any other local system in Hindu South Asia, the organization of castes, or *jat*, in Narikot is loosely based on the classical varna system. At the top are "those who wear the sacred thread" (*tagadari*). This group encompasses the Brahman and Ksatriya varnas who traditionally filled the role of priests and warriors, respectively. The Chetris, whose name is derived from Ksatriya, fall into this group, as do the Thakuris. The middle-ranking group, roughly comparable to the Vaisya in the varna system, are called *matwali* or "those who drink liquor." At the bottom of the scale are the low caste or *pani na calne jat*— "those from whom water is not accepted." As Campbell (1978:87) has noted, this version of the varna model, which prevails throughout much of rural Nepal, differs from the classical Hindu system in that it collapses the two lowest categories: the Sudra who in the classical model were touchable and inside society and the untouchables who were outside it. In fact the distinction is present in Nepal, as Höfer's work (1979:45) has shown. In the old legal code the impure or "water unacceptable" castes are further subdivided into those who are touchable and those who are not. However, since most of the members of the former low-caste but touchable group are Newar service castes, who generally inhabit only the more highly diversified urban areas, the distinction has little significance in most rural hill communities such as Narikot, where only untouchable Parbatiya low castes are found.[4]

The women I studied were Brahman and Chetri members of the high-caste tagadari group. Brahmans and Chetris are viewed by themselves and others as in some sense forming an identifiable group sharing a single cultural heritage and social structure. Among all but the highest Brahman group, some degree of intermarriage with other ethnic groups has been tolerated; nevertheless, the Brahman and Chetri of Nepal have largely retained the features of their Indo-Aryan ancestors (see Haimendorf 1966). According to their own traditions, sometimes recorded in long genealogies, they, along with some of the untouchable service castes, are the Parbatiya or "people from the hills." Both high-caste and untouchable Parbatiya are the original Nepali-speaking peoples, who, the tradition continues, migrated to the Himalayas from northern India at different periods and eventually formed the bulk of the conquering army of Prithivi Narayan Shah, when he invaded the Kathmandu Valley in the eighteenth century. The account of K. B. Bista (1972) while supporting this view, presents a considerably more complex picture. Bista contends that "It is a difficult matter with a few exceptions to know the original status" of most Chetri, and points out that certain family names could originally have been Rajput, Magar, or even Tibetan (1972:16). But despite such early looseness in the criteria for membership in the Chetri caste, the language, religion, and social structure of the Parbatiya Brahman and Chetri leaves little doubt that, as a group, they are linked with the Hindus of North India[5] and distinct from the high-caste Newari Hindus of Kathmandu Valley's ancient urban centers.

At the apex of the caste hierarchy are the Upadhaya Brahmans, who alone may serve as hereditary priests (*purohit* and *puret*) for Chetri families. Since they embody and maintain the highest ritual purity—in terms of both marriage and ritual food restrictions—all other castes will accept dal-bhat cooked by Upadhaya Brahmans.

The offspring of a union between an Upadhaya Brahman man and a Brahman widow or divorcee are known as Jaisi Brahman. The status of this fairly numerous group is definitely lower than that of the Upadhaya Brahmans. Jaisis may not serve as priests or accept certain ritual gifts (*dan* or *daksina*). But there is some ambiguity about the Jaisi's standing with respect to other "twice born" castes, because while they refuse to take dal-bhat from Chetris, Chetris also refuse to eat this food when cooked by them.

A further division among the Brahmans, and one which cuts across the Upadhaya/Jaisi division, is that between the Purbiya and the Kumai Brahmans, who trace their origins respectively from the East and the West. Once again, the relationship between these two groups is not clear, and each claims superiority over the other. In Narikot, where there were only Purbiya Brahman residents, that group was considered higher, and village Chetris said that they would call only Purbiya as their priests.

Next to the Brahmans in rank are the Thakuris. They, like the Chetris just below them, belong to the second of the four varnas, the Ksatriya or warrior caste, and they count the royal Shah clan in their number. However, as Haimendorf (1966) has pointed out, in their more Mongolian features and in their social structure (notably the permitting of matrilateral cross-cousin marriage) they differ from both the Brahmans and the Chetris.

Among the Chetris too there are numerous subdivisions resulting from irregular marriages of various types. The children

of a Brahman man and either a Chetri or Matwali woman are
known as Khatri (or Khatri Chetri or K.C.). They take the surname of their Brahman father but rank as Chetri. As with the Jaisi
Brahmans, this reduction of status is usually a permanent one for
the descendants of the union, although I found in a Nepali book
on the subject a statement implying that offspring through the
female line can eventually be reinstated as Brahmans:

> When a daughter is born of such a marriage [Brahman husband,
> Chetri wife] then she should be married according to tradition. And
> in this manner when such marriages [presumably to Brahman males]
> of such daughters have been performed for seven generations, then
> the daughter of the seventh generation becomes a Bahuni [female
> Brahman] instead of a Chetrini [female Chetri]—and this directive is
> also found in the shastras. [Sharma n.d.: 23, my trans.]

A further division in the Chetri caste is that between *jharra*
and *thimbu* or "pure" and "mixed" Chetri. Jharra Chetris are the
offspring of orthodox Hindu marriage (*kanyadan biha*) between
jharra men and women. Thimbu Chetris are born from several
different types of irregular unions. One example would be the
union of a Chetri man with a Chetri widow or a Chetri woman
who has left her first husband. In this case both husband and
wife may be themselves pure full-status Chetri to begin with, but
the fact that orthodox marriage must be a *kanyadan* or literally
the "gift of a virgin" obviously precludes second marriages for
women. Although a man who makes a second marriage retains
his full ritual status, a woman loses her caste standing on her
second union, and so this union and its offspring cannot be given
full status. A second type of irregular union might be one between a Chetri man and a woman from the middle-ranking Matwali castes. As long as a man never takes dal-bhat cooked by
such a wife he retains his full caste status, and his children,
though thimbu, are still Chetri.

Though Narikot villagers know the thimbu or jharra status
of every Chetri, this makes little difference in daily interaction.
There is, however, an important difference in ritual status. Jharra
Chetris will not take boiled rice from thimbu Chetris, nor will
they give their daughters to them except, perhaps, when a thimbu
family is extremely rich and powerful. In such cases, as Haimendorf (1966:53) points out, the thimbu Chetris are trading their
worldly prestige and wealth for the ritual status of a full-caste
bride (usually from a poor hill family) in the hopes that such a

match might eventually help restore jharra status to their descendants. One other ritual occasion in which jharra/thimbu status is important is in the annual or biannual celebration of *devali* when the lineage gods are worshiped (see chapter 4). At that time only jharra males may actually perform the sacrifice and worship ceremonies.

Leaving aside the question of the higher twice-born Newari castes, who exist in a kind of "separate but parallel" status with respect to the high-caste Parbatiya the remaining castes and ethnic groups all fall under the rubric of Matwali or "liquor-drinking." From the Brahman-Chetri point of view this large middle-ranking group includes most Newar and other Tibeto-Burman peoples such as the Magar, Gurung, Tamang, Limbu, Rai, Sherpa, and Tibetans. It also includes anthropologists and other foreigners.[6] Members of this group are *cokho* (clean, pure). They are touchable, and water, as well as cokho food (uncooked food, or food cooked with clarified butter) can be accepted from them by high-caste individuals. Women from this group can also be kept by high-caste men as second-class wives.

Below the Matwali group and at the bottom of the hierarchy are the untouchable *pani na calne* or *sano jat* (low caste) groups. As their name quite literally suggests, other groups will not take water that they have touched. In this group are the three major untouchable Parbatiya artisan castes, the Kami (blacksmith), Sarki (leatherworker), and Damai (tailor-musician) groups. It also includes untouchable Newari groups such as the sweeper (*cyame*) and butcher (*kasai/pore*) castes, though no members of these groups live in Narikot.

In Narikot, relationships between Brahman-Chetri and members of the Matwali group are quite relaxed and informal. Unlike such middle-ranking groups in most rural Indian communities, the Tibeto-Burman Matwali groups of Nepal remain to varying degrees outside the Hindu system. It is true that many (especially the Magar and Gurung) have adopted all the parts of the Hindu tradition in a process that seems roughly similar to Srinivas' (1966) "sanskritization" in India. But in most groups these Hindu traditions are tempered with strong elements from their persisting Buddhist beliefs and less rigidly hierarchical social structures. Indeed, among certain groups like the Sherpa and other Tibetan peoples from Nepal's northern border regions, Hindu ideology seems to have had little effect at all, except perhaps in the acknowledgment of certain groups as untouchables. At any rate, whatever respect a Tamang or Gurung from around Narikot might show to a Brahman would be the result of the Brahman's age or wealth and political power rather than his ritual or caste status. Of course, the hierarchical Hindu ideology remains the given framework for certain kinds of interaction between high-caste and middle-caste individuals. No Matwali, no matter how wealthy (and there are some wealthy Matwali in adjoining villages), would expect even the poorest Brahman to eat dal-bhat cooked by his hand. But outside the ritual sphere, deference in daily interaction is a function of more secular factors.

Such an essentially secular or "democratic" relationship does not hold, however, between high-caste and untouchable parbatiya groups. Although many untouchables of the younger generation in Narikot have sought less demeaning, or at least more anonymous, employment outside the village, their elders still maintain their inherited service/patronage relationships with high-caste families. This is the system known in India as *jajamani* and which Bista (1972) calls the *kamaune* system in Nepal. Here, each service-caste family performs its specialized tasks for one or more high-caste patron families in return for a biannual grain payment. In addition, untouchables are given a rice meal whenever they come to work and uncooked provisions whenever they do extra work or give special service at a family celebration (like the Damai musicians at a wedding). The principal difference between Indian jajamani and kamaune in Nepal is that the latter is much simpler, usually involving only three untouchable service castes: the Sarki for leatherwork and carpentry; the Kami for ironwork; and the Damai for tailoring and occasional music. In India the number of service castes is often much greater, including the sweepers, barbers, washermen, and potmakers, as well as barber or sweeper women who serve as midwives.

As I mentioned earlier, Brahmans and Chetris do avoid the touch of the service castes.[7] They also use non-honorific forms of address to them and do not generally allow them inside their houses. Likewise, the demeanor of untouchables toward their high-caste patrons is often tinged with obsequiousness—a behavior totally absent in the interaction between Matwalis and the higher castes. The most extreme example of such subservient behavior I observed in Narikot was that of a thin, middle-aged Damai widow who had two young children to support. She had almost no land and very little skill as a seamstress. Had it not been that her patron families felt obliged to employ her despite the badly sewn garments she made, she would, as she herself openly acknowledged, have been reduced to beggary.

A similar hereditary relationship exists between Chetri *jajman* ("he who sacrifices") and their Brahman *puret* (priests). Such family priests are expected to officiate at certain calendrical festivals and at important family ceremonies such as weddings, naming ceremonies, funerals, and the like. In return for his ritual expertise and his ability (however marginal) to read the sacred Sanskrit texts, the puret is regularly given a payment during the Dasai festival. He also receives a small gift of money, *daksina,* and uncooked or ritually pure foods whenever he presides at a ceremony. Even though daksina and other occasional religious gifts, *dan,* given to Brahmans are meant to acknowledge their higher ritual status, some Brahmans—especially if they are wealthy or highly educated—feel that it is somehow demeaning to accept them. The priest of one village family is now such a wealthy man that he will come only for the most important ceremonies. At other times the family must call on poor neighboring Brahmans who are glad to give ritual service in return for daksina.

The Brahmans and Chetris who form the subject of this study include both Upadhaya and Jaisi Brahmans, Khatri Chetris, and Chetris of both pure (jharra) and mixed (thimbu) status.[8] Despite these internal subdivisions in terms of pedigree, the Brahman-Chetri are a recognizable cultural unit sharing essentially the same mythic and social structures. Of course there are divergences. Brahmans do some things differently from Chetris, but they share an ideology that accounts for these differences— i.e., the Hindu caste ideology that places Brahmans at the ritual apex (as priests) and Chetris (as warriors) below them. Thus, for example, although Brahman women do not wear stitched blouses when cooking while Chetri women do, both groups understand that this difference is a function of the greater purity required in Brahman cooking. Likewise in Narikot only the Chetris include in their weddings the separate *swayambar* ceremony where the bride "chooses" her groom (see chapter 3). This ceremony is recognized as appropriate to them and not to Brahmans because in the old texts only the daughters of Ksatriya kings had such rites. For the most part, however, the description and analysis in this book applies equally (unless specifically noted) to all the subdivisions within the Brahman-Chetri group.

Patrilineal Organization

Besides the vertical stratification of caste with its subtle internal gradations in ritual status, Brahmans and Chetris are also divided horizontally into agnatic units called *thar* and *gotra*. Every Brahman and Chetri belongs to a thar and a gotra. Men become members of their father's thar and gotra; women assume their husband's. As Haimendorf (1966:30) has pointed out, these units are not ranked hierarchically: "No [Chetri] *thar* is inherently superior or inferior to any other Chetri clan [*thar*]." The same could be said of Brahman thar and gotra. The fact that a Brahman man gives his Khatri children (from whom he cannot take boiled rice) his own thar and gotra suggests that neither are primarily indices of ritual status. In fact, almost all gotra and many thar[9] cross-cut caste boundaries. Thus, for example, an individual belonging to the Bhandari thar and Bhardwaj gotra could be anything from a full Upadhaya Brahman to a Jaisi, a Hamal (with Brahman father and Thakuri mother), or a jharra Khatri-Chetri or even a thimbu Khatri-Chetri—depending on how far afield his ancestors had married.

But beyond such general definitions it becomes difficult to say with much preciseness just what thar and gotra are. Informants tend to conceive of both loosely as agnatic descent groups. This belief is especially strong with regard to gotra because of the tradition of the gotra rishi: each gotra bears the name of an ancient sage or rishi who is somehow considered to be the patrilineal ancestor of everyone born into that particular gotra.[10]

These mythological rishis are ideologically important to Brahman-Chetri agnatic organization in that they provide conceptual basis for the cherished ideals of patrilineal continuity and purity of descent. These ideals are expressed in individual genealogical records (*bamsawali*). Families take pride in the length of their genealogies. Yet, although some I collected spanned seven or eight generations (and one spanned fourteen), most village families had records of only the last four or five generations. Beyond these specific genealogies, lineages depend on their gotra affiliation which links them (however obscurely) with a rishi ancestor of unimpeachable purity and makes them part of a patrilineage older than the Vedas themselves. Gotra provides a kind of "spiritual pedigree," and many religious ceremonies, especially those honoring the ancestors, require the invocation of one's gotra name to establish one's ritual legitimacy before the gods and ancestor spirits.

Because of the conceptual importance of gotra as a "spiritual" descent group, it is considered a sin to knowingly marry within one's own gotra. The definitive text on the subject, the *Gorkha Thar Gotra*, states quite plainly that

> it is not permissible to give a bride to a member of one's own gotra.
> . . . If a son is born [from such a marriage] then [that son] will most
> certainly be one who is accursed, damned (*candal*). . . . He will
> take you to hell and he will destroy the heaven of both the mother
> and the father. When one marries with a member of his own gotra
> then society will spit upon him, and the one who has married thus
> will not show his black face and will hide. [Sharma n.d.:18, my
> trans.]

A further quotation from this passage specifies that gotra endogamy is banned because it is seen as a kind of incest. "If one does marry [a woman of one's own gotra] without knowing and then finds out . . . one should not sleep in the same place with her. The shastras advise that such a wife is to be treated as if she were one's sister" (Sharma n.d.:19). For marriage purposes then, the gotra is treated as if it were in fact a single agnatic group descended from the same forefather.

Yet, despite the conceptual importance of gotra, some informants—many of them women—were unable to give their own gotra name when questioned. With considerable embarrassment they had to ask a relative or even wait to consult the family priest. Probably this is because the gotra has little use in daily life. It is not used for identification: people use their thar rather than their gotra as a surname. Nor do members of the same gotra automatically have any genealogical links with each other or any mutual economic, ritual, or social obligations. In fact, beyond the observation of strict gotra exogamy, members of the same gotra do not constitute a kin group in any behavioral sense. Like caste, gotra is a pan-Hindu phenomenon, with the same named units appearing throughout India. What T. N.

Madan (1962:67) writes about Brahmanic gotra in Kashmir holds for the Brahman and Chetri of Nepal: "The sagotrā (of the same gotrā) Brahmans of a village may be an agnatic kin group with known genealogical ties but Brahmanic gotrā are distributed all over India and are not kin groups in any specific sense." In short, belonging to the same gotra is a necessary but by no means sufficient criterion for determining social agnatic relationship.

The same could be said about thar membership. Although villagers sometimes refer to their thar as if it were a clan or even lineage unit, thar, strictly speaking, is really nothing more than a last name shared by many different descent groups. Individuals with the same thar may or may not be agnatically related. Yet because of the vague sense of the thar as an extended patrilineage, there is a preference to marry outside one's thar. Unlike gotra exogamy, however, there is no specific marriage prohibition here, and I encountered several cases of thar endogamy in the genealogies I collected.

The largest functional agnatic unit in Brahman-Chetri society is the kul (clan, lineage), whose members not only share the same thar and gotra but, more important, worship the same kul devta or lineage gods. The obligations which kul members have toward each other—in terms of observing birth and death pollution and performing communal worship of the lineage gods—sharply distinguish the kul from either gotra (which requires only exogamy) or thar (which requires nothing).

Theoretically, a single kul could continue to grow for centuries, so that its members—on the model of "descent" from the mythic gotra rishis—could trace their patrilineal descent in an unbroken line for many generations. In this ideal expansion the kul embodies, more vividly than even the gotra, the central Hindu values of agnatic solidarity and purity of descent.

Despite these values, however, actual kul seldom span more than five or six generations. Quarrels, migrations, and lack of fastidiousness in maintaining genealogy records all contribute to the process of fragmentation whereby a single lineage group splinters into new kuls. In fact, the kul unit is also called "branch" or "limb" (sakha, haga), revealing an image of the kul as an offshoot of some larger, less defined patrilineage. Thus, the actual size and generational depth of a kul can vary from the minimum of a single family or household to the ideal of a large clan.

Often very large or prestigious kuls within a thar are

named after the location of the *kul ghar,* ancestral home (such as the Sijapati Bista, the Bista lineage whose ancestors came from Sija in the far west). Kuls may also be named after a famous person in their ranks, like the Jung Thapa, whose ancestor married the granddaughter of Prime Minister Jung Bahadur Rana. Many smaller, less famous lineages, however, have no names. Likewise, in time, the larger named lineages fragment again into several new kuls, each having the same name but worshiping their lineage gods separately. It is the group whose members worship lineage gods together at a single shrine and observe at least minimal death and birth pollution for each other that forms the structural basis of the kul, rather than the named lineage whose significance in most cases is now only historical.

The organization of Brahman-Chetri patrilineal descent groups can be schematically represented by a series of widening circles surrounding an individual (see figure 3). The larger thar and gotra units are represented by circles *asymmetrical* with respect to ego and his kul, since both his thar and his gotra may contain individuals to whom he is not actually related.

Within the intersection of the two circles representing thar and gotra are a series of *concentric* circles surrounding ego. Individuals within these circles have the same thar and gotra as ego and are at least potentially members of ego's own kul.

At the closest range, usually spanning between two and four generations, is the *parivar,* family or household. This group, which holds property jointly and observes most life-cycle and calendrical rituals together, is by far the most important patrilineal unit in Parbatiya society. The clearest single indicator of proximity of agnatic relation is the length of time that one is obliged to observe birth and death pollution for another. Members of the same household must observe the maximum ten days for birth and thirteen days for the death of a member.

Beyond the parivar are units of increasing generational distance and proportionally decreasing ritual obligation. In the ideal scheme represented in figure 3, death pollution observances vary only with the proximity of agnatic relation. In fact, of course, such observances vary also according to the orthodoxy and respective caste status [11] of the families, the geographical distance separating households, [12] and above all, whether the two families are members of the same kul.

Theoretically then, the *sapindi bhai* (lit. brothers sharing in the same rice ball offering), which encompasses five genera-

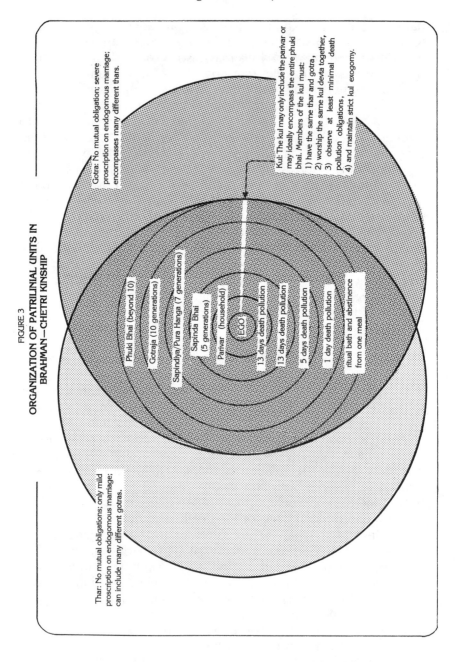

FIGURE 3
ORGANIZATION OF PATRILINIAL UNITS IN
BRAHMAN—CHETRI KINSHIP

Gotra: No mutual obligation; severe proscription on endogomous marriage; encompasses many different thars.

Kul: The kul may only include the parivar or may ideally encompass the entire phuki bhai. Members of the kul must:
1) have the same thar and gotra,
2) worship the same kul devta together,
3) observe at least minimal death pollution obligations,
4) and maintain strict kul exogomy.

Phuki Bhai (beyond 10)

Gotraja (10 generations)

Sapindiya/Pura Hanga (7 generations)

Sapinda Bhai (5 generations)

Parivar (household)

EGO

13 days death pollution

13 days death pollution

5 days death pollution

1 day death pollution

ritual bath and abstinence from one meal

Thar: No mutual obligations; only mild proscription on endogomous marriage; can include many different gotras.

tions including ego, are linked by the mutual obligation to observe thirteen days' death pollution and by the fact that they must all offer *pinda,* a ceremonial rice ball, to the same great-great-grandfather. This offering takes place during the ceremony on the twelfth day after a death in the family of a member (see chapter 3). Agnatic relatives up to and including seven generations removed are called either *sapindiya* or *pura haga* relatives. They should observe five days' death pollution for each other. Agnatic relatives between eight and ten generations removed are called *gotraja* and receive one full day of mourning. Relatives separated by more than ten generations become *phuki bhai,*[13] for whom one merely observes the rituals of bathing and abstaining from one meal after news of the death is received (*chak khalko*).

This scheme was given (with absolute confidence) by a respected and very learned Brahman pandit who occasionally served some of the more important families of Narikot. Other informants, however, were less certain about these divisions and their ritual obligations. Though they all knew in general that obligations decreased in proportion to the distance between ego and the relative in question, many gave different answers to questions on ritual obligation or said they would have to consult their family priest for the specifics. In addition, Bista (1972:40–41) reports another version of the birth and death pollution obligations, as recorded in the National Code of 1955.[14]

The reason for this apparent confusion lies, I believe, in the fact that ultimately death and birth pollution obligations are not solely determined by such idealized schema. A more significant factor in determining these ritual obligations is the actual extension of the kul.[15] And the kul, in response to the kinds of fragmenting tendencies mentioned earlier (i.e., disputes, migration, and blurring of precise records), can vary in size from the ideal of the open-ended phuki bhai grouping to the minimum of a single parivar unit. Members of a kul spanning only five generations would not observe the funeral obligations beyond the sapindi bhai even in the unlikely event that they were aware of their distant extra-kul relatives. The rules given here, then, come into play only for a large kul whose family priests have maintained precise records and whose members continue to reside close to the ancestral home. Otherwise, kul members who can no longer trace their precise interrelations simply assume the phuki bhai relation and observe the minimal restrictions. Probably no family actually lives up to—or even knows—its full phuki bhai obligations. Nevertheless, even though these rules are not consistently observed, they still serve to substantiate the concept of an unbroken patriline, much the way gotra exogamy does.

However, it is the parivar or family which most fully embodies the patrilineal ideals of male authority, respect for elders, and agnatic solidarity. For in addition to the kinds of ritual obligation which bind members of the kul together, the parivar also shares a common economic base. As in many peasant societies, this most important kinship unit is also the major unit of production and consumption in rural Nepal. Members of one parivar hold and work land as a group. They also generally share a single hearth and live under one roof. Members are hierarchically organized under the eldest male, who is the focus of authority and respect. To most perfectly express the ideal of agnatic solidarity the parivar should be a joint or extended family consisting of a man, his wife or wives, his brothers, their wives, all their unmarried daughters, sons, sons' wives and their children. Yet in fact the collateral joint family with adult married brothers living together after the death of the father is an almost unknown phenomenon. Even the lineal joint family—a man and his married sons—is a highly mutable structure which, despite the ideological pressure for remaining together until the death of the father, often fragments before that event into separate parivars or household units based on the nuclear family.[16] Like the kul then, the parivar varies greatly in size, with the ideal being large and the reality often much smaller.

The Household Economy

As might be expected in such a strongly patrilineal society, the authority over household and property management rests nominally with the senior male. Of course, in the reality of daily decisions about work, food distribution expenditures, and long-term property management, seniority and maleness are not the only principles behind authority. Especially in large extended families, women and junior males use many strategies to influence these decisions. In later sections of this book I will focus

on these strategies and their effect on family and kinship structures (see also Bennett 1981:93–107). At present, however, we
will be concerned with the less political side of how a household runs, in terms of financial management and the kinds of
tasks assigned to men and women, respectively.

The household economy in Narikot is based firmly on
agriculture. Though only a minority of households grow enough
produce to sell for cash, all but a few raise most of their own
food.[17] There would be more surplus to sell were it not for the
fact that all but four Narikot families share-crop at least part of
their agricultural land and hence must turn over 40–50 percent
of its yield to their landlords.

The main crop is rice, which is transplanted in the irrigated bottom lands before the onset of the monsoons and harvested four months later. Rice cannot be transplanted to nonirrigated, terraced land until the rains have begun. Corn is planted
in the early spring on high or sloping nonirrigated land and harvested in midsummer. Sometimes beans are planted between
corn rows and allowed to grow up the stalks after the corn has
been cut. Other topland fields are plowed after corn harvest and
planted with a crop of barley, millet, soybeans, or peanuts. Bottom land is planted in winter wheat in the late fall, and the
wheat is then harvested in April–May. Potatoes are also planted
on bottom land in January and harvested in late April.

After the winter wheat is planted, there is a slack period
of several months. From then on, and especially in the peak
May–June rice planting period, villagers are particularly busy in
the fields.

The senior male in the family organizes and oversees the
agricultural work. He must meet with the other village farmers
to set up his planting schedules, and then make sure he can hire
any extra labor he will need on his planting days. In the parma
system each household sends several members (usually women)
to whomever is planting (weeding, harvesting) on a given day.
In return, that household gets an equal number of free laborers
when its planting day comes. Members of poorer families with
less land to cultivate often work for wages instead of labor exchange. The wage for a male laborer in 1975 was six rupees
and two measures of flattened rice plus midday snacks and a
few cigarettes each day. Women earned only three rupees and
one and a half measures of flattened rice for a day's work.

The amount one must work in the fields is a clear measure of one's status. Any man who can afford to pays someone else to do the heavy farm labor for him. None of Narikot's respected elders, nor indeed any of the younger generation of men who have gone to school, would demean themselves by doing physical labor.[18] Senior affinal women in high-status families and married daughters on short visits to their parents are not sent to the fields, and favorite wives are sent less often than other wives and daughters-in-law.

Certain agricultural tasks are categorized as either men's or women's work. Men drive the oxen[19] and do the plowing (except for Upadhaya Brahmans, whose caste status bars even the poorest of them from this particular job). Men turn over the soil in dry fields or in the irrigated paddies to prepare for the planting of rice seedlings. They build and maintain the irrigation ditches and the mud walls between the paddies, and they do the first threshing of the wheat. Most of the agricultural work, however, is done by *parma* or labor exchange groups, and the major responsibility for arranging and scheduling the work of these groups falls to women (Bennett 1981:93). It is women's job to prepare a ploughed field for planting. This is done by pounding the rough dirt clods with wooden mallets. Women must also transplant the individual rice seedlings, and it is usually their job to carry manure to the fields. Harvesting, carrying crops to the house, weeding, and hoeing the soil are done by both men and women. Animal husbandry also is not linked to any particular sex, though usually it is a daughter-in-law's job to cut the huge loads of grass and fodder needed daily for each cow or buffalo. Pasturing goats and cows and bathing the water buffalo in the river or pond during the warm season are considered easy tasks which older children can perform.

In addition to their substantial input in the fields, women are also responsible for the storage, processing, and preparation of what is harvested. They must spread the grain out to dry, raking it frequently to see that it all gets exposed to the sun and hauling it inside if rain threatens. They must remove the corn from its stalk, storing some in neat bundles hung from the house eaves or from a tree and husking and shucking some for storage in baskets inside the house. They must also thresh the wheat straw a second time by beating the stalks on flat stones to shake loose any grain that is left.

A major part of women's work in food processing is husking the raw paddy to get edible grain and grinding the corn,

Women return from cutting grass for the family livestock. *Photo by Ane Haaland*

wheat, etc. into flour. Twenty years ago all rice had to be husked either by hand, using a heavy wooden pounder tipped with a metal ring, or on the footmill (dhiki). It takes three people to operate the footmill at maximum efficiency, and even then it takes three hours to process 25 kilograms of rice—barely enough to last a family of ten for seven meals. Most households in Narikot now take paddy to the electric mill which was opened in the early seventies and processes paddy for five paisa a pathi (approximately 2½ kilograms). But households with enough female labor still use the footmill to save money. Corn and wheat is now all ground at the village mill for twenty-five paisa a pathi In the old days women had to transport the grain to and from water mills that were several miles away and took payment in grain rather than cash.

One of the most time-consuming female tasks is cooking the two daily meals. Women must first make the fire with wood they have chopped (though men may have helped with this) or with cowdung chips they have collected and dried. Families that can afford it prefer to eat rice or unleavened wheat bread as their staple diet. Others must eat either unleavened bread made of barley, millet, or corn, or dhiro—a thick mush made of boiled corn or wheat flour that is considered the poor man's food. Along with this, dal (spiced lentil soup) is served and, if the family can afford it, one or more vegetable curries and a raw vegetable condiment. Families that can afford meat more than two or three times a year are very rare; but when meat is cooked it is the men's job to slaughter the animal and cut it into small pieces. In those households where women, for religious reasons, will not cook or eat meat, the men must cook it themselves outside. If there is extra milk from the livestock the women must churn it to make butter and then refine it into clarified butter. Even for a small family on an ordinary day, cooking a meal takes at least two hours, and cleaning up another forty-five minutes to an hour. During the rice-planting season women must also prepare and carry to the fields large amounts of spicy condiment and popped corn or roasted soybeans as an afternoon snack for the people working in their family's fields that day.

Child care is primarily a woman's job. But older men who spend a great deal of time around the house enjoy playing with toddlers and young children—teasing them, singing to them, and getting them to dance. The less pleasant tasks like feeding, cleaning up after messes, bathing and oiling children usually fall to women—though I have observed fathers bathing their children. If the mother of a nursing child has to work in the fields, she might strap the child to her back with a shawl. But if there are other women at the house to look after her child she may leave it there, and return during the day to feed it. Some adult villagers whose parents lived in a small nuclear family remember with a vivid horror being tied up and left at home when their mother had to work in a distant field. But usually there are many women in a household, and child care is a task happily shared by all.

The women in Narikot have few crafts to occupy them during the slack agricultural season. They do make floor mats out of braided rice straw, and cushions out of corn husks or sacred *kus* grass. Some women have learned how to knit, and though they can seldom afford good wool they often pull apart tattered sweaters and reknit them. Many women are also adept at simple sewing—making pillows, baby mattresses, and even mosquito nets from old saris. They may also remake their husband's torn clothes to fit a child. A few women from high-status homes know how to embroider pillowcases and sari slips, though their output is limited by the high cost of thread. The main avenue of aesthetic expression for Narikot women seems to be in religious worship which, as we will discover in the next chapter, is also largely their responsibility.

Women do the housecleaning. As a daily task this starts with the application of a fresh purifying coat of cowdung mixed with mud (*gobar*) to the door posts and front porch—an unpopular early-morning job that, significantly, must be done by daughters-in-law and never by daughters. Women sweep, hang out quilts to sun, and straighten the beds. They also do the laundry. Yet all these tasks around the house are considered preferable to being sent out to the fields to do farmwork or cut grass. Work in the home is considered easier and more refined, and the number of women a family can keep at home is a sign of their wealth and status.

Another responsibility of the senior woman, who carries the keys to the storeroom, is to keep track of the family's supply of cooking oil, salt, spices, etc. She has no money to buy these supplies herself, but must inform the household head when something is running low so that he can bring it from the bazaar. She must also inform him of any ritual supplies like incense, special fruits, etc., that may be needed for an approaching festival.

The household head is responsible for providing the cash

needed to buy these and other items that cannot be produced by the family. If he heads a family that has surplus grain to sell for cash, he will merely sell some of the grain, usually to a familiar Newari merchant[20] in a nearby bazaar town. Narikot farmers try to store their grain and delay selling it as long as possible, since aged grain brings a higher price. Furthermore, the longer they can wait after the harvest seasons, the less grain is available to drive down the market price. In storing the grain themselves, however, they risk theft and loss by rats.

The heads of less fortunate families must bring in the necessary cash by other means. If they or their coresident adult sons have education or influence, they will try to get work in town with the army, government service, or some private firm. Only a few men of Narikot have very important or lucrative jobs. Most work as accountants, clerks, cooks, or drivers and some have only a night watchman's post. For almost all such men, the village continues to be the center of their lives—even if they can only return on Saturdays and holidays. An older man is often content to give up his own job as soon as his son has found one. In fact, many more young men who are still living with their fathers have jobs in town than do the older heads of households. This pattern perhaps relieves some of the inevitable tensions of the extended family, because the son, off in town living in a barrack or inexpensive rented room, has some measure of independence. On the other hand, this independence sometimes generates new problems. The son begins to want some of the expensive pleasures of town living—such as cinemas, good clothes, hotel-restaurant meals, perhaps even a second "love-marriage." He may resent having to turn over most of his salary to his father for the support of his mother, wife, and children back in the village.

Those people who have neither sufficient land to feed themselves nor the education or influence necessary to get a post in town must work as occasional laborers. A few of the poorest must work as full-time servants. Members of this unfortunate latter group are those marginal individuals without families or land—deserted and divorced women, widows, and people who cannot marry because they are physically handicapped. Behind their backs they are called *bhat-mara* because they have no source of rice (*bhat*) but what others will give them for their labor. They are given room, board, and clothing, but usually little or no money.

It is difficult to get reliable figures on income and expenditures for Narikot households. Villagers do not ordinarily think in terms of annual or even monthly budgets, nor do they keep records of such things. A sum of money from grain sales or someone's salary is simply spent as household needs arise until it is gone. To give some idea of household economics, however, chart 1.1 presents the approximate expenses as reported by the head of a typical, fairly comfortable ten-member Narikot household. The account covers one year when the family had no special expenses.

Such a household would probably sell almost Rs. 3,000 worth of grain, earning the rest of its income through the salaries of its working members and by selling milk, eggs, etc. A poorer and more typical family could reduce its monthly expenses to Rs. 60 by cutting out tea, sugar, tobacco, and other luxuries. Less would be spent for the Dasai festival and the family's new clothes. With fewer fields there would be no cost for field hands—though the family might have to spend some money for food grains.

Usually only the household head (or one of his adult sons to whom he delegates the authority) actually makes any purchases. Other members of the family approach him with their requests and he decides the priorities. Certain things must come first, like cooking supplies and laundry soap for the women, school fees, fertilizers, medicine for a family member who is sick, basic ritual supplies, and tobacco. At Dasai the household head's burden is especially heavy because every member of the

Chart 1.1 Estimated Living Expenses for a Ten-Member Household, 1973

Monthly	Rs.	Annual	Rs.
Oil	30	Field labor (including cigarettes and rice	
Jira, mirch (spices)	3	beer)	1,300
Salt	4	Fertilizer: Rice	400
Sugar/Tea	26	Wheat	100
Milk	14	Festivals	
Puja (worship items)	6	Dasai (including new clothes)	1,100
Soap	15	Sraddha (including payments to Brahman	
Tobacco	16	and priest)	200
School fees	15	Others	200
Hair oil and cream	2		Rs. 3,300
Medicine	10	Monthly expenses	1,692
Monthly total	Rs. 141	Annual total	Rs. 4,992

family expects a new set of clothes, while at the same time the family must slaughter a goat and prepare special costly food for visiting relatives. At rice planting time too, the household head must buy new blouses for all the women in his house, pay the wages of the extra laborers he needs, and provide cigarettes and rice beer for those of his field hands who drink.

But even aside from Dasai, there are always requests: the household head's youngest wife asks sweetly for a new sari, his twelve-year-old son for pocket money at school, and his shy, sullen daughter-in-law hints indirectly that her little daughter needs new shoes and she herself could use some hand soap. Then the roof on the cowshed caves in, the buffalo dies, or it is time his eldest daughter was married and a good proposal has come. There is never enough money for all these things. In some years if the crops are poor or he loses his job, even basic expenses are difficult to meet. And the cost of a modest wedding (which on the average is at least double an annual family budget) can rarely be paid without borrowing. As a result, most villagers are involved in a network of interest-free loans with friends and relatives.

It is difficult for an outsider to understand why anyone gives such friendly loans, since (having given a few myself) they are seldom paid back promptly and one risks losing a friend in the process of dunning him for payment. Nevertheless, most villagers say they feel an obligation to give a loan of two or three hundred rupees if they have the money and there is a real need. It is also clear that such generosity is required if one is to achieve and maintain the status of a respected elder in the village.

For larger sums one must go beyond the village. Sometimes Newari merchants will make a loan at between 25 and 40 percent interest a year. The government's Agricultural Bank may loan large sums at lower rates if they can be convinced that the money will be used for agricultural purposes rather than to finance a wedding. Men who have been in the army or government service a number of years are eligible for an advance on their future salary. Otherwise a valuable piece of the wife's wedding jewelry may have to be pawned, though men say they feel ashamed to do this. And as a last resort there is always the dreaded prospect of selling or taking out a mortgage on one's land.

As a footnote to this brief look at household economics and as a prelude to our subsequent study of conflict in the joint family, we might note the high incidence of domestic theft in Narikot. During my period of research several fairly large sums of money or grain were stolen *within families*. There is a general atmosphere of distrust—even of young children—in one's own extended family, and everything that can be is kept under lock and key. Predictably, it is the relatively powerless members of the household who tend to steal: children, servants, and daughters-in-law. Children's thefts (usually of food or petty cash) are viewed more or less as naughty pranks until the age of twelve or so. But thefts by servants or daughters-in-law are considered serious offenses. Resentment is probably a major motivation in such cases, since both servants and daughters-in-law are in some sense "outsiders" in the family. They labor the hardest and yet have the least say in how the family resources are spent. At the same time, the high value placed on the internal solidarity of the family usually protects the domestic thief from serious legal consequences. Rather than lose face in the community by seeking police action, the family invokes its own sanctions against the offender.

Notes

1. The panchayat system in Nepal is essentially the same as that in India except that political parties are not permitted. The system consists of a series of elected councils or *panchayats* at the village, district, and national level. For a discussion of panchayat democracy in Nepal see Rose and Scholz (1980:41–57, 83–93) and Borgström (1980).

2. The main impetus for the fund drive came from a group of young men not actually on the school committee who got together and made up a list of what they thought each villager could afford to pay. Several who were on the school committee were assessed very large sums, up to Rs. 300 each, which they had to and did pay to maintain their prestige in the village.

The current value of the Nepali rupee is 13.10 to the dollar.

3. Höfer (1979:136–41) points out that the hierarchy presented in the Mulki Ain is not always consistent or unambiguous—especially with regard to the placement of the higher Newari castes.

4. The exception may be certain hill communities where the Muslim Curaute caste are residents. Since this group belongs in the category of touchable but water unacceptable (Höfer 1979:136), the distinction would no doubt be important in such communities. (See also Harvey Blustain, 1977.)

5. For discussion of similarities in the kinship structures of high-caste Hindus in North India and the Brahman-Chetri of Nepal, see Bennett 1978.

6. Apparently this latter group has enjoyed a certain upward mobility within the caste hierarchy during the last century. In the National Code of 1854 all foreigners (Mlecck) ranked at the very bottom of the impure but touchable castes from whom water could not be accepted (Höfer 1979:45).

7. If contact occurs, the affected high-caste person must be purified by a simple ceremony called *cito katne*, in which a person of equal or higher ritual status sprinkles the polluted person with pure water.

8. The term Khatri or Khatri-Chetri is ambiguous. It means specifically only that an individual is descended from a Brahman father. But (like the term Chetri) it says nothing about the individual's jharra or thimbu status, which depends (as for Chetri) on the status of the mother. Thus, it is possible to have a Khatri-Chetri of thimbu status (Brahman father, Matwali mother) who has no Chetri blood at all.

9. That is to say, any Brahman thar by the process of crosscaste marriage can have Khatri-Chetri members and thus, over time, can become Chetri thar as well. Only a few Chetri thar (among them Thapa, Basnet, Bista, Karki) are exclusively Chetri, having no Brahman ancestry.

10. The number of rishis usually cited in Hindu mythology is seven. The seven sages are Jamadagni, Gautama, Bharadvaja, Atri, Viswamitra, Kasyapa, and Vasista. However, there are many more than seven gotras, and thus presumably many more than seven founding gotra rishis. The *Gorkha Thar Gotra* (Sharma n.d.) lists 36 gotras as current in Nepal, but gives no indication as to whether the list is considered complete. G. S. Ghurye (1972) says the number of existing gotras reaches into the hundreds in some of the traditional treatises. He, however, believes that the "long list of gotras with 800 units or more such as Baudhayana presented in his 'Pravaradhyaya' [must incorporate] a large number of lineage names, names of units forming preceptor pupil successions of various schools of vedic learning and even the names of the original clan-units of the indigenous people who secured admission into the ranks of Brahmins!" (Ghurye 1972:226).

11. For example, a Brahman family observes only nine days of death pollution for its Khatri relatives even at close proximity. Likewise, Khatri offspring cannot offer pinda made of rice to their Brahman ancestors, who are purer and of higher ritual status than they. Instead, they must offer pinda made of barley flour.

12. If news of a distant relative's death arrives after the thirteen-day mourning period following his death, then only the *chak khalko* (abstaining from one meal) restrictions are observed.

13. The term *phuki bhai* is also used for individuals with whom ego has no known genealogical ties, who are not members of ego's kul, but who have the same thar and gotra as ego. In such circumstances there are no mutual death pollution obligations.

14. Bista (1972) has constructed the following table from the *Mulki Ain, v.s.* 2012 (1955), "Asoc barneko" section, pp. 93–111:

Relation	Days of Pollution for	
	Birth	Death
(a) members of the same lineage after thirteen generation	0	0
(b) between 8 and 13th	0	3
(c) between 3 and 8th	3	10
(d) separated by 3 or less	10	13

15. Residential proximity is also a factor. Members of the same village who share the same thar and gotra but belong to separate kul and have no known genealogical connections may observe chak khalko restrictions as if the deceased were a phuki bhai relation.

16. A survey which I conducted as part of the USAID-funded Study on the Status of Women in another Parbatiya village related to Narikot through marriage revealed that only about 36 percent of the high-caste households were extended families (Bennett 1981:45).

17. In 1975 one household in Narikot sold between Rs 8,000 and 9,000 worth a

year, seven households sold between Rs 2,000 and 3,000 worth annually, and ten households sold between Rs 200 and 300 worth annually. The rest broke even or had to supplement their own harvest with purchased grain. Only the two Damai households and one Chetri family are completely without farmland in the village.

18. For further discussion, see Stone 1975.

19. Narikot shares two pairs of oxen, which in 1975 rented with their plowman for Rs 16 a day.

20. Recently several Narikot farmers trusted an unknown dealer who had just settled in a nearby village and who had promised a larger percentage of profit. The man decamped in the night with the grain, leaving his wife (who was almost stoned out of the village) and the enterprising Narikot farmers several thousand rupees poorer. Even in a case of such blatant wrongdoing, the villagers would not call the police.

CHAPTER 2

Religion: Conceptual Framework and Some Central Oppositions

The Concept of Dharma

The Brahmans and Chetris of Narikot are Hindus. As they put it: "We follow/obey the Hindu religion," *Hamiharu hindu dharma manchau*. I have translated *dharma* as "religion" here, but it has a much broader meaning than "religion" has in contemporary usage, where it tends to be confined to the realm of the theological and spiritual. As Mary Douglas has pointed out, religion in contemporary Western thought has been increasingly considered a matter of belief and individual intellectual commitment, specifically opposed to ritual conformity, which is often considered empty of meaning and "not compatible with the full development of the personality" (Douglas 1970:22).

For the Hindus of Narikot, ritual and belief are still unselfconsciously integrated—so much so that villagers tend to speak of dharma in terms of action, as something one *does* (or at least should do), rather than something one believes in. In Nepali usage the word *dharma* encompasses the performance of specified rites and ceremonies, and obedience to ritual prescriptions appropriate to one's place in the social structure, as well as general ethical behavior covering individual actions of compassion, honesty, etc. Whether it is the result of ritual conformity or individual decision, dharmic action grows out of, harmonizes with, and is indeed part of the social, moral, and metaphysical order of things.[1] Dharma is *duty*, compelling because it is conceived to be grounded in the nature of reality. In this sense, the statement that Clifford Geertz made about religion could also serve as a definition of dharma:

> Never merely metaphysics, religion is never merely ethics either. The source of its moral vitality is conceived to lie in the fidelity with which it expresses the fundamental nature of reality. The powerfully coercive "ought" is felt to grow out of a comprehensive factual "is" and in such a way religion grounds the most specific requirements of human action in the most general contexts of human existence. [Geertz 1973:126]

Because village Hinduism is so involved with ritual and the "specific requirements of human action," some anthropologists have stopped at this level in their interpretation of it. S. C. Dube writes:

> Clearly Hinduism as it is practiced in the village is not the Hinduism of the classical philosophical systems of India for it possesses neither the metaphysical heights nor the abstract content of the latter. It is a religion of fasts, feasts and festivals in which prescribed rituals cover all the major crises of life . . . spiritualism cannot be said to be the keynote in the life of the community; far from it, the religion appears to be a practical one. [Dube 1967:93]

But even the sheer practicality of Hindu dharma depends on its metaphysical meaning for the people who follow it, and is thus inseparable from their spiritual and philosophical concerns, their conceptions about "the most general contexts of human existence." In other words, village rituals command the authority to "cover the major crises of life" *by virtue* of the fact that they are symbolic expressions of the very "abstract content" Dube would deny them. Despite the difference in the way they are articulated, the fasts and festivals of Narikot and the "classical philosophical systems of India" share certain basic Hindu values and concepts about the structure of reality. They are varied forms of a single dharma which unifies all aspects of Hindu experience from the social to the spiritual.

The Samsara/Mukti Opposition

The Hindu world view is structured by certain fundamental conceptual oppositions. One of the most pervasive is the opposition between *samsara,* the phenomenal world, and *mukti,* release or salvation. To my informants samsara (or *sansar,* as they called it) means the world as they, in their unenlightened state, experience it. Turner's (1931) Nepali dictionary describes samsara as "the round of birth and death." Transmigration of the soul, however, is only one manifestation of the general instability and contingent nature of samsara. Village informants described samsara as an unending and untrustworthy fluctuation between different physical, emotional, ritual, social, and economic states. These states tend to be cast as opposites of one another: happiness and sorrow, hunger and satiety, wealth and poverty, pleasure and pain, and, in the longer range, birth and death. Despite its uncertainty, samsara is ultimately just, because it works according to *karma,* the law of moral cause and effect whereby an individual's evil actions are eventually repaid through his own suffering. But the individual, limited by the finite consciousness of his present incarnation, often experiences the fluctuating fortunes of samsara as arbitrary. The working of karma is so subtle, and its time scheme so vast, that the individual could never hope to grasp the detailed moral accounting which has brought about his present state.

The villager's emphasis on instability is consistent with the dominant Hindu conviction that samsara is ultimately unreal. In Hindu metaphysics, change and its concomitant multiplicity belong to the realm of "conditional reality." It is "delusion" resulting from individuation and the subjective consciousness. Informants, of course, never described samsara to me in such abstract terms; nor would they dismiss the phenomenal world as unreal. But they have expressed it as provisional—as in some sense an obfuscation of a higher level of reality.

This is, I think, what one village informant meant when she spoke of the need to look at the world with "the mind's eye" as well as one's "outside eyes." We were speaking about dharma in its broader sense and about how one determines ethical or "right" action in areas not prescribed by ritual dharma. She quoted a proverb, "Sri Ram says, Sri Ram says, keep the inner and outer consciousness open; Keep both eyes open" (*Sri Ram bol, Sir Ram bol; Caitya bhitro bahiro rakne khol; Duwai akkha khol*). And then she went on to explain:

This means open your eyes which are on the outside and those which are inside and look. And then meditate upon God's name. If you stare only on the outside, then there's nothing within—you are empty. But when you open your mind's eye and look, then you know if you do this, then this is what will happen and if you do that, then that is what will happen. . . . They say that when such a person dies [who has thus meditated and assessed the true karmic results of her actions in samsara], then that person doesn't have to be reborn as a human being, that person will live in heaven (swarga). A life like this, in which one has a son but hasn't money, will not have to be suffered.

The final portion of her explanation reflects the fundamental Hindu belief that under certain circumstances an individual's soul (atman) can attain mukti or release from samsara into transcendent reality. However, village concepts about the nature of this reality are hazy and often blend with beliefs about what happens to the ordinary, unenlightened soul after death. Some, like the informant quoted above, seem to conceive of transcendence rather literally as entry into swarga, "heaven"— that pleasant celestial realm of the gods that villagers have heard described in vivid and luxuriant detail whenever religious texts are recited.

Most villagers, however, tend to see swarga and narka or hell as part of the samsaric round. One earns swarga or narka as one earns a good or bad rebirth in the next life. Both are conceived as karmic reward for one's actions. As one old woman explained, "there is no such thing as swarga. This is swarga, this is narka. If you have done dharma then after you die you become human. Haven't you seen people who are born without eyes, hands, or feet? They are all people who have committed sin (pap) in their past life."

In the course of my work two distinct modes or levels of immortality emerged, each with its own dharmic path: the transcendent immortality, or true mukti, for the enlightened soul; and the "conditional immortality" of the unenlightened individual still bound into samsara. It became clear that swarga is used in reference to both types of immortality. It stands as a kind of literal equivalent for the abstract concept of mukti, and it also represents one version of conditional immortality—a kind of reward in the afterlife for the unenlightened but reasonably virtuous individual.

Village concepts about conditional immortality center on the belief that after death the ordinary individual is transformed, through the ritual ministrations of his or her son, into an ancestor spirit, pitr, and goes to dwell in the pitrlok, the abode of the fathers. The exact nature of existence in the pitrlok varies among different informants. Many speak of it as a pleasant place equivalent to heaven or swarga. Others seem to conceive of the pitrlok as a kind of neutral limbo where one exists prior to rebirth. Still others thought that some spirits who had not been virtuous in their previous lives, or who had died in a state of ritual impurity, would not be allowed to enter the pitrlok at all, but would instead either have to go to hell or haunt the world of the living in the form of a "hungry ghost." We will explore these ideas in more detail in the section on death rituals in the next chapter. But it is clear that ideas about the nature of conditional immortality are complex, and in some respects mutually inconsistent. For example, informants were never very certain about how the idea of transmigration dovetailed with their belief in the soul's existence in the pitrlok. Yet most of them were quite comfortable with a certain looseness of fit between different belief structures and levels of conceptualization. And from a certain perspective, transmigration and existence as an ancestor spirit *are* consistent representations of the essentials of conditional immortality. Neither releases the soul from the needs and desires, the suffering and uncertainty of samsara. Just as the newly reborn soul is once again subject to its bodily needs and dependent on its parents for sustenance, so the ancestor spirits are still subject to the same needs in the afterlife, and dependent on their own living progeny to "feed" them in annual commemorative rituals.

Although villagers are uncertain about the exact nature of conditional immortality, they are confident about how it is achieved. They must follow the rules, rituals, and morality of conventional Hindu religion and they must produce male offspring. This, in essence, is the "householder's path" (*grhastha dharma*). Here the ideals are those of social and familial responsibility. The householder must earn a living because, as one informant reported, "it is the duty of the householder to support everyone—from the insects to the gods." The householder is also expected to marry and have a family. Because of the importance of having sons to perform the funeral ceremonies necessary for the soul's admission to and continued sustenance in the pitrlok, the householder's path coincides to a large extent with the values of patrilineal ideology—especially regarding the importance of maintaining lineage continuity.

According to the householder's dharma then, one contributes to and participates in samsara and receives his rewards there—whether it is a pleasant sojourn in swarga or a high rebirth. But even as they faithfully and scrupulously follow this path, most villagers are aware that this path shares the provisional nature of samsara and that true *mukti* or release is something categorically different from swarga or any kind of rebirth no matter how magnificent. They know that ultimately release is achieved not by the rituals of conventional religion, nor through the mediation of the patriline, but by abandoning the family, caste, and worldly wealth of their present birth and renouncing samsara altogether. The same woman who spoke above about doing dharma to receive a good rebirth went on to express her concept of mukti. We were discussing whether she would prefer rebirth as a woman or a man in her next life. She said:

> But if it were possible for me to do great dharma, then I wouldn't be a man or a woman. I would try to receive mukti. Mukti means— it is better to keep the soul (*atma*) away from all the *maya* [infatuation, magic, love; used colloquially to mean love] for the husband and for the children. If you are too immersed in maya then you are too caught up with your husband and your children and you come back again. Sometimes you are born in your own children's wombs. . . . It becomes peaceful if the soul is kept apart. But you must work very hard for this. I think that the *mahatma* [great souls, saints] receive it—this mukti. They spend a whole month in meditation, neither eating nor drinking. They don't even sleep. They don't move at all. They receive the vision of God in peace. After they die they will not be born again. . . . They are ascetics (*tyagi*). There is one mahatma. He had a very big and beautiful house in Balaju, and others in Chetrapati and Dhoke Dhera. But he has forsaken all of these. He became an ascetic at the age of thirteen. His dharma is very great.

Village informants, then, seem to conceive of two levels of immortality and two approaches to dharma: one based on participation in and contribution to the ongoing processes of organic and social life; and the other—ultimately higher—based on control, withdrawal, and final denial of these processes. The ascetic's path to transcendent immortality (*sanyasi dharma*) is in many ways the opposite of the householder's path. The ascetic seeks to escape from samsara by strictly controlling the needs and desires of his body and the emotions that perpetuate his involvement in the unceasing round of birth and death. The ascetic must renounce family, caste, and all the pleasures of the flesh to become a celibate, homeless mendicant. He must wander from house to house, begging for food, and he must practice harsh forms of austerity (*tapas*) to discipline his senses and wean himself away from samsara.

In Narikot there are no ascetics. No one has left home to become a naked *sadhu* or holy man. And in the course of my fieldwork no one—male or female—expressed the intention or even serious desire to take up the ascetic path.[2] Although, like the informant quoted above, villagers believe in principle that great spiritual powers and ultimate mukti can be achieved by the ascetic saint, most are very skeptical about the actual sadhus who come begging at their own doors. They would often claim that most such "ascetics" were either lazy, untrustworthy charlatans who were unwilling to earn an honest living with their own labor, or that (especially in the case of female ascetics) these unfortunate individuals had been driven to a life of mendicancy by financial necessity rather than by a genuine desire for mukti.

Narikot is a village of solid householders. Yet, paradoxically, conventional village religion is itself deeply permeated by ascetic values. Through its symbolic forms—the myths and rituals which express the householder's view of samsara and structure his passage through it—the householder's path incorporates the contradictory values of the path of the ascetic.

The Symbolism of Purity and Pollution

One of the clearest instances of the penetration of ascetic values into conventional religion occurs in the rules of purity and pollution that structure so much of village thought and behavior. To the outsider first encountering village Hinduism, the preoccupation with ritual purity seems almost obsessive and its meaning obscure. But once it is placed in the context of asceticism and the samsara/mukti opposition, the parallel opposition between pollution and purity (jutho/cokho) assumes central symbolic importance.

The very organic processes that the ascetic seeks to control—eating, urination, defecation, copulation, menstruation, birth and death—are what the village householder perceives as polluting. The villager, of course, cannot avoid his involvement with these life processes. They are the very basis of his individual existence, of the collective existence of the patrilineal unit and, indeed, of the entire society of which he is a member. His constant fluctuation between states of purity and pollution is symbolic of his entanglement in the instability and unreality of samsara. Through the rituals of conventional religion he attempts to maintain the balance in favor of purity. But for the householder, purity—symbolic of renunciation and release into transcendent reality—is always a fleeting state, achieved with effort and soon lost again.

In the course of a normal day the Hindu villager is constantly affected by varying degrees of pollution which, to follow his dharma, he must counteract with appropriate ritual purification. When he awakes the clothes he has slept in are mildly polluted (*bitulo*), and so is his body after his morning trip to the fields. He counteracts this impurity by washing (though not always with a full bath), cleaning his teeth, even scraping his tongue and gargling out "old" saliva, and then putting on another set of clothes. If he is a Brahman, he must put on a dhoti (which is wrapped, rather than sewn, to cover the lower half of the body) to prepare himself for the next two events in the day— worship and eating. For these activities he must be in a relatively high state of purity, and stitched clothing is considered less pure than unstitched clothing. Then, before the morning meal, while he is still in a state of purity from all-night fasting, he should perform the daily worship of the household gods (*nitya puja*). Actually, except in certain orthodox Brahman households where a fossil stone sacred to Visnu (*saligram*) is kept, this worship is usually performed by women, who must also have bathed and changed clothes. Even the gods are slightly impure after they have "slept" at night and must be bathed before they can be "fed" grains of rice, fruits, fried breads, or sweets and then offered fresh flowers.

Next comes the morning meal. Eating a rice meal is not a leisurely, convivial event.[3] Although a good host will tell his guest to eat slowly so that he might have room for more, in fact family meals are eaten rapidly with little unnecessary conversation. There is a sense of vulnerability which pervades the cooking and eating of *dal-bhat* (lentil broth and boiled rice), the ritually relevant foods. For one is liable to pollute others or be

oneself polluted—even to the point of losing caste—if the conditions under which the meal is cooked and served are not
carefully regulated.[4]

To get a sense of the complex logic of pollution beliefs,
let us look in some detail at the ritual surrounding the morning
and evening rice meals.

The hearth where rice is cooked must be kept extremely
pure. No one of a caste lower than that of the household, no
one in a state of temporary impurity, and no one who is wearing shoes may enter the hearth area. Gobar (cowdung mixed
with mud paste), used in many contexts to create a pure or sacred space, must be spread over the entire cooking and dining
area after every meal before another meal can be cooked. Peripheral tasks like cutting vegetables, carrying water—even
cooking roti (unleavened bread) and curries—may be performed
by unmarried girls, uninitiated boys, or members of clean Matwali castes. Lentil broth and boiled rice, however, can only be
cooked by a full-status adult member of the family's caste or
above. If the family is Brahman, then the woman who cooks
must remove her blouse (which has been stitched, and hence is
not entirely pure) and wrap the end of her cotton sari around
her breasts. The cook may not eat or even taste the food until
she has served everyone else. For if she were to do so she
would be polluted by the contact between food and the saliva
of her own mouth, and if she again touched the food then it
would all become jutho or polluted and hence inedible for all
members of the family who have achieved full adult caste status
(see chapter 3). For the same reasons, those who are eating are
careful not to touch anyone else or any common vessel. Each
stays in his own eating square, and second helpings are dropped
or poured onto the plates from a safe distance by the cook.

At the beginning of the meal, people wash their hands
and feet so that nothing unclean will be brought into the eating
square; and when the meal is over, people wash their hands,
mouth, and feet to remove the impure leftover food. Though
these pollution rules are more lax for children, they begin to
learn them almost before they are toilet trained. Adults' reaction
to being approached by a toddler with rice still smeared on his
hands and face is as strongly negative as their reaction to an
unwashed bottom.

To villagers these daily rituals of purification hardly seem
like ceremonies but are more like simple acts of bodily hygiene,

personal grooming, or dining etiquette. Unless there is accidental contact with some unclean object, with a person of untouchable caste, or for an adult male with a menstruating woman,
these rituals are sufficient for the kind of neutral purity required
on an ordinary day.[5] But when the family is observing some
auspicious life-cycle or calendrical rite that requires a higher state
of purity, or when death or childbirth has put the family (or one
of its members) in a state of severe pollution, strong purification
rituals are required. As we will learn, these rituals can be long,
complex, and taxing to perform.

Hindu ritual contains a whole symbolic arsenal of purifying activities. Specifically *ascetic* activities like fasting (full or
partial), sexual abstinence, all-night vigils, and even temporary
vows of silence are extremely powerful. There are various types
of ritual gifts, such as *daksina* (gift of money), *sidha* (gift of one
measure of uncooked rice, curd, fried breads, vegetables, and
spices—i.e., all the ingredients of a meal), *godan* (literally, the
"gift of a cow," usually represented by a leaf plate with some
coins on it), and other kinds of *dan* or religious gifts. All bring
merit and purification to the donors when given to ritually superior individuals (i.e., Upadhaya Brahmans and certain categories of kin). The utterance of certain mantras has a purifying effect, as does contact with *prasad,* the offerings of fruit, flowers,
rice, red and yellow powders, etc., made to the gods and then
received back by the donors as a kind of blessing.[6]

In addition, almost every category of physical object or
substance seems to be ranked in the conceptual hierarchy of
purity and pollution that structures samsara. This means that some
elements, such as fire, water, gold, and in some contexts earth,
have active purifying powers that can be used to nullify pollution. Other substances in this category are the five products of
the cow (milk, curds, clarified butter, dung, and urine) as well as
certain plants (such as kus grass, dubo grass, the tulsi plant, the
pipal tree, etc.)

Besides these few items that have active purifying powers, many other physical substances and objects fall into one of
two ranked categories: those which are less permeable to pollution and hence can be purified, and those which must be destroyed once they have been in contact with a polluted object.
For example, a clay pot which has been touched by a low-caste
person or a menstruating woman must be thrown out, while a
metal pot may be purified with water and used again. In other

words, metal is purer than clay. Among metals, gold is ranked highest, then silver, copper, brass. Likewise, wool is considered more pure than cotton; baked brick purer than unbaked; running water purer than stagnant water; uncooked food and food cooked in clarified butter purer than cooked food—especially boiled rice and lentil broth, which as I mentioned earlier is particularly vulnerable to pollution. The list goes on and expands to classifications of such diverse things as the parts of the body, the cardinal points, the directions left and right, the male and female sex, the days of the lunar fortnight, the months of the year, the kinds of supernatural beings, even the kinds or castes of human beings—all of which are ranked according to their relative purity and auspiciousness.

The many Hindu purification rituals are all based on this conceptual framework, using, for the most part, the same symbolic vocabulary of ritual acts (fasting, bathing, etc.) and physical substances (fire, gold, cowdung, etc.) in different combinations and strengths. Ritual purification is extremely important in village religion as a means by which the opposing values of asceticism are symbolically incorporated into the householder's life. Ritual purity, attained by obeying the rules and performing the ceremonies of conventional religion, is at least on one level a metaphor for ascetic purity attained through renouncing samsara and performing harsh austerities. Both kinds of purity require discipline and set limits to the bodily and egotistical desires of the individual. Significantly, the strongest rules for maintaining ritual purity have to do with the regulation of sex and eating, both areas where the desires of the flesh are strong.

Means to Conditional Immortality

The householder's dharma involves several other strategies for achieving conditional immortality, all of which are themselves deeply entwined with concepts of ritual purity. One important strategy which I touched on earlier is the effort to build up merit (*punya*) or "good karma" during one's present lifetime. Whether this merit is believed to earn a better rebirth or a pleasant sojourn in heaven (or perhaps some combination thereof), there are two principal ideas about how it is accumulated.

One way is through the performance of not only the required rituals (which merely keep the "karmic score" even), but also special rituals that either increase the balance of merit or, if one has committed a specific sin (*pap*), cancel out the sin and restore the balance. Some of the special ceremonies that took place in Narikot during my fieldwork were *Satya Narayan puja* (worship of Visnu), *Rudri* (worship of Siva), *Saptaha* (reading of the *Bhagavata Purana* by seven Brahmans in seven days) and *Navaha* (nine days of readings from sacred texts). The first two are modest domestic rituals that usually employ only the family priest and perhaps an assistant. They can be completed in a few hours and involve only minimal expenses for offerings to the gods and gifts or payments to the priests. The Saptaha and Navaha rituals, however, are much more arduous and expensive to perform. A special enclosure must be erected, a more learned priest must officiate, more lavish offerings and ritual gifts must be given, and the whole village is invited to attend. But of course the merit earned from these rituals is also proportionately greater.

It is usually women who urge that family resources be used to sponsor these special rituals. Although male Brahman priests must be called in to officiate, it is the senior women of the patron family who organize and run the event. They find out exactly what ritual materials and offerings will be needed, what purifications must be done, and what special foods must be prepared. They recruit husbands and sons to make the necessary purchases and to construct the ritual enclosures, and they call upon neighbor women to help prepare food and make ritual leaf plates. These special rites, along with major life cycle ceremonies such as weddings, give women an important opportunity for self-expression beyond the immediate family—one of the few legitimate "public" areas in which women can seek to enhance their prestige at the community level.

As has been observed of the Hindu women of North India (Lewis 1958; Luschinsky 1962; Jacobson and Wadley 1977), the women of Narikot are responsible for most of the ritual activities within the household. Although the textual traditions have generally been the exclusive preserve of male Brahman priests and although there are certain important patrilineal rituals which can only be performed by initiated males, women have their own areas of ritual expertise. Daily worship of the household gods and celebration of the numerous minor calendrical festivals, as well as the essential maintenance of the ritual purity of

On a freshly plastered circle of cowdung a woman ends her religious fast with an offering to the sun god Surya. *Photo by author*

the family kitchen, are all in the hands of women. Women seem to derive great satisfaction and pride from performing *puja* or worship ceremonies for the gods, though these rituals often involve rising in the pre-dawn darkness to bathe in an icy river, making a long trip on foot to a distant temple, or fasting for a full day. In fact, as men will readily admit, in most households the women are far more fastidious about ritual purity and far more involved in religious and devotional matters than men are. For example in Narikot it was usually women who undertake voluntary religious fasts (*barta*) on a weekly or monthly basis. On any given Sunday, Tuesday, new moon, or full moon day (as well as countless other auspicious days during the year) one would find many Narikot women abstaining from their regular meals and taking only a little fruit or milk in order to earn merit.

Merit can also be gained outside the ritual context by moral behavior, such as honesty and marital fidelity, and through simple humanitarian acts of kindness and compassion. Villagers frequently mentioned the giving of alms as a way to build up merit. Informants believe that God (Bhagwan) keeps a very strict account of what one gives, and one woman told a kind of King Midas story to illustrate her belief. The story was about a rich man who had given an entire house of gold to a Brahman as dan. After this magnificent gift he felt his charity obligations were fully discharged and henceforth refused to give anything to the many starving beggars who came to his house. His wife however, was a very religious woman who followed not only the rituals but also the spirit of dharma. Whenever her husband wasn't looking, she would sneak out and give at least a handful of barley flour to the beggars. When the man died and reached the afterworld, he found only his cold and empty golden house. There were no beds, no clothes, and no food. It was only because a woman's merit is transferred to her husband that this man was spared hunger and misery in the afterlife: in one room of the golden house he found the barley flour his wife had secretly managed to give away as alms.

Another related path by which the householder can seek conditional immortality is through devotion to God or even to the many personified forms of God. In many ways this strategy overlaps with the quest for merit. Indeed, all the special meritorious rituals listed earlier, as well as most of the normal calendrical rites, bring merit *because* they are dedicated to the gods. For the villager, to whom the concept of mukti is rather remote,

God or Bhagwan is a more congenial cipher for ultimate reality, and the *devta*, or personified forms of Bhagwan, are a more comprehensible focus for religious efforts.

Villagers have little difficulty combining a firm belief in the unity of God with the blatant multiplicity of the forms which the deity takes for those enmeshed in samsara. As one woman explained to me:

> All the devta are the same for us. Only their names are different. But if one devta eats meat [i.e., takes blood sacrifice] and another doesn't; if one is strong and another isn't—what is there to say? Devi [the goddess] eats meat and Mahadeo [Siva] doesn't. Ganes eats and Kumar doesn't. The Panc Kumari [five virgin goddesses] accept *bhog* [blood sacrifice]. It is just a matter of whether they take bhog or not. But Bhagwan is the same. Now, you and I are different and we are different from the Damai [untouchable tailors], but all this is only a difference of color and caste. All our souls are the same. It is the same with Bhagwan. Only the name differs.

Despite this metaphysical unity of Bhagwan and the devta, there is a definite practical difference between them in village religion. Bhagwan is the name used to refer to the deity in ethical contexts. Almost like a personification of karma, Bhagwan is believed to keep track of one's good and bad deeds—the accumulation of merit and sin—over the countless incarnations of the soul. One pleases Bhagwan by ethical and humanitarian acts rather than through the performance of ritual. It is the devta who are the object of the constant puja ceremonies that take place in the homes of Narikot Hindus.

Puja is a central feature of the householder's religious life. It is a means for achieving a good rebirth or entrance to heaven in the afterlife and also a means for achieving one's worldly goals in this life—though some informants claimed that one had to choose whether to reap the fruit of one's merit in this life or to save it for the afterlife. The concept of puja is simple: one pleases the gods by sharing one's resources with them, and they reciprocate according to their varying powers and natures.

As I mentioned earlier, there is a hierarchy of spiritual beings in Hindu thought,[7] and villagers relate differently to each level of the hierarchy. For the few priests in the village who have some Sanskrit training, *Atma* or the universal soul (with which the individual soul or *atma* is joined when true mukti is attained) is the highest and most undifferentiated form of divinity. However, very little attention is given to this vague meta-physical entity. For most villagers the highest form of divinity (in the sense of the most abstract and universal) is Bhagwan. At the next level, among the devta who must receive worship, Visnu in his ten incarnations (including Ram Chandra and Krisna), Siva, and the many forms of the goddess Devi are the highest. When pleased, these deities are able to help their devotees, granting wealth, sons, and protection in this life and also granting con-ditional salvation, i.e., admission to swarga, in the next life. Be-low these three principal gods are Surya, the sun god (also a form of Visnu), and Agni, the fire god, both of whom are pow-erful in granting purification to their devotees. Kumar (the six-headed warrior son of Siva) and Ganes (Siva's elephant-headed son) are at about the same level in the hierarchy as Agni and Surya. These are all Great Tradition gods that are found through-out Hindu culture.

The next form of divinity, the kul devta, is specific to each lineage group or kul. These gods display a much more demand-ing nature, and their powers seem to be largely confined to af-fecting the present life of their devotees. The great gods, of course, can be demanding too, but the kul devtas are particu-larly so. As one woman explained:

If I don't respect/obey (mannu) the kul devta, if I have no considera-tion and forget to offer up what I've cooked . . . , then there will be trouble. There will be pain for my body; there will be losses in the house. If the kul devta becomes angry it will cause trouble for the members of the family and bring harm to the children. Whatever is cooked must be offered up to the kul devta—but it is sufficient just to think about Bhagwan and remember his name.

In the intermediate levels between gods and men are various beings such as the nag (snake godlings), the Seven Rishis, Bhumi, the earth god, and of course, the pitr or ancestor spirits. These must all be worshiped to avoid or counteract mis-fortunes in this life that occur if they are neglected. But these beings have no power to affect the villager's existence in the afterlife or to help villagers achieve conditional immortality.

Finally, at the lowest level of the hierarchy are the bhut and pret. These are malevolent spirits of the dead, who have been unable to enter swarga or the pitrlok. They must be pro-pitiated with offerings of food, etc. But they are propitiated only after they have caused trouble to the living.

To become a devotee of Bhagwan or one of the three great gods is one of the householder's principal means of achieving conditional salvation. In fact, according to some of my informants, if an individual's *bhakti* or devotion is fervent enough, that bhakti itself can be an alternate path to unconditional salvation. Just as the ascetic frees himself from his attachments to samsara through austerities that control the senses and emotions, so the devotee loses his attachments by becoming totally absorbed in his passionate devotion to the deity. For most villagers, however, worship is more a matter of respect and obedience, perhaps mingled with some fear and gratitude, than a matter of fervent bhakti.

The final means of achieving conditional immortality in the householder's path is one we have already encountered: the production of male offspring who will perform the ceremonies necessary to insure the soul's admission and continued sustenance in the pitrlok. These four interrelated strategies—the maintenance of purity, the accumulation of merit, devotion to the gods, and the production of male offspring—serve as alternatives to ascetic renunciation. In the following chapter we will see how these alternatives are articulated through the symbolic forms of the life cycle rites (*samskara*) of the householder.

Notes

1. "Order" is, in fact, one of the Sanskrit meanings of *dharma*: "that which is established or firm." In certain technical philosophical usage *dharma* means "the nature, character . . . or essential quality of a thing" (Monier-Williams 1959).

2. Several women did express interest in eventually becoming disciples of a religious master (*guru*) and possibly even going to live in an *asram* under his guidance as a member of a religious community. But these women all stressed the devotional rather than the ascetic nature of this kind of religious life.

3. Poorer families will have the cheaper wheat or corn mush (*dhiro*) instead, the rules for which are slightly more lax.

4. Interestingly, one is also vulnerable to witchcraft at mealtimes. The most common way of casting a spell over someone is to put something in their food or simply to recite a spell while looking at the food which will be eaten by one's victim.

5. If there is physical contact with an unclean object (such as human excrement) the affected part must be washed. Though it is not a conscious ritual, the automatic reaction of a villager to the sight or smell of unclean things seems to be to clear the throat and spit as if to dissociate themselves from the offending presence by cleaning the mouth of saliva. Ritual purification after contact with an untouchable, as I mentioned earlier consists of a simple ceremony in which the person is sprinkled with pure water

(*cito katne*). The impurity of contact with a menstruating woman must be removed by bathing, changing clothes and sacred thread, and drinking water that has been touched with gold (*sun pani*), the purest of metals.

    6. The great purity of prasad is further attested by the fact that (except for prasad of food or water, which should be consumed) it is placed atop the devotee's head, the purest part of the body.

    7. The basic outlines of this hierarchy are taken from J. G. Campbell 1976.

CHAPTER 3

Life-Cycle Rites
for the Householder's Path

The central oppositions and some of the harmonies we saw in the last chapter are expressed most clearly in the completed ceremonies surrounding birth, death, and the transition to adulthood—the *samskara* or life-cycle rituals of Narikot's Brahman-Chetri community. In tracing these ceremonies it is possible to learn a great deal about Hindu kinship—especially about the ideology and behavioral obligations of the patriline, which appear to be the dominant concerns of the orthodox samskara. It is interesting that most of the formal life-cycle rituals described here center on males. For example, initiation with the sacred thread is exclusively for males, while the menarche rite which in many ways marks the equivalent transition to adulthood for females (to be discussed later) is not even considered a samskara. Likewise most of the wedding rituals and particularly the long and complex death rituals are predominately expressive of the male point of view. Nevertheless, by noting the roles women play, and more important, the roles they do not play in these rituals, we can begin to ascertain how women are viewed—at least in terms of the dominant patrilineal institution.

Birth Pollution (*Sutak*)

Since birth, like death, is one of the most radical assertions of man's involvement with the organic processes of life that govern samsara, it is consistent with the Hindu world view that birth should create severe pollution. This pollution, however, affects only the new mother. The infant has not really activated its karma and entered fully into samsara; thus the ordinary rules of purity and pollution do not yet apply to it. This is not to say that the infant is without karma. The very situation of its birth—its sex, the caste and wealth of its family, its physical and mental equipment—all these things represent the results of good and bad actions in past lives. However, because the infant is not yet socially or spiritually responsible for its actions, it cannot yet generate *new* karma. The first three of the five major rites pertaining to the life-cycle (*samskara*) are directed toward bringing the child into samsara, into full responsibility for its ritual purity and its social and ethical actions. This state of full adult responsibility is appropriately called *karma caleko* or "activated karma."

But before tracing the child's development into full religious and social being, let us look at the effects of its birth on the ritual purity of its mother and family.

Ideally, one Brahman priest told me, purification should begin with conception, but in village practice there are no prenatal ceremonies.[1] Pregnancy is ritually recognized after the fifth or sixth month, when the life breath (*sas*) is believed to have entered the embryo. The woman then becomes "two-bodied" (*duijiu*) and is barred from participating in religious ceremonies, especially memorial rituals for the ancestor spirits (*sraddha*), and from cooking boiled rice for adults. This latter restriction is not always followed in poor families where there is a shortage of female labor.

The formal period of birth pollution (*sutak*) begins with the cutting of the cord and extends until the morning of the eleventh day after birth.[2] During this period patrilineal relatives within five generations may not worship their household gods, participate in rituals honoring the lineage gods, or perform any other religious ceremonies.[3] But they are not themselves in a negative state of pollution. They may move freely among other members of the community and need not observe food restrictions. Only the mother is untouchable. In fact female family members and midwife attendants *do* touch her to oil, massage, and generally assist her. But they must bathe and change clothes before touching others.

Several minor ceremonies occur during the ten-day birth pollution period.[4] In most families an astrologer, usually of Jaisi

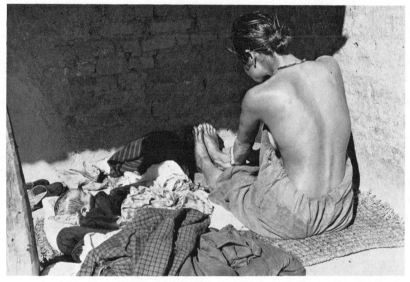

A newly delivered mother suns herself and her infant during the eleven-day period of birth pollution called "sitting in a corner." Once she has borne a child she need no longer feel shy about exposing her torso and breasts as she rubs oil on herself and her baby. *Photo by author*

Brahman status (*jyotis*), will be consulted to make sure that the child was not born under a sign hostile to his father. Only then is the father allowed to see his child.[5] The cutting of the cord involves certain ritual elements. It must be cut over a coin or a betel nut, tied off with new undyed thread, and buried by the mother herself if she is able. A votive light must be left over the spot. On the sixth night, when Bhabi, the goddess of fate, comes to write out the child's fortune on its forehead, a pen, a book, and a lamp must be placed beside the sleeping child. The lamp must be kept burning all night so the goddess can see to write out a long future for the child.

Name-Giving (*Nuharan*)

The first formal rite in a child's life is the name-giving ceremony (*nuharan*), which is performed on the morning of the eleventh day. On this day the family priest gives the infant its secret religious name. The child's father will also give his thar and gotra name to the child, thereby accepting it into the family's caste and patriline. This ceremony marks the end of the birth pollution period. The new mother can leave the dark room in which she and the child have been staying. As preliminary steps in her purification, she must bathe and wash her hair, clothes, and bedding. The child's father must also bathe and change his sacred thread.

Before the morning meal the family priest arrives, and inside the house on the ground floor he prepares an auspicious astrological design made with rice flour (rekhi) on an area which has been freshly spread with a purifying coat of cowdung paste. Here he will perform a Vedic fire ceremony (hom) and call upon various gods to bless the child. At one point in the fire ceremony the priest asks the exact time of the child's birth and then consults his astrological almanac to determine the letters that will begin the child's name. The father then tells the priest his thar and gotra and gives him tika, an auspicious mark of blessing which is placed on the forehead. The priest writes the child's name with yellow saffron paste on a pipal leaf, which is placed on the child's bed, after which he whispers the child's name into its ear three times. The priest then holds the child over the sacrificial fire and bounces it in the air three times.

The next part of the ceremony seems to be the village equivalent of the "first outing" (niskarmara) which in orthodox tradition was celebrated, like the prenatal ceremonies, as a separate rite (Pandey 1969:89). The child's mother or grandmother covers it with a shawl and carries it outside, places its feet on the ground, and then removes the shawl, allowing the child its first view of the sun.

Next, the priest gives a tika mark to the baby, the father, and other members of the family. He then prepares a mixture of ghee, curds, cow urine, milk, and honey with great purifying powers (panc amrt). This is offered to the lineage god and the household god to purify them and then given to each family member to drink. The family members, thus purified, come to the Brahman to have protective yellow strings tied to their wrists. The child's father must then give tika and daksina (a small gift of money to a ritually honored person) to the daughters of the house. The family may also have the child's horoscope written out by their astrologer on the naming day.

With the name-giving, which establishes the child as a

member of its father's patriline, the child's entry into this particular rebirth has begun. As yet, however, the concern with purity
and pollution which characterizes samsara only peripherally affects the child. Until the child receives its first rice at the age of
six months (see the next section), the nursing link between
mother and child seems to protect it from pollution. Mother's
milk is an extremely pure food, and informants explained that
infant feces and urine are not so polluting as those of adults
because the infant's only food is its mother's milk. Nursing children are not affected by the pollution of birth or the menstrual
pollution of their mothers.

The baby's lack of involvement in purity and pollution is
apparent in the funeral rites which are appropriate for an infant
who dies before the age of six months. It is buried instead of
cremated in the usual Hindu manner; and distinction is made
between a premature stillborn child and one who has had a
name-giving ceremony and has lived for several months. After
the burial hole is dug, a dish of milk is placed at the bottom and
buried with the child or fetus. Five days later milk is again placed
over the grave, and a new set of clothes is given as dan to a
Brahman child of the same sex as the deceased. During these
five days the child's mother and father may eat only once a day,
avoiding salt or oil, and may not worship the gods. Other close
patrilineal relatives eat only one meal on the first day; after
bathing the next day, they are again pure.

The symbolism involved in burying the very young child
becomes apparent when we note other kinds of individuals who
are buried rather than cremated in Hindu society. J. G. Campbell
(1976:118) has noted that besides infants, honored saints and
smallpox victims are also buried. He suggests that all three of
these categories are in some way outside the community for
whom normal Hindu ritual applies. The saint because he
achieved mukti, and the smallpox victim because he is believed
to be possessed by the smallpox goddess (Sitala), have both
transcended the normal human state. They no longer need the
final symbolic purification of the body which the cremation fire
brings. Infants do not need this purification because they have
not yet fully reentered the samsaric involvement with purity and
pollution.

First Rice (*Pasne*)

In time, of course, the nursing link must weaken and the child become a separate social and ritual entity. The beginning of this process is celebrated in the second life-cycle rite, the rice feeding ceremony (*pasne*), where the child receives its first rice meal. The rite is performed at five months for a girl child and six months for a boy.[6] The ceremony is simple. A priest or astrologer is asked to consult his astrological calendar and name an auspicious day and hour for the child to be given his first rice. Sometimes the family cooks a rich milk-and-rice pudding (*khir*), which is first offered to the gods in a public temple before being fed to the child. Often, however, the ceremony is performed at home, either with rice pudding or an ordinary rice meal. The child, dressed in new yellow clothes, receives its first rice from a senior male member of its father's household. This person usually scoops the rice onto a coin and then into the child's mouth. The coin is then given to the child. All the other assembled relatives "whom the child must respect" then feed it in order of their rank. First the child's paternal relatives take their turn. Next its mother's brothers (*mama*) and any other maternal relatives who have been called to the ceremony feed the child.

As we have seen, cooked rice is a particularly vulnerable channel for the transmission of pollution. It is a key cipher in the symbolic structure of caste organization. Status in the complex hierarchy of ritual purity is determined and expressed by the giving and acceptance of cooked rice. The eating of its first rice, then, signals the child's initial involvement in the sphere of purity and pollution. Villagers say that a child's first teeth come in at the time of its rice-feeding ceremony. In fact, teething may occur later, but these two events are conceptually associated. If a child dies after the first teeth appear (some informants say after the rice ceremony), it will be cremated with the same rites given to any other individual who has not reached full adult status (i.e., boys who have not had their initiation ceremony and unmarried girls). The child's parents will observe five days' death pollution (rather than the full thirteen days for a full-status adult) and the rest of the paternal relatives will observe only three days. What is important here is the association of the child's first food pollution with the fact that, in the event of death, the child's body now requires the stronger ritual purification of cremation.

The burial rituals which sufficed before are now symbolically inadequate.

The full transformation from a nursing infant to a karmicly responsible adult member of the Hindu community is a slow process that follows the same pattern which can be observed in the progression from the naming ceremony to the rice-feeding ceremony: increasing vulnerability to pollution, coupled with increased responsibility to participate in the rituals of purification offered by the householder's path. Children, as I have said, are exposed to pollution beliefs from a very early age, but the rules which apply to them are much more lenient than those which apply to karma caleko adults. Although they are discouraged from doing so, children may even eat rice from an untouchable until their adult teeth come in. As one woman recalled of her childhood:

> They say that I used to go to the house of a Damai even and eat there! Mother used to tell me that I shouldn't eat in such persons' homes, but I used to go to the Damai's house and say, "Sister-in-law, give me some rice. Put some clarified butter in it." Mother used to say that when your baby teeth fall out and new teeth grow, then from that time you mustn't eat from the hands of an untouchable or you will lose your caste. She used to say that if I did eat then she wouldn't let me back into our house. She used to teach me in this way, and if I didn't listen to her then she would scold me and beat me.
>
> The Newars in our village used to say "Bring the children of the Lieutenant (*laftan sab*). We shall give them food." And they used to give us food. I have taken liquor and rice beer also during the festival of Sansari Mai. You are allowed to drink until you are married. Once I was drunk and they had to carry me back, but I don't remember. I was quite small then.

While this woman's mother was obviously uncomfortable about her child taking food from untouchables, she was not concerned when her child took food and liquor from Newars, even though Brahmans and Chetris (especially women) are strictly forbidden to take liquor. Until a male has been initiated and until a female is married—that is, until they are karma caleko—they may take liquor and cooked rice from any of the clean castes. By the same token, such individuals cannot, as we mentioned, cook rice for those of their own caste who are karma caleko.

Initiation (*Bartaman*) into Caste and Patriline

Before I describe the initiation ceremony, which is the next life-cycle rite for the Hindu male of Narikot, I should mention that there is an important female rite that will be described in detail in my discussion of female body symbolism in chapter 6. This rite, which occurs at menarche, is called colloquially "staying in the cave" (*gupha basne*). It is not considered one of the orthodox life-cycle rituals (*samskara*), though certainly it conforms to the pattern of initiating increased responsibility for pollution and consequent involvement in purification ritual. Women however, have no real equivalent to initiation. They become karma caleko only through their marriage ceremony, whether it occurs after or before the menarche rite.

The rituals I am describing in this chapter are all part of the dharma of the householder, which strives toward the perpetuation of the patriline and the attainment of individual "conditional immortality" through one's progeny. Both these related goals would seem to be antithetical to the path of asceticism. Yet, if we look at the symbolic means by which the householder attempts to achieve these goals, we see that these life-cycle rituals represent a continual process of compromise with— one could even say co-optation of—the ascetic path that the householder has chosen not to follow.

One of the basic compromises is the cycle of the four *asramas* or life stages. As Wendy O'Flaherty (1973:78) put it:

The tension which is manifested in metaphysical terms as the conflict between the two paths to immortality, between Release and *dharma* of conventional society (in particular, the *dharma* of marriage and procreation) appears in social terms as the tension between different stages of Hindu life. These four stages provide a superficial solution in temporal terms: first, one should be a *brahmacārin* (chaste student), then *grhastha* (married householder), then *vanaprasthā* (the man who dwells in the forest with or without his wife), and finally the *sanyāsin* (the ascetic who has renounced everything).

This traditional schema attempts a resolution of the conflicting dharmas or paths by making the householder's dharma govern only a certain portion of a man's life. However, in the Hinduism of Narikot the last two stages of increasing renuncia-

tion are hardly ever realized. There are no ceremonies practiced to initiate the *vanaprastha* and *sanyasi* stages of life. In fact,
the vast majority of villagers look forward to spending their last
days in as much comfort as their sons can provide. There is a
marked tendency for older people to spend more time in religious activity, but this almost always takes conventional forms
of piety, rather than ascetic renunciation.

For a high-caste male of Narikot, who will in all proba-
bility spend the rest of his life as an ordinary householder, the
brahmacarya stage remains as the one brief period in his life
during which his conduct fully expresses the values of asceticism, as opposed to the worldly values and concerns which will
henceforth tend to dominate his life. During the *bartaman* or
initiation ritual, all the tension between the two paths is focused
on the contrast between the initiate's role as chaste student and
his upcoming role as a householder. Traditionally, a boy[7] was
to leave his own parents' home during this stage to live and
study in celibacy in the house of his guru. He was to return
home to be married and become a householder only when his
studies were complete. But like many other aspects of the as-
rama theory, the actual experience of the brahmacarya stage in
Narikot is very different. For village boys Vedic study and the
ascetic life are only symbolically enacted during the bartaman
ceremony that initiates this stage. Although this ritual is sometimes performed several years in advance of a boy's wedding,[8]
very often the bartaman is performed just a day or so before the
marriage ceremony. Here it becomes a necessary preliminary
rite within the wedding ceremony.

None of this, however, lessens the conceptual importance of the brahmacarya stage or of the bartaman ceremony as
its symbolic enactment. For the ascetic purity that the initiate
achieves in his bartaman is essential to the many changes that
the ceremony will bring about in his status. With his bartaman a
boy becomes karma caleko—ritually and morally responsible for
his own actions. This means that the merit and demerit of all his
actions begin to matter in the final accounting of his karma,
which will then determine his next rebirth.

As part of his karma caleko status, the initiate also assumes full membership in the two groups which largely identify
his place in Hindu society: his caste and his lineage. Since caste
membership is based on the maintenance of purity, it is consistent that the purification achieved by passing through the brah-

macarya stage is part of the initiation into full caste status. Once he has received his sacred thread at his bartaman, a Hindu must observe all caste restrictions at the peril of losing his own caste status. From people of castes lower than his own, he must take only pure food (*cokho*, food which is uncooked or cooked with clarified butter). He must refuse liquor and certain kinds of meat, and he may not take water from or allow himself to be touched by untouchable castes or menstruating women.

With regard to initiation into the lineage, however, the reason for this emphasis on ascetic purity is less obvious. Had we not already had some intimation of the paradoxical interpenetration of ascetic and householder ideals in Hinduism, we might reasonably expect the lineage, with its absolute dependence on progeny, to be utterly hostile to celibate asceticism. But this is not the case. O'Flaherty has demonstrated in her study of Siva mythology that asceticism and fertility are closely related in Hindu thought. "Although in human terms, asceticism is opposed to sexuality and fertility, in mythological terms, *tapas* [asceticism, austerities] is itself a power-creative force, the generative power of ascetic heat" (O'Flaherty 1973:41). Though householders and ascetics use the power of tapas in different ways, it is a means to both their respective modes of immortality. They share the idea that control/abstinence produces purity/power. Within this ideological framework spiritual power and sexual power are conceptual equivalents.

In a sense, the whole set of purity and pollution rules that we encountered in the householder's daily life represent a kind of minimal tapas—the imposition of some restraint and control on natural man. But it is tapas aimed not at the ascetic's radical goal of direct individual release but at the conventional goals of the householder—chief among which is immortality through offspring. Hence the tapas of sexual restraint that a boy enacts during his initiation can be seen as favorable to the interests of the lineage because it prepares him for the subsequent stage of marriage. As O'Flaherty puts it (1973:56), "Since one of the most important requirements of a bridegroom is his virility (the purpose of marriage being to beget children), the man of chastity is a good choice by virtue of the sexual powers amassed by his continence."

The Preliminary Rituals (*Purbanga*)
      Let us look now at how the values of asceticism are in-
tegrated into the life of the householder through the symbols of
the bartaman rituals. On the day before the bartaman certain
rituals collectively called *purbanga* (preliminary), must be performed.[9] After the purbanga rites the bartaman cannot be delayed by pollution from a death or a birth in the family.
      In the first of these preliminary ritual activities (called the
bhar bandan), an altar is built for worship of the *matrka* or mother
Goddesses, the ancestor spirits, and various other gods. (See figure 4.) The northeast corner of one room is purified with cowdung paste, and seven dobs of cowdung, representing the seven
matrka, are placed on the eastern wall of the room. Each dob is
decorated with a piece of sacred dubo grass, rice grains, and
auspicious red powder. As shown in the figure, sixty other
matrka[10] are represented by grains of red-colored rice, or in some
houses, more dobs of cowdung, placed on a low wooden seat.
Two Brahmans must place two stalks of sugar cane, onto which
a container of yogurt and a basket of dried fish have been tied,
in the corner of the room where the matrka are represented.
These stalks with the container of auspicious items are called
the *bhar*. When the bhar is in place, the family priest worships
the two sets of female goddesses with a ritual called *matrka
puja:* first a sari (which later goes to the wife of the priest) is
offered to the sixty matrka on the wooden seat; then the seven
matrka on the wall are worshiped.
      The initiate's father next offers a single *sidha* (a leaf plate
with the ingredients of a meal) to Bhumi, the earth god, as "rent"
for using the earth during the ceremony. He then offers three
sidha to all the gods and three to the collective ancestor spirits.
Then comes *abhyudayika sraddha*. This last ritual in many ways
represents the reverse of the death rituals or *sraddha* which will
be described at the end of this chapter. Unlike the death ceremonies, the abhyudayika sraddha performed before bartamans,
weddings, and certain other special meritorious rituals is auspicious. The rice ball fed to the ancestors during the death sraddha is replaced with a festive variant made of raisins. The sacred
thread of the person making the offerings remains in its auspicious normal position, and red powder, associated with fertility,
replaces the ascetic yellow powder used in death ceremonies.
Also, the ancestor spirits, who are generally viewed as irascible
and vaguely threatening beings, are believed to be pleased by

FIGURE 4

THE PURBANGA RITUALS

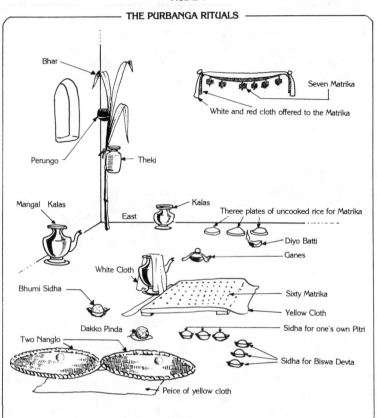

Bhar

Seven Matrika

White and red cloth offered to the Matrika

Perungo — Theki

Mangal Kalas

East

Kalas

Theree plates of uncooked rice for Matrika

Diyo Batti

Ganes

White Cloth

Bhumi Sidha

Sixty Matrika

Yellow Cloth

Sidha for one's own Pitri

Dakko Pinda

Two Nanglo

Sidha for Biswa Devta

Peice of yellow cloth

Seven Matrika - gobar with pieces of dubo grass decorated with red acheta and worshipped with libations of hot ghee

Theki: wooden vessel containing yogurt

Ganes: a supari (betel nut) in a leaf dish containing uncooked rice and a piece of red cloth

Two nanglo: winnowing baskets each containing a kasar ball made of rice flour, molasses and water

Bhar: two sugarcane stalks

Perungo: basket containing bananas, bundle of sal leaves, palung (spinach greens), dried fish, daneuro (a long fried bread), chura (beaten rice) and kasar (rice flour and molasses sweet)

Sixty matrika: grains of acheta on a pirka (wooden seat)

Dakko pinda: ball of dak (raisins), amala (tart fruit) bayer (jujube seeds) offered to pitri the bartaman. After a boy has been initiated he is eligible to perform death ceremonies and have this done for him in turn when he dies. The ancestors are pleased that a new male relative will be able to feed them with annual offerings as long as he is alive, and when he dies, join them in pitrlok.

After the abhyudayika sraddha, there are two rites performed by two married Brahman women which are devoted to the decoration and worship of a holy water vessel (mangal kalas) and the preparation of special sweets called kasar made of flour and molasses.

Next comes a ceremony called "digging pure earth" (cokho mato korne). For this two unmarried Brahman girls (kanya keti) must go out to the fields to get the earth needed to build the sacred enclosure where the bartaman will be performed.[11] Two virgin Brahman girls are also required for another ritual in which the rice that will be used in the upcoming bartaman ceremony and the subsequent feast is brought out into the sun to dry. The girls must also perform a ritual in which turmeric, saffron, and mustard seeds are roasted in a clay pot and ground into a paste. This paste will later be rubbed over the initiate's body by his sisters before the bathing ritual which takes place the next day.

Finally, the family Damai is called for a ritual in which he ceremonially finishes sewing clothes required the next day for the bartaman. Some time after these purbanga ceremonies the sacred enclosure (jagge)[12] is established in the family courtyard.

One preliminary rite remains. In the evening the initiate's father or the family priest must prepare the boy's hair for ceremonial tonsure the next day. A brass tray is brought to the room where the matrka puja was performed. On it are scissors and an iron razor for cutting hair, a porcupine quill that is white in three spots and black in two, twenty-seven pieces of kus grass, two brass cups containing butter, yogurt, clarified butter from a cow, and dung from a red calf. There are also three pieces of yellow cloth which have been made into bundles each containing mustard seeds, barley grains, dubo grass, sandalwood powder, curds, rice grains, and cowdung. These bundles are tied into the boy's hair by his father or the priest, one by each ear and one at the back of his head. Then a yellow turban is tied around the boy's head and he can go to sleep.

Hair Cutting (*Chewar*)

The day of the bartaman begins as the priest conducts a vedic fire worship ceremony inside the sacred enclosure and supervises the initiate's father in offering seven *godan*. Each godan is a leaf plate containing money which is offered to the priest. Each represents an occasion in the initiate's life when ideally a fire ceremony should have been performed.[13] Thus on the day of the bartaman the father compensates for his previous lack of orthodoxy and prepares his son ritually for the subsequent steps of his initiation.

The tonsure is the first rite actually requiring the son's participation. The boy sits in his mother's lap faced away from her "toward the moon." His sisters sit beside them (see figure 5) with a brass tray which has been given by the boy's maternal uncle to catch the cuttings of his hair. Now the father[14] comes and sits before the boy, still in his mother's lap, and wets the boy's hair with warm water. He removes the yellow cloth bundle tied near the right ear, and with the porcupine quill from the brass tray prepared the night before, he divides that hair into three strands. Three pieces of kus grass from the twenty-seven pieces on the tray are then braided into the strand nearest the top of the boy's head. At the auspicious moment set by the astrologer, the father takes the razor in his left hand and touches it to the boy's head and then takes the scissors in his right hand and cuts the strand braided with kus. Meanwhile, the priest is chanting mantras and performing a fire ceremony in the altar at the center of the jagge enclosure. The same fire altar is used throughout the entire bartaman, but the different stages of the ceremony (each of which in orthodox practice would have been a separate rite with its own fire worship) are represented by different bricks to the south and north of the central altar.

The rest of the boy's hair is ritually sheared in a similar way until all twenty-seven pieces of kus have been braided into the boy's hair and cut. After this the father rinses the boy's head with hot water and then (if the village has one) he calls the Nau (barber) who finishes shaving the boy's head, leaving only the Hindu top knot (*sika*).

The boy's sisters (real or classificatory) must catch all the hair in the brass tray and wrap it in yellow cloth with a mixture of yogurt, flattened rice, sweet fried bread, and some of the kasar sweets made during the purbanga ceremony. (Then the sisters must take the bundle down to be washed away by the

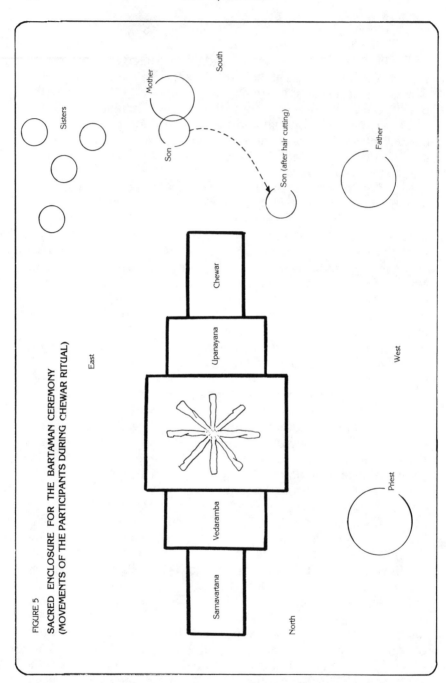

FIGURE 5

SACRED ENCLOSURE FOR THE BARTAMAN CEREMONY
(MOVEMENTS OF THE PARTICIPANTS DURING CHEWAR RITUAL)

river. Finally they rub their brother's body with the yellow paste which was prepared the previous day and bathe him in a large copper vessel.

Investiture with the Sacred Thread (*Upanayana*)
   After he has been bathed, the boy must feed the sons of three Brahmans with a special sweet (*dai pera*). Then the boy and his father take seats beside the priest and offer three more special godan. These purify the boy of three kinds of pollution incurred during his lax and carefree childhood, when he wandered where he liked, said whatever he wanted, and ate what he pleased. The rituals also serve to instruct the boy that he must henceforth behave strictly according to caste rules.
   Next, the person who is playing the role of the boy's guru—his father if the boy is a Brahman, or if he is Chetri the family priest—gives the boy the items he will need as an ascetic student or *brahmacarin*. He receives the skin of a black deer (preferably with horns, feet, and tail intact) to be used as a bed. This is worn over one shoulder. Around his waist a rope of sacred *mudje* grass is wound three times and knotted three times while the priest reads a special mantra. He is given a loincloth made of wild ginger leaves to wear on the rope, and a poncho-like garment of yellow unstitched cloth. Then he is given a wooden staff in his right hand, and a bag, with separate compartments for dal, rice, and alms, is tied to a stick and placed in his left hand. Finally, a yellow cloth is tied around his newly shaven head.
   In a later part of the ceremony (*upanayana*), the guru invests the boy with his sacred thread (*janai*). Both boy and guru then drink three times from water poured into their hands. The boy presents his guru with gifts[15] and offers him godan. Then, at the auspicious time, the guru teaches the boy the most sacred verse in Vedic literature, the *gayatri* mantra.

Begging for Alms (*Bhiksa Magne*)
   After the guru completes his sacrifice to the fire, it is time for the boy to go on his rounds as a yogi begging for alms (*bhik*) in the *bhiksa magne* ceremony. At this point there is an interesting change in the father's role. Until now (at least among the Brahmans) he has aided his son in becoming an ascetic brah-

macarin. He has cut his son's hair and given him the accoutrements of ascetic life. But now the father's role is reversed. The father becomes anti-ascetic and begins preparing his son for life as a married householder. Informants say the boy must "sneak away" from his father to become a yogi "just as Sukla Dev left his father in the middle of his bartaman because he wanted to continue to study rather than get married." The myth of Sukla Dev which one informant told to explain this part of the ceremony is perhaps worth recounting here.

The boy Sukla Dev left his bartaman because he decided that he did not want to marry. He would be a pure ascetic untainted by contact with women and other worldly pleasures. So his father Bias sent him to study with a wise king, having already told the king of his son's stubbornness. When Sukla Dev arrived at the king's palace, the king said he would accept Sukla Dev as a student only if he could pass a test. He told Sukla Dev to take a vessel filled to the brim with milk and circumambulate the palace and the palace gardens without spilling a single drop. Sukla Dev did so, walking slowly and concentrating with all his might on the vessel of milk so as not to spill any. When he had completed the circuit he returned to the king quite pleased with himself, for he hadn't spilled a drop. But the king asked him what he had seen on his tour. Had he seen the lovely fruit gardens or the beautiful women leaning from the harem windows? Sukla Dev had to admit that he had seen nothing but the vessel of milk. The king laughed and said that he was not ready to be a true ascetic until he could carry the milk without spilling it and see the beauties of the palace women and gardens at the same time.

The myth makes it clear that the bartaman must prepare a boy to be pure (preserving the bowl of milk) and fertile (enjoying women and fruit gardens) at the same time—which is, of course, the ideal of the householder stage. Sukla Dev's father and the wise king work together to balance the boy's somewhat smug ascetic fanaticism. This need to balance the opposition between asceticism and fertility helps to explain the father's double role in the bartaman. As "great teacher" (maha guru) and representative of the ancient rishis, the father leads the boy into a life of celibacy and Vedic study. But when the boy's asceticism threatens to become too extreme during the alms-begging ceremony, the father, as representative of the patriline, tries to lead his son back to householder values.

Among the Chetri the division of these roles is sharper because the family priest, not the father, takes the part of the pro-ascetic guru who teaches the gayatri mantra, leaving the father alone to disapprove of his son's symbolic departure from home as a yogi. But Brahmans are nonetheless consistent about maintaining the opposition of roles, even if both are played by the same person. The father alone among all the relatives does not give alms to his own son. When asked why, informants at a Brahman bartaman gave two reasons. They said the father does not give because, as representative of a patriline ideally supposed to provide for all its members, "He is ashamed that his son is so poor he has to beg, so he must ignore him." Other informants said that the son may not beg from his father because the father is his guru, and it is not respectful to beg from one's guru. Instead, one must offer the guru gifts, as the boy did before the guru taught him the gayatri and as he does again at the end of the alms ceremony when he places everything he has collected at the feet of his guru-father.

This interpretation of the opposing roles of the father is further supported by the fact that there are abrupt reversals of a similar nature in the roles of two other principal actors in the bartaman drama: the boy's mother and his maternal uncle. At the beginning of the alms ceremony the uncle comes forward to give a small plate for collecting the alms (bhiksa patra) and a large cone-shaped basket in which to keep them (soli). The uncle accompanies the boy on his three begging trips around the sacred enclosure and carries the basket for him. At this stage of the bartaman the mother's brother is clearly pro-ascetic and antagonistic to the boy's father (or in the case of the Brahmans, that part of the father's role which is pro-fertility). However, in the final stages of the bartaman, the uncle's role also switches, and in the end it is he who convinces the boy to return and be married.

Likewise, the boy's mother at first appears to support her son's career as a wandering ascetic. In each of the three trips around the sacred enclosure, she is first to give alms. After her, the boy's sister, his father's sister (phupu), and then other relatives and neighbors in turn offer their alms. Yet the mother will be the first to welcome her son back to his home and to eventual marriage after his "religious journey." She alone will receive her son's bheti (gift of money to respected person), and he will touch her feet with his forehead (dhok) in respectful greeting on his return. When asked why the mother and not the father received this respectful greeting, one informant explained that it was "because weddings and household affairs are the business of the women."

The Beginning and End of Vedic Study
(Vedarambha and Samavartana)

When the boy has completed his three begging rounds he places the uncooked rice, money, fruit, and pure fried food he has received as alms at his guru's feet. After receiving his guru's permission, he eats some of what he has collected. The boy offers another godan to the family priest (who for Chetris is also the guru), then performs the special fire ceremony which is supposed to mark the beginning of a four- to twelve-year study of the Vedas (Vedarambha hom). Immediately after this ceremony, however, another godan and fire worship are offered marking the end of studenthood (samavartana). The boy touches the feet of his guru, adds fuel to the sacrificial fire, and then bathes in water from eight different vases placed on the circumference of the sacred enclosure.

After the boy has bathed, his father gives him luxurious new clothes that he will need as a householder.[16] His sisters decorate him with yellow and red tika or forehead marks, black kohl around his eyes, garlands of flowers and dubo grass, and, if the family can afford it, a golden armlet and a necklace. But the boy has still not been drawn back fully into "worldly" life. In the final scene of the drama he is carried off on a "pilgrimage to Banaras" to worship at a local temple lying somewhere east or north of his home. His mother's brother goes with him and, as we noted earlier, convinces him to return home and marry the beautiful girl his parents have selected.[17] On his return, after first touching his mother's feet, the boy gives tika marks and daksina to several Brahmans and to his sisters. Then the family feasts all the relatives and neighbors who have given alms to their son.

Marriage (*Kanyadan biha*)

Marriage, as we have already seen, marks the beginning of the productive and socially responsible householder stage for which, in the case of males, the bartaman is a necessary preparation. As such, marriage is a major expression of the value of fertility and conventional religion in the continuing Hindu conflict between the ideals of the householder and those of the ascetic.

Besides this, marriage also reveals a great deal about the relative status of men and women, and about the structures of caste and kinship. These social dimensions of marriage are also "religious," in that they are deeply involved in the symbolic structures of Hinduism and expressive of the Hindu world view. Nonetheless, in this section I have not fully expanded the analysis of marriage to all these levels of meaning, but rather present the wedding rituals with a minimum of interpretation. To more adequately "unpack" the meanings of marriage in Narikot, we will need to return to it again in the contexts of kinship and women's status.

There are several kinds of marriage of varying degrees of formality, but the orthodox marriage described here (*biaite* or *kanyadan biha*) is the most important and the only one that qualifies as a full life-cycle ritual. *Liaite* marriage where the man simply "brings" the woman into his household, either as a first or as a second wife, is also common. Liaite unions with a previously unmarried woman are ritualized by a simple ceremony involving the worship of a sacred water vessel with votive lamps (*deo kalas puja*) or by the *swayambar* ritual (to be described below) where the bride places a garland around the groom's neck. In the case of a woman who has been married before, there is only the "changing of clothes" (*luga pherne*) ceremony in which a woman simply puts on a new set of clothes given her by her new husband. Children of such a marriage, as we saw earlier, are of less than full caste status.

Orthodox marriage in Narikot is always arranged between the parents of the bride and groom. Though the potential groom rarely takes an active role in the search for a suitable girl, he does retain a much greater freedom to reject his parent's choice than the girl does. The idea of courting is completely antithetical to the structure and ideals of *kanyadan* marriage, which is based on the father's gift (*dan*) of his virgin daughter

A new bride decorated and ready to be given in marriage as a "virgin gift."
Photo by author

(*kanya*) to the groom's family. Nevertheless, the boy may well get a chance to look over the girl who should not (but usually does) know she is being "seen."

Agreeing on the Match (*Kam Kuro Chinne*)

If the boy considers the girl attractive enough, and more important, if the two families find each other's caste and social standing acceptable, the parents set a time for the *kam kuro chinne* ceremony to formalize the agreement. This ceremony can take place at either the bride's or the groom's home or some neutral place like a temple.[18] The bride's and groom's family priests are there, and they settle on a mutually agreeable auspicious date for their clients' wedding. With great diplomatic tact the father of the bride tries to find out how large the groom's party (*janti*) will be, since he must feed them all lavishly, and what kind of work his daughter will be expected to do in her in-laws' house. When these matters have been agreed upon, the bride's father says to the groom's father, "From today I turn over my daughter to your son" (*Aja dekhi mero chori hazoor ko chora lai takrae*). This is a momentous statement, for once it is said, if anything should go wrong causing the marriage to be cancelled, the girl's reputation is compromised and it will be difficult to find her a suitable husband.

The bride's father then gives the groom's father a leaf plate containing pan, a banana, and a betel nut. Then he gives tika to his prospective son-in-law, places sacred dubo grass in his hands and touches his feet.

"Choosing" a Husband (*Swayambar*)

The *swayambar* or "self-choice" ceremony in which a girl "chooses" her husband is in Narikot only done among Chetris, because, they explain, their Ksatriya forefathers made this type of marriage, as is recorded in the Puranas.[19] Puranic swayambars were grand affairs where thousands of princes and their armies turned out in hopes of being chosen by the princess. A Chetri girl in Narikot, on the other hand, is presented with but a single suitor whom she is probably too embarrassed even to look at during the ceremony.[20] Yet it is a revealing ritual, because it seems to express a very different (and rather romantic) view of marriage and of the bride's role than is evident in the principal rite of the wedding, the bride-giving or *kanyadan*. In the kanyadan ritual, marriage is clearly conceived of as the transfer of an item of property (the bride) from one agnatic group to another.

The swayambar also brings about an important change in the bride's status. It is the bethrothal ceremony, and after her swayambar a girl is considered to be a member of her husband's gotra rather than her parents'—though there is some uncertainty about whether the transfer is complete until after the kanyadan ceremony. All informants agreed, however, that if the bride should die after the swayambar,[21] the groom's family must perform funeral ceremonies and observe a full thirteen-day death pollution. This means that not only has her gotra changed, but she has became karma caleko, a responsible adult, and thus is entitled to adult funeral rites. At the same time, if the groom should die after the swayambar, his death pollution affects the girl and she becomes a widow.

The ceremony, which takes place at the bride's house, is simple. The groom arrives with his family priest and a small party of male relatives. The bride (her face hidden with the end of her sari) sits with the groom before a purified area in the bride's courtyard. Here the bride's priest and the groom's priest together worship the god Ganes, a burning votive lamp, and a sacred water vessel (*kalas*), and then give tika to the bride and groom. Then the bride must take a brass water vessel (*karuwa*) with a spout that has kus grass in it and walk three times around the groom clockwise pouring water. This is called *ayu baras* ("extending the lifespan") and is meant to ensure her husband a long life. She must then put a garland of dubo grass around the groom's neck to signify that she has chosen him as her husband. At this point the groom's friends may clap and cheer. Then the groom puts a flower garland, a ring, and a red tika mark on the bride. She gives tika in return, bows (*namaste*) to the groom, and withdraws. The bride's people then feed the groom's party with yogurt, flattened rice, tea, and other pure foods before they depart.

Preliminary Rites and Erection of the Sacred Enclosure
(*Purbanga* and *Jagge Halne*)

The purbanga ceremonies for the wedding are basically the same as those described for the bartaman, except that they

Chart 3.1 Marriage Sequence

Rituals in the Groom's House	Rituals in the Bride's House
Agreeing on the match (kam kuro chinne)	
Initiation with sacred thread* (bartaman)	
	Betrothal—"choosing the husband" (swayambar)
Preliminary rites (purbanga)	Preliminary rites (purbanga)
Erection of the sacred enclosure (jagge halne)	Erection of the sacred enclosure (jagge halne)
Propitiation of the planets (graha santi puja)	
	Food gifts to the bride (sai pata)
Departure of the groom (janti jane)	
"	Arrival of the wedding party (janti parsane)
Women's night of festivities (ratauli)	
"	Welcoming (barani)
"	Washing the bride's feet (gora dhune)
(Women in groom's house join two wicks together)	The gift of a virgin (**kanyadan**)
"	Secret oblation (**gupti ahuti**)
Ratauli continues	Worship of the grinding stone (sila puja)
"	Playing with dice (pasa khelne)
"	Looking in the mirror (aina herne)
"	Roasting the puffed rice (laba bhutne)
"	Feeding curds (maur khuwaune)
"	Putting vermilion in the bride's hair (sidur halne)
"	Exchanging places (thau sarne)
"	Groom's feast (janti bakhri)
"	Bride's feast (runce sapro)
"	Farewell to the bride (dulai anmaune)
Waving the lamps (arti syauli)	
Barring the door (dhoka chekne)	
Joining the braids (cultho jorne)	
Filling up the grain measure (pathi bharne)	
Showing the storeroom (bharar dekhaune)	
Looking at the bride's face (mukh herne)	
Fire ceremony (cathurthi hom)	
Ritual games in groom's enclosure	
Catching fish (macha marne)	
Eating the polluted food (jutho khane)	
Drinking water from the groom's foot (gora pani khane)	
Bride's feast (bahu bhater)	
	Return of the bride and groom (dulan pharkaune)
	Feeding a snack (khaja khuwaune)
Meeting the in-laws (sasu/sasura cinne or samdhi/samdhini bhet)	

*This ritual may have been done several years earlier.

must begin simultaneously in the bride's and the groom's houses. (See chart 3.1, the marriage sequence.) To effect this a paper is sent from the groom's side specifying the time that his astrologer and priest have picked as auspicious for beginning the ceremonies. This can be as many as seven days before the kanyadan—though it is usually done the day before the groom's party leaves for the bride's house.[22]

The other purbanga ceremonies take place at both the bride's and groom's houses much as they are described in the section on bartaman.[23] However, if the groom is undergoing his bartaman immediately before the wedding, the purbanga rituals are only performed once at his house and not repeated for the wedding.

The establishment of the sacred pavilion in the bride's and groom's family courtyards (jagge halne) can be done anytime after their respective purbanga ceremonies are complete. Despite the apparent informality of this procedure—friends and neighbors all participate and discuss what should be done—there are definite ritual specifications as to how the sacred enclosure is to be built. For brevity many of these have been recorded in the drawing of a typical wedding enclosure in figure 6. During the course of the wedding many items are added and taken away from the pavilion as they are needed, but this simplified drawing presents the basic points.

At the groom's house a ritual to propitiate the nine planets (graha santi puja) must be done in the groom's newly erected pavilion. This is to protect the groom by ensuring that the nine planets (graha) and the gods they represent are all pacified or favorably disposed toward the groom and his upcoming marriage. Toward the end of the worship of the planets there is a ritual where the groom must see his face reflected in melted clarified butter contained in a leaf plate. As the groom stirs the butter with a piece of kus grass, the officiating priest asks him if he can see his face, prompting him to say yes, since that will mean that the planets are set right and the gods are pleased.

Departure of the Groom's Party (Janti Jane)

During the final stages of the propitiation of the nine planets the Damai musicians arrive, along with the men who will carry the groom in his sedan chair, the trunk of clothes for the bride, the groom's bhar (tied sugarcane stalks from his altar

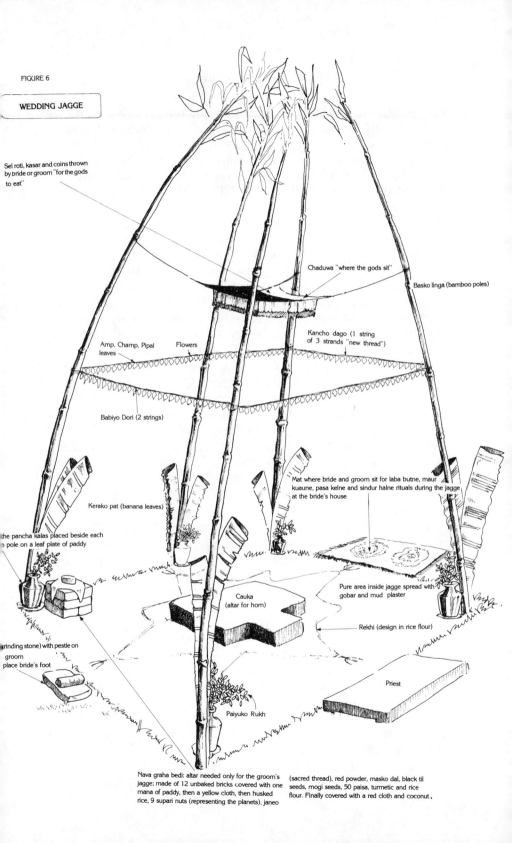

FIGURE 6

WEDDING JAGGE

Sel roti, kasar and coins thrown by bride or groom "for the gods to eat"

Chaduwa "where the gods sit"

Basko linga (bamboo poles)

Kancho dago (1 string of 3 strands "new thread")

Amp, Champ, Pipal leaves

Flowers

Babiyo Dori (2 strings)

Mat where bride and groom sit for laba butne, maur kuaune, pasa kelne and sindur halne rituals during the jagge at the bride's house

Kerako pat (banana leaves)

the pancha kalas placed beside each pole on a leaf plate of paddy

Pure area inside jagge spread with gobar and mud plaster

Cauka (altar for hom)

Rekhi (design in rice flour)

rinding stone) with pestle on groom place bride's foot

Priest

Paiyuko Rukh

Nava graha bedi: altar needed only for the groom's jagge; made of 12 unbaked bricks covered with one mana of paddy, then a yellow cloth, then husked rice, 9 supari nuts (representing the planets), janeo (sacred thread), red powder, masko dal, black til seeds, mogi seeds, 50 paisa, turmetic and rice flour. Finally covered with a red cloth and coconut.

room) and his sacred water vessel (mangal kalas). The musicians are fed with pounded rice, curries, and curd outside the house and given a cash payment of about fifteen to twenty rupees. The Damai who usually serves the family is also given a large turban. The bride's trunk of clothes is covered with red cloth and bound to a bamboo pole so that it can be carried by two men. The water vessel is also covered with red cloth and decorated with garlands of puffed rice and streaks of red and yellow powder. The groom is dressed in entirely new clothes—usually the traditional Nepali tunic and pants (mayalpos-suruwal) with a modern suit coat on top, socks, shoes, and a new cap (topi). If possible, he wears a watch, a fountain pen stuck in his suit coat pocket (to show that he is literate), and perhaps sunglasses to complete the sophisticated image. Even his sacred thread must be new. His sisters will have given him a garland of flowers and one of kus grass. After emerging from the house dressed in splendor, he must circle the pavilion three times behind the man who carries his bhar and water vessel, sprinkling red rice grains and water as he goes. Then the groom sits in his sedan chair and his mother feeds him a curd mixture (sagun).[24] He gives her a gift of some coins (bheti) which she will later pay to his bride for the privilege of seeing the bride's face. The motley Damai band has begun to play, and the groom with his party of male friends and relatives sets off for the bride's village.

Women's Night of Festivities at the Groom's House (Ratauli)
        The next event which takes place in the groom's house after the men's wedding party has departed is ratauli. This is not a ceremony so much as a night-long celebration for the women of the groom's family and their female neighbors. The occasion is a joyous one. The women of the groom's house must stay up all night, keeping a light burning and the door of their house open. In addition, two small wicks of mustard oil are placed in the kitchen and joined together into a single flame at the precise moment that the kanyadan ceremony is scheduled to take place at the bride's house.[25] The most important part of the ratauli, however, is the dancing, male impersonation, and sexual joking that take place. It is ordinarily considered "shameless" (laj namanne) for a woman to dance or sing, but on this night the groom's mother and sisters must dance. Other women join them and the festivities last on and off through the whole night and the next day until the wedding party returns with the bride.

Food Gifts to the Bride (*Sai Pata*)

Meanwhile, the focus of the wedding has shifted to the bride's house. Sometime before his party actually arrives the groom must send *sai pata* to the bride's house. The *sai pata* is a gift of food, including *masala* (a mixture of coconuts, betel nuts, raisins, nuts, and sweets) curd, fried breads, spinach greens, *kasar* (the molasses sweets prepared during the purbanga ceremonies), fruits, and other pure foods. These are all arranged on trays for maximum show and carried to the bride's house, along with the groom's sacred vessel and his bhar. The groom's bhar and vessel are carried into the room in the bride's house where worship of the mother goddesses took place, the *matrka puja* room.

On one of the trays is a piece of paper giving the time of the party's arrival and the auspicious time for the kanyadan ceremony. Along with it is a collection called literally the symbols of a woman with a living husband (*saubhagya saman*) and consisting of red bangles, red hairbraid, a comb, a mirror, a box of red powder, and red beads; there is also a piece of cloth on which the groom's handprints have been impressed in yellow turmeric. Under the direction of her family's priest, the bride must place her handprints on the cloth, thus signifying her acceptance of the groom and his party. This cloth is then placed in the matrka puja room.

Arrival of the Wedding Party (*Janti Parsane*)

As the party approaches the bride's house with horns blowing and drums beating, the bride's father (who has bathed and put on a dhoti) goes out to the main village path for the arrival ceremony. Preceded by a woman carrying the bride's sacred water vessel and a man with the bride's bhar, the bride's father must circle the groom clockwise three times, sprinkling him with flowers and rice grains. Then the bride's family and village friends all join in throwing rice on the groom's party as it enters the courtyard of the bride. The groom's bhar and water vessel are brought out by the bride's people and placed in the sacred enclosure.

Welcoming (*Barani*)

Now the *barani* or the welcoming of the groom takes place. The groom stands outside the pavilion in the bride's courtyard while the bride's father (or her elder brother) circles the groom three times pouring water from a copper vessel. Then after the bride's father and priest have worshiped a fire lamp, the water vessel, and the god Ganes, a yellow cloth is held up between the groom and bride's father while the priest chants the appropriate sacred verses. This is called "putting up an obstacle" (cheka rakhne). The groom passes some money under the cloth, which the bride's father doubles and passes back. Then the bride's father brings the groom into the sacred enclosure (if the groom is young enough he is carried) and seats him facing east on a wooden stool covered with yellow cloth. The bride's father sits on a round mat of braided kus grass facing the groom and begins to sprinkle him with kus grass and puffed rice. He then gives a tika mark and two garlands to the groom (one of flowers and one of dubo grass). The groom then cups his hands and receives a large leaf plate. In it is a new dhoti, an unshelled coconut, and two bundles tied in the corners of a yellow cloth, each containing kasar balls, pan, a sacred thread, betel nut, and a tiny piece of gold.

Then the bride's father takes a conch shell containing water and touches the groom's hands, shoulders, stomach, knees, and ankles. Informants say that this is to make the groom's body pure. The groom gives tika and prasad to the bride's father, who then takes him by the thumb and leads him forward.

After the welcoming ceremony there is usually a hiatus in ritual activity while the bride's people feed the groom's party and the other wedding guests. The bride remains hidden inside her parents' house, resting for the kanyadan ceremony, which often occurs in the early hours of the morning. The bride's parents, if they are doing the kanyadan that night, must fast to be ritually pure for this most meritorious of all religious acts. The groom sleeps outside the bride's house or on a porch of a neighbor's house. The rest of his party, if they sleep at all, do so huddled on porches, under trees, or in a nearby tea stall.

The Gift of a Virgin (Kanyadan)

The kanyadan ceremony usually takes place on the first floor of the bride's house. There the bride's people have set out a bed complete with mattress, sheets, quilts, pillows, and mosquito net which will be given to the groom as sayya dan or the "gift of a bed." There is also a chest—or among the more wealthy, a wardrobe—containing saris, blouses, petticoats, a shawl, umbrella, etc. for the bride. And there is a trunk with a set of clothes and shoes, perhaps even a watch or radio, for the groom. Tethered in a corner is a cow, which must also be given to the groom. All this, plus whatever jewelry her parents can afford to give her, and the gifts given to her by the relatives who must wash her feet (see below), make up the bride's dowry (daijo).

It is important that the kanyadan be performed at the auspicious astrological moment (lagan) as determined by the priest. Sometime before that moment the priest begins performing the preliminary fire-worship ceremony, and the bride's women friends wake her and begin to prepare her. This is called "decoration" (sinar garnu), and is a very important part of the wedding for the women. Using makeup, hairpins, ribbons, and so on they dress the bride's hair and do her makeup with great care and lavishness. They dress her in the sari—always red or pink— that her father has given her, and put a red net veil embroidered with sequins over her head.

The bride is led downstairs and seated on the bed to the right of the groom for the foot-washing ceremony (gora dhune). Her father places a large copper vessel[26] before the couple and they put their feet in it. He then pours water over the hands and then the feet of his daughter, catching the water and sprinkling it back on himself; then he pours more water over her feet and drinks of it three times. Then he gives his daughter some money, she bows (namaste), and he bows deeply to her, touching his forehead to her foot (dhok). The bride's father then washes the groom's hands and feet in the same way[27] and then gives a red tika mark to both bride and groom.

This procedure is repeated by the bride's mother, her mother's co-wives, her father's brothers and their wives, her father's sisters, her brothers and elder sisters, her mother's brothers and their wives, sons, and daughters (if they are older than the bride), and, if they are present, her mother's sisters. Women do not actually touch the groom's feet (as they may only touch the feet of their own husbands). Also some relatives wash the bride's feet but not the groom's, since only those who must call the groom "son-in-law" or "brother-in-law" (juai) must wash his feet.[28]

Each relative who honors the bride by washing her feet must also offer a gift of money, household utensils, clothing, or ornaments to the bride (*gordhuwa*). By participating in the foot-washing ceremony they receive some of the religious merit which the bride's parents get by doing the kanyadan.

After the bride's and groom's feet have been washed by her relatives, the groom presents the bride with wedding gifts from his family. This will include a trunk of saris, petticoats, etc. and a smaller box containing makeup, hair oil, and whatever jewelry the groom had bought (or borrowed for the occasion) to decorate the bride. The most important gifts are the wedding sari (always red or pink) and a necklace of red beads which the groom places around the bride's neck after the foot-washing ceremony. The red beads, usually divided in the middle by a small cylinder of beaten gold, are one of the principal signs of a married woman.

For the kanyadan ceremony the couple remain seated on the bed. The bride's father takes his daughter's right hand and holds a conch shell above her hand with his other hand. The groom places his hands beneath those of the bride and her father to receive the *kanya* (virgin, daughter). The bride's mother then pours water, which falls onto the conch shell, over the father's and bride's hands, and then into the groom's hands before reaching the large copper pot below. The mother must continue pouring the water while the priests chant a Sanskrit recitation of the bride's and groom's male ancestors for three generations (*sakhacarna*). It begins by stating that the bride is the great-granddaughter of her father's father's father whose name, thar, and gotra were such and such; then on to her grandfather and father. This is all repeated three times. Then the great grandfather, grandfather, and father of the groom are also repeated three times in the same way with their names, thar, and gotra. When this recitation is finished, the kanyadan is complete, and the bride's father hands her over to the groom, who grasps her thumb.

Meanwhile, an assistant priest will have been worshiping the sacred knot (*lagan gatho*), which is tied during the kanyadan. This knot is made of two white pieces of cloth, one given by the groom's side, the other given by the bride's people. The cloth from the groom's side must form the top of the knot. A sacred thread, betel nut, and a rupee note must be bound up in the knot, which is then tied around the bride's waist after the kanyadan.

The final rite in the kanyadan, which is almost an echo

of the kanyadan itself, is the *gai dan*. Here the bride's father gives the groom a cow. First the cow is worshiped by the bride's father, who sprinkles it with water, rice, and red powder. Then he puts over the cow's back a red cloth (the equivalent of the bride's wedding sari) with some money tied in one corner (the equivalent of the relatives' gifts to the bride). Then, taking barley grains, sesame seeds, and kus grass in his hands, he grabs the cow's tail (as he earlier took his daughter's hand) and gives it to the groom while a chanting priest pours water over their joined hands.

After this ceremony the groom returns to his friends in the wedding party and the bride is taken upstairs to rest. She will later be decorated and dressed once again, this time in the sari and jewelry given by the groom, for the ceremonies which take place outside in the pavilion the next day.

Status Reversal in the Bride's Pavilion

The dynamic of a Brahman-Chetri wedding is probably most clearly expressed by the progression of rituals which take place after foot-washing and kanyadan in the bride's pavilion. During the course of these rituals the bride's status undergoes a reversal with respect to the groom—a reversal that will hold for all her future relations with him and his family. During the foot-washing ceremony the bride's status was elevated above all her consanguineal relatives, who washed her feet. During the kanyadan she, as the virgin daughter being given as a religious gift, is at the height of her purity and sacredness. At the beginning of the pavilion rituals her status with respect to the groom is also high. The couple sit together on the southern edge of the sacred pavilion with the bride in the place of honor on the groom's right, as she was during the kanyadan. But as we shall see, the bride does not remain in this position for long.

For the first ritual the priest sits on the western side of the pavilion and a shawl is held up hiding the couple from him and from the sacred fire. This is called the "secret oblation" (*gupti ahuti*). Informants explain that the cloth is held up because it would be disrespectful to the fire god Agni, "who is like a guru," were the bride and groom to look at each other instead of at the fire. The priest then instructs the couple, thus hidden from Agni, to look at each other (which the bride rarely has courage to do). Then, as he chants and offers clarified butter and barley

seeds into the fire, the bride gets up and leads the groom (who
is holding on to the "tail" of her sacred knot cloth) around the
fire clockwise to the western side of the pavilion. There the
bride's brother gives her a handful of puffed rice. The groom
puts his hand on the bride's shoulders while she throws the puffed
rice on the fire. Then the groom takes the bride by the hand and
leads her to the northern side of the pavilion. There, where the
priest sits, is a grinding stone and pounder decorated with three
stripes of vermilion powder. The groom must now touch the
bride's foot and place it on the pounder. In several of the weddings I saw (including pictures of the king's wedding) the groom
touched the bride's foot with a handkerchief rather than with
his hand. When I asked an older priest about this, he expressed
great impatience with the present generation of young men
whose pride would not let them touch their wife's foot with
their bare hands even during this important rite. He went on to
explain that the purpose of this rite was to ensure that the wife
would henceforth be subservient to her husband. By showing
respect for his bride while she still has the high ritual status of a
virgin girl, the groom validates his right to receive respect from
her during their subsequent married life, when she is no longer
a virgin and has thus lost her initial high status. The priest blamed
the fact that men nowadays seemed to have more trouble keeping their wives in line on the modern groom's reluctance to do
this rite properly.

After this ceremony the couple continues (with the bride
in front) circling clockwise around the pavilion. They make two
more trips, the bride first offering the puffed rice given by her
brother to the fire and the groom then touching her foot at the
grinding stone each time. After the third trip, the couple sits down
again at the southern side of the pavilion for the ritual games.

Informants explain that these games are to cheer the bride,
since she is unhappy about leaving her parents, and yet it is
inauspicious for her to leave her natal home weeping after kanyadan. At the weddings I observed, the brides, their heads still
covered with a gauzy veil, were very subdued during these rites.
However, the groom's party and the bride's wedding guests did
socialize and joke during this period.

The first game is usually "gambling with cowries" (*pasa
khelne,*) which informants say is done in imitation of the divine
couple Siva and Parvati, who are fond of gambling together. The
bride and groom "play" by tossing betel nuts or cowrie shells

Ritual games between the bride and groom are conducted in the sacred enclosure (*jagge*) at the bride's house after the *kanyadan* ceremony. *Photo by author*

onto the mat before them. In this game, as in all the others, a victory for the bride means she will bear a son; if the groom wins, she will have a daughter. But from my observation the bride is usually too reticent at this point to really compete seriously. While the couple are playing, they are supposed to look at themselves in a mirror that has been placed on the mat between them. "Looking in the mirror" (aina herne) is supposed to indulge their youthful vanity by letting them see themselves adorned in wedding finery. Also during the gambling a woman from the bride's side who has been engaged as a ritual servant[29] and one from the groom's side stand over the couple with a piece of new cloth stretched between them. On the cloth are grains of puffed rice, which the two servants jiggle by moving the cloth back and forth. This is called "roasting the puffed rice" (laba bhutne). The gambling ends abruptly with puffed rice spilling all over the couple when one of the women succeeds in yanking the cloth out of the hands of her opponent.

The next game is "feeding the maur." Here a brass plate containing maur—curds, sugar, and sesame seeds—is set between the bride and groom. The bride must divide the maur into two portions with her fingers and then offer some to the gods. Then she and the groom compete to see who can feed the other first.

The next rite is a more serious one: "putting on the vermilion powder" (sidur halne), which marks the climax of the rituals in the bride's sacred enclosure and the point at which the bride's status vis-à-vis the groom undergoes a radical reversal. The groom offers vermilion powder first to Ganes, then to the sacred fire, and then to his sacred vessel, which has been placed in the northeastern corner of the pavilion. A white cloth is extended from this vessel, into which all the groom's house gods have been invoked, to the bride's forehead. The groom then sprinkles a line of vermilion powder from the vessel to the bride's forehead, where he places a red line in the part of her hair. So important and powerful is this line of vermilion that no one except the bride's immediate relatives are allowed to see it. As soon as she has left the enclosure the bride's female relatives cover the vermilion with a handkerchief—for if a witch should see the first vermilion mark, she could easily curse the bride to be barren or to be possessed by an evil spirit. The next morning (at the groom's house), only after the bride has bathed and put on fresh vermilion, the handerchief can be removed.

As Campbell (1976:92) has suggested in his analysis of Kangra Rajput weddings, the red powder in the part of the bride's hair symbolizes the groom's sexual possession of her. It is said that only after the groom has placed the vermilion mark can the bride call him husband.[30] Though Brahman and Chetri women never interpreted the mark itself in sexual terms, they did speak about the sexual connotations of the marriage rituals:

> If the husband wants sex and you refuse, that is definitely a sin. Because while you are being married then all the rites are performed. The groom touches your breasts and feeds you his polluted food. All these things are done then, and if you don't [let the husband have sex] later, then it is a sin. . . . When our marriage is being performed then the father of the bride has to touch the feet of the groom. Then the priest tells him to touch the groom's knees and here and here and finally the conch shell is placed on the groom's navel. That embrace, the touching of the breast—all this is done to show that all bonds have been broken.

Two things support the interpretation of the vermilion mark ritual as symbolic of the bride's defloration. One is the fact that the bride's parents may not witness the ritual. The second is the fact that afterward, the bride's status vis-à-vis the groom has been reversed. She is now definitely *lower* than him. The change in the bride's status is immediately expressed by the "changing place" rite (*thau sarne*) which comes next. The groom stands and removes the bride from her seat on his right to the less honored position on his left. The bride must then grasp the groom's coat and ask him to sit (on her right). She then touches his feet (*dhok*). From now on she will always sit on his left and greet him by touching his feet.

Two Feasts (*Janti Bakhri* and *Runce Sapro*)
　　After the pavilion ceremonies are concluded attention shifts to the wedding feasts. Two separate feasts are prepared. One, the "portion of the groom's party" (*janti bakhri*) is cooked and eaten by the groom's side on some public land in the bride's village from supplies given by the bride's family. The party sends one leg (*sapro*) of the goat to the bride's feast, which is called the "tearful leg" (*runce sapro*). The groom must eat twice; once with his own friends and once again with the bride at her feast. After the wedding couple have eaten, the bride's guests are fed in order of caste rank.

The Bride's Farewell (*Dulai Anmaune*)

Then it is time for the saddest part of the wedding, the "farewell to the bride" (*dulai anmaune*). Once again the bride's women friends decorate and dress her in her wedding finery. They take extra pains now, because they know that the women of the groom's house will give the bride a very critical inspection when she arrives. They also tie seven knots in the drawstring of her petticoat, which the groom must untie that night.

Then the couple enters the matrka puja room, where the bride performs a final worship of her family gods. The bride's mother then ties pan, betel nut, and a rupee note very tightly into the groom's waist cloth. This knot will later be untied by the bride's new mother-in-law (*sasu*) and the contents used in the ritual games in the groom's house. Then the bride's mother says to the groom, "If you kill her the sin is yours, if you keep her the merit is yours" (*Mare pap, pale punya*). The bride's father gives a tika mark and a garland to the groom and then the bride. Both are fed curds, then the bride's bhar and ritual vessel are taken out in a procession around the pavilion. Behind follows the father,[31] carrying or leading the bride. As the Damai band plays, father and daughter circle the pavilion three times and then the bride's father puts her into the sedan chair brought by the groom's party. With the bride in the front and the groom behind (in his own sedan chair) the wedding party leaves the bride's village. At this point, even though informants say one should not weep at a kanyadan, almost all the bride's relatives and friends and the bride herself are weeping.

Arrival: Waving the Lamp and Barring the Door (*Arti Syauli* and *Dhoka Chekne*)

Before the party returns with the bride to the groom's house, the groom's sisters decorate their foreheads with a special tika mark of white rice flour and water. When the Damai band accompanying the party can be heard, a circle is purified with cowdung paste in the sacred enclosure erected earlier in the groom's courtyard. A copper tray with five compartments (*panc pala*), a ritual vessel, and a special "lamp" made of seven rice-flour cups, each containing clarified butter and a wick, are placed in the circle. The bride's sedan chair is carried over the spot and held there while the groom's sisters do a brief ritual called "the shadow of the lamp" beneath her (*arti syauli*). It involves waving a lighted lamp before the vessel and worshiping it with flowers, rice grains, and dubo grass. Then the bride is lowered and the sisters circle her sedan chair three times clockwise, with the sister in the lead pouring water from a spouted water vessel. The groom's sisters then give tika, a flower garland, and curds first to the groom and then to the bride. The bride is helped out of her sedan chair by her husband's paternal aunt (phupu) and led toward the house. She is preceded by the groom's vessel and bhar. On reaching the door, however, the bride finds the way blocked by the groom's sisters. This is a kind of ritual joking called "barring the door" (dhoka chekne.) Only after the bride has promised them each a new blouse (which she must give formally at a later date) is she allowed in the house. Inside the door seven piles of paddy have been heaped on the floor leading to the family altar (usually in the kitchen area) where the matrka puja was done during the purbanga ceremonies in the groom's house. Each pile is topped with a leaf plate containing a lighted wick, which the bride must extinguish with her foot as she steps on the piles of grain to reach the altar. Then with the help of the groom's priest, the couple worships the vessel and the seven matrka.

Games with the New Mother-in-Law

In front of the matrka the "joining of the hair-braids" rite (cultho jorne) is done. The bride and her new mother-in-law put their heads together, and strands of their hair are entwined and anointed with clarified butter by the priest. Narikot informants say this is done so the two women will not quarrel.[32] If there are co-wives of the new bride, the rite must be done with them also.

Now the bride goes to the door while her mother-in-law remains at the altar and they both sweep the piles of grain toward each other. Then the two women play the ritual "filling a grain measure" game (pathi bharne). The groom's mother fills a measure with grain and hides in it the money, sacred thread, and betel nut which the bride's mother had tied into the groom's waist band. Then the grain is dumped out into a winnowing tray, and the two women compete to see who can find the objects first. This must be done three times. Then the paddy is heaped on a winnowing basket, and bride and mother-in-law carry it upstairs alone to put it away in the storeroom, a rite called "showing the storeroom" (bharar dekhaune).

Looking at the Face of the Bride (Mukh Herne)
    The final ceremony of the day—and perhaps the most uncomfortable for the new bride—is the mukh herne, "seeing the face." The bride is seated, always slumped over with downcast eyes, while the women of the family, starting with the groom's mother, lift her veil to look at her face. They must place some money in her lap, and for that they buy the privilege of being as critical as they like in their comments about her. After her mother-in-law has seen her face, the bride must touch her mother-in-law's feet with her forehead (dhok dine). The other women of the family also have their feet touched by the bride. And then it is time for the neighbor women to come and see the bride and evaluate the new member of their village.

Fire Ceremony and Ritual Games in the Groom's Pavilion
    The next day the final rituals in the groom's pavilion begin with a special fire ceremony called the caturthi hom.[33] This fire ceremony is not strictly part of the marriage; some poor families do an abbreviated version on "rented" land in the bride's pavilion. But most families do it, because it is "custom" and because it is an auspicious way to say farewell to the gods who were invoked for the wedding.
    Then when the fire ceremony is complete, family and neighbors gather for the final ritual games. The bride and groom are seated once again on the southern side of the pavilion. A large copper vessel is placed before them filled with muddy water, leaves from used leaf plates, and stones. The priest takes the paper on which the auspicious time for the kanyadan was written and wraps it around a stone to make the "fish" for the "catching fish" game (macha marne). First the groom hides it in the vessel among the dried leaves and the bride searches for it. Then the bride makes the groom search. This ritual is accompanied by much joking and teasing from the groom's village friends and the groom himself. At one wedding I observed, the groom tricked the bride by only pretending to hide the fish in the vessel. He held it in his hand where all the villagers could see it while the bride searched and searched in the muddy waters of the pot.

Next comes the "eating of polluted food" ritual (*jutho khane*). Several ball-shaped sweets (*kasar*) are placed on a tray before the couple. The groom takes a bite out of one, thus making it jutho or ritually polluted, and the bride must finish it. This is repeated several times; it expresses the bride's subservient status and respect for her husband. The groom then gives her some money. From this day on she will always take her food from the jutho plate of her husband, and he will often leave some special food on his plate for her as a gesture of affection.[34]

As a final expression of the bride's subservience to her husband, another foot-washing ceremony (*gora pani khane*) must now be performed. Two days before in her parent's home the bride's feet were washed by her relatives. Now her position is completely reversed, and she must wash her husband's feet and drink the water. After she has done so she is supposed to grab the groom's big toe and refuse to release it until he gives her money. Henceforth she must wash his feet and drink the water before every rice meal where her husband is present.

After these ceremonies comes the bride's feast, where the groom's family first eat dal-bhat cooked by the bride. The bride and her mother-in-law together must cook some *khicari*, rice and lentil cooked together, at the family hearth. This signifies that the bride is now karma caleko, and that all members of her husband's family may eat from her hands. At the bride's feast the bride and groom eat together, and they are served first. (Ordinarily the daughter-in-law eats alone after everyone else has been served.) The bride is given food on two separate leaf plates. She takes a little from each and the jutho leftover food is thrown away. The groom's family must feast the friends, relatives, and neighbors whom they invited to the wedding. Everyone will be served in order of caste rank. If the groom's family is Chetri, they will have called in a Brahman to do the cooking so that their Brahman neighbors may also eat the food.

The Bride's Visit to Her Natal Home (*Dulan Pharkaune*)

The main wedding ceremonies are now complete, but there remains the bride's subsequent return to her natal home, or *maita*, with her new husband. This journey is called "the return of the bride" (*dulan pharkaune*) and by orthodox account the bride should return to her maita only after the fifth night after the kanyadan—the night during which according to orthodox tradition the marriage may be consummated.[35]

Before the couple returns to the groom's house, the bride's family must give them at least a measure of rice, some lentils, and a tray of *masala* (lit. "spices") including a sacred thread, betel nut, and pan as well as sweets. Various curries, pickles, and fried breads are sent. They must also return an amount of money greater than the sum their daughter received during the ceremony when the groom's female relatives paid to see the bride's face. These ritual gifts to the groom's family are called "feeding a snack" (*khaja khuwaune*).

The Bride's Father Visits His In-Laws (*Samdhini/Samdhi Bhet*)
As a final gesture of good will and generosity, the bride's people, if they can afford it, may do a ceremony called either "meeting the mother and father-in-law" (*sasu/sasura cinne*) or "meeting the child's mother and father-in-law" (*samdhini/samdhi bhet*). For this the bride's father journeys to his daughter's house and presents his *samdi* or child's in-laws with a tray of spices and sweets as lavish as he can afford and a new sari, blouse-piece, and petticoat for his child's mother-in-law. Until this is done the bride's new mother-in-law must hide from the bride's father if he should visit his daughter's house. The point of the ceremony is to ease the relationship—which tends to be formal and strained—between the two families.

Death Ceremonies

Four Levels of Ritual Obligation
The ceremonies of the final life-cycle rites—those concerned with death—are in a sense never really complete. Theoretically death observances, *sraddha,* continue forever through phases of lessening intensity and individuality. The most personal and demanding are those during the first thirteen days after death, *kirya basne.* Then there is a period of regular monthly rituals and mourning, *masik sraddha,* during the first year after death. A third phase of annual rites—*ekodhista sraddha*—is observed on the lunar anniversary of an individual's death by his or her male descendants for three generations. Finally, there is a collective honoring of all the ancestors, *sora sraddha,* during

the fortnight preceding the fall festival of Dasai every year for as long as the lineage itself survives.

Indeed, the death rituals taken collectively embody with extreme clarity the belief already stressed as so central to village Hinduism: that the householder attains immortality, albeit "conditional" immortality, through his or her progeny. The rituals express village ideas about the nature of this mode of immortality and about the responsibility of the living patrilineal unit toward its deceased members.

The Ancestors' Place in the Hierarchy of Spiritual Beings

As mentioned earlier, the pitr or ancestor spirits are immortal—but theirs is a circumscribed and somewhat contingent immortality, very different from the transcendent immortality of the devta, gods, or mahatma, saints. In village conception the pitr are clearly neither gods nor saints. They are firmly described as "dead people" (moreko manche). They are still involved in the periphery of the samsaric round, dependent on their patrilineal descendants for sustenance and comfort in the afterlife. Devta, on the other hand, have never been caught up in samsara, except for an occasional incarnation as part of their divine play; and the saints have achieved release and thus escaped samsara altogether through their austerities and ascetic renunciation.

Gods are free of the needs and, to a large extent, of the emotions, which control human beings. Of course they still enjoy the pleasant sights, smells, and food offered to them in puja. But they do not need these things as the pitr need the food and water which their descendants offer them in sraddha. Also, though the gods do feel pleasure and anger (which is occasionally expressed in the good and bad fortunes of men) their emotions are not as petty and vindictive as those of the pitr. As one village saying goes: "The gods give but the ancestors destroy" (Devta haru dinchan; pitr haru harchan). I was first confused when informants repeatedly told me that the pitr were bigger or greater than the gods (pitrharu devta bhanda thulo chan). But they explained that this meant that the pitr are more likely to give them trouble than the gods. They are more dangerous, not because they are higher or more powerful but because they are still under the control of samsaric needs and emotions.

This differentiation between saints and gods on the one

hand and pitr on the other is reinforced by the distinction which is sometimes made between swarga, heaven, and the pitrlok, the abode of the ancestors. As we saw earlier, swarga is conceived by some villagers as a kind of literal equivalent to the metaphysical concept of mukti, release or salvation. It is the reward for fastidious obedience to the householder's dharma just as true mukti is the reward of strict adherence to the discipline of the ascetic's dharma. Swarga is the splendorous realm of the gods, and its inhabitants want for nothing. The pitrlok, however, with its continuing dependency, is more like an extension of samsara than a transcendence of it. As one village man explained: "If I could be sure that my mother had gone to swarga, I would not do sraddha for her. She would not need it there. But who can see the results of karma? She may be going hungry and thirsty in the pitrlok if I don't do her sraddha."

The Pitr and the Patriline
        Another facet of the pitr's peculiar nontranscendent immortality is their continuing connection with their patrilineal unit. Each pitr or group of pitr is known and honored by only a small segment of Hindu society, while the gods are more accessible and worshiped much more widely.[36] Those who honor the same pitr are somehow related. There are many levels of ceremonial obligation which reflect the proximity of relation to the deceased and to the other individuals who honor the deceased as one of their pitr. Indeed, exactly who has what ceremonial obligations to which specific pitr is one of the clearest indicators of (1) the ideology of mutual rights and duties within the patriline; (2) how the living members of the extended patriline are organized into family units; and (3) how a patrilineal unit is connected to other patrilines through marriage.
        There are roughly four levels of ceremonial obligation towards one's pitr which, as I mentioned before, are marked by decreasing intensity and individuality. (See chart 3.2.) The first three levels (i.e., kirya basne, masik sraddha, and ekodhista sraddha) are confined to pitr from one's own patriline—who by birth or marriage share one's own gotra and thar. The fourth level of obligation extends not only to all deceased karma caleko members of one's own lineage for three ascending generations, but also to women who have married out of the lineage and certain close affinal relatives. The affinal and more distant consanguineal relationships included at this level seem to be largely coex-

tensive with the category of more distant relatives whom one calls *natadar*.

The performance of the first three kinds of ceremonies is a matter of clear undisputed obligation. A man who fails to perform his father's or mother's kirya, for example, automatically loses caste. Performance of the first three levels is seen as a duty connected with the right to inherit land, which is preeminently the son's right. In the absence of sons, the principles determining who does kirya, and the closely related question of who inherits the land, can become confused. The latter especially is an area of ambiguity and stress in Brahman-Chetri family structure to which we will return in our discussion of kinship.

At the moment let us look briefly at who is responsible for kirya and who is eligible for land inheritance. Informants tend to speak as if the two were always the same, but in reality the order of precedence does not exactly coincide. For example, in the absence of wife or son, a deceased man's widowed daughter-in-law stands to inherit his land, but one of his brothers should do kirya for him. If, because of some particularly bitter quarrel with the deceased, the brothers refuse, the daughter-in-law of the deceased could simply pay a male Brahman to observe the rituals in her stead. Although a wife does inherit a share in her husband's ancestral property equal to her son's share, women are not considered as efficacious as men in performance of the rituals, since "a woman might menstruate and become impure during the thirteen days of kirya basne."[37] Even if a bereaved woman were past menopause however, villagers preferred a male as chief mourner. Informants said that, except for cremation (which is an all-male ceremony), a woman *could* perform kirya if there were no one else, and if she were too poor to pay a male Brahman to stand in for her. But no villager could recall ever seeing a woman do the kirya rituals.

The order of precedence given here for inheritance of ancestral property (ansa) holds largely for kirya responsibility *if the women are removed*. The order of inheritance which villagers tended to give for the death of male ego is the following:

1) wife (equally with the sons)
2) sons
3) son's sons
4) son's wife
5) daughter (with permission from ego's brothers)[38]
6) brothers
7) brother's children.

Life-Cycle Rites

Chart 3.2 Sequence of Death Rites: The Four Levels of Ritual Obligation*

Level of Ritual Obligation		Sequence	Ritual
First level: kirya basne		before death	dying person moved to river or Tulsi; given water to drink and cow's tail to hold
		death occurs	women of the household lament; wife removes bangles and unbraids hair; chief mourner shaves his head
	day 1	as soon as possible	malami (all-male funeral procession)
		" "	cremation
		first night after death occurs	ksetrabas/koro barne
	day 2	morning of day after death	dhikuro sraddha
	day 3	third day after death	" & asthiasanchayana
	day 4		dhikuro sraddha
	day 5		" "
	day 6		dhikuro sraddha
	day 7		" " & pateya sraddha
	day 8		dhikuro sraddha
	day 9		" "
	day 10		destruction of dhikuro
	day 11		egharau sram (& abyabdika sraddha)
	day 12		sapinda sraddha
	day 13		suddha santi
Fourth level: sora sraddha, abhyudayik sraddha, tarpan		theoretically, in perpetuity during the lunar fortnight before Dasai (on the lunar date which corresponds with the death of the father of the male household head).	1. sora sraddha
		before auspicious family rituals such as weddings and bartamans.	2. abhyudayik sraddha
		every day (in orthodox families), and as part of all sraddha rituals.	3. tarpan
Second level: barakhi or masik sraddha		beginning of the first year after death (day 11 of kirya basne period)	abyabdika sraddha

Level of Ritual Obligation	Sequence	Ritual
	29 days after death	unamasik sraddha
	1 month " "	duitya sraddha
	45 days " "	tripaksika sraddha
	2 months " "	tritiya sraddha
	3 months " "	caturtha sraddha
	4 months " "	pancama sraddha
	5 months " "	sasta sraddha
	6 months " "	unasarna sraddha
	7 months " "	saptama sraddha
	8 months " "	astama sraddha
	9 months " "	nauma sraddha
	10 months " "	dasama sraddha
	11 months " "	ekadasa sraddha
	1 day less than a year after death	unabdika sraddha
	12 months—first anniversary of death	duwadasa/barakhi sraddha
Third level: ekodhista sraddha	subsequent lunar death anniversaries for next three generations	ekodhista sraddha

*See text for explanation of terms.

For a woman's death, the sequence of inheritance is:

1) sons
2) sons's sons
3) husband
4) co-wife's sons
5) co-wife's son's sons
6) daughter (with permission from husband's brother)
7) husband's brothers
8) husband's brother's children
9) own brothers.

This order is by no means universally applied, since in the absence of a spouse or direct male descendant, sentiment and sheer politics come into play. For instance, a powerful son-less widow who hated her co-wife's son could maneuver to pass her share of her husband's ancestral property on to her own daughter instead. Nevertheless, if we leave the politics of land inheritance aside for the moment, the order of precedence for kirya responsibility itself gives clear expression to the Hindu ideals of the parent/son bond and of patrilineal solidarity.

The First Level of Obligation: The Thirteen Days of Death Pollution (*Kirya Basne*)

Even after the most peaceful death of an elderly person, there is a transitional period during which the deceased becomes a *pret*—a ghost or malevolent spirit—and for thirteen days hovers in vague discontent near the family home. This is the period of death pollution (*sutak*) for the family of the deceased and his close agnatic relatives. It is also a time of severe austerity and social isolation called "sitting in mourning," *kirya basne*, for the chief mourner (*kirya putra*). The main rites of the kirya basne period center around four transformations: (1) disposing of the corpse, (2) feeding the pret and reconstituting its "body," (3) changing the pret into a pitr, and (4) purifying the family and the chief mourners, and in the case of a father's death, recognizing the chief mourner's new status as head of the household.

Cremation

As soon as the life breath has ceased, the body becomes a dangerous and highly polluting object.[39] It is immediately wrapped in new white or saffron-colored cloth,[40] sprinkled with yellow powder, kus grass, and tulsi leaves, and tied to one or two bamboo poles so that it can be carried to the river. Only male caste fellows may make up the funeral procession (*malami*), and they must be barefoot and clad only in a dhoti or shorts.[41] They walk in silence except for the periodic blasts from a conch shell, which is sounded to warn others that the inauspicious procession is coming. Until the corpse has been cremated, the members of the funeral procession cannot speak to, or touch, anyone of lower caste than themselves. Likewise, the corpse itself must be carefully guarded against pollution from the touch of an animal, an untouchable, or anyone of caste lower than the deceased.

The corpse is bathed in the river. One measure of rice and some money are tied in a white cloth and placed on the corpse's chest, and a small piece of gold is placed in the mouth to purify it. When a man dies, his widow's bangles and marriage beads (which she is no longer privileged to wear) are also placed on his chest. Napthalene (*kapur*) and clarified butter are also put on the body, which is then wrapped in new clothing.

Meanwhile, the funeral pyre (cita) is being prepared. It must contain at least a small piece of the sacred sandalwood and tulari wood, as well as some kus grass. Then the corpse is carried once counterclockwise (ulto, backwards, the inauspicious direction) around the pyre, placed on top, and sprinkled with yellow powder, kus and tulsi leaves. One member of the funeral procession removes a small portion of the flesh from the corpse and buries it in the sand near the river. This is the share for the demon who eats corpses (krbyad rakhsa ko bhag). If this is not given, one informant explained, the demon will be angry and will return with the funeral procession to trouble the bereaved family.

The chief mourner, who had shaved his head before he left the house with the funeral procession, now bathes in the river. Then, taking a firebrand (dag batti), he walks counterclockwise three times around the funeral pyre. Then he puts the firebrand into the mouth of the corpse. He lights the bundles of straw on the rest of the pyre while the family priest recites a mantra invoking the fire god Agni to burn the corpse. Finally when the corpse is burnt a piece of bone (astu) is taken. This is wrapped in white cloth and thrown into the river, where it will be "carried to heaven."[42] What is left of the funeral pyre is cleared away and the ground beneath it washed with purifying river water and sprinkled with cow's milk. The chief mourner must then bathe and offer six cremation rice-balls (cita pinda) of uncooked rice to the deceased on the site of the funeral pyre.[43]

Before returning, the chief mourner must again bathe and change to a fresh dhoti. The members of the funeral procession also bathe. A new fire is built and sprinkled with clarified butter, and a thorn branch placed on the ground beside it in the direction of the path back to the village. The chief mourner and the members of the funeral procession must walk over the fire and the thorn branch on their way back to the village "so sickness and demons cannot follow them back to the house from the burning ground." As they walk they reverse the normal order, with the youngest men in front and the oldest man in the rear.

The Mourning Enclosure (Ksetrabas)

When the chief mourner returns he enters a room which has been purified for him with gobar. He will spend the rest of the day and night in severe mourning called koro barne or kse-

trabas (literally "staying in a field of purity"). He is separated from all other members of the family within an enclosure of new, undyed string (*kacho dhago*) which is strung around the room.[44] Within the enclosure, on the south-facing side, a clay pot (*ghaito*) filled with water and milk is suspended over a "cup" made by hollowing out a mound of ritually pure cowdung. A small hole is made in the pot and stuffed with kus grass, thus allowing the water and milk mixture to drip slowly into the cup of dung. Beside it is placed a clay dish containing seven kinds of grains and seeds (*sapta dhanya*) on top of which is a sesame oil lamp, which is kept burning. The family priest must offer a *pinda* or rice-ball beside the dish of seven grains.

On the day of death during the koro barne period when he remains within the ksetrabas enclosure, the chief mourner may not take rice.[45] His only food may be fruit and sugar water. For the next nine nights he must sleep within the enclosure with his head to the north on just some straw and a woolen blanket.[46] He may not drink water from a glass or metal vessel. Instead, water is brought from the well or a spring and poured into small cups called *khoca*, each made of a single sal leaf. The chief mourner must untie the knot in his *sika* (lock of hair which Hindus may not cut). He may not wear any stitched clothing—only a dhoti, a shawl, and a handkerchief as a head covering on his newly shaven head. He may not touch anyone, enter other people's houses, or even speak to individuals of castes lower than his own. Nor may he say the sacred gayatri mantra which he was given at his initiation or participate in any kind of worship beyond the kirya ceremonies.

New widows observe the same restrictions as the chief mourner. They may, however, wear a stitched blouse—so long as it is turned inside out. They do not generally shave their heads (unless they are very old or very orthodox), but refrain from oiling, combing, or braiding their hair.

In terms of purity and pollution these kirya basne restrictions can be looked at in several ways. Though they are similar in many respects to other sets of temporary ascetic rules aimed at making the individual pure before a certain religious act,[47] they have another important aspect. For besides protecting the chief mourner from pollution by outside forces, the restrictions also protect others from him, because he is in a state of extreme pollution (*bitulo*). The death of a close relative has severely lowered his ritual status. He is deeply involved with the deceased in his ceremonial obligations and has, in a sense, taken on the pollution of the corpse itself. Hence he must practice this strict asceticism both to purify himself so that he can resume his normal status and to purify the deceased, who exists during the mourning period as a ghost dependent on the chief mourner's ministrations for release. The pret itself is an unclean being—somewhere between a corpse and a pitr on the ritual scale, and if there is any irregularity in the chief mourner's observation of kirya basne, the deceased will not be freed from its ghost form.

Reassembling the Body (*Dhikuro Sraddha*)

On the morning of the first day after death, when ksetrabas fast is over, the nine days of *dhikuro sraddha* begin, when a mound (*dhikuro*) is built on which the deceased will be ceremonially fed. During this time the chief mourner is feeding the spirit of the deceased each day in its ghost form, and also assembling a new "body" for the deceased. For the pinda which he offers—cooked rice formed into a ball with curd, sugar, bananas, and black sesame seeds—are both the food and the body of the deceased.[48] The pinda offered on the first day forms the head and throat. The second day's pinda becomes the chest, and so on until the back, genitals, upper legs, calves and feet, hands, and male or female "seed" are formed on successive days. Finally on the tenth day with the final pinda the reassembled "body" of the deceased, said to be about eighteen inches high, gains the power to breathe and eat and is ready to make the year-long journey to the pitrlok.

The first day's dhikuro sraddha begins when the chief mourner bathes in the river or any running water. During this bath he offers sesame seeds and water to the deceased. He finds a stone and sprinkles it with kus grass, sesame seeds, and water and then fills a copper vessel with water for the sraddha and his own use.

Under the direction of the family priest (who never enters the area), the chief mourner clears an area on public land near the water, covers it with a cowdung paste, and makes the dhikuro or mound of dirt where the spirit of the deceased will come as a ghost to be given food and water.

This feeding must be repeated for nine days or up to the tenth day after death. A tripod of sticks is placed over the mound, and a clay pot with a hole in the bottom—the same one used in the ksetraba enclosure—is suspended over it. (See figure 7.) The pot is filled with a mixture of water and milk so that it will drip steadily over the dhikuro mound. Within the purified area a fire is built on which the chief mourner must first cook rice for the pinda offering and then for his own single daily meal. Only after offering pinda to the ghost (as well as substances like sandalwood paste, sheep's wool, raw sugar, and a piece of iron) may the chief mourner cook his own sparse meal of rice and clarified butter. The meal is eaten on leaf plates and stirred with a piece of wood, which are all thrown away after the meal because of the extreme impurity they have absorbed through contact with the chief mourner.

When he is finished, he fills the vessel suspended over the dhikuro mound with water, removes the pinda, and throws it into the river. Then he spreads the whole area with a fresh coat of cowdung paste, places thorn branches over the tripod to keep the animals from polluting the dhikuro, and goes home.

After the last dhikuro sraddha is completed on the tenth day after death, the dhikuro must be destroyed. First the string and the plate of seven types of grains are brought from the koro barne room in which the chief mourner has been sleeping and placed on the dhikuro mound. Then the chief mourner offers sweets to the dhikuro and removes the tripod and its suspended clay pot. After dividing the mound into four sections with a piece of gold wire wrapped with kus grass, he breaks up the mound, shatters the clay pot, and snaps the koro barne string. If the deceased was his father or mother or anyone to whom he owed respect, he must break up the mound with his head—as if touching his head to the deceased's feet one last time. If the deceased was the chief mourner's wife, he uses his chest to push away the mound, and for his younger brother or any other junior person, he need only use his knee. Then he takes some dirt from the dhikuro mound and mixes it with the seven kinds of grain. He walks several paces away from the abandoned mound and, turning his back on it, he walks backwards, throwing dirt and the mixed grains behind him until he has reached the place where the mound was.

Informants explained to me that during the period of mourning following death, "everything is backwards." That is somewhat of an exaggeration. The reversals are not always so graphic as in the ritual destruction of the dhikuro, but certainly many behavioral norms are suspended. The ritual status, clothes,

FIGURE 7
DHIKURO SRADDHA

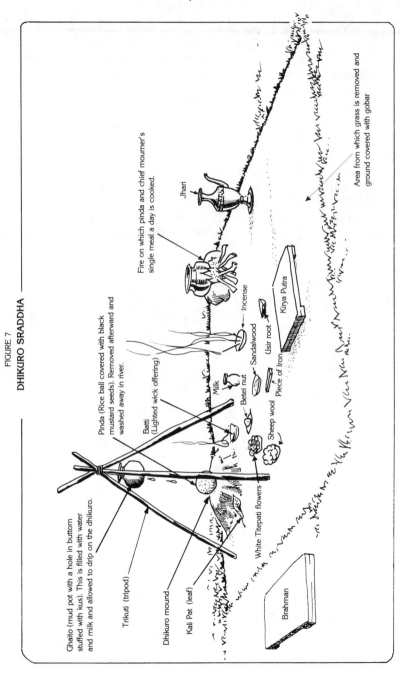

Ghaito (mud pot with a hole in buttom stuffed with kus). This is filled with water and milk and allowed to drip on the dhikuro.

Trikuti (tripod)

Dhikuro mound

Kali Pat (leaf)

Pinda (Rice ball covered with black mustard seeds). Removed afterward and washed away in river.

Batti (Lighted wick offering)

Fire on which pinda and chief mourner's single meal a day is cooked.

Jhari

White Titepati flowers

Milk

Betel nut

Sheep wool

Sandalwood

Usir root

Incense

Piece of Iron

Kirya Putra

Brahman

Area from which grass is removed and ground covered with gobar food, speech, and even sleep of the chief mourner (and to a lesser extent the family and wider kin group) have been drastically altered. He has been in what Van Gennep (1909) describes as a "liminal state," cut off from the gods and from his fellow villagers, involved almost exclusively with the spirit of the deceased.

With the dismantling of the dhikuro, however, the return to normality begins. During the next three days the chief mourner and his family will be drawn progressively back into ordinary social intercourse. As soon as he has destroyed the dhikuro, the chief mourner bathes in the river, shaves his head again, drinks purifying cow urine, and changes his sacred thread. He is now pure enough to end his most acute separation from society by touching first a cow and then his Brahman priest with a piece of kus grass in his hand. From now on he may touch members of his own caste and those above him. The restrictions against touching lower but normally touchable castes still remain until the thirteenth day, though he may at least speak with them now. Also, after the tenth day he no longer has to eat outside but may begin to take his food in the house.

The Eleventh Day (*Egharau Sram*)

On the eleventh day after death a series of other ceremonies are performed. These ceremonies are largely intended to help release the deceased's soul from its worldly sins and to assist the soul in reaching the pitrlok rather than hell. On its quest to reach the pitrlok, however, the soul must undertake a very difficult and dangerous journey through the other world. Several features of the eleventh day rites, therefore, are geared toward providing the soul with the necessary supplies it will need: food, clothing, a bed, even a toothbrush. By giving these to the officiating priest as *sayya dan* (literally "gift of a bed") it is believed that they are transferred to the deceased. Very poor families may give replicas of the more expensive objects such as the bed, but often the sayya dan is quite lavish and constitutes one of the major expenses of the initial death rituals. After the sayya dan a series of rice-ball offering are made—seventeen in all—which initiate and prefigure the offerings that will be made periodically throughout the upcoming year of mourning.

The Ghost Becomes an Ancestor Spirit:
The Rice-ball Ceremony (Sapinda Sraddha)
      On the twelfth day one of the most important of the death
rituals is performed: the sapinda sraddha, in which the deceased
in transformed from an inauspicious ghost to an ancestral spirit.
This is done by mixing his or her pinda with pinda representing
the family's three most honored patrilineal ancestors.[49] Once
again the chief mourner must bathe in the river and drink cow's
urine to purify himself. Then he prepares an area by sprinkling
it with "white" mud and sesame seeds and dividing it into three
separate areas (areas A, B, and C in figure 8) with lines of white
rice flour. Area A is for the gods. Kus grass figures placed in
plates of uncooked rice are set out, one representing Bhuswami
(the late father of King Birendra) and three representing the bis-
wadeva, all the gods. Area B is for the pitr of the chief mourner.
Three kus grass figures are set out to represent the father, grandfather, and great-grandfather of the deceased. In area C a single
kus figure is set out to represent the deceased, who is still a
ghost.
      Several offerings are made to these throughout the sap-
inda sraddha. The significant feature of these ceremonies is that
in the beginning after each offering the chief mourner makes to
the ghost in area C, he must purify himself (by drinking cow's
urine) before crossing over to area B or A to worship the pitr or
the gods. The deceased in ghost form is still unclean, and this
impurity must not be transferred to the gods or the pitr. During
the course of the ceremony, however, the offerings to the ghost
and those to the pitr are ritually joined. Water from the ghost's
leaf cup is poured into leaf cups containing water offered to the
pitr. Likewise, the pinda of the deceased is divided into three
parts, which the chief mourner must press firmly into the three
pindas that have been offered to the deceased person's father,
grandfather, and great-grandfather. Thus symbolically the distinction in ritual purity between the deceased and his ancestors has
been removed. The deceased is no longer a pret, but has become a pitr ready to begin the journey to the pitrlok. Now the
chief mourner returns home and a feast is given in which twelve
Brahmans are fed (baun bhojan). Up to this point, no auspicious
worship had been done in the bereaved household, but now
that the deceased has been released from ghost form, the ban
on worship is lifted. So before the feast the auspicious elephant-

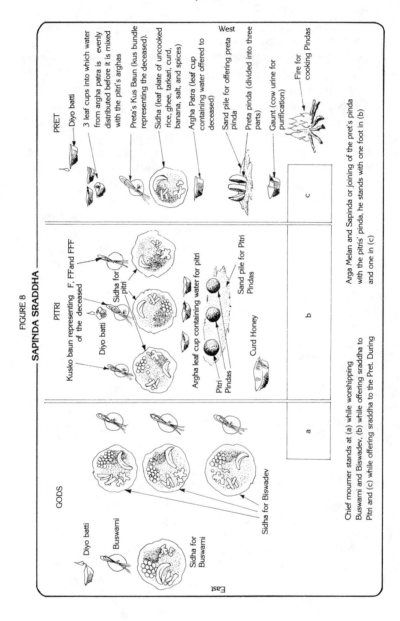

FIGURE 8

SAPINDA SRADDHA

GODS

Diyo batti

Buswami

Sidha for Buswami

Sidha for Biswadev

East

PITRI

Kusko baun representing F, FFand FFF of the deceased

Diyo batti

Sidha for pitri

Argha leaf cup containing water for pitri

Pitri Pindas

Curd Honey

Sand pile for Pitri Pindas

PRET

Diyo batti

3 leaf cups into which water from argha patra is evenly distributed before it is mixed with the pitri's arghas

Preta's Kus Baun (kus bundle representing the deceased).

Sidha (leaf plate of uncooked rice, ghee, tarkari, curd, banana, salt, and spices)

Argha Patra (leaf cup containing water offered to deceased)

Sand pile for offering preta pinda

Preta pinda (divided into three parts)

Gaunt (cow urine for purification)

West

Fire for cooking Pindas

a

b

c

Chief mourner stands at (a) while worshipping Buswami and Biswadev, (b) while offering sraddha to Pitri and (c) while offering sraddha to the Pret. During Arga Melan and Sapinda or joining of the pret's pinda with the pitris' pinda, he stands with one foot in (b) and one in (c) headed god, Ganes, is worshiped. The chief mourner may also retie his topknot.

The period of death pollution ends on the thirteenth day with a series of rituals called literally the "pure and peaceful" (*suddha santi*), which must be completed before midday. A simple sacred enclosure is constructed in the family courtyard, and a fire worship ceremony is performed. Then "in case anything has been forgotten" in the kirya basne rituals, a golden vessel (actually it is usually a clay pot containing a tiny piece of purifying gold) filled with curds, clarified butter, and milk is given to a Brahman. This is the "ghost vessel" (*pret ghara*) intended to insure the release of the deceased from the ghost form. Then, after certain gifts are given to the family priest, a feast is prepared and given to the members of the funeral procession.

The Second Level of Obligation: The Year of Mourning and Its Monthly Rites (*Barakhi* and *Masik Sraddha*)

After the ceremonies on the thirteenth day the chief mourner and his family are once again pure (*cokho*). The chief mourner can now mix freely with others and eat all the ordinary foods, except that he must refrain from milk for a year in the case of his mother's death and curds in the case of his father's death. He may wear stitched clothing and shoes again—but the clothes must all be white, and the shoes only of cloth or rubber rather than leather. Widows also must wear white for a year and never again wear red—even as a tika mark or hair braid. They should not oil or braid their hair for a year and should not see any males from their natal home (*maiti*) for a year.

The chief mourner may do daily household puja if there is no one else, but he may not use red powder in the worship. Nor may he receive anything but yellow tika during the year. He should not enter a temple or take prasad. Likewise, neither he nor the members of his household may go to other households to receive tika during the Dasai festival. He may attend weddings, but no weddings or initiations should be performed in his household. The one exception here is in the case of the widower, who may marry and bring home a new wife forty-five days after his first wife's death.

At intervals during the year of mourning a series of monthly rites or *masik sraddha* must be done to assist the deceased on his journey to the pitrlok and make sure he has sufficient nourishment on the way. As can be seen from chart 3.2 at the beginning of this section, there are actually sixteen rather than twelve masik sraddhas. As mentioned earlier the first of the memorial offerings (adyabdika sraddha) which marks the beginning of the year after death is actually performed during the kirya basne period on the eleventh day after death.[50] The actual cycle of monthly offerings however, begins one day short of one month after the death (*unamasik*) and is completed on the first anniversary of death (*barakhi sraddha*) when the year of mourning is over.[51]

During the year of mourning the normal annual memorial ceremony (ekodhista sraddha) of other deceased relatives of the same generation as the person who died, but junior in age/sex ranking, are not performed. Thus, when ego's mother dies he may do his deceased father's ekodhista sraddha during barakhi, but not the reverse.

Except for the final barakhi sraddha, none of the monthly sraddhas involves rice-ball (pinda) or water offerings (*tarpan*) which are so central to most sraddha ceremonies. The deceased, represented by a figure made of grass, is worshiped with offerings of a lighted wick, a clay pot full of water, and two plates of *sidha* or uncooked food.

The barakhi sraddha, however, which marks the end of the year of mourning and the arrival of the deceased in the pitrlok, is more elaborate. It is similar in structure to the annual ekodhista sraddha and sora sraddha rituals to be described below. In fact, the barakhi marks the transition between what I have called the second level of obligation and the third. It is actually the first of the ekodhista sraddha, which are henceforth to be performed every year on the lunar death anniversary of the deceased as long as his or her son, grandson, or great-grandson is alive.

The Third Level of Obligation: Annual Commemoration (*Ekodhista Sraddha*)

The ekodhista sraddha obligations are more diffuse than those for kirya basne or barakhi and more dependent on the particular organization of family units within the patriline. For example, if all a man's sons are living in a single household (the ideal situation), when he dies they will all cooperate in a single joint ceremony for his death and subsequent annual ceremonies. But if, as usually happens on the death of the father, the brothers separate into individual households, then after the kirya and barakhi ceremonies, which are done jointly in the house of the eldest, the subsequent annual memorial for the father will be done separately by each of the brothers in his own household.

Figure 9 illustrates some of the principles which regulate these shifts in responsibility for ekodhista sraddha.

When three brothers A, B, and C share a single household they do ekodhista sraddha together for their father, grandfather, and great-grandfather. They also participate together in the sraddha for B's and C's deceased wives and A's deceased son Y. (No sraddha is done for A's daughter Z because she was married and is now the responsibility of her husband P's patriline.)

After the brothers A, B, and C divide the joint patrilineal estate and set up separate households, the situation changes.

FIGURE 9

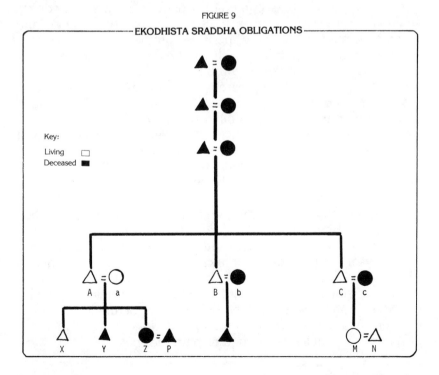

EKODHISTA SRADDHA OBLIGATIONS

A man makes offerings of food to his father's spirit during the annual *ekodhista sraddha* ceremony. *Photo by author*

Though all the brothers continue to perform separate ekodhista sraddha in their respective households for their father and mother, in many cases only the elder brother A, as senior representative of the patriline, will continue the observances for the grandfather and great-grandfather with their wives. A's brothers B and C will also cease to participate in the sraddha for A's son Y. And B and C will each do their own wife's sraddha alone without the help of the other brothers.

The number of individual pitr whom a given family must honor with separate annual ceremonies, then, usually depends on the family's generational depth and on whether its household head is the eldest living brother. For male ego B (who is not a senior brother) ekodhista obligations may extend minimally to his father, his mother, and his wife and son, since they predeceased him. Other factors, however, can increase the ranks of the household's dependent pitr who must be ritually "fed" once a year on their death anniversaries. For example, when B dies his ekodhista will probably be done by A and after him by A's son X, since B had no living offspring of his own. Otherwise one does not do sraddha for one's brother or uncle. C's sraddha, on the other hand, will probably be done by his daughter's husband N. N belongs to another patriline, but since C had no male offspring, N has, in opposition to the usual patrifocal practice, gone to live with his wife's father and become a "house son-in-law" (ghar-juai, one who lives with his wife's parents). Though C's brothers must give their permission,[52] N will inherit C's property and do sraddha for him.

Although at least the eldest brother's family should perform ekodhista for three ascending generations, many families cease doing the full ceremony to be described below for their great-grandfathers. Instead of offering the usual rice ball and water libation they simply offer a plate of uncooked rice, spices, vegetables, curd, and fried bread called sidha to their family priest on the great grandfather's death anniversary. Those who are well off or very orthodox perform the full ekodhista sraddha, since it is felt to benefit the family if the great-grandfather's spirit is happy. As the village saying goes: "If you want to become wealthy, perform your great-grandfather's sraddha" (Dhan kamāunu paryo bhane kupro bā ko śrāddha garnu).

The Fourth Level of Obligation
(Sora Sraddha, Abhyudayik Sraddha, and Tarpan)

The most important among the fourth-level death rituals is the sora sraddha, which is performed once in every Brahman-Chetri household during the lunar fortnight before the annual fall Dasai festival.[53] It is a collective ceremony in which food offerings are made to many ancestors at once. These same ancestors should be remembered with daily offerings of water (tarpan),[54] and again with occasional offerings of food and water during the abhyudayik sraddha described earlier as a necessary preparation (purbanga) for any auspicious family ritual such as an initiation or a wedding.

The fourth level—consisting of these three observances—is the most open in terms of the range of kinship categories which can be included and one's freedom about whether or not to maintain the obligation. A list is given later in this section of some twenty-five categories of pitr—many affinally related in collateral and ascending generations and even some fictively related—which may be included in sora sraddha and tarpan observance. In practice villagers are quite haphazard and casual about keeping the record of names and gotras of the pitr which the priest must recite during the sora sraddha and tarpan ceremonies. Some villagers showed me their lists and were somewhat embarrassed to see that the lists were actually incomplete—with many of the gotras of affinal relatives unknown and even their names missing. Since the kin terms are given in Sanskrit and the priest recites all the names, villagers pay little attention to the specifics of which pitr are being invoked. When the priest does not know the name or gotra of a certain ancestor he addresses it as "what's his name" (yatha nam) and gives the gotra as kasiv, which is a "catch all" gotra for those who have no gotra. One family showed me a rather sketchy list of twenty-three ancestors which their priest had written out for sora sraddha. The head of the household was surprised when I mentioned that at the sora sraddha ceremony I had observed he had only offered sixteen pinda instead of the required twenty-three. The oversight of seven pinda was blamed on the family priest, who, my informant complained, "is always in a hurry and does sloppy work." Nevertheless, the incident indicates a certain laxity in keeping up sora sraddha and tarpan obligations, and it is easy to see how names get dropped from the list after a generation or two.

This blurring of connection and obligation is part of the phenomenon described earlier that occurs between members of the wider patrilineal kin groupings. As the genealogical chart in figure 10 illustrates, mutual observation of death pollution restrictions for deceased members drops from the full thirteen days among sapindi bhai, agnatic relatives within four generations, to a simple observance of bathing and abstaining from a meal (chak khalko) among phuki bhai, agnatic relatives ten generations removed and beyond. After five generations (i.e., beyond the sapindi bhai grouping) precise connections tend to be lost, and unless contact has been maintained through residential proximity, even these attenuated obligations usually lapse unless the relatives are members of a single kul. Members of a kul group know vaguely that they share common pitr. This is, after all, the basis of their relatedness. The obligation to observe death pollution for a deceased member (however minimal it may be) is an acknowledgment that the deceased is in some peripheral way one of their pitr.

Among the sapindi bhai, however, the relationships and their concomitant obligations are much clearer. They are, as we

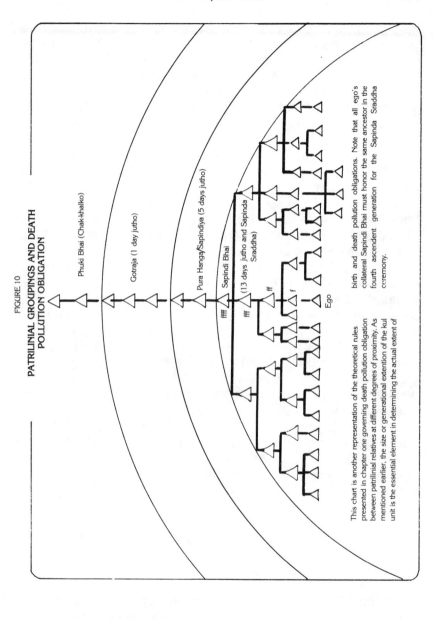

FIGURE 10

PATRILINIAL GROUPINGS AND DEATH
POLLUTION OBLIGATION

Phuki Bhai (Chakikhalko)

Gotraja (1 day jutho)

Pura Hanga/Sapindiya (5 days jutho)

Sapindi Bhai

(13 days jutho and Sapinda
Sraddha)

ffff

fff

ff

f

Ego

This chart is another representation of the theoretical rules presented in chapter one governing death pollution obligation between patrilinial relatives at different degrees of proximity. As mentioned earlier, the size or generational extention of the kul unit is the essential element in determining the actual extent of birth and death pollution obligations. Note that all ego's collateral Sapindi Bhai must honor the same ancestor in the fourth ascendent generation for the Sapinda Sraddha ceremony.

have seen, ritualized in one of the most important death ceremonies, the sapinda sraddha, where the pinda offering to the
deceased is ritually joined with the pinda of his three ascending
patrilineal ancestors—those for whom the deceased had to do
ekodhista sraddha during *his* lifetime. As the simplified diagram
in figure 10 shows, this means ego offers a pinda to his paternal
great-great-grandfather for the last time during the sapinda sraddha ceremony. This pitr, who is the common ancestor of all
ego's sapinda bhai, will no longer receive separate ekodhista
sraddha from ego and the other members of his generation. His
immortality continues vaguely in the pitrlok. But his living descendants' direct memory of him has faded, and their specific
obligations to him are finished—just as their connections and
obligations to each other through him will be lost and attenuated in succeeding generations.

The ritual forms of the sora sraddha ceremony (to be described below) clearly express the status of the pitr vis-à-vis their
living descendants and the gods. The person performing the
sraddha plays a subservient but succoring role toward the pitr—
very much like the Hindu host/guest relationship. The pitr are
honored and their needs lavishly attended to through water libations and offerings of sidha and pinda. But, like a guest, the
pitr should not remain too long. There is a certain relief on the
part of the participants when the ceremony is over and the pitr
sent back to the pitrlok. For the family has satisfied its obligation
and feels that, since they have made the pitr "happy," the pitr
now have a reciprocal obligation to make the family prosper—
or at least not to be angry with them—during the coming year.
This belief is expressed toward the end of the ceremony when,
before bidding the pitr farewell, the individual performing the
ceremony takes the pitr's blessing and asks that they help the
family (here gotra) to increase and prosper.

Besides expressing the somewhat uneasy relationship between the pitr and its living relatives, the symbolic forms of the
sora sraddha—indeed of all types of sraddha—also articulate the
position of the pitr with respect to the gods. As figure 11 shows,
there are several ways to offer the *tarpan* or water libations
which are part of most sraddha rituals. The different parts of the
hand from which the libation is poured are ranked with respect
to purity and auspiciousness. That which is dedicated to the gods
(the fingertips) is the purest; that which is dedicated to the pitr
(the space between the thumb and forefinger) is the lowest. It is

FIGURE 11

RITUAL FORMS EXPRESSING THE DISTINCTION BETWEEN GODS (DEVTA) AND ANCESTOR SPIRITS (PITRI)

Right hand

TARPAN: libation of water poured from a spouted copper vessel (argha) containing kus grass, sandalwood, rice grains, sesamum seeds, barley and flowers. Different hand positions are used when offering tarpan to:

I. Devta — Straight from fingers — Argha

Water

Auspicious

Copper Bowl

2. Sanakadi (mind born sons of **Brahma**) — from little finger side, Kayatirta

Intermediate

3. Pitri — From between thumb and forefinger

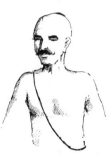

Inauspicious

Janai (sacred thread) worn in different positions when worshipping:

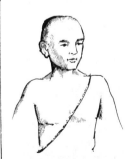

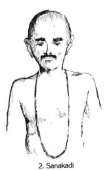

I. Devta
Sabhya
Auspicious

2. Sanakadi
Intermediate

3. Pitri
Abasabhya
Inauspicious

the same with the position of the sacred thread. The reverse of the ordinary auspicious position, over the right shoulder (sabya) must be worn when approaching the pitr. There is considerable emphasis on reversal and inauspiciousness throughout the various stages or levels of the death ceremonies, used to express the separation (from living humans on one side and the immortal transcendent gods on the other) which death has imposed on the pitr. For example, sora sraddha may be done only after midday, while the gods are usually worshiped early in the morning. Anything offered to the devta is offered with the palm facing downward and preferably to the east or west; [55] offerings to the pitr must be made with the palms facing up and toward the south. Likewise, the gods may be offered barley grains (which are planted and sprout during Dasai, symbolizing fertility and renewal) while the pitr are said to prefer black sesame seeds as offerings. We have already encountered one of the more vivid indications of the separation imposed by death in the strict ban on the color red in the worship of the pitr (except for abhyudayik ceremonies performed for weddings and other joyful occasions). Red powder (which symbolized the sexual possession of the bride in the marriage ceremony) may not be mixed with the unbroken rice grains (acheta) given to the pitr, as it usually is when offered to the gods. No red flowers may be offered, nor may red tika marks be given during or after the ceremony. Informants explain that the ancestors don't like the color red. They like white and above all, yellow. Hence all flowers and tika given during the sraddha are yellow or white—colors associated not only with death, but with ascetic withdrawal and purity.

On the day before sora sraddha the person who will be performing the ceremony (ego in figure 11) must purify himself with a ritual fast.[56] On the morning of the sraddha he bathes himself without soap because soap is impure (bitulo) and "the pitr don't like the smell of soap." He puts on a fresh dhoti and a new sacred thread. The women of the household are busy preparing a special meal—usually with the favorite sweet rice-milk pudding called khir—for as many Brahmans as they can afford to invite. Villagers say that the pitr are pleased when Brahmans and the family's young children are fed during a sraddha. The Brahmans are believed to somehow transmit the food they receive to the pitr. In fact, during the ceremony itself a Brahman (sometimes several) must be fed while sidha plates of uncooked food are being offered to the pitr. As one Chetri woman explained, "When the sraddha is being performed . . . they feed the priest with fruits, pickles, and curries. If the priest is fed, then it is like feeding the pitr." Another informant from Nuwakot district explained the Brahmans are like visible pitr during the ritual feeding.[57]

Before the actual sora sraddha ceremony begins, the householder who is performing the ritual greets his priest and the other Brahmans he has invited[58] by washing their feet and drinking some of the water as a gesture of respect. Then he enters the sraddha area (see figure 12) and purifies himself by drinking cow urine, dung, milk, curds, kus grass, and water (pancagabya) and by performing the prayascitta godan, a gift of a cow or coins symbolizing a cow, made for expiation of former sins.

Then it is time for the series of tarpan or water offerings mentioned previously. The first is offered in the auspicious manner (see figure 10) to Brahma and all the other gods. Ego pours the water while the priest recites the names of the gods. Then ego changes his sacred thread to the intermediate position (like a garland round his neck) and offers tarpan to the Sanakadi, the seven ascetic, mind-born sons of the Brahma. Although the sons of Brahma are human, they are so removed by their ascetic purity from samsaric change and pollution (i.e., they were not born of women; they do not marry; and they remain forever at the innocent age of five) as to be semidivine—which is the way they are treated in the symbolic forms of sraddha.

The third libation is offered to the seven dibya pitr or kabyabat. These beings are definitely below the Sanakadi, but sometimes they are described as kings of the pitr and sometimes as the pitr's servants who bring sraddha offerings from the world of men back to the pitrlok. At any rate, for their tarpan the sacred thread is switched to the inauspicious abasabya position over the left shoulder.

Finally tarpan is offered to ego's own pitr, not only in his own thar and gotra, but those from his mother's brother's side, other affinal relatives, and even special fictive relatives. It is perhaps worth giving the long list of possible pitr categories here in the order in which they would be recited by the priest. Each male pitr is invoked together with his wife (sapatni) and each female with her husband (sadaba sapatya)—though in a few cases important spouses are mentioned separately. The actual number of pitr categories, then, is almost double the list given here:

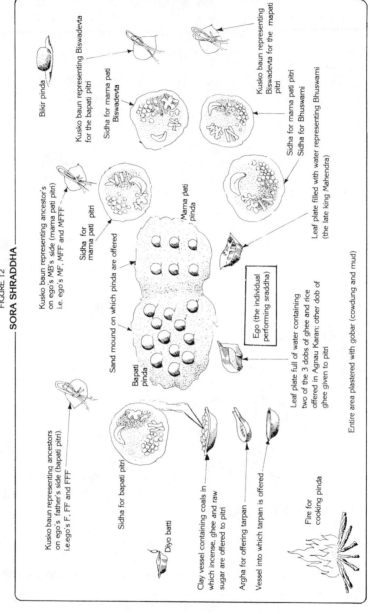

FIGURE 12
SORA SHRADDHA

Bikir pinda

Kusko baun representing Biswadevta

Kusko baun representing Biswadevta for the mapati pitri

Kusko baun representing Biswadevta for the bapati pitri

Sidha for mama pati Biswadevta

Kusko baun representing ancestor's on ego's MB's side (mama pati pitri) i.e. ego's MF, MFF and MFFF

Kusko baun representing Biswadevta for mama pati pitri pitri

Sidha for Bhuswami

Sidha for mama pati pitri

Sidha for mama pati pitri

Leaf plate filled with water representing Bhuswami (the late king Mahendra)

Mama pati pinda

Sand mound on which pinda are offered

Ego (the individual performing sraddha)

Bapati pinda

Kusko baun representing ancestors on ego's father's side (bapati pitri). i.e.ego's F, FF and FFF

Leaf plate full of water containing two of the 3 dobs of ghee and rice offered in Agnau Karan; other dob of ghee given to pitri

Sidha for bapati pitri

Clay vessel containing coals in which incense, ghee and raw sugar are offered to pitri

Argha for offering tarpan

Vessel into which tarpan is offered

Entire area plastered with gobar (cowdung and mud)

Fire for cooking pinda

Diyo batti

1. father (*pitr*)
2. father's father (*pitamaha*)
3. father's father's father (*prapitamaha*)
4. mother (mata)
5. father's mother (*pitamahi*)
6. father's father's mother (*prapitamahi*)
7. mother's father (*matamaha*)
8. mother's father's father (*pramatamaha*)
9. mother's father's father's father (*brida pramatamaha*)
10. wife (*patni*)[59]
11. son (*choro*)
12. daughter (*chori*)
13. father's brother (*thulo/sanoba*)
14. mother's brother (*mama*)
15. brother (*daju/bhai*)
16. brother's wife (*bhauju*)
17. father's sister (*phuphu*)
18. mother's sister (*thuli/sani ama*)
19. sister (didi/bahini)
20. wife's father (*sasura*)
21. wife's mother (*sasu*)
22. the person who taught ego the gayatri mantra (*gayatri guru*)
23. person who gave special initiation (*diksa guru*)
24. persons initiated by ego (*cela*)
25. ritual friend (*mit/mitini*)
26. ritual friend's son or daughter (*mit chora/chori*)
27. those who have no living relatives (*aputra pitr*)

Probably no one has dead relatives in all these categories and, as we said, there is a certain laxity in keeping up the complete list. Nevertheless the list presents a clear picture of how extensive the fourth level of obligation can be. Also whereas in the first three levels of the death rituals the emphasis has been predominantly on patrilineal linkages, here we see that several categories of affinal relatives have been included. Indeed, as can be seen in figure 12, there is a careful symmetry in the sacred enclosure and in the sora sraddha ritual itself between the patrilineal ancestors (*bapati pitr*) and those on the mother's brother's side (*mamapati pitr*)—and by extension all other categories of affinal relatives. All the offerings which are made to conclude the sora sraddha ceremony, including sandalwood paste, flowers, grains, strips of cloth representing clothes, clarified butter and, of course, the pinda, are given separately to the two groups of pitr.

Notes

1. According to the orthodox Brahman traditions, as explained to me by a village pandit, a father should perform the propitiation or expiation ritual (*prayascitta*) whereby he takes a purificatory bath before going to his wife to beget a child. Then during the time of conception itself the family priest should be performing a Vedic fire sacrifice (*hom*) in the family courtyard, with a special ceremony called *garba dan*, "placing the seed in the womb". During the pregnancy two other ceremonies should be performed: one called "quickening a male child" (*pumsa bana*) and one in which the pregnant woman's hair is oiled and ceremonially parted by her husband (*simantonnayana*).

In fact, this same informant explained, these ceremonies are only performed ex post facto and in a much abbreviated form many years later during the initiation of a male child.

2. As Höfer has pointed out, *sutak* refers to "the state of impurity a) of a woman in confinement and b) of the bereaved after the death of one of their relatives" (1979:50). However, it was my observation that people generally used the term *jutho* to refer to death pollution and *sutak* to refer to birth pollution—perhaps because of the association of the latter with the term *sutkeri*, which refers to the new mother during her confinement.

3. If the family is in the midst of a wedding or some ceremony which would be costly to cancel, they leave the cord uncut until the ceremony is irrevocably under way.

4. The descriptions of these and the *nuharan* and *pasne* ceremonies are largely taken from Bennett 1976.

5. Informants reported that if the child's sign was unfavorable he would be sent away to live with another family and not allowed to see his father until the number of years specified by the astrologer has elapsed. I know of only one case where a child was sent to live with his mother's family because of such an incompatible sign.

6. Females are usually connected with odd numbers and males with even in Hindu symbolism. For example: coitus on odd number days after the menstrual period is said to result in a female child, even days a male; girl babies start to move in the womb during the fifth month, boys during the sixth.

7. According to my pandit informant the ceremony could be performed for males between the ages of 5 and 16 for a Brahman, 8 and 22 for a Chetri. And in fact the age range for performing the initiation ceremony displayed a wide variation.

8. An early *bartaman* may be done by a wealthy family that can afford two separate ceremonies or by a poorer Brahman family hoping for extra income after their son has been initiated to full caste status and is eligible to perform sacrifice for his patrons and receive religious gifts.

9. For weddings the same *purbanga* ceremonies are done simultaneously at the groom's and the bride's houses.

10. Some informants said there should be sixty-four piles of rice and that they represented the sixty-four female ascetics who accompany Siva (*causatthi yogini*) rather than the matrkas.

11. The girls are supposed to use a small golden hoe (*kuto*) and a silver mattock (*kodali*) which, of course, are not found in village homes, so they use their hands, which because of their virginal state are equally pure.

12. See figure 6 and description in the section on marriage.

13. Besides the prenatal ceremonies mentioned earlier, there are three other occasions for which a fire ceremony and appropriate religious gifts to Brahmans *should* have been offered. Of these the *jatakarma* (in which a symbol of the goddess Saraswati—*bij mantra*—is written on the child's tongue in honey and clarified butter with a piece of gold wire) is observed, if at all, by the simple custom of putting clarified butter and honey or sugar water (*bakut*) in the mouth of a newborn child. The first rice (*annaprasana*) is done but usually without a fire ceremony, and the ear piercing (*karna vedha*) may or may not be done as part of the name-giving but is not marked by a separate ceremony. In fact, to this point the only hom that has been offered for the child was at his name-giving.

14. Some informants reported that tonsure was performed by the priest; others said that the boy's maternal uncle performed this rite.

15. A white dhoti, a shawl called an *uparna*, and, if the family can afford it, a golden ring.

16. Traditionally this was a turban, a special shawl called a *dosala*, shoes, tunic, and pants, and an umbrella.

17. This scene is enacted even when the boy is very young and his parents have not even begun to look for a bride.

18. If the families are poor they may arrange for the entire wedding to take place at a temple and thus save on the expense of feeding their village neighbors.

19. Less conservative Brahmans in the Trisuli area, however, have begun recently to perform the swayambar when the bride and groom are past puberty. They say it is done to ensure love between the bride and groom and is "like a love marriage." Linda Stone, personal communication.

20. No informants could recall any instance of a groom being refused, though some of the women seemed pleased with this novel idea.

21. The swayambar can be done several months or weeks before the main wedding ceremony or combined with it (which reduces expense and risk to the girl) but it must be done before the *kanyadan* ceremony.

22. As in the bartaman, after the purbanga ceremonies birth, death, or even the bride's menstrual pollution cannot cause the marriage to be postponed.

23. There are some variations between families and villages in the way the matrka puja is done. But the giving of a sari and various other offerings to the matrkas seems to be the central feature. The bhar are also consistently present at the altars in both the bride's and groom's houses.

24. Among the Brahman-Chetri of Nuwakot district the category of women who must feed the groom sagun is larger: MFBW, FZ, MZ, MM. Linda Stone, personal communication.

25. Linda Stone, personal communication.

26. This copper vessel (*karkaulo*) is also part of the bride's dowry, a gift from her parents.

27. Informants explain that after the bride's parents die, the groom must offer them a libation (*tarpan*) during the yearly *sora sraddha* because they have washed his feet during this ceremony. (See the last section of this chapter.)

28. Linda Stone reports an exception. The bride's elder sister, who must call the groom "brother-in-law," does not wash his feet.

29. The bride's servant (*lokanti*) usually accompanies her to the groom's house, returning with her for the ritual visit home (*dulhan pharkaune*).

30. Linda Stone, personal communication.

31. It can also be her mother's brother (*mama*) or elder brother but it must be "someone who loves her."

32. Linda Stone reports a different explanation from informants in the Nuwakot area, who say this rite is to make the bride "similar to the groom's mother" who used to do all washing, cooking, and other work for the groom. This work must henceforth be done by the bride.

33. A pandit informant said that the *caturthi hom* should be done on the fourth day after the kanyadan, as its name indicates. But almost always it is done on the first day after the wedding party returns, when the village is feasted by the groom's family.

34. In a joint family, where the women eat last, the tastier, better-quality foods are often finished before the women eat. A husband can see that his wife gets some by leaving some on his own plate.

35. In fact my informants told me the marriage is often consummated earlier, on the first night in the groom's house when the couple are given a room together.

36. The one exception that comes to mind here is the *kul devta*, who is also linked to a specific patrilineal unit, and shows the same irascibility that the *pitr* do.

37. Though most sraddha symbolism seems to confirm that the pitr have lower ritual status than the devta, they are in one important sense considered more fastidious (or perhaps simply more vulnerable to pollution) than the devta: a woman can worship the gods six days after beginning her menstrual period; but she may not cook, carry water for, or participate in sraddha until the seventh day. As in so many of the restrictions surrounding the pitr, the rule is explained in terms of the pitr's anger.

38. Informants were apparently unaware of the recent amendments in the Nepalese National Code which place the daughter unequivocally before brothers, thus doing away with the need for the brothers' permission. Likewise, when asked about inheritance, no villagers mentioned the new law (passed in 1975 International Women's Year) giving unmarried daughters over the age of 35 equal inheritance rights with sons.

39. Linda Stone reported to me the interesting procedure followed among Brahmans and Chetris of Nuwakot district when in the case of an accidental death or suicide, the body cannot be recovered. On inquiry I found the same procedure is followed in Narikot.

After several days of search have proved ineffective, an image or *putali* (doll) of the deceased is made with kus grass and wheat flour and it is burned in place of the actual body. Coconut bark is used for hair, a piece of banana for the nose, pomegranate seeds for the teeth, *ritha* berries for the eyes. The sexual identity of the image is important; if the deceased was a woman, the image is given a piece of new red cloth for a sari, marbles for breasts, and a banana is placed horizontally between the legs to indicate the vagina. Men's images are dressed in yellow cloth and the banana is placed vertically to represent the penis. Mercury is placed between the legs of both male and female images to represent male and female seed (*bij*), respectively. Despite the substitute ritual cremation, a person who has died under such circumstances is almost certain to become a pret.

40. A woman who dies while her husband is still alive is wrapped in red.

41. If the deceased had no male descendants or collaterals, his wife or daughter must pay someone of his own caste to burn the body.

42. For the wealthy and for the king, a Brahman wearing a dhoti goes all the way to Banaras or Ridi Bazaar, where he places the astu in the Ganges. For a poor man any river will do, since it is believed that all rivers are the Ganges.

43. Cita pinda are offered to various places that the corpse has polluted: the place of death (*mrtusthan*); the door (*dhoka*) through which the corpse was carried if death occurred indoors; the places where the funeral procession rested on its way to the cremation ground (*bisramsthan*). Three pinda are offered to the cita, or funeral pyre itself.

44. If the deceased had more than one son, all are chief mourners and participate in the following rituals together. If he has no sons, his widow will still observe koro barne, though a male will probably do most of the other rites. For Brahmans the string enclosure is in the shape of a triangle; for Chetris it is a square.

45. If the death occurs late in the day after a rice meal has been eaten, the first day does not count as ksetrabas. The chief mourner must remain in the enclosure that night, the following day and through the second night without eating rice.

46. Ordinarily villagers never sleep with their head to the north, since that would

put their feet towards the abode of Yama in the south and their head towards the pitrlok in the north, which is considered an inauspicious alignment.

47. One of the strictest and most important of these is the *havisyak basne* or *havasya basne* fast. This fast is observed before worship of the lineage gods (kul devta), foot-washing (gora dhune), and other occasions when the individual must reach a state of great purity. The person, if male, must shave his head (though few observe this now), cut nails, bathe, wear freshly cleaned clothes, and avoid sexual intercourse. He or she may eat only one rice meal a day of pure vegetarian food.

48. *Pinda* in Monier-Williams' Sanskrit dictionary is given not only as "ball" and "roundish lump of food," but also as "body" and "embryo in early stages of gestation." Informants also describe the pinda as the body of the pitr to whom it is offered. One priest even went so far as to explain that the black sesame seeds were the pitr's "hair."

49. If the deceased is a male this would be his father, grandfather, and great-grandfather. If the deceased is a woman, the pitr involved would be her mothers-in-law for three ascending generations (H F W: H F F W: H F F F W). When a young man dies whose father is still alive, the pitr involved are his grandfather, great-grandfather, and great-great-grandfather.

50. At that time seventeen rice-ball offerings are made: one for the abyabdika sraddha and sixteen others in a ceremony called *sodasi sraddha* (literally, "sixteen offerings") which prefigures the entire masik sraddha cycle.

51. *Barakhi* refers to the ceremony which completes the year of mourning and to the year of mourning itself.

52. Should A or B object to the property moving into another patriline and refuse permission, other villagers will bring pressure on them to allow the property to go to M and her husband N. The brother's permission here seems to be mainly a bow to the concept of patrilineal solidarity in the face of the general consensus that a direct lineal descendant—even if female—has more claim to the individual's property than the individual's collateral relatives do.

53. The lunar fortnight actually makes up only fifteen of the sixteen (*sora*) days during which *sora sraddha* may be performed. The sixteenth day falls on *ghata stapana*, the beginning of Nauratha (nine nights of Durga) of the Dasai festival itself. The only sraddha which may be done on this final day is the *mahatmya sraddha* for ego's mother's father. However, only one pandit informant knew of this and none of the villagers questioned said they had ever performed it. Each family does *sora sraddha* on the lunar date (*tithi*) during the fortnight which corresponds with the death of the father of the male household head.

54. Only in a few very orthodox families, water libation to the ancestors is performed every day when the household gods receive worship. In such households (almost always Brahman) men do the daily nitya puja rather than women. In most households tarpan is offered along with the pinda given during sora sraddha and abhyudayik sraddha.

55. Women also face either east or west when giving birth, as these directions are considered auspicious.

56. The havisyak basne described in note 47.

57. Linda Stone, personal communication.

58. In addition to their regular family priest, Brahmans can also call their son-in-law (*juwai*) or sister's son (*bhanij*) to serve in the ritually superior position of priest. If possible, they call other relatives in this category for sraddha. For Chetris any full Upadhaya Brahman may be invited for the ritual feeding.

59. Though technically speaking, ego could be female, my priest informant assumed ego was a male and gave all the kin terms from a male point of view. If a female did the ceremonies, she would begin with her husband's father, etc., and continue in the same order as above. The first ten kin terms here were given in Sanskrit, the rest in Nepali.

CHAPTER 4

Complementary Kinship Structures: The Dual Status of Women

Now that the rough conceptional scaffolding of the Brahman-Chetri world view is in place, it is time to return to our main subject—the women. It is already clear that Narikot society is strongly patrifocal. Women in this scheme are the submerged members of society, and indeed this is how they appear in day-to-day village interaction and in the women's own expressed view of themselves. One informant described women as *sano*, a word that literally means "small" and is used for untouchables or to indicate low rank in any hierarchy. She explained, "They have to offer obeisance to all the others. A man is respected/obeyed by all, but who is there that will respect us women?"

Of course, this is emphatically not the whole picture. Although the patrifocal model groups agnatic males together and gives affinal women low status, these same males owe ritual deference to their own kinswomen. The partial reversal of women's status in their consanguineal and affinal groups suggests the presence of a secondary model within the Brahman-Chetri kinship—a model reflecting values other than those of the dominant patrilineal ideology. I will attempt to uncover this secondary model and to explore the alternative image of women that it conveys, but my first concern will be to elucidate the values of the patrifocal model. For it is there, in her affinal group where her status is determined by patrifocal values, that a woman's most important social roles, wife and mother, are enacted.

My initial question is: why are affinal women given low status within Hindu patrilineal ideology?

Female Sexuality and the Purity of the Patriline

Village women themselves suggest one answer when they are questioned about their status and about the difference between the positions of men and women. Almost every woman I interviewed expressed her low status in terms of her sexuality and the vulnerability of her reputation. One remarked:

> Our caste (jat) is very different [from men's]. A man can go where he pleases day and night without having to explain anything to anyone. But a woman cannot go anywhere without being called *phuri* [looking for trouble]. If you are a man, then there is no one who can order you around or possess you. But if you are a woman, then you are always afraid to say anything because you don't know what your husband or your mother-in-law or father-in-law will say. . . . A bad woman can do what she likes and say what she wants to say. But a good woman will always fear what others will say. Like when I go to the market and I'm late—then even on the way home I worry that something will happen or someone will say something. If you walk when it's dark, then others will say that you're a harlot. Whereas a man can go out whenever he wants to and no one can say anything.

Another woman put it even more vividly:

> if your husband talks with someone and laughs with them, then there's nothing you can say. But if some man talks with you and laughs with you, then [your husband] will get angry. So when this happens, then is not the woman lowly (*nic*)? Even during sex she has to lie beneath the man!

Inevitably, women cited affinal relatives—the in-laws or husband—as the people who were suspicious of their behavior and concerned about their reputation. The patriline's purity of descent is made vulnerable by the affinal women who must bear its next generation. It is obvious that if a woman's sexuality is not guarded, the offspring of other men, from other lineages and even other castes, may be mistakenly incorporated.

But beyond the need to clearly establish the pedigree of

its next generation, there is another reason for the patriline's concern with the sexuality of its affinal women. This concern arises from the by now familiar contradiction in Hindu culture between the desire to maintain the continuity of life and to withdraw from it—between the householder and the ascetic. In Hinduism the patriline is the epitome of continuity: it links the individual to his ancestors and the ancient sages or rishis as well as to his descendants on whom his own hopes of heaven and future rebirth depend. Through its members' meticulous performance of the arduous death pollution and annual commemorative ceremonies, the patriline represents that part of Hinduism which seeks salvation through progeny and conventional ritual. However, the strain of Hindu thought which follows the ascetic route of abstinence and discipline is also a crucial part of the ideology of the patriline. Through gotra affiliation each patriline traces its symbolic descent from one of the rishis, or ascetic forest dwellers. As O'Flaherty (1973:81) has demonstrated, the rishis' wives with their distracting sexuality only deluded the rishis and obstructed their spiritual pursuits. This theme permeates Hindu thought: sexuality weakens and destroys spiritual power attained through ascetic practices. In this view, women—again specifically affinal women, whose roles within the patriline are sexual and procreative—are seen as threatening to the spiritual purity of a core group of agnatic males. Campbell (1976:140–45) has suggested that the patriline's ideal self-image could best be represented by an unbroken line of celibate holy men, such as is found in the mythological lineages of the North Indian Nath cults. There, as elsewhere in Hindu mythology, male offspring are produced by a series of miracles instead of by normal sexual intercourse between men and women. Fertility, and thus continuity, is achieved without the loss of purity entailed by the householder's involvement with women.

In fact the whole structure of the male initiation ceremony can be seen as an enactment of this: the boy is "reborn" into his full adult status through the ascetic practices and sacred texts taught by the male guru. It is this second spiritual birth without the help of women that sets the twice-born high-caste males apart from women and from the lower castes (neither of whom may wear the sacred thread) and symbolizes their greater purity.

Of course, on the biological level total abstinence is incompatible with the continued existence of the patriline. Since absolute ascetic purity is impossible for the patriline as a social institution, purity of descent becomes its structural equivalent. Sexuality is legitimate if it is disciplined by rules of gotra exogamy and caste endogamy, so that the "right women" are obtained in marriage. Thus, the patriline's concern with female sexuality as a threat to the legitimacy of the descent line is, on a deeper level, a concern for its own spiritual purity.

We recall the emphasis on asceticism in the bartaman ceremony which initiates the Hindu male into both caste and gotra membership. The young boy must renounce his family and lineage for the life of a celibate student. The sacred thread which a boy receives at his initiation is not only the emblem of caste rank, and full lineage membership; it is also a symbol of spiritual purity and of the initiate's link with his ascetic rishi "ancestors." Informants explain that the rishis are actually *in* the sacred thread that they wear. The lives of adult Brahman-Chetri males are beset with rules to keep the sacred thread—and by extension, its wearer—from being defiled. Thus the sacred thread is placed over the ear during defecation and changed altogether after contact with a menstruating woman, or following a birth or death in the patriline. Like purity of descent, these rituals of physical purity are the householder's equivalent of the absolute purity of the rishis—a purity which the householder cannot himself actually attain.

The importance of the rishi as an ideal of male purity is evident in the yearly Janai Purni festival, where Brahman and Chetri men purify themselves to receive new sacred threads. The men say they must bathe 360 times on Janai Purni "because the rishis used to bathe every day [360 times a year] and we don't so we make up for it on this day." On the day before, all initiated males observe a purifying fast involving, among other things, sexual abstinence (*havasyak basne*). Then early in the morning all high-caste men go down to the river carrying their new sacred threads and the ritual items they will need to purify themselves and to worship the rishis.

After stripping to his loincloth, each man takes pure earth (*cokho mato*) in his left hand, makes three balls out of it, and covers them with his right hand. Then he recites a mantra invoking the mud to destroy his sins. He next takes the first ball of mud and rubs it over the lower half of his body; the second ball is rubbed from the waist up and the third ball from the head down over the whole body. Then dipping his entire body in the river, he bathes.

He repeats the process twice, rubbing himself with cowdung and then ashes—but since the ashes are sacred to Siva, they may only be rubbed on the purer part of the body, i.e., above the waist. Then he takes some strands of dubo grass and sprinkles himself three times with water from the river. He does the same thing with *datiun* leaves and finally splashes water on himself 360 times with a sprig of kus grass before taking a final plunge in the river.

When all the men have finished bathing and put on clean clothes, they gather in a large circle for the rishi puja. A copper tray containing all their new sacred threads is placed in the center along with the sacred water vessel, a votive lamp, and a betel nut representing the god Ganes. After these have been worshiped, various items are offered to the sacred thread[1] and then to the rishis. The Brahman priest who is leading the worship instructs each man to remember his own gotra name as he is making his offerings to the rishis. During the worship the priest intones the following mantra: "Let our sacred thread give us brilliance, strength, and life" (*tej, bal, ayurda*).

After the joint worship each man approaches the priest, gives him a sacred thread and a small gift of money (*daksina*), and puts a new sacred thread on himself while reciting the same mantra. Later in the day each family's priest will come to the house and tie a yellow protective thread on the right wrist for all men and the left for all women. Thus, through bathing and worship of the rishis on Janai Purni, high-caste men are able to restore the power and purity of the sacred thread which the past year's existence as a householder—above all their contact with female sexuality—has dimmed.

Women in Patrilineal Ideology

I have selected three of the major ritual complexes in Brahman-Chetri culture for an analysis of women's place in the patrilineal organization of Hindu society. Each ritual expresses a different aspect of what I have been referring to as the "ideology of the patriline." By ideology I mean the values, beliefs, and principles of organization that structure the dominant patrifocal model of kinship and largely determine the status of women in Brahman-Chetri culture.

It is evident from the initiation and the Janai Purni rituals that male purity is highly valued by the patriline. The importance of male purity is also expressed in the rituals to be discussed, but what emerges most clearly as the core of patrilineal ideology is the ideal of agnatic solidarity. Linked with this central patrilineal value is the belief that besides endangering male purity, women also threaten male solidarity. In each ritual complex the cooperation of agnatic males is central. Women—both affinal and consanguineal—are not entirely excluded, but they are definitely peripheral and ritually inferior to the men who participate in these ceremonies.

Death Rituals
     The first of the ritual complexes I will examine is the set of death rituals that I described in the last chapter in more detail. I noted then that the complex of death-pollution and memorial rites establishes the primacy of the parent-son bond both for individual immortality and for the collective existence of the agnatic kin group. The death rites show that—in the spiritual realms at least—the successful working of the patrifocal model depends upon the production of male offspring.
     Categorically, death rites are performed by sons, as the use of the word Kirya putra for "chief mourner" suggests, putra meaning literally "son." However, there is a corollary principle: for performance of the funeral rites, any male—as long as he is of sufficient caste purity—is preferable to a woman, even a wife or direct lineal female descendant. This brings about the dissonance I mentioned earlier between the order of precedence for kirya basne responsibilities and that for land inheritance. Women are included in the latter but not in the former.
     In the ideal situation—i.e., when there is a male heir—the order for both kirya responsibility and land inheritance is the same. There is then a reciprocal relation between the economic basis of the patrilineal group—the land—and its spiritual basis—the quest for immortality.[2] To put it somewhat crudely, the son ensures his parents' salvation in exchange for their land. Informants always explained the relationship between funeral responsibilities and inheritance this way, when in actuality the person who inherits the patrilineal property may well be a female relative who must ask a male agnate of the deceased or hire a Brahman to do the rituals. This kind of situation (and also

to a lesser extent when a more distant collateral relative inherits and does kirya) is disturbing to the villagers—almost as if the rituals lose some of their efficacy when they are not performed by a son. Informants without sons say they have "no one" to do their kirya, though in fact there are many other relatives (including a daughter's husband who is a member of another patriline) and any number of unrelated Upadhaya Brahman males who are ritually qualified to perform the rituals. But the further away the chief mourner gets from the category of son, the greater the sense of disorder and anxiety about the spiritual future of the deceased. A deceased person who has no relatives at all to do his kirya (bewarsi) is considered dangerous to the community. Even though other villagers get together and pay someone to perform the death rituals for him, a bewarsi is extremely likely to become a ghost and haunt the village, causing illness and misfortune.

The same feeling of imbalance and uneasiness is evident in cases of irregular marriage where the son's inferior ritual status (received through his mother) debars him from performing his father's funeral rites.[3] Such Khatri or thimbu sons, as we saw earlier, receive their father's thar and gotra name and his general caste status, and yet, ritually speaking, they remain on the periphery of the patrilineal group. Like women, sons of mixed parentage are not "pure" enough to participate fully in certain of the most important ritual activities of the patrilineal kin group—i.e., funeral rites and worship of lineage gods. Like women, they are members but not full members.

Though recent laws give thimbu sons equal inheritance rights with full-status jharra sons and thus full participation in the patriline's economic continuity, they still cannot contribute to its spiritual continuity. A jharra Chetri woman who had been unable to bear a son referred to this in her account of the Khatri son born to her Newari co-wife:

The co-wife's son was beautiful. They said that he would be like my own son and that I should help look after him. They can say that but there was grief in my heart. I felt very sad and wept that I hadn't had my own son. Later my husband also felt anxious and worried. Others told him that to have a son by such a wife was no use. Such a wife was for pleasure only. Her son was a half-breed (thimmar). He would not be able to carry his father [in the funeral procession] when he died. He wouldn't even be able to touch his father's rice! Khatri sons are no use to us when we die. He cannot perform our kirya. The Brahman will do it. Although the other wife has sons they are just to take the wealth. They will get money, property, land, whatever there is.

Devali—Worship of the Lineage Gods (Kul Devta)

A second ritual complex which expresses another dimension of patrilineal ideology is the kul devta cult—the communal worship of lineage gods. While the death rites can be seen as an expression of the patriline's "vertical" extension through time, the kul devta cult represents the patriline's "horizontal" spread or sphere of influence in the present. The former is principally concerned with the lineal dimension of kinship, the latter with the collateral dimensions. In ritual the memorial rites are an embodiment of the parent-son bond and the continuity which it establishes between previous and future generations of a single branch of the patriline. The worship of the lineage gods, on the other hand, is chiefly concerned with the presently living generations of a single lineage—with the solidarity and the worldly prosperity of the brothers (daju-bhai) across as many branches of the lineage as possible. As I mentioned earlier, the kul, whose members all belong to the same thar and gotra and who worship their lineage god(s) together, is the largest functional unit in the patrilineal organization of Brahman-Chetri society. Members observe at least minimal birth and death pollution for each other, and no communal worship of the lineage gods can take place if birth or death pollution is being observed in any member household. The kul can be as small as a single household (parivar), but it generally encompasses at least several households— usually an agnatic group of three or four generations' depth— who are separated but still live near each other. The ideal, of course, is a kul so large that its members can no longer trace exact relationships to each other. The reality of lineage factions and migrations usually cause the kul to splinter before such grandeur can be achieved. The average kul in Narikot encompasses between four and ten households. But two families belong to great kuls that include members from more than a hundred households all over the valley (one has its large permanent shrine in Narikot), and several families belong to kuls of more than thirty households.

K. B. Bista (1972) has described the organization and rituals involved in worship of lineage gods at length. I present

here only a short summary of what he has written on this worship in support of my own analysis of the *devali* ritual complex
and its relationship to the patriline. It is difficult to make such a
summary because both Bista's work and my own observations
indicate that for almost every generalization one can make about
the worship of lineage gods there is some lineage group that
does things a little differently. There is no single unifying Sanskrit text laying down the standard of ritual orthodoxy.[4] Yet, the
way the kul is organized for worship and the overall structure
of the devali ritual do appear to be uniform in Brahman-Chetri
culture throughout the middle hills of central Nepal.

Usually each kul worships a number of deities—some of
whose names may be recognizable as gods of the great tradition
of Hinduism, such as Siva, Ganes, or Durga (Bista 1972:63). Generally villagers tended to identify any deity that did not accept a
blood sacrifice (*bhog*) as Sankar (Siva) and those that did as the
goddess Devi or as Bhairav (the terrifying form of Siva). Some
form of the Devi was present in every kul group in Narikot. The
actual identity of the individual divinities does not much concern the worshipers, since, as Bista points out: "Whatever their
functions and manifestations in general belief and practice, when
they are kul devta, they have only one limited function which
is always the same . . . [that is] to protect the family from ca-
tastrophe and to assure that it will attain wealth, prosperity, and
male descendants" (1972:58, my trans.).

To assure that the lineage gods will continue to bestow
prosperity and fertility on the kul, each household must regularly set aside for the lineage gods some of the special foods
cooked during important ritual events such as naming ceremonies
or marriages.

The most crucial obligation toward the lineage gods is
the periodic communal worship called *devali*. A kul may celebrate devali as often as twice a year or as infrequently as once
in several years on the full moon day of Baisakh (April–May),
Jesta (May–June), or Mangsir (November–December) (Bista
1972:73).[5] At that time, the lineage gods, represented by stones,
are carried in procession to a shrine from the house of the eldest male lineage member, where they have been stored. This
shrine, which may be a permanent one made of brick or a temporary structure of branches made anew each devali, is usually
located in a secluded spot on a hilltop or in the woods where
outsiders cannot easily see the ceremony (Bista 1972:66).[6]

Though Bista does mention one kul that allowed anyone to watch their devali (1972:68), for most the secrecy of the ceremony is of utmost importance. Only pure initiated males may actually enter the interior of the sanctuary and directly participate in the worship (Bista 1972:79). Other male lineage members may observe from the outside, while female lineage members (like nonmembers) must not witness the sacrifice to the main gods at all.[7] Indeed, women are as peripheral to the worship of the lineage gods at devali as they are to the performance of death pollution and memorial rituals. They may plaster the shrine with cowdung before the ceremony and may carry some of the ritual implements in the procession that takes the gods (always hidden from the women's view) to the shrine. The most important function women have in the devali ceremony, however, is making clarified butter and curds from the milk produced by the family cows and preparing special foods from these milk products which will be offered to the lineage gods by the men of the family.

The heart of the devali ceremony, which centers on blood sacrifice, is a purely male affair. Its organization reflects what Doherty (1974:9) has called the "preoccupation with status" within the patriline. The status he refers to is that of age, whereby the younger person always owes respect to the elder. This principle determines that the eldest purebred member of the lineage must be the ritual "headman." He will keep the lineage gods in his house, organize the devali celebration, and give his blessing (in the form of tika, the auspicious forehead mark) to all the male kul members at the end of the ceremony (Bista 1972:91). If the kul is a large one, there may be four or more headmen—again chosen in order of age rank and named respectively jetha eldest, mailo second, sailo third, kancho youngest, the way all siblings are designated in the patrilineal joint family.

The other officiants of devali are the pujari, who actually offer the puja items and sacrifice the goats and chickens under the direction of the eldest headman. All the ritual officiants, the head of each participating household, and the wives of household heads must bathe, fast, and abstain from sexual intercourse.

These temporary ascetic restrictions (havasyak basne) are necessary for household heads, since they must be in a high state of ritual purity to carry the family's puja offerings to the shrine, and are equally necessary for their wives, since they must cook the special foods that are offered to the lineage gods. The

An uncastrated male goat is sacrificed for the worship of the lineage gods.
Photo by Gabriel Campbell

officiants and lineage members who have gone to the shrine must remain pure by fasting until the devali ceremony is over—usually in the late afternoon. But the purity of the pujari (or the ritual headman if he enters the inner sanctum) is even more crucial to the successful propitiation of the lineage gods, since these officiants have closest contact with the deities—and among some groups, Bista reports the belief that the pujari who beheads the animals is actually possessed by the lineage gods. Thus, the pujari chosen must not only be purebred, karma caleko status, but his wife may not be menstruating at the time of devali, since her state of pollution affects his own ritual purity.

One other officiant common to many kul of Narikot, is the lineage god *dhami*—a man who becomes possessed by the lineage gods during the annual devali. Unlike the ritual headman, the dhami is not chosen by seniority. Rather, when the incumbent dhami feels he is too old or weak to carry on, a ceremony is held in which a lineage god is invoked to "choose" one of the dhami's gathered "sons" as its vehicle. The god then enters this individual, causing him to tremble and speak with the god's voice and enabling him to pass certain tests like walking on fire. The retiring dhami then teaches the new initiate a mantra for invoking the lineage god.

During devali, the dhami is possessed by the lineage god(s) generally on the eve of main ceremonies. At this time the lineage god tells the congregation what offerings and sacrifices it desires. Then during the evening after the devali ritual the lineage god is invoked again to say whether it was satisfied with the worship it received. At both of these sessions, male and female members of the lineage as well as outsiders may ask the god for advice about their problems having to do with health, fertility, prosperity, and family relationships. "Will our daughter-in-law return from her parents' place after the last quarrel?" "What must Ram's wife do to have a son?" "Will it benefit Kancha if he goes to India to seek a job?" "What is the cause of my son's illness?"

Bista (1972:95–100) also reports several groups in which the dhami is possessed throughout the ceremony—leading the procession to the shrine and drinking the blood of the sacrificial goats. Of the twenty-seven different kul represented in Narikot, eleven have dhami and of those, three take blood during the sacrifice.

The ritual activities of devali seem to move between two different levels of patrilineal organization: the family and the kul. During the days preceding devali and on the morning of the sacrifice, each family unit prepares its contribution for the communal worship. At this level women are included. Married sisters and daughters, with their husbands and families, are invited. The wife of the head of the family, assisted by other women, cooks the fried breads and prepares the *sidha* plate of uncooked rice and other foods and the tray of offerings which will be presented to the lineage gods.

On the morning of devali when all the puja offerings and the animals are ready to be taken to the devali shrine, the mistress of the house goes to the courtyard where she throws some flowers and rice grains on the people who are departing with the offerings. This rite is called "*sait garnu*" which means good or auspicious departure. [Bista 1972:80, my trans.]

The men who leave the house and go to present the family's offerings at the shrine are participating in a communal expression of patrilineal solidarity that extends beyond their individual family units to the entire lineage. Devali represents the temporary reversal of the patrilines' persistent tendency to splinter into smaller units. The oft-repeated sentiment that brothers would get along if only their wives didn't set them against each other is here enacted. For on the afternoon of devali, the kul temporarily reestablishes the single joint family from which all the participating household units originated. There are no women—only classificatory brothers (the *daju-bhai*), under the leadership of their eldest member, the senior ritual headman. Haimendorf (1966:42) has succinctly described the reciprocal economic obligation which binds the joint family together: all members "are subject to the father's authority and expected to place their earnings at his disposal. In return they are entitled to maintenance and their legitimate needs are met out of the family purse." For devali the senior ritual head plays the role of father to the entire kul. Each family's representative must present its offerings for the lineage god to him. In turn family members receive the meat of their sacrificial animal and their share of the *prasad* (offering returned to the worshiper as blessing after the god has accepted it). At the end of the ceremony they also receive a blessing from the headman. On one level, this exchange can be interpreted as a replication of the ideal reciprocal relation between the individual and his own joint family described above. The more households it comprises and the more branches of the lineage it draws together (and of course the more lavish the sacrifice the group can afford), the greater the prestige of the kul and the more pride each member derives from being part of it. When asked why they thought large kuls were better, informants invariably mentioned that this provided more "brothers" to back them up in a quarrel or help their sons enter government service. However, from our earlier discussion of Brahman-Chetri patrilineal organizations, it is evident that the size and extension of a kul is equally important for symbolic reasons: the larger the kul, the more perfectly it embodies the deeply held value of agnatic solidarity.

Dasai
        The third ritual complex which brings the values of patrilineal ideology into particularly clear focus is Bara Dasai. For Brahmans and Chetris, this fall Dasai festival is the major religious and social event of the year. Its mythic and ritual symbolism is at the very core of the people's spiritual interpretation of their world. Most important, the symbolism of Dasai also reveals much about the ideology of gender and in particular, the meanings attached to the female sex within this Brahman-Chetri world view. I will return to this aspect of the Dasai rituals subse-

quently. Here, however, we will explore the social aspects of Dasai which are so deeply entwined with its symbolic importance. From the social point of view, Dasai is, above all, a celebration—an enactment—of the complex status relationships that bind kinsmen together.

A detailed "map" of each individual's place in the hierarchical organization of the kin group is revealed by the ritual exchanges between kin during Dasai. These exchanges—which consist of tika marks, ritual greetings, and ritual gifts of money— begin at the climax of the two week long festival on the tenth day of the light half of the month of Asauj (September–October) and continue until the full moon day. This kinship hierarchy is emphatically not a simple one. On the contrary, it operates through a web of overlaid hierarchies—some reinforcing each other, others in uneasy conflict, and some even in complete opposition. In other words, the Dasai exchanges clearly reveal that the dominant patrifocal model is not the only model operative in Brahman-Chetri kinship. There are multiple principles of determining status within the system, and there are two distinct sets of values by which the individual is ranked. It will become evident that, even though the values of patrilineal ideology are those most strongly articulated at Dasai, the patrifocal model alone cannot explain all the relationships expressed in the ritual exchanges.

Dasai begins, as I have said, in the second lunar fortnight of the month of Asauj. It is preceded by memorial rituals in the first lunar fortnight of Asauj in which the household "feeds" all its deceased kin (sora sraddha). During Dasai, each household will also feed as many living relatives as possible (both consanguineal and affinal) with the special Dasai foods—goat meat, yogurt, and pounded rice. The head of each household must present every household member with a new set of clothes. It is extremely important to villagers that they be able to wear new clothes for the interfamily visiting that takes place between the tenth day of the festival and full moon day. For many people, these are their only new clothes for the entire year, and even if the household head has to borrow on the coming rice harvest, he is obliged to give everyone something. Dasai is also the time to take care of house repairs and give the house a new coat of mud "paint" (gray-white on the inside and red on the outside) so that the family will appear prosperous to holiday visitors.

Dasai is the worship of Durga, the warrior goddess. In

each household an altar to the goddess, called the *Dasai ghar,* is established on the first day of Navaratri, the nine nights of Durga which begin the festival. In this central feature of Dasai, the worship of Durga, we find that women are once again peripheral to the main rituals. The Dasai ghar (see figure 13) is always in a locked, darkened room from which all but initiated males of the household (and for the Chetris, the family priest) are barred. Menstruating women are not even allowed to be on the same story of the building as the goddess. Thus, if the family has set up the Dasai ghar on the ground floor, any menstruating women must sleep and eat out on the porch or in an outbuilding during their period of pollution.[8]

Early in the morning of the first day of Navaratri, the head of the household must bathe himself and then go to a nearby Durga temple. Most of the men in Narikot walk several miles to the famous Gujeswari temple at Pasupati because they feel that that manifestation of the goddess there is more powerful than those at nearer temples. Each household head will visit the goddess's temple every morning during the Navaratri period and bring back the offerings for the whole family before he worships the goddess in the family's own Dasai ghar. Every night he must worship Durga by offering a lighted lamp at her altar.

On the first day of Dasai household members collect sand from the river beach. The head of the household then makes a bed of sand in the corner of the Dasai ghar and also puts some in leaf plates. He plants the damp sand with barley seeds. More of the seeds are mixed with cowdung, and this mixture is used to decorate a clay pot filled with water. The goddess is invoked into this vessel (*ghanta*). The rest of the altar is set up as pictured in figure 13, with Durga represented again by a long curved knife (*khukuri*) or with a sword tied with a red and white cloth. On the first day and every day thereafter until the tenth day, the head of the household must offer rice grains, red powder, fruits, flowers, incense, a lighted lamp, and fried breads to Durga. If he is literate he will read part[9] or all of the *Candi Path*—a hymn of praise to Durga that tells of her victories in battles with various demons. Otherwise, he may simply worship the holy book itself or pay a Brahman priest (either at the temple or in the village) to read it in his name.

On the seventh day of Dasai (called *Phulpati*) a bundle made of flowers, sugarcane stalks, and bel patra leaves (also called the *phulpati*) must be placed inside the Dasai ghar.

FIGURE 13
THE DASAI GHAR

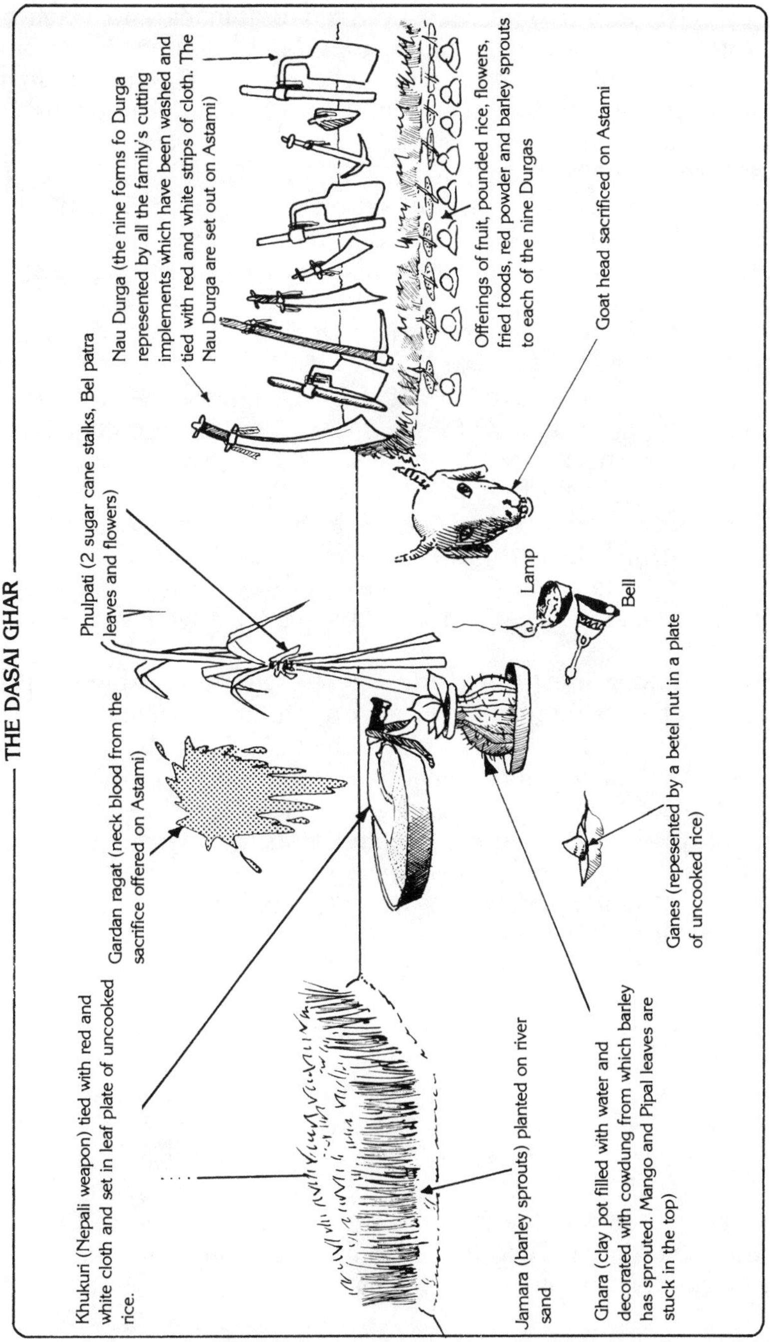

Khukuri (Nepali weapon) tied with red and white cloth and set in leaf plate of uncooked rice.

Phulpati (2 sugar cane stalks, Bel patra leaves and flowers)

Nau Durga (the nine forms fo Durga represented by all the family's cutting implements which have been washed and tied with red and white strips of cloth. The Nau Durga are set out on Astami)

Offerings of fruit, pounded rice, flowers, fried foods, red powder and barley sprouts to each of the nine Durgas

Goat head sacrificed on Astami

Gardan ragat (neck blood from the sacrifice offered on Astami)

Lamp

Bell

Ganes (repesented by a betel nut in a plate of uncooked rice)

Jamara (barley sprouts) planted on river sand

Ghara (clay pot filled with water and decorated with cowdung from which barley has sprouted. Mango and Pipal leaves are stuck in the top)

There is a difference between Brahmans and Chetris in the rituals they follow on the eighth day of Dasai.[10] In Brahman households all initiated males gather in the Dasai ghar in the morning. They collect all the household's cutting implements— knives, axes, farming tools, etc.—and after washing them, they set them up on a clean banana leaf in the Dasai ghar. Nine betel nuts (or other small fruits) are set on piles of rice in front of the row of weapons and consecrated as the Nau Durga or nine forms of Durga. They are worshiped with rice grains, flowers, red powder, fried foods, etc. Then, after reading from the Candi Path the men of the household sacrifice a black uncastrated male goat (boko) to the goddess.[11] The blood from the animal's neck is allowed to spurt over the Nau Durga represented by the cutting instruments and onto the main knife representing Durga. Some of the neck blood may be saved and given to any women in the family who are barren or who suffer from menstrual problems, since the blood is believed to have a beneficial effect on these female problems. The severed head of the goat is placed before the altar, while the family and their visitors eat the rest of the animal. The tail portion however, is given to the family Damai.

Among most Chetri the Nau Durga are worshiped late at night between midnight and two or three in the morning in a ritual called kal ratri, "black night." Though Haimendorf (1966:42) states that the object of such worship is the lineage gods rather than Durga, he has accurately described the organization of the rite: "Sons separated from their father join at this time in celebration in their father's house, and after his death they and their children continue to perform the rite jointly as long as one of them is alive."

As in the worship of the lineage gods, though on a smaller scale, the patriline expands beyond the bounds of the single household for the kal ratri ceremony. Though each household has its own separate Dasai altar, the kal ratri sacrifice is performed in the Dasai ghar of the eldest male in the immediate lineage. The family priest is summoned to read the Candi Path and perform a fire worship ceremony in the Dasai ghar. When the priest is halfway through the fire ceremony, one lineage member sacrifices the goat, whose blood is offered to Durga as described above. Then the animal's liver and heart are cut into 108 pieces and offered by lineage members into the fire.[12] After this meat is roasted, it is taken out of the fire and eaten with salt and black pepper as prasad from the goddess.

The tenth day, also called tika day, is the climax of the Dasai festival. It is the day when Durga celebrates her victory over all the evil demons who had in epic times threatened the gods and men with total destruction. After bathing and before the morning meal, the head of the household offers final worship to the goddess and then the Dasai ghar is opened to the whole family, women and children included. A mixture of yogurt, red powder, and uncooked rice is prepared for giving the auspicious tika marks. The head of the household cuts a bundle of the yellow barley sprouts (jamara) which have been growing for nine days in the dark cloistered room. He first decorates himself with tika and barley, which are considered to be the sacred prasad of the goddess. Then one by one each member of the household receives his or her tika and barley in the Dasai ghar. Later that day and for the next few days relatives visit each other's houses, where they receive tika and barley sprouts and are fed with meat, curd, and pounded rice.

The giving of tika involves a whole complex of ritual actions, each of which conveys a message about the status relations between the giver and the receiver. I shall return to these rituals a little later. However, as I have mentioned, there are two different dimensions of value expressed in Brahman-Chetri kinship, and hence two different hierarchical models within which a person's status can be determined. One individual's relationship to another might very well be marked simultaneously by inferiority in one realm and superiority in another. Before these models can be elucidated through detailed examination of the Dasai tika rituals it is necessary to clarify what the two "dimensions of value" are.

An Alternative Model: Filiafocal Status

Up to this point we have been exclusively concerned with the dominant patrifocal model. We have seen its organizing principles at work in the rituals of birth, male initiation, and marriage, in the death rituals, in the worship of lineage gods, and in the Dasai ceremonies.

As has been repeatedly emphasized, the cardinal value and first organizational principle of the patrifocal model is *the solidarity of agnatic males.* Besides this, two other hierarchical principles operate in several ritual contexts: first, *the superiority of males over females* (of the same generation), and second, *the superiority of age over youth—*which has the corollary of reversing the first principle, so that senior consanguineal females rank higher than junior males. These principles structure the formal relations between male agnates as with affinal women. In secular contexts these principles also apply to the relations between a man and his female consanguineal relatives (or a woman and her consanguineal relatives).

There is, however, another dimension of value in Brahman-Chetri kinship which influences relations between affines and cross-sex relations between consanguineal relatives. These latter relationships are in fact, based on the *sacredness of kinswomen.* One example of this sacredness which we have already encountered is that of the bride vis-à-vis her natal relatives, who demonstrate her ritual superiority over them by washing her feet during the wedding rituals. Another ritual which gives strong expression to the special status of consanguineal women is Bhai Tika or Brother Tika. This important festival will be discribed in greater detail subsequently, but it centers on the spiritual protection which the sister offers her brother (by garlanding him, giving him gifts of pure food, and placing a special multicolored tika on his forehead) and the worship and economic protection which he offers her (by touching her feet and offering gifts of money and clothes).

I have elsewhere (Bennett 1978:121–40) analyzed this second dimension as an example of Victor Turner's concept of "communitas." Turner (1969:96) uses this term to distinguish the broader, spiritual egalitarian values of a society from the "differentiated and often hierarchical system of politico-legal, and economic positions" which he calls "structure." The structure/communitas opposition provides a useful framework in which to consider the reversal of women's status that takes place as women move from the context of their affinal group to that of their consanguineal kin. Certainly the patrifocal model, which assigns low status to affinal women, would seem to correspond to Turner's notion of "structure." This is especially true in respect to the patriline's involvement in inheritance and property rights and its emphasis on rank and authority relations within the

At the completion of a memorial ceremony to the ancestor spirits a father displays his filiafocal deference for his daughter by washing her feet. *Photo by author*

group. As Turner noted, "the patrilineal tie is associated with property, office, political allegiance, exclusiveness and particu-laristic segmentary interests. It is the 'structural' link par excel-lence" (1969:114).

Further, the combination of sacredness and affection with

which consanguineal women are viewed does suggest the notion of communitas. To quote Turner again (1969:117): "Where patrilineality is the basis of social structure, an individual's link to other members of his society through his mother and hence by extension and abstraction 'women' and 'femininity' tends to symbolize that wider community and its ethical system that encompasses and pervades the political-legal system."

But although Turner's analysis can well be applied to the Brahman-Chetri situation, it does not, on closer scrutiny, entirely fit. Turner stresses the egalitarian nature of communitas, in which all members of the group in question are undifferentiated by rank or status. But in the particular kinship relation under consideration here, that between consanguineal men and women, rank and status are not abolished; they are reversed. Women do not become equal to men; they become higher. Hence, the phenomenon we are discussing is not antistructure (which Turner equates with communitas) but rather alternative structure—an alternative to the dominant patrifocal model.

Therefore, despite the fact that the relationships between consanguineal men and women in Brahman-Chetri society are indeed expressive of the broader spiritual and affectional values of communitas, I have felt it necessary to adopt a new term, *filiafocal*, to describe this alternate model. This term parallels "patrifocal," which indicates a system of relations based on respect and obedience to the father—i.e., a male relative of the first ascending generation with respect to ego. It is significant that, although the filiafocal principles inform all relationships with—and through—kinswomen, the focal point of the filiafocal model is the daughter, a female relative in ego's first descending generation. With this focus on the daughter, the filiafocal model reverses the two patrifocal principles of status determination, male over female and age over youth. These two reversals are crucial to understanding the relations between a woman and her consanguineal kin.

The filiafocal status principle with the widest ramifications for Brahman-Chetri kindship, however, is that which affects affinal relations. This is the principle whereby *wife-takers rank over wife-givers*.[13] Here it is necessary to return to the concept of the *kanyadan* or "gift of a virgin daughter" which is the central ritual in orthodox Hindu marriages. The logic of the *dan* or religious gift is pertinent here. Campbell (1976:102) notes that dans "should be given upwards to Brahmans and the purer and

more valuable the item is, the more merit is received from giving it." The ritual in which consanguineal relatives of the bride
(except females junior to her) must wash her feet assumes her
significance in this context. As an expression of the bride's sacredness and superior purity vis-à-vis her consanguineal relatives, it emphasizes her appropriateness as a religious gift. Furthermore, the fact that, if it is to bring merit, one must give a
dan "upwards" to a person of higher ritual status helps to explain what Dumont (1966:101) has called the "hypergamous
stylization of wife-takers as superior and wife-givers as inferior
[which] pervades the whole [Hindu Indian] culture." As Haimendorf (1966:32) has pointed out, there are no ranked clans
among the Chetri of Nepal (or the Brahmans). Even so, marriage
itself creates a ritual superiority of the groom's people—and
hence a hypergamous situation—where there was formerly
equality.

Through this ad hoc hypergamy associated with the sacredness of consanguineal women, the filiafocal model has a
profound effect on affinal relations in Brahman-Chetri kinship.
As figure 14 shows, the ranking of wife-takers over wife-givers
places each patrilineal unit in the middle of a three-stage hierarchy—above those from whom it takes wives and below those
to whom it gives them. Each male is in a position of inferiority
vis-à-vis groups to whom his father has given a sister or to whom
he has given a sister or daughter. He must respect members of
these groups. On the other hand, he is superior to the groups
from which his mother, his wife, and his son's wife have come.
The consanguineal relatives of all these kin, male and female,
must respect him.

The hypergamous hierarchy is expressed through various
ritual interactions (such as the Dasai tika exchange), forms of address and, most vividly, by the affinal prestations which begin
with the wedding kanyadan and continue thereafter in the same
dan pattern. That is to say, wife-givers exchange material goods
(including their daughter) for spiritual merit and a certain amount
of social prestige. Although initially during the wedding, the
groom's family does give some gifts, the bride's family gives far
more back—and continues to do so for a long period of time.[14]
Furthermore, the gifts from the groom's family go to the bride
herself and not to her family. As S. J. Tambiah (1973:97) noted:

> The wife-givers are persistent gift givers and lavish hosts while they
> are at the same time excluded from intimate social contact with the

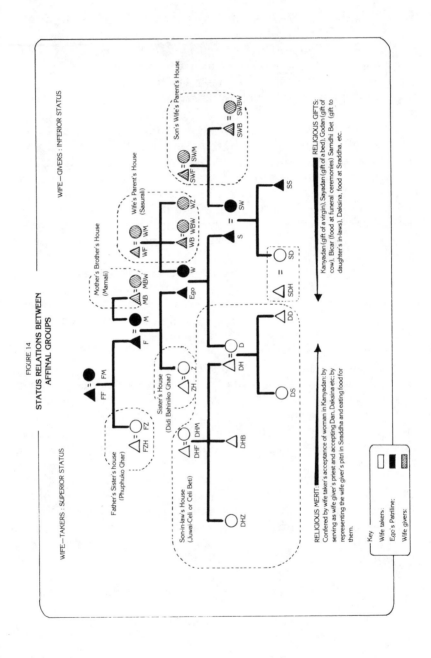

FIGURE 14
STATUS RELATIONS BETWEEN
AFFINAL GROUPS

WIFE—TAKERS : SUPERIOR STATUS

WIFE—GIVERS : INFERIOR STATUS

Father's Sister's house
(Phuphuko Ghar)

Mother's Brother's House
(Mamali)

Wife's Parent's House
(Sasurali)

Son's Wife's Parent's House

Sister's House
(Didi Bahiniko Ghar)

Son-in-law's House
(Juwai-Celi or Celi Bet)

RELIGIOUS MERIT: Confered by wife taker's acceptance of woman in Kanyadan: by serving as wife giver's priest and accepting Dan, Daksina etc: by representing the wife giver's pitri in Sraddha and eating food for them.

RELIGIOUS GIFTS: Kanyadan (gift of a virgin), Sayadan (gift of a bed), Godan (gift of cow), Bicar (food at funeral ceremonies) Samdhi Bet (gift to daughter's in-laws), Daksina, food at Sraddha, etc.

Key
Wife takers:
Ego's Patriline:
Wife givers:

receivers as this would smack of equality. . . . In conformity with the pattern of the gift, the bride's father makes it a point of honor not to receive anything in exchange other than the reflected glory of his son-in-law's family, which will be higher than his own.

Tambiah's description here of affinal relations after a hyperga-mous marriage between ranked clans in North India is for the most part an apt characterization of affinal relations among Par-batiya Hindus in Nepal. The only difference is, as noted above, that in Nepal there are no ranked clans and the husband's higher ritual status is a product of the marriage itself. There is, as Hai-mendorff (1966:59) noted, a preference to marry daughters to families who are wealthier and/or closer to the capital city. Nevertheless, most kanyadan marriages tend to take place among families who are of the same ritual status and also share roughly similar socioeconomic levels.

In Narikot, however, I did encounter an extreme case of socioeconomc hypergamy where a woman from a hill family (with military connections) was married into a wealthy aristo-cratic family in Kathmandu. Though the gifts involved were far more lavish than is ordinarily the case, the woman's description reveals how the prestige and pride of her family of birth were felt to be at stake in their affinal prestations:

As dowry (daijo) father gave numerous pots and utensils, trunks, safes, and wardrobes. This was because he wanted to show that we were very wealthy. He gave me silver spoons, plates, cups, and water vessels and a different set of silver utensils to his son-in-law. They gave me fifteen sets of clothes from my maita [natal home]. Those clothes were embroidered with gold and silver.

Later, after her first child was born and she was returning to her husband's house after the customary postnatal stay in her maita, the flow of gifts continued:

When it was time for me to leave then mother prepared rice-flour doughnuts and other sweets, bananas, and filled a vessel this big with meat kabobs—all as koseli [polite gift to an honored person] for my mother-in-law. The people from my ghar [husband's house-hold] shared and ate everything. My husband's paternal grand-mother (budi sasu) said: "How much food this one has brought! She has brought enough flattened rice to last for the whole month." They used to send me good clarified butter and utensils and twelve-thirteen measures of flattened rice. When I gave birth to my daugh-ter they sent musk such as you can't even find these days. And after her naming ceremony had been performed on the eleventh day they gave me the mattress, quilt, and pillows that had been brought from my maita for me. They had also sent a separate bed for my daughter . . . and all that was required for the baby—pillows, covers, five pairs of clothes, and a whole pile of cloths for diapers. They gave me seven dhotis, five saris, five blouses, and five pairs of shoes.

Of course my other sisters only received the ordinary things, but as I was married into a wealthy family, they had to show fitting behavior. They had to show off by giving many things.

This account represents an extreme case—and one which has perhaps been exaggerated by an old woman looking back. Yet it does represent a cultural paradigm that other villagers also refer to and follow, albeit on a more modest scale. Unless there is an open quarrel and a woman's ghar has previously refused such gifts, the maiti (woman's family of birth) always send a gift of special foods[15] for the in-laws when their daughter returns to her husband's house after a visit. The maiti also feels honored if anyone from their daughter's ghar comes to a family celebration, and special attention is always paid to see that such in-laws are well feasted. On the other hand, a woman's father is reluctant even to go to his daughter's ghar, and until she has borne a child he would certainly never take food offered to him there. Along these same lines, several informants emphasized that it would be shameful and a great sin to keep any of the money or gifts given to the bride by her consanguineal relatives in the foot-washing ceremony instead of sending it with her to her husband's house.

The same pattern of affinal prestations reflecting the three-stage hierarchy between ego and his wife-taking superiors and hs wife-giving inferiors is present in the death rituals. Ego must invite his son-in-law, daughter, and their children (juwai-celi) to all sraddhas held in the house. The ancestors are said to be pleased when they, along with unmarried daughters, are fed at the memorial feast and are given tika marks and a small gift of money (daksina). Some informants explained that the daughter, her husband, and their children represent the ancestors. To feed the daughter and her family of marriage is to feed the ancestors, just as these ancestors are fed through ritually superior Brahman priests who accept cooked food during part of the sraddha ceremony. Among those Brahmans who do not have hereditary priests, the sacredness of the daughter's family of marriage is underlined by the fact that the son-in-law or sister's son is often called to act in the ritually superior role of family priest.

In contrast, the family of ego's mother's brother (*mavali*) his wife's family (*sasurali*), and his son's wife's family, i.e., wife-givers of three generations (indicated by cross-hatching in figure 14), are pointedly *not* called to a sraddha in ego's house. Informants say that members of these groups would be "embarrassed" and probably refuse to eat if they should unknowingly visit ego on a sraddha day. This notion is part of the broader ideological principle whereby it is considered wrong to take anything from ritually superior persons (whether Brahman or wife-taking affine) to whom one gives ritual gifts (dan or daksina). Significantly, the only role the wife's family has in Hindu death rituals is that of making two gifts to ego's family during the mourning period. One is a special mixture of "pure" foods that will be used for some of the funeral feasts (to which, of course, the wife's family do not come) at the conclusion of the thirteen days of death pollution. The second gift, made by the woman's natal home when their daughter has been widowed, is a set of clothes (any color but red) for her to put on when she takes off her white clothes of mourning after the barakhi ceremony, which is held a year after her husband's death.

There are three types of prestation directed toward the daughter's in-laws, distinguished by the terms *koseli, dan,* and *daksina.* While all are gifts given to superiors, the last two specifically imply that superiority of the receiver is in the ritual rather than the political or economic realm. At the same time, however, koseli and dan despite the underlying sacred nature of the latter—are reflective of the donor's honor, pride, social prestige (*izat*), as well as his quest for merit. In fact, Turner's Nepali dictionary glosses koseli as "present or bribe," making its secular nature explicit. In other words, in the course of fulfilling his more spiritual filiafocal obligations to honor his son-in-law and daughter, there is much room for the donor to gain (or lose) worldly prestige through the lavishness of the wedding, dowry, and subsequent gifts.

Daksina, the third type of gift, tends to be more exclusively an index of the ritual or spiritual hierarchy. Though, of course, there is some variation, the size of the daksina gifts tends to be standard and such gifts are much less an arena of display. Like dan, daksina is primarily a religious gift given to a Brahman or relative who is one's ritual superior *in the filiafocal model.*

Unlike dan, however, it is given not only to Brahmans and wife-taking affines but also to ego's own daughters and sisters, both before and after they are married. It is, thus, the most consistent and thorough index of status relations in the filiafocal dimension of Brahman-Chetri kinship.

The Dasai Tika Exchange

With the meaning of daksina in mind, I return to the discussion of the Dasai festival and the ritual of the tika exchange. By understanding individual acts in the ritual code as expressive of either patrifocal or filiafocal hierarchical principles, it is possible to resolve the apparent paradox of tika exchange: that an individual can be simultaneously superior and inferior to another. This "paradox" of the Dasai ceremony is, by extension, relevant to Brahman-Chetri kinship structure as a whole.

In the Dasai tika exchange there are two main ritualized interactions: (1) the giving of tika, which expresses status relations exclusively within the patrifocal model;[16] (2) the accompanying salutations and gifts of money, which may be expressive of status relations within either model.

The first interaction is relatively straightforward and easy to decipher. The person who gives the red tika mark and yellow barley sprouts is superior to the person receiving them (by the patrifocal principles of respect for age and male superiority). Likewise, the patrifocal inferior must travel to the house of the superior to receive tika—although while he (or she) is there he may give tika to his inferiors in that household.

The second interaction is more complex. The inferior greets the superior first with ritual salutations ranging from touching the feet (gora dhokne) of highly respected relatives to a simple folded-hands gesture (namaste).[17] The namaste gesture is simply returned by the superior. The more extreme deference of foot-touching is answered with the blessing gesture (asik) in which the superior touches the inferior's bent head and expresses the wish that the inferior might prosper, make a good marriage, bear a son, or pass an exam (as the case might be) during the coming year.

However, only by noting the nature of the gift of money

which the inferior presents to the superior at the time of ritual salutation is it possible to determine whether the relationship in question is entirely structured by the patrifocal principles or whether filiafocal principles are also operating. Thus if the gift of money is placed on the superior's feet before the salutation, it is called *bheti* and indicates the giver's inferiority within the *patrifocal* model. Bheti directly reinforces the status relations established by the giving of the tika. Bheti is offered only to males or senior affines—situations where status relations are completely determined by the patrifocal ranking principles.

But between other kin the Dasai ritual exchanges also reflect the filiafocal principles of the sacredness of consanguineal women and the superiority of wife-takers. The pattern of such exchanges sometimes reinforces the status hierarchy set by the patrifocal model and sometimes reverses it. In these cases the gift of money which is given at the time of salutation is called *daksina*. Since we are already familiar with daksina, we know that the person who receives it ranks above the donor in the sacred hierarchy. It is, thus, a most appropriate cipher in the tika-exchange "code" for deference within the filiafocal model. For example, when a man gives tika to his daughter, he is demonstrating his superiority over her in the patrilineal dimension. But when he also places the small daksina gift of money in her hands, he is indicating that in the sacred or filiafocal dimension she is superior to him.

The Dasai tika exchanges are set out in considerable detail in chart 4.1. In column 2 the main ritualized actions of the Dasai tika exchange are listed. Each of these actions is a coded expression of either patrifocal or filiafocal status relations between ego and the relative listed in column 1. By using the following rules, these status relations can be restated simply in terms of whether ego is higher or lower than a given individual in the patrifocal model:

(1) Ego gives tika = (+).
(2) Ego receives tika = (−).
(3) Ego receives bheti = (+).
(4) Ego gives bheti = (−).

Whenever bheti is exchanged we know immediately that there is no filiafocal influence on the status relation. Furthermore, since the person who gives tika is always the recipient of bheti the two interactions reinforce each other. Thus, whenever

Chart 4.1 Dasai Tika Exchange

Key:
A = asik, blessing gesture
B = bheti, gift of money placed on feet of a patrifocal superior
D = daksina, small gift of money to filiafocal superior
GD = gora dhok, touching forehead to feet; highest respect
MGD = modified gora dhok; hands inserted between forehead and feet
N = namaste, folded-hands gesture
T = tika, forehead mark

RELATIVE Key: △ = Ego as male, ○ = Ego as female

	RELATIVE	NEPALI TERM (1)	DASAI EXCHANGES (2)	EGO'S PATRIFOCAL STATUS (3)	EGO'S FILIOFOCAL STATUS (4)
1	△ F	ba	Ego gives B and GD (Ego should be thinking of his gotra name as he dhoks his father) Ego receives T and A.	− / −	
2	○ F	ba	Ego receives T and D. Ego gives MGD and receives GD.	−	+
3	△ FF	hazur ba	Ego gives B and GD. Ego receives T and A.	− / −	
4	○ FF	hazur ba	Ego receives T and D. Ego gives MGD and receives GD.	−	+
5	△ FFF	jiju ba	Ego gives B and GD. Ego receives T and A.	− / −	
6	○ FFF	jiju ba	Ego receives T and D. Ego gives MGD and receives GD.	−	+
7	△ MF	mama bajeh also matamaha	Ego receives T and GD, D. Ego gives MGD and receives GD.	−	+
8	○ MF	mama bajeh	Ego receives T, GD, and D. Ego gives N.	−	+
9	△ MFF	jiju bajeh	Ego receives T, GD, and D. Ego gives N (must go to MFFS house).	−	+
10	○ MFF	jiju bajeh	Ego receives T, GD, and D. Ego gives N.	−	+
11	△ FB	thulo ba, jetha ba, kaka	Ego gives B and GD. Ego receives T and A.	− / −	
12	○ FB	thulo ba, jetha ba, kaka	Ego receives T and D. Ego gives MGD and receives GD.	−	+

Chart 4.1 Dasai Tika Exchange (Continued)

No.	Symbol	Term	Description		
13	△ MB	mama	Ego receives T, D, and GD. Ego returns N (must go to MB's house).		-	+
14	○ MB	mama	Ego receives T, D, and GD. Ego returns N (must go to MB's house).		-	+
15	△ M	ama	Ego gives B and GD. Ego receives T and A.	- / -	
16	○ M	ama	Ego receives T, D, and GD.	-	+
17	△ MM	hajur ama	Ego receives T and D, gives N.	-	+
18	○ MM	hajur ama	Ego receives T, D, and GD.	-	+
19	△ MFM	jiju ama	Ego receives T and D, gives N.	-	+
20	○ MFM	jiju ama	Ego receives T, D, and GD.	-	+
21	△ FM	hajur ama	Ego gives B and GD, receives T and A (ego goes to FM's house).	- / -	
22	○ FM	hajur ama	Ego receives T, D and GD, gives N (goes to FM's house).	-	+
23	△ FFM	jiju ama	Ego gives B and GD, receives T and A.	- / -	
24	○ FFM	jiju ama	Ego receives T, D, GD, and A.	-	+
25	△ FZ	phupu	Ego receives T, gives GD and D (goes to FZ's house).	- / -	
26	○ FZ	phupu	Ego receives T, D, and GD, returns N (goes to FZ's house).	-	+
27	△ MZ	thuli ama, sani ama	Ego gives B and GD, receives T and A (goes to MZ's house).	- / -	
28	○ MZ	thuli ama, sani ama	Ego receives GD, T, and D (goes to MZ's house).	-	+
29	△ B(elder)	dai	Ego gives B and GD, receives T and A (goes to B's house).	- / -	
30	△ B(younger)	bhai	Ego receives B and GD, gives T and A.	+ / +	
31	○ B(elder)	dai	Ego receives T, D, and GD, returns N.	-	+
32	○ B(younger)	bhai	Ego receives T, D, and GD, returns N.	-	+
33	△ FBS(elder)	dai	Ego gives B and GD, receives T and A (goes to FBS/'s house)	- / -	
34	△ FBS(younger)	bhai	Ego receives B and GD, gives T and A.	+ / +	
35	○ FBS(elder)	dai	Ego receives T, D, and GD, returns N.	-	+
36	○ FBS(younger)	bhai	Ego receives T, D, and GD, returns N.	-	+
37	△ FZS(elder)	bhanij dai	Ego gives T, D, and GD (FZS comes to ego's house), ego receives N.	+	-
38	△ FZS(younger)	bhanij bhai	FZS comes to ego's house, ego gives T, D, and GD.	+	-

Chart 4.1 Dasai Tika Exchange (Continued)

39	○ FZS(elder)	dai	Ego receives T, D, and GD, returns N.	-	+
40	○ FZS(younger)	bhai	Ego gives T, receives D and GD.	+	+
41	△ MBS(elder)	dai	Ego receives T, D, and GD, returns N.	-	+
42	△ MBS(younger)	bhai	Ego receives T, D, and GD, gives N (Ego is potential priest for MBS and therefore receives T from him as jajaman).	-	+
43	○ MBS(elder)	dai	Ego receives T, D, and GD, returns N (Ego goes to MBS's house which is her mamali.	-	+
44	○ MBS(younger)	bhai	Ego receives T, D, and GD, returns N (Ego goes to MBS's house which is her mamali).	-	+
45	△ MZS(elder)	dai	Ego receives T, gives B and GD (Ego goes to MZS's house).	-	
46	△ MZS(younger)	bhai	Ego receives B and GD, gives T and A.	+	+
47	○ MZS(elder)	dai	Ego receives T, D, and GD, returns N (Ego goes to MZS's house).	-	+
48	○ MZS(younger)	bhai	Ego gives T, receives D and GD (MZS comes to ego's house).	+	+
49	△ Z (elder)	didi	Ego gives T, D and GD, receives N.	+	-
50	△ Z(younger)	bahini	Ego gives T, D and GD, receives N (Z goes to Ego's house).	+	-
51	○ Z (elder)	didi	Ego receives T, D and GD, gives N.	-	+
52	○ Z (younger)	bahini	Ego receives T, D and GD, receives N.	+	-
53	△ FBD(elder)	didi	Ego gives T, D and GD, receives N (meet at FB's or FBD comes to ego).	+	-
54	△ FBD(younger)	bahini	Ego gives T, D and GD, receives N (meet at FB's or FBD comes to ego).	+	-
55	○ FBD (elder)	didi	Ego receives T, D, and GD, returns N.	-	+
56	○ FBD(younger)	bahini	Ego gives T, D, and GD, receives N.	+	-
57	△ FZD (elder)	bhanji didi	Ego gives T, D, and GD, receives N and A.	+	-
58	△ FZD(younger)	bhanji bahini	Ego gives T, D, and GD, receives N and A.	+	-
59	○ FZD (elder)	bhanji didi	Ego receives T, D and GD, gives N (FZD comes to ego).	-	+
60	○ FZD(younger)	bhanji bahini	Ego gives T, D and GD (FZD comes to ego).	+	-
61	△ MBD (elder)	didi	Ego gives T, D, and N, receives N.	+	-
62	△ MBD(younger)	bahini	Ego gives T, D, and N, receives N.	+	-
63	○ MBD (elder)	didi	Ego receives T, D, and GD, gives N.	-	+

Chart 4.1 Dasai Tika Exchange (Continued)

No.	Relation	Term	Description		
64	○ MBD(younger)	bahini	Ego receives T, D, and GD.	–	+
65	△ MZD (elder)	didi	Ego gives T, D, and GD, receives N.	+	–
66	△ MZD(younger)	bahini	Ego gives T, D, and GD, receives N.	+	–
67	○ MZD (elder)	didi	Ego receives T, D, and GD, gives N.	–	+
68	○ MZD(younger)	bahini	Ego gives T, D, and GD.	+	–
69	△ S	choro	Ego receives B and GD, gives T and A.	+	+
70	○ S	choro	Ego receives B and GD, gives T and A.	+	+
71	△ BS	choro	Ego receives B and GD, gives T and A.	+	+
72	○ BS	bhada	Ego gives T, receives D and GD.	+	+
73	△ ZS	bhanij, jholi ko devta	Ego gives T, D, and GD, receives N.	+	–
74	○ ZS	choro (jholi ko devta if he is younger sister's son, but not if he is elder sister's)	Ego gives T and A, receives B and GD.	+	+
75	△ SS	nati	Ego gives T and A, receives GD and B.	+	+
76	○ SS	nati	Ego gives T and A, receives GD and B.	+	+
77	△ SSS	panati	Ego gives T and A, receives GD and B.	+	+
78	○ SSS	panati	Ego gives T and A, receives GD and B.	+	+
79	△ DS	nati, jholi ko devta	Ego gives T, D, GD and A, receives N (DS comes to ego).	+	–
80	○ DS	nati, jholi ko devta	Ego gives T, D, GD, and A, receives N (DS comes to ego).	+	–
81	△ DSS	panati	Ego gives T, D, GD, and A, receives N.	+	–
82	○ DSS	panati	Ego gives T, D, GD, and A, receives N.	+	–
83	△ DDS	panati	Ego gives T, D, GD, and A, receives N.	+	–
84	○ DDS	panati	Ego gives T, D, and A, receives N.	+	–
85	△ D	chori	Ego gives T, D, GD, and A, receives N or MGD.	+	–
86	○ D	chori	Ego gives T, D, GD, and A, receives N or MGD	+	–

Chart 4.1 Dasai Tika Exchange (*Continued*)

87	△ BD	bhatiji	Ego gives T, D, GD, and A, receives N or MGD.	+	–
88	○ BD	bhadai	Ego gives T, D, and A (BD comes to ego's house).	+	–
89	△ ZD	bhanji	Ego gives T, D, and GD (ZD comes to ego).	+	–
90	ZD	chori	Ego gives T, D, and GD (ZD comes to ego).	+	–
91	△ DD	natini, jholi ki devta	Ego gives T, D, and GD (BD comes to ego).	+	–
92	○ DD	natini, jholi ki devta	Ego gives T, D, and GD (DD comes to ego).	+	–
93	△ DDD	panatini	Ego gives T, D, and GD.	+	–
94	○ DDD	panatini	Ego gives T, D, and GD.	+	–
95	△ SD	natini	Ego gives T, D, and GD.	+	–
96	○ SD	natini	Ego gives T, D, GD, and A, receives N (SD must come to ego)	+	–
97	△ SSD	panatini	Ego gives T, D, GD, and A, receives N.	+	–
98	○ SSD	panatini	Ego gives T, D, GD, and A, receives N.	+	–
99	△ FZH	phupaju	Ego gives B and GD, receives T and A.	–	–
100	○ FZH	phupaju	Ego receives T, D, and GD, returns N.	–	+
101	△ WB(elder)	jethan	Ego receives T and D, GD among Brahman, N among Chetri, returns N (ego goes to sasurali).	–	+
102	△ WB(younger)	salo	Ego receives B and GD, gives T.	+	+
103	△ ZH(elder)	bhenaju	Ego gives B and GD, receives T.	–	–
104	△ ZH(younger)	juwai	Ego gives T, D, and N, receives N.	+	–
105	○ ZH(elder)	bhenaju	Ego receives T, gives MGD (may receive D if ego is not being considered as potential wife; ego goes to ZH).	–	?+?
106	○ ZH(younger)	juwai	Ego gives T, D, and N.	+	–
107	HZH(elder)	dai	Ego gives T, D, and N.	+	–
108	○ HZH(younger)	nande bhai	Ego gives T, D, and N.	+	–
109	△ WZH (elder)	sadu dai	Ego gives B and GD if Brahman, N if Chetri, receives T (usually don't meet at dasai).	–	–
110	△ WZH(younger)	sadu bhai	Ego receives B and GD if Brahman, N if Chetri, gives T.	+	+

Chart 4.1 Dasai Tika Exchange (*Continued*)

No.	Symbol	Term	Description			
111	△ SWF	samdhi	Never exchange T, do not meet on dasai.			+
112	△	samdhi	Never exchange T, do not meet on dasai.			-
113	△ SWM	samdhini	Never exchange T, do not meet on dasai.			+
114	○ SWM	samdhini	Never exchange T, do not meet on dasai.			+
115	△ DHM	samdhini	Never exchange T, do not meet on dasai.			-
116	○ DHM	samdhini	Never exchange T, do not meet on dasai.			-
117	○ SWF	samdhi	Never exchange T, do not meet on dasai.			+
118	○ DHF	samdhi	Never exchange T, do not meet on dasai.			-
119	△ W	swasni, joi, srimati	Ego receives B and GD, gives T and A.	+	+	
120	○ HS(elder)	amaju	Ego receives T, and gives D and GD.	-		
121	○ HZ(younger)	nanda	Ego gives T, D, and GD.	+		-
122	△ WZ(elder)	jethi sasu	Ego receives T, D, and N.	-		+
123	△ WZ(younger)	sali	Ego gives T and N (ego may give D if WZ is so young as not to be potential marriage partner).	+		-?
124	△ BW(elder)	jethi bhauju	Ego gives B and GD, receives T and A (usually ego does not give GD because he is embarrassed, so he gives N).	-	-	
125	△ BW(younger)	buhari	Ego receives B and MGD, ego throws rice grains and barley shoots to give T without touching.	+	+	
126	○ BW(elder)	bhauju	Ego receives T, D, and GD, returns N.	-		+
127	○ BW(younger)	buhari	Ego gives T, receives D and GD.	+		+
128	○ HB(elder)	jethajyu	Ego gives B and MGD; ego is sprinkled with rice grains and barley shoots but may not be touched by jethajyu.	-		
129	○ HB(younger)	devar	Ego receives B and GD and gives T and A.	+		
130	○ HBW(elder)	didi, jethani didi, thulo didi	Ego receives B and GD, gives T and A.	+	+	
131	○ HBW(younger)	deurani, bahini	Ego gives T, receives N returns N.			
132	○ WBW(elder)	jethani didi	Ego receives T, D, and N.	-		+
133	△ WBW(younger)	bahini	Ego receives B or gift of spices (masala) and N, gives T (WBW comes to ego's house; if B is given ego must return money).	+	+	
134	△ DH	juwai	Ego gives T, D, and GD (if Brahman) or N (if Chetri) receives N (DH comes to ego's house which is his sasurali).		+	-
135	○ DH	juwai	Ego gives T, D, and GD (if Brahman) or N (if Chetri) receives N (DH comes to ego's house which is his sasurali).		+	-
136	△ SW	buhari	Ego receives B and GD, gives T and A.	+	+	

Chart 4.1 Dasai Tika Exchange (Continued)

137	○ SW	buhari	Ego receives B and GD, gives T and A.	+ / +	
138	○ HBS	choro, bhatija	Ego receives B and GD, gives T and A.	+ / +	
139	△ WBS	bhada	Ego receives B and GD, gives T and A.	+ / +	
140	○ HZS	bhanij	Ego gives T, D, and N.	+	-
141	△ WZS	choro	Ego receives B and GD, gives T and A.	+ / +	
142	○ HBD	chori	Ego gives T, D, and GD, receives N.	+	-
143	○ HZD	bhanji	Ego gives T, D, and GD, receives N.	+	-
144	△ WBD	bhadai	Ego gives T, D and N.	+	
145	△ FW(not ego's mother)	thuli/sani ama, sauteni ama	Ego gives B and GD, receives T and A.	- / -	
146	△ MH (not ego's father)	thulo/ sano ba	No exchange		
147	○ Co-wife	sauta	Elder gives T to younger (younger should give B and GD, but most do not; give N instead).	+ ?	
148	△ step child	jharkelo chori/ choro	Ego gives T.	+ ?	
149	△ ritual friend	mit	Ego gives and receives T simultaneously, each give N simultaneously.	NA	NA
150	○ ritual friend	mitini	Ego gives and receives T simultaneously, each give N simultaneously	NA	NA
151	△ ritual friend's wife	mitini	Ego throws T on mitini, N simultaneously (must not touch each other).	NA	NA
152	○ ritual friend's husband	mit	Ego receives thrown T as if mit were jethaju (must not touch each other).	NA	NA

bheti appears on the table, there is a double notation (e.g., +/+) in column 3, which indicates ego's patrifocal status with regard to the relative in question; and column 4, which indicates the filiafocal status rleations, is in these cases always blank. For example, let us take the very first instance which appears on the chart, the case of a man meeting his own father on tika day. We see from column 2 that the man will receive tika from his father. This means that he is, as would be expected, lower than his father in the patrifocal system, and therefore rates a minus sign in column 3. Since he must also give his father bheti (and touch his father's feet) there is another indication of his inferior patrifocal status vis-à-vis his father, and so another minus sign appears in column 3. However, because relations between father and son are not at all affected by filiafocal principles, the fourth column appropriately contains no notation at all in this case.

When daksina rather than bheti is given we know that filiafocal principles are influencing the status relation between ego and the relative listed in column 1. The rules here are very simple:

(5) Ego gives daksina = (−)
(6) Ego receives daksina = (+)

The applications of these last two rules are given in column 4 of the table. Often, as is the case with daughters and sisters and their respective offspring and spouses, the filiafocal status relation encoded in column 4 is reverse of the patrifocal relation encoded in column 3.

For example, a man (and his wife and their children) travels to his wife's parent's home (sasurali) and to his mother's brother's home (mavali) to receive tika from his wife's father and his mother's brother, respectively, because these two rank above him by patrifocal reckoning of superior age. This means a minus in column 3. However, as wife-givers, members of his wife's parents' and mother's brother's households rank beneath him in the filiafocal dimension. Therefore, these two relatives must give him daksina, and ego rates a plus in column 4 (see nos. 13, 102, and 110 in the chart).

The same contrast between status in the patrilocal and filiafocal dimension is even more evident in the case of a woman who is visiting her own natal home (maiti) or her mother's brother's home (mamali). Thus in her maiti she will receive tika from her father, mother, and brothers and from her mother's brother and his wife in her mamali, since all these relations rank above her in the patrifocal model. Yet in addition to the daksina gift they must also all show her the most extreme form of deference by touching her feet in the gora dhokne salutation, while she responds with only the less extreme modified gora dhokne (for her father and mother) or the ordinary namaste gesture with folded hands (for her brothers and mother's brothers). Thus in relationships where the filiafocal dimension comes into play we find that the salutations exchanged often reinforce the daksina gift and express a status relationship that is just the opposite of the patrifocal tika exchange.

However, between certain relations, as, for example, male ego and his father's sister (FZ), the filiafocal status relationship reinforces the patrifocal relationship. As a senior agnatic female, ego's paternal aunt must be respected in the patrifocal

dimension. In addition, ego owes this woman filiafocal deference inherited from his father "because the son must respect
whomever his father respects," and ego's father owes filiafocal
deference to his sister. Ego receives tika and gives daksina. This
gives him a minus in columns 3 and 4 (see no. 25).

There is no need to go into each of the many relationships represented in the chart. The principles behind the Dasai
tika exchange are consistent, and they accurately reflect the
symbiosis of the two dimensions of value in Brahman-Chetri
culture. Of course, this symbiosis between patrifocal and filiafocal principles is not without its points of stress and ambiguity,
which sometimes affect the tika ritual itself.

One such example which deserves mention here is the
relation between parents-in-law (nos. 124–31 on the chart). This
is in many ways a particularly strained relationship, and there is
a heavy emphasis on both sides on maintaining family pride.
Parents of the girl (who as wife-givers must be deferential to all
members of the son-in-law's family) often believe that their
daughter is being overworked and ill-treated in her marital home,
and for this they tend to blame the husband's parents rather than
the husband himself. The husband's parents, on the other hand,
often feel that the bride's people have not been sufficiently generous with dowry and koseli gifts; more important, they are suspicious of the bride's continuing attachment to her maita. Though
all affinal relations are marked by distance-respect behavior, in
the relations between parents-in-law, distance prevails. We have
already noted the reluctance of the bride's father to visit his
daughter in her husband's home. The most striking expression
of avoidance, however, occurs in the context of the Dasai tika
ritual. As the table indicates, parents-in-law do not exchange
tika at Dasai (nor do they at any other time). This suggests—at
least in the context of the tika ritual—that through avoidance
parents-in-law suspend the problem of their uneasy patrifocal
status relation. The principles of respect for age and male superiority have no real bearing on how these in-laws interact. That
interaction is entirely determined by the filiafocal principle of
the superiority of wife-takers over wife-givers. This principle is
apparent in the ceremonial presentation of gifts to the daughter's new father-in-law and mother-in-law after the wedding and
on any other occasion when parents-in-law should happen to
meet. In all such contexts, the bride's parents show deference
to the groom's. It is also extremely significant that, unless this

formal ritual (*samdhi bhet*) is performed, the mothers of the married couple can never meet each other. In many cases the ceremony is never performed at all, and thus avoidance behavior is maintained at its maximum expression.

Two significant areas of informant uncertainty became evident while I was making this chart. Although these areas are not marked on the table itself, they reflect the villagers' ambiguity as to whether patrifocal or filiafocal status relations should be acknowledged in a given situation.

The first concerns greetings. I received confusing comments on this issue until I learned to distinguish between formal ritual greetings, such as are exchanged at Dasai and other ceremonial occasions "inside the house," and secular greetings exchanged in public "on the path." Villagers seem to feel that patrifocal deference (especially in its less extreme forms) is more compatible with these secular situations. Informants reported being ashamed or embarrassed (*laj lagyo*) to show filiafocal deference or even extreme patrifocal deference *in public* to anyone but their most important patrifocal superiors (i.e., parents, grandparents, husband, or husband's mother). Instead, for everyday secular greetings, all but the most ostentatiously "religious" citizens of Narikot replace the filiafocal deference shown in formal greetings with patrifocal deference. For instance, in secular contexts, a daughter is the first to offer namaste to her father, mother, etc. as a sign of respect for her (patrifocal) superiors, even though these same relatives must touch her feet in formal ritual situations. In cases where extreme patrifocal deference is required (as to male ego's elder brother, elder brother's wife, etc.), informants said they usually dispense with any informal public salutations, since "it is disrespectful and proud to give just a namaste greeting to someone whose feet you are supposed to touch."

In short, the divergences between the ritual greetings that appear on the chart and the everyday greetings point to areas of ambiguity or stress in the kinship system where the idealized status relation does not accurately reflect the "political" reality. Daughters are actually under the control of their patrifocal superiors. As one informant put it: "In daily household matters the daughter has to respect and obey the father: in religious matters the father has to obey and respect the daughter" (*Kunai ghar ko bebaharma chori le bau lai mannu paryo: dharma ko kura ma bau le chori lai mannu paryo*). Likewise, younger brothers frequently chafe at actually respecting and obeying an elder brother "as if he were their father," which is the ideal expressed in the ritual greeting.

Another important aspect of the tika ritual not evident on the chart but about which informants displayed uncertainty was the order of precedence for giving tika. The order of precedence between families is very clear and displays a marked patrifocal bias. On the tenth day of Dasai one receives and gives tika first in one's own family and then in nearby patrilineally related households. After that, usually during the next day or two, men and their wives and children journey, as we mentioned earlier, to their wife-giving affinal relatives. For married women this means a return to the natal home to receive tika, daksina, and special Dasai foods from their parents, brothers, etc. Informants are emphatic, however, that a woman may not receive tika from anyone else until she has touched her husband's feet and received tika from him—or if he is absent, from some senior member of her husband's household. To purposely avoid receiving tika from her husband (e.g., by staying in her parents' house during Navaratri) is tantamount to asking for a divorce.[18]

But informants are less consistent about the order of precedence *within* their own immediate family on the morning of the tenth day. Always the first tika mark is received by the male head of the household "as prasad from the Devi" when he has finished the final worship on the tenth morning. He places a dab of the mixture of uncooked rice grains, yogurt, and red powder on his own forehead and places the barley sprouts on his head. Then he calls the rest of the family to receive their tika from him in order of their rank. But here confusion arises. Some informants gave patrifocal rank (i.e., household head's younger brother, ego's wife, brother's wife, sons in order of age, son's wife, unmarried daughter, etc.). Others insisted, on occasion, that unmarried daughters and granddaughters are given tika and daksina first, strictly according to filiafocal ranking (i.e., youngest first). One informant whom I questioned about this inconsistency said that in the past tika used to go to brothers, etc., first, and that probably in the remote hills things are still done this way. But he strongly expressed the view that to honor his unmarried daughters was an act of higher dharma.

Notes

1. Navatantu, lit. nine threads—though the sacred thread of a high-caste jharra male contains only six strands.

2. This relation is evident in the Nepali word for patrimony, *pitradhan*, or literally "wealth of the ancestors."

3. He may perform the death rites for his own mother, since she is also of lower caste standing than the father.

3. Bista (1972) does mention a text which the lineage headman (Thakali) reads during the sacrifice, but he doesn't give its name or any other information. All but three of the twenty-seven kul groups I investigated in Narikot reported that they read the *Candi Path* during their devali ceremonies. The same text—a hymn praising the bloody exploits of the goddess Candi (a form of Durga) and beseeching her protection—is also used at Dasai during the worship of Durga (see chapter 8.)

5. Also, Linda Stone reports that in the Nuwakot district some Brahman kul celebrate devali only when one of their male members gets married.

6. Bista reports (1972:117), and my own observations also indicate, that some kul—especially small ones—perform devali in the ancestral home or *kul ghar*.

7. In some lineages each household worships Gairu, the guardian diety of cattle, separately in their own cowshed on returning from the communal worship at devali, and women may observe this rite.

8. Normally for Brahman-Chetri households in Narikot a menstruating woman could sleep inside the house so long as she was not in the same room as her husband. The Brahmans and Chetris of Jumla and other more remote areas of Nepal, however, never allow a menstruating woman in the house.

9. A short section of the *Candi Path* called the *Durga Kabac*, which beseeches the goddess's protection, is often read.

10. Khatri-Chetris, who are descended from Brahmans, follow the Brahman custom.

11. Some families may also offer a male goat at the temple, in which case the head is brought home and placed on the Dasai ghar and the body is consumed by the family. Wealthy families may offer a goat every morning of Navaratri, as is done in homes of the Rana aristocracy. Most goat meat that is consumed on nonritual occasions comes from gelded male animals called *khasi*, but for Dasai and other occasions requiring sacrifice only uncastrated males, or *bokos*, may be offered.

12. Linda Stone (personal communication) reports the number 66 in this context among the Chetris of Nuwakot.

13. For discussion, see Dumont 1961; Dumont 1970:chap. 5; Doherty 1974; and Bennett 1978.

14. Tambiah (1973:70, 85) makes the important point that these gifts which accompany the bride and continue to follow her to the husband's house represent *stridhanam* (Sk. woman's wealth)—the classical Brahmanical concept of the *moveable* property which a patrilineal group gave to their consanguineal women as dowry, since they were not normally eligible to share in the joint estate of their birth.

15. Notably fried rice-flour doughnuts (*sel roti*), clarified butter, flattened rice, vegetable preparations, pickles, fresh fruits and vegetables, and possibly even a load of corn or paddy or a cow.

16. With the notable exception of mother's brother's son younger than ego, who gives tika to ego.

17. Between the full gora dhok and namaste there are several intermediate gestures. For example, women may not give gora dhok to any man but their own husband, and so they do a modified dhok gesture in which the thumbs are placed on the forehead and the woman's fists touch the ground in front of the honored person. In a less extreme form of deference (still higher than the namaste) a woman may bend her head and touch

it to the raised end of her sari which is worn over her chest. Among men a gesture of intermediate deference is the *hath* (hand) *dhok* in which the inferior bends over as if to touch the honored person's foot, but is stopped by the other's hand extended to his forehead in the *asik* or blessing gesture. Brahmans must show the extreme deference of gora dhok to many relatives—most notably the son-in-law—to whom Chetris need only give namaste.

18. Incidentally, the same might be said for any of the central kinship relations. Unless there are reasons of distance or ill-health, the failure to exchange tika with any of the above-mentioned patrilineal or affinal groups signals a severe break in the relationship.

CHAPTER 5

Status and Strategies: Patrifocal and Filiafocal Dimensions in a Woman's Life

Turning now from the formal expressions of the complementary patrifocal and filiafocal models documented in the
Dasai rituals, let us look at how these two dimensions of status
affect the lives and relationships of actual women. It will be
recalled that the group in which a male will find his main social
and emotional identity is the patriline into which he was born.
Since marriage is patrilocal, his principal roles as son, husband,
and father are enacted within the same family. In fact, the major
rituals we have reviewed all indicate an ideal of society organized around discrete groups of agnatically related males. But,
as the last chapter showed, women's position with respect to the
patrilineal institution is extremely ambiguous. Women are never
full ritual members of these patrilineal groups; rather they *are
the links between them*. Although a daugher is a "member" of
her natal lineage to the extent that this linkage is important in
determining whom she can marry,[1] she can never become a full
member. Emotionally, of course, there is a strong attachment to
her family of birth and childhood—the maiti. After marriage,
however, a daughter must leave her natal home and go to live
with her husband. Only then, in her ghar or husband's family
(lit. house) does a woman achieve her full religious and social
identity. Only after marriage, when she has assumed her husband's thar and gotra, does she achieve the same full adult, karma
caleko status that boys achieve at their initiation. As mentioned
earlier, a woman is identified with her husband's patriline for

the performance of her funeral rites and for the annual memorial ceremonies—though she may be included in the collective
memorials (*sora sraddha*) of her maita. The death of a daughter,
whether she is married or unmarried, requires only a five-day
period of mourning by her consanguineal group.[2] Her husband's
family, on the other hand, must observe the full thirteen days of
death pollution for her.

The transient nature of a girl's stay in her maita is evident
by the saying, "Daughters go to another's house and repair the
walls of that house" (*Chori arkako ghar jancha: arkako bhitta
talcha*). "House" or *ghar* here is a clear metaphor for the daughter's affinal patrilineal group, to which she must go after marriage and to which she will contribute her labor and her fertility.

The Unmarried Girl

Though most women retain a strong emotional loyalty to their
maita, the impermanence of their tie with the natal home in-
duces contradictory feelings. Some women expressed guilt that
they could not stay and care for their parents the way their
brothers could. "When you are born with the karma of a daughter," explained one informant, "then you appear to be cruel.
No matter how much you love your mother and father you are
unable to look after them and take care of them when they
need help. A daughter has to look after another's home."

Other women feel a certain resentment at being sent
away—though usually it is expressed more as a general bitterness about the status (or as the informant above put it, the karma)
of women rather than anger at the maiti for enforcing it. As one
informant said: "They kept my brothers even when they were
well grown up, but me—as soon as I was fourteen they began
to say that I was grown up and that it wouldn't do for me to
grow older at home. So they married me off." Although they
were reluctant to express it, some women confided that they
felt resentment specifically against their fathers for giving them
away hastily to an unsatisfactory household that had not been
thoroughly checked out, or for giving them a meager dowry
which brought forth criticism from their in-laws.

All the women I interviewed seemed to have perceived

the superior position of boys from an early age. Some recalled that milk and yogurt were given only to sons, and that boys did less work. All the older women said that only boys had been allowed to go to school when they were young. Several women used the phrase "treated me like a boy" to describe the particularly indulgent and affectionate behavior which certain of their favorite relatives showed toward them. One woman remembered her early jealousy toward her own little brother:

> I was two years old when my little brother was born. When he was being given a bath, then they say I saw his *tuturi* [penis] and I wept saying, "Brother has a tuturi, why don't I have one too! Please make one for me!" I told father that he should make me into a son! I used to weep and tell father I didn't want to be a daughter. Father put a cap, coat, and tunic and pants (*mayalpos suruwal*) on me and made me into a son. I used to say that I didn't have a tuturi like my brother's and he would make one out of mud and put it on me. When I said that wasn't what I wanted he used to say he would make it for me the next day.

When I asked this informant why she wanted to be a boy she emphasized two things: one was the restrictions placed on her to protect her reputation, and the other was the hardship of being sent away at marriage to work in the house of demanding strangers.

The impending trauma of marriage is constantly referred to during a girl's childhood. One frequently hears a young daughter of four or five being laughingly teased—or sometimes angrily scolded—with the threat that her parents will hurry and marry her off to get rid of her. I once observed a girl of four in near hysterics after her mother and older brother had teased her about marrying her off to the son of a Newari potmaker who had come to the courtyard to sell his wares. The adults—including the low caste potmaker, who was a stranger to the village—found the situation amusing, but the little girl was plainly terrified. Even after she stopped screaming she spent the rest of the afternoon clinging to her mother's sari.

Girls see the whole family—men and women—sobbing in a rare public display of emotion when their older sisters and female cousins are sent off at marriage. When these married sisters return to their maita they tell of hard work, little sleep, and fault-finding mothers-in-law in their ghars. And too, unmarried girls see plainly that the daughters-in-law in their own joint family do much harder work than they do.

One of the most popular games, which every woman I interviewed remembered playing, is "marriage" (biha). Not only is the ceremony itself enacted with great attention to detail, but other common scenes of married life are portrayed. As in the following passage, girls quarrel over the roles because everyone wants to be the mother-in-law or the husband and no one wants to be the bride:

My older cousin Sano Maya used to pretend to be the mother-in-law. "If I am the mother-in-law, I will play with you. Otherwise I won't," she would say. So she used to be the "mother-in-law" and we used to be the daughters-in-law. Then we would bring corn, and soybeans, and some pickle from our homes. We used to give these to the "mother-in-law" as koseli. We learnt this from seeing our sisters-in-law do it. . . . We had to give koseli to our "mother-in-law," who was Sano Maya. She used to pretend to get up early in the morning and plaster the doorway with cowdung. That is a job that the daughter-in-law must do, and so she would pretend to get angry and say, "I, the mother-in-law, have gotten up and my daughter-in-law is still asleep!" And then she would scold us.

Another woman remembered the same game (and, interestingly, she too stressed the importance of koseli as affinal prestation):

Sometimes I would be the groom and she would sometimes be the bride. . . . There were no boys. Only we girls used to play. We would say that we would have our children married and we would [pretend to] cook special fried breads for the wedding. . . . We would say that today we go to our children's in-law's (samdhi) to bring our daughter back and we would put some koseli on a tray and cover it with a red cloth and take it along. . . . The bride used to weep when it was time for her to leave her parents. "Don't weep. Why do you weep? Tomorrow we shall be coming to see you." We would say this to try to console her.

There is another rather poignant version of the marriage game which, though I did not observe it myself, all my older women informants remembered playing as children. Although it is strikingly similar to the Rala Rali rituals in Kangra in which images of Siva and Parvati are married and then destroyed,[3] the marriage of dolls enacted by Nepali Brahman-Chetri girls seems to be more a spontaneous game than a formal ceremony. As one woman described it:

During Dasai we used to play groom-and-bride (dulha-dulhai) with dolls. We used to make these dolls. Sometimes we used black thread to sew on the hair, and then make it into one plait or sometimes two. . . . We would prepare the sacred wedding enclosure and everything else for the marriage. . . . We would take them all to the houses and have them married off. Then they used to be thrown into the river. Before throwing them into the river we would put good clothes on them and put eyeliner and vermilion powder on them [sindur—placed in the bride's hairline at weddings]. They say that the dolls have to be thrown into the river. When we had thrown them into the river we would return home, weeping all the way and crying out, "My children are dead!" Then we were consoled by the elders and told that we would all have to go that way; then we would keep quiet.

The Marriage Crisis

It is clear that female children grow up with a strong awareness that their stay in the maita is transient and that their existence is peripheral to that of their natal patriline. While sons of the family remain members of the consanguineal group, daughters become identified with the affinal group and its patriline. For it is there, in her husband's house, that a woman will fulfill her most important structural roles in the dominant patrifocal model—as wife and mother.

However, this identification with her ghar after marriage is neither immediate nor total for a young girl. Usually she visits her maita frequently and maintains strong emotional and ritual ties with her consanguineal relatives. As Karve (1953:79) put it, "a woman's soul moves in two worlds," and, as will become apparent, the opposition between maiti and ghar marks a drama that plays throughout a woman's life. It is this tension between her consanguineal and affinal ties, or between her filiafocal and patrifocal roles, that makes a woman's position in the kinship system ambiguous.

To the groom's family the bride is viewed as an "outsider," an affine who is somehow dangerous to the central patrifocal value of agnatic solidarity. Obviously, this suspicion about her is greatest in the first months and years after marriage, before she has children that give her common interests with the patriline. It is at this stage that she may be held responsible for any misfortunes that befall her in-laws, and it is at this time that her behavior will be most critically watched and controlled by them. One of my informants (the same hill girl mentioned earlier who had been married into a very wealthy family) tells of how, but for the timely death of the Rana Prime Minister, she would have been held responsible for the loss of much of her husband's family's wealth:

> In those days there was the rule of the Ranas here. Bhim Shamshere, who was ruling, was saying that he would do away with all the *birta* [the land given as gift by the king]. And so it seemed that our birta too would be taken away from us. When I had been married, my mother-in-law had thought to herself that if this daughter-in-law was one of *lacchin* [auspiciousness, good luck] then they wouldn't lose their land. The servants told me that my mother-in-law had said this and that it was to be seen that my fate and destiny held for me. But I was just a child and didn't worry. I felt that it didn't matter whether they kept me or sent me away—as I had my maita after all! Seven days after I was married a bugle was sounded at the Dharara. In those days if a bugle was blown at that place you knew the ruler had died. When the bugle was sounded then everyone was happy. It was the reign of Mohan Shamshere, and he didn't take away the land. Even to this day we still have it. All my husband's brothers showed affection for me because their birta hadn't been lost. "This daughter-in-law is good. She is one of lacchin," they said. . . . And my mother-in-law knew that her son and her daughter-in-law had been well matched and she was happy.

Most brides are not so lucky, and from my observations, the judgment of the ghar tends to fall much more often on the negative or at least neutral side. There seem to be certain standard accusations made about the daughter-in-law. She will very likely be accused of taking pieces of her wedding jewelry back to her maita and pretending that it is lost. Much of the jewelry women are given at weddings (aside from that which is loaned by neighbors for the occasion) is "borrowed" back later by the husband or other family members. There is a great deal of ambiguity as to whether such jewelry represents the bride's personal property (*stridhanam*) or the joint wealth of her affinal family, and there is great resentment when any of it disappears. A more serious common accusation is that the daughter-in-law has stolen something—such as a brass vessel or some grain—that is clearly family property. One daughter-in-law I interviewed sensed this mistrust and guarded against possible accusations, even though she and her mother-in-law get along quite

A married daughter on a visit to her natal home shares a cigarette and a relaxed moment with her mother. *Photo by Ane Haaland*

well: "I don't know whether she trusts me or not. But I am
afraid of doing anything in another's home. She tells me to fetch
things out of the locked storeroom (*bhandar*) but I tell her that I
can't."

Another complaint which I frequently heard about a bride
is that she is really older than her husband and that the family
lied about her age to get her married, or that her family said she
had some accomplishment—like knitting, reading, etc.—which
she doesn't really possess. All these, and many other variations,
express the common feelings of suspicion and disappointment
with affinal women.

This harsh scrutiny is ritually exemplified by the customary viewing of the bride after she has been brought to her husband's house. All the family and village neighbor women pay a
rupee or two for the privilege of looking at the new bride's
face, which had remained covered during most of the wedding
ceremonies. For that small price they buy license to minutely
examine and criticize the bride, her features, and the gifts sent
with her by her parents. I have heard brides called dark, small-

eyed, buck-toothed, and acnied as they sat meekly with down-cast eyes during this ritual. In one case the dowry the bride brought was deemed meager and of poor quality, so the mother-in-law took back two of the saris which the groom had given to the bride during the wedding and gave them to her own daughters!

One young woman summed up the position of the daughter-in-law very accurately:

> You feel shy and embarrassed with your mother-in-law and hus-band's elder brother. When you are in your own house then you can do what you like. But if you are in another's house and if you happen to talk a little too loudly, then they'll think that you are ill-mannered. They will say that you have no decorum (sobath) and they will scold you. In my parents' house I can run about and scold my little sisters and brothers. But in my husband's house, even if my husband's younger sister does something I can't say anything. In-stead, I worry that if I scold her they will say, "What sort of woman is this? She answers back to her husband's younger brothers and sisters! Her parents seem to have had no control over her!" . . . You mustn't say a single word to them! You have to do whatever they tell you to do. If they tell you to pour water from this side, then you so do. It is not the same as your parent's home. It is diffi-cult in another's house.

The Husband/Wife Relationship

To her husband's family the bride is at once a dangerous in-truder and a vitally needed source of progeny and labor. The tension caused by her presence is evident both in her pre-scribed role relations with her affines and in the severe gap which tends to open between her ideal role and her actual strat-egies, especially in her relationship with her husband.

Toward her husband (logne, sriman) the wife's public role is one of respect-avoidance. Young wives rarely address their husbands in the presence of others and then only indirectly through a third party. One woman, remembering her early years as a daughter-in-law, said, "I could only speak to my husband in our room. If I were to talk with him outside then it would be laj [shame, embarrassment]. He didn't talk with me nor I with him."

There is a studied mutual ignoring between husband and wife when a young husband returns on leave from his job in town. Beyond the formal greeting in which a woman touches the feet of her husband, not a glance or word is exchanged between the two. The wife goes about her chores—perhaps even going out to cut grass on the hillside to show her unconcern—while the husband sits down with his father and mother to tell them the news from town.

This minimizing of the husband/wife relation in the joint family has as its corollary the playing down of the dependent son's fatherhood. Usually a dependent son's child (until it is six or seven) is taught to call its father *dai*, elder brother, and its grandfather *ba*, father, as long as its grandfather is the head of the household. My observations also indicate that the child tends to be played with and fondled more by the grandfather than by the father as long as the father is dependent.

The emotional bonds which would form the basis for a move to split the joint family into nuclear units are kept publicly at a low level in the interests of agnatic solidarity. T. N. Madan (1965:134), noting a similar lack of public interaction between husband and wife among the Kashmiri Brahmans, draws the same conclusions: "The growth of an exclusive loyalty between any two members of a household is disruptive to the ideal of joint family living. Since a daughter-in-law is a relative stranger, the development of such a loyalty between her and her husband is looked upon with particular disfavour."

Similar to the young bride's public behavior before her husband is her behavior toward her father-in-law, her husband's elder brother, and, in fact, any elder males of the patriline.[4] There is no purdah in Nepal such as that described by Jacobson (1970) for middle India. Nevertheless, the idiom of purdah is used to express a woman's respect-avoidance relationship with senior affinae males. A daughter-in-law usually pulls the end of her sari up to cover her head in front of her father-in-law, and she is expected to always do this in the presence of her husband's elder brother. This latter relationship seems to be the most restricted. A woman and her husband's elder brother may never touch each other—even to exchange tika at Dasai (see no. 128 in chart 4.1). Instead of placing the tika mark on his sister-inlaw's forehead, the elder brother-in-law sprinkles it over her without any contact.

Jacobson, in discussing the respect-avoidance relation between daughter-in-law and the elder males of her conjugal household, stresses its functions as a distancing technique in "situations of ambivalence, ambiguity and imminence of role conflict"—situations, in short, like the presence of a new affinal woman (1970:485). I have already noted that respect-avoidance between husband and wife functions to minimize conflict between the roles of son and husband for a young married man. It also serves to eliminate suspicion of sexual relations between the daughter-in-law and her father-in-law or elder brother-in-law by replacing ambiguity with strictly prescribed mutual behavior patterns.

Respect-avoidance also protects the bride, who is apt to be overwhelmed and uncomfortable in the presence of so many critical strangers. Although in Nepal there is no actual veil to hide behind, I have observed daughters-in-law whose blank faces, downcast eyes, and silence made them seem almost invisible. In sum, respect-avoidance behavior serves almost like a mutually protective membrane separating the new female affine who has been taken into the agnatic corporate body. "It is a symbolic statement that she was—and to some extent still is—a member of another kin group" (Jacobson 1970:20).

An equally important part of the husband/wife relationship—ideally in both public and private aspects—is the extreme respect which a wife must show her husband. The most forceful expression of the wife's deference is in the ritual in which the woman washes her husband's feet and drinks that water by splashing some of it into her mouth (gora pani khane). Village women, except when they are ritually impure through menstruation or childbirth, do this before every rice meal. They also eat off the unwashed plate from which their husband has eaten and consume whatever food he has left for them. Both the plate and the leftover food are considered jutho or polluted; likewise the water from washing the feet, an impure part of the body, is considered defiled. The wife's consumption of her husband's foot water and his leftover food is a symbolic statement that he is so high above her that even his impurities are pure for her.[5]

Except when open quarrels erupt (and the case histories to be recounted will show that they do erupt), the wife's public behavior toward her husband is always marked by humility and deference. She must walk behind him, carry burdens for him, eat after he has finished, refer to him in honorific terms (while he uses the lower form in addressing her), and generally try to serve him in every way possible. A single verse from a work by

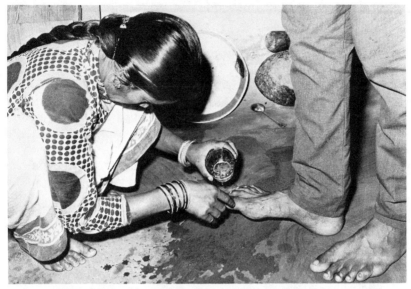

A wife washes her husband's feet before drinking the *gora pani*, or "foot water," in a ritual expression of patrifocal deference performed before each meal. Many women say they do not even feel hungry until they have performed this rite. *Photo by Alice Wagont*

the nineteenth-century Nepali poet Bhanubhakta Acharya, "Instructions for the Bride" (*Badhu Siksa*), gives the flavor of the ideal wifely attitude (Acharya 1968: v. 28, my trans.):

> Let her go before the lord of her breath,
> Her husband, and do what he commands.
> If he asks for his tobacco to smoke,
> Then she should fill his waterpipe immediately.
> Let her give him raisins, grapes, almonds,
> Sweets, coconuts—whatever there is,
> And let her come forward with a bowl of oil
> So that she can anoint his feet with it.

The accepted rationale for this worshipful attitude is, of course, religious. Bhanubhakta tells the bride that she should "through her devotion recognize her husband as god" (v. 1), and that there is "no other dharma for a wife which is as great as that of serving her husband" (v. 32).

All the village women I spoke with held the same view: that it was their dharma to be obedient, respectful, and pleasing to their husbands. Of course, even the most pious women had no illusions about their husbands. Far from believing them to be gods, the women saw them as quite human, often with more than their share of human failings. But that did not change their acceptance of the wife's duty to treat her husband *as if* he were a god.

However, besides a woman's publicly accepted religious motivation to please her husband through service and humility, there is also her own private political motivation. For a woman's position in her ghar depends a great deal on her husband. Although, out of his respect for his parents, the husband cannot openly show any affection for his wife, there are many indirect and covert ways of expressing his regard for her. If the husband gives this support to his wife, and, more important, if he fathers children with her, her status in the household is considerably improved. As one distraught daughter-in-law who felt that her husband no longer cared for her said, "If the husband doesn't love you, no one in the household loves you." She went on to tell about her junior sister-in-law whose husband had demonstrated his regard in a publicly acceptable manner by buying and cooking meat for his wife to strengthen her after childbirth. "Now," she said, "even the mother-in-law is nice to her and doesn't ask her to do the hardest chores, which she should do because she is junior. Instead *I* have to do them and my husband doesn't even notice."

The public ideal of religious devotion and service to the husband may well coincide with a woman's private strategies to secure her own position in the household, and perhaps even, eventually, get her husband to split off from the joint family altogether. All depends on winning the husband's affection, and women know that their wifely services and the deference that increases his self-esteem and prestige within the family are a good path into their husband's heart.

It is, I think, significant that often the submissive "devotional" act of rubbing oil on the husband's feet, such as Bhanubhakta described, becomes in private a prelude to sex. Women explained to me that after they have rubbed oil on their husband's feet at night, they begin massaging his calves and move slowly to his thighs until he either becomes aroused or dismisses them.[6] Thus can a woman transform an openly accepted form of deference into private seduction.

Women told me frankly that sex, as the means to have children and as the means to influence their husband in their favor, was their most effective weapon in the battle for security and respect in their husband's house. Most women professed that they themselves did not really enjoy sex, and they were, I noticed, uncomfortable talking seriously about their own physical and emotional responses. On the other hand, there was a great deal of vigorous sexual joking carried on among the women—sometimes even within earshot of the men. Unmarried girls were told that first intercourse would burn the vagina just as chili-peppers burn the tongue. The suggestive nature of keys being fitted into locks or of the shapes of bananas and cucumbers (and which of their neighbors was thought to relish these foods the most) was a source of endless joking among the women.

However, though some women did confess to having enjoyed sex when they were "young and healthy," and all seemed to enjoy joking about it, my impression was that even those women who did have good sexual relationships felt it somehow improper to admit their own sexual pleasure. On the contrary, when they were serious about their sex lives, they spoke of sex as a way to influence their husbands.

And it is just this which makes a woman's affinal relatives suspicious of her, even though her behavior toward them is so respectful and even servile. For they know that in most cases her goals must eventually run counter to the ideal of agnatic solidarity and that the public restraints placed on husband/wife relations to protect that solidarity do not persist in the bedroom.

In this context, a young man's attraction to his wife may be interpreted by his family as a betrayal of them. Hence, romantic affection and sexuality are expressed covertly, both because of the pervasive ascetic values of Hindu culture and because these emotions represent a shift of loyalties dangerous to the joint family and the patrilineal ideals it embodies. Romantic sentiment in the early years of marriage is expressed with secret gifts of food and clothes. Some of the koseli gifts from a wife's maita, which should be given to her mother-in-law, are saved and given to the husband at night. A little money from a job or grain sale, which should be turned over to the father and used for the household equally, is kept aside and used to buy clothes, hair ribbons, or sweets for a man's wife and his own children. The comments of two informants give a sense of such covert transactions:

Later on [my husband] began to show love (maya) for me, and I too felt love for him. He would ask me what I wanted to eat and would bring it to me right there in the room. There never used to be want of good things to eat in my room. He would bring good clothes for me without letting anyone in the house know about it. He would tell me that I should say that I had brought the clothes from my maita and that I should wear them.

In the second example below a woman recalls when her paternal uncle caught her father in the act of sneaking sweets to her mother. The mischievous uncle dressed in women's clothes and masqueraded as his brother's beloved wife:

In the old days when father worked in the city he would bring good things to eat for all us children—there used to be ten-twelve of us. He would give us the things which were cheap, like biscuits, and he would keep the special food to give to mother later. . . . First he would take his meal, and grandmother would talk with her son who had come from the city. And then he would come back to his room to sleep after having had his rice; he would give mother the delicious stuff to eat. My uncle Ram knew what was going on, and he said to grandmother, "Kancha brings things to eat from the city but he doesn't give us any. . . . Next Friday when Kancha comes home you put a sari, long-sleeved blouse, and earrings on me. I shall put vermilion in the parting of my hair, and when he comes I shall touch his feet as if I were his wife."

He wanted to see whether my father would recognize him—and he also wanted to eat that bundle of delicious food. My grandmother agreed. . . . So he put on mother's sari, blouse, and earrings—his ears were pierced so he could even put on the earrings—and he put on cream, a vermilion mark in his hair, and tika on the forehead and went there on the day that my father was to come. Of course it wasn't very bright and there was just a kerosene wick burning.

All the children were there [and when my father came] he distributed sweets to all of us. Then, as we had agreed beforehand, we all left the room. Father went and sat on the bed and lit a cigarette and Uncle Ram went up just like mother used to do and touched father's feet. Father said, "What is it, *pat?*" Pat means one with a slim body. Father handed Uncle Ram a bundle of food and said, "Here. Take this and keep it. None of the children are around."

At that point Uncle Ram laughed and said, "Ha! Ha! The *poko* [bundle] will be eaten by the *pat!*" He went downstairs and called all the children asking if they would like some treats. Father was speechless!

In this instance, the young husband's duplicity was treated as a joke, as it might well be when the joint family is otherwise operating harmoniously. However, when tensions are already high, the same action on the husband's part would have been cause for increased resentment, or even the spark to ignite an open quarrel. In such a situation, the greater share of blame and resentment would have fallen on the wife for having wheedled and beguiled her husband into such an act of disloyalty. The scenario of the harmonious coexistence between parents and their sons which is shattered by the devisive self-interest of the sons' wives was consistently presented to me by informants. Even the women see tensions and quarrels within the joint family as caused chiefly by members of their own sex. One woman recalled that in her maita when she was a child, "the men used to get along with each other. Their behavior was friendly. But the women used to quarrel a lot with each other. Even when the co-wives were getting along, then the sisters-in-law would fight. That is why the family broke up."

My observations, however, do not entirely support this popular view. Although the women are apt to be much more vocal than men, relations between males in the joint family are often equally strained. Both Haimendorf (1966:40) and Doherty (1974:37) have noted that among the Brahmans and Chetris relations between male agnates are highly competitive and tend to lack mutual trust. Brothers vie with each other for prestige, land resources, and even marriageable women (Stone 1976:50). Although this competitive situation may be used by women or even aggravated by them, they do not create it. In fact, my observations indicate that, as long as brothers (or sons and their parents) are getting along with each other, the squabbles of the women are ignored or (if they are more serious) mediated by the men or senior women. It is only when a man has decided that it will be to his advantage to separate that the women's fights are taken up by the men.[7] It must, of course, be granted that many wives do take an active part in convincing their husbands of the advantages of separating from the joint family. But the tensions between parents and sons—and especially between brothers—are, in most cases, already present. It is only the high value placed on the ideal of agnatic solidarity which casts the scheming affinal women as the sole cause of strife within the joint family.

The Mother-in-law/Daughter-in-law Relationship

Probably the most common reason for a woman to encourage her husband to separate from the joint family is the demanding presence of the *sasu* or mother-in-law.[8] The mother-in-law/daughter-in-law (*sasu/buhari*) relationship is traditionally fraught with tension. In Narikot a woman is pleased when her son marries. In fact the *ratauli* celebration on the night before her son brings a bride (see chapter 3) is one of the few occasions when a woman is expected to dance in public. It marks the culmination of her long and difficult transition from a lowly incoming bride to a senior affinal woman. She who was beneath everyone in the patrifocal model will now receive patrifocal deference from her new daughter-in-law. Moreover, her new daughter-in-law will be expected to do all the hardest work—carrying manure, cutting grass, working in the fields, husking rice, and scrubbing pots. She is thought of as her mother-in-law's servant.

Bhanubhakta's "Instructions for the Bride" also describes her proper daily behavior toward her mother-in-law (Acharya 1968: vv. 2, my trans.):

Let her go and fall upon
Her sasu's lotus feet,
And beseech to be told
What service she may perform.

When she has completed all her duties
Let her massage her sasu's feet
So that her sasu becomes drowsy
And drifts easily to sleep.[9]

In Narikot families daughters-in-law are, even now, expected to greet their sasu by touching their foreheads to her feet. They must also drink the water from washing their sasu's feet before each meal, ask if they may wash her clothes, and rub oil on her feet at night.

Despite such services most mothers-in-law I observed remained, at best, indifferent, and more often harshly critical of their daughters-in-law. This may reflect the fact that the two women are in subtle competition for the loyalty of a single man—the husband of one and the son of the other. The bride's relation to her husband in public and private is necessarily "two-faced."

The mother-in-law knows that the bride's public deference to her may well be hypocritical—and that, even while the bride is silently massaging the mother-in-law's feet, the girl is likely to be thinking of the next chance she will have to complain to her husband or neighbors about what a heavy workload her mother-in-law gives her. I have encountered several instances where a woman forbade her daughter-in-law to wash her feet any longer after discovering that the daughter-in-law had spoken or done something against her (often quite minor) behind her back. This has the effect of humiliating the daughter-in-law and of mobilizing family sentiment against her by bringing her "hypocrisy" out into the open.

Somewhat surprisingly in the face of all this suspicion, I found that most brides enter their husband's family with what appears to be a genuine hope of winning their mother-in-law's confidence through services and deference, and with no conscious intention of splitting up the joint family. This—and of course motherhood—is the only culturally acceptable strategy for securing their position as married women, and the brides I observed seemed to be trying to make it work. Ironically, it may be because this open strategy so often fails that the daughter-in-law is driven to the sullenness and scheming that weaken the solidarity of the joint family.

With such tension between the two women, the birth of a daughter-in-law's first child often marks a crisis point in the relationship. The daughter-in-law may cease to wash her mother-in-law's feet and drink the water, and her open service may begin to slacken. After the shy young bride has become the mother of one or two children—especially sons—her status has increased considerably, and she may feel that the authority of her mother-in-law no longer has to be accepted without question. It is then that quarrels may erupt openly, and the husband, whose first loyalty is supposed to be to his mother and father, may be put to the test.

In the case history presented below, the stress on the young husband who is torn between parents and wife is clearly evident. Although there were certainly other contributing factors—such as the pressure of studying for his B.A.—this tension between lineal and conjugal ties appears to have been at least partially responsible for precipitating a long period of acute depression.

This history was told to me by a young woman who believed that her brother had been bewitched by his wife as a means of getting him to separate from his parents. The fact that my informant (along with her parents and brothers) believed the sister-in-law would, to achieve her own ends, bring her husband to such a state of helplessness and near death shows the depths of suspicion in which affinal women are held:

My elder sister-in-law used *tuna* [black magic] against my brother so that he would separate from mother and father. He had said he wouldn't separate from them until the day he died. So sister-in-law said some spells over some food and gave it to him to eat. This caused my brother's mind to become restless and upset. It went on in this way until he left off studying for his B.A. He would think about things of no relevance. . . . and he was unable to answer properly when someone asked him a question. . . . he would sit pulling at the knots in his hair like this. Mother and father tried all sorts of cures. A local practitioner [*janne manche*, lit. "a knowing person"] told us that it was the work of sister-in-law. . . . They placed some rice grains in a plate like this and they would call my brother's name. They also felt his pulse. A coin is placed on the plate as offering and then the practitioner tells you that so-and-so is responsible for the affliction. The practitioner would ask for eggs and a chicken. My parents brought all the things needed for the puja, like incense, rice-grains, etc., and then they would perform the puja. The practitioner would carry off two–three hundred rupees. But my brother wouldn't get cured. We called in someone who has been a military nurse and we called a shaman (*jhakri*) but my brother didn't get well.

Later sister-in-law said that she wouldn't live with an insane person and she went to her maita. The practitioner would say that she was responsible, and she would say she wasn't! And if sister-in-law was there, then my brother's face would light up and he would seem happy. If she wasn't there, then he wouldn't even come down to eat rice with us. . . . She didn't come for three-four years and my brother was bedridden during that time. . . .

When three–four years had passed we took my brother to sister-in-law's maita, where she was staying. He didn't want to go, but we put him in his clothes and took him there. He stayed in sister-in-law's maita for twenty-two days. . . . His in-laws gave him treatments, and he became slightly better. . . . He was all right for nine months, and then he relapsed again. . . . He became more seriously ill and we thought he was going to die. That is why everyone said that his son's initiation ceremony should be performed [so that his son could do funeral ceremonies for him when he died]. We thought he probably wouldn't even live through the winter. Mother and father were really worried, because no matter what they did it looked as if their eldest son wouldn't live. Father used to weep, saying that he saw sons of all the others all dressed up and walking around, while his son was lying bedridden.

Then mother went to her sister's home. The two sisters talked and mother wept about her plight. Her sister consoled her and said that this was her karma that her daughter-in-law had turned into someone like that. There happened to be a guest staying in that house, and he said: "Well—are you both going to talk among yourselves and weep, or will you tell me what the trouble is?" Mother replied, "What to do? My son is about to die." The guest asked whether mother hadn't found a practitioner who could help. Mother told him that they had spent all their wealth, and still her son hadn't been cured. She said she wished that she would die before her son did. The guest said that there was a practitioner at Koteshwar who would be able to tell whether my brother would live or die.

When mother heard this she said that she would call that person. Because she knew that she couldn't spend all their resources on one son alone, since there were other children who had to be thought of, she said that [if the practitioner said] my brother would live she would spend money on him; otherwise, she would accept fate. My brother's condition became so bad that when my father called him to come and eat it would take him hours to respond.

That practitioner came and said that he needed incense, vermilion, and one measure of rice and a rupee. Then he told us that sister-in-law was trying to separate my brother from us and take him away. When my father asked him if he could cure my brother, the man said that he would try but he couldn't promise. At that time, sister-in-law was at her maita, and the practitioner said that she must stay there or he wouldn't perform the treatment. We agreed, and he began the treatment and performed the puja, which lasted through the night. He ate a meal in the morning and went away saying that he would return after fourteen days.

Father and mother didn't believe in him because all the others had said just the same thing. But this man said that my brother would be completely cured on the fourteenth day, and if he wasn't then he would never be cured. Father kept waiting. My brother wouldn't go upstairs, so we made a bed for him downstairs and he would eat and sleep there.

On the evening of the thirteenth day I cooked rice and gave it to everybody. At that time only my younger sister-in-law was there. . . . She took the utensils out to wash them. And my brother was just lying there. He had gone back to bed without even washing his hands after eating! So I washed his hands and mouth. I thought of how much money we had spent trying to cure him, and here he was sleeping with his hands jutho! I thought that there was probably nothing that could be done for him now.

Father and the others were upstairs sleeping. Only my younger sister and I were downstairs when suddenly my brother woke up in a rage! He threw off the quilt like this, and looked around like this. We were afraid so we took the lamp and went upstairs. . . . I told mother what my brother had done and said maybe he would talk after all. So mother went downstairs and called his name. "Shyam Krishna?" she said. In the past even if we called him like that fifty times he wouldn't answer. But now he said, "Hazur" [respectful affirmative]. Mother said, "Son? Shall I bring a mosquito net and put it up for you?" He answered that he wouldn't need one. Then she asked if he wanted some water and he said he didn't.

He had become very thin and wasted, and he looked like a pole. He could hardly talk, and when mother asked him anything he spoke very slowly. . . . Mother wept when she saw her son who hadn't talked for so long talking now. She went upstairs and told father that their son was talking; father rushed down and fell down the stairs in his haste!

My brother bent over and began to weep, saying that he had given us all so much sorrow and trouble. And when we saw my brother weeping, then father and all the rest of us began to weep also. In the end my brother had to console us! . . . And then we made some tea and all of us drank it and talked through the night. And when we asked my brother what he used to feel, he said that he had felt as if horses, cars, rivers, and streams were pouring over him and covering him. And when he would start up thinking he would try to escape, he would find that the window had shrunk. And he would feel as if the house were falling down. He would feel as if he had to climb crags on a path which no one could tread. That's how he used to feel every day. And then when it was time for all this to end and he was about to sleep, my brother dreamed he was riding away on a huge chariot. He dreamed he was wearing cloth shoes, and when he wanted to get off the chariot his shoe fell off. He tried to pick up the shoe but it had fallen into a deep crevice, and when he bent over to pick it up he woke with a start. . . . Only then did he become aware of his surroundings.

It was four in the morning when we had finished talking with him. . . . He didn't remember a single thing of what had happened in all those years. He didn't remember what he had eaten or what he had worn or done. That was the kind of illness he had.

Sister-in-law was called back from her maita. My brother said he wouldn't marry another wife. "What has happened has happened," he said. "I can't carry two headstraps [to support a load] on my one forehead." He said he already had a son and a daughter. All he wanted now was to get his son married. Sister-in-law came back after two years. She was sent an invitation for my marriage. We must give invitations, and when she came after receiving the invitation she stayed on. . . . Everyone is friendly with her, as she

only did those things to her husband and not to anyone else. . . .
Of course it is a sin (*pap*) for sister-in-law. If she hadn't arranged
that black magic no one else would have done it to him. When we
speak about it to her face she denies it all, but the practitioner says
that she is the one. . . .

My brother is quite happy now. He says that we will never
separate. The sisters-in-law say that we should separate. But my
brother tells them that if they want to live separately, then they can
do so—but he says the brothers will stick together. If the brothers
are friendly with each other, then the sisters-in-law have to get along
with each other also.

The story as it is related here stands as a paean to agnatic
solidarity. Certainly it demonstrates the tenacity of patrilineal
ideals and the deep mistrust of affinal women. The irony is that
my informant herself managed to get her husband to separate
from his parents within little more than a year of marriage. Her
account of that incident has a very different tone:

My mother-in-law used to nag a lot. She gave me so much misery,
but she wouldn't give good food either. I talked with my husband,
and he said there was no need to suffer like this once in a lifetime
even. . . . I did not know anything about the work in the fields.
. . . When the marriage had been settled then my father told my
father-in-law: "My daughter can do all the housework and cook.
But she doesn't know how to go outside and carry loads in a basket." At that time my father-in-law replied that I wouldn't have to
do the outside work and that he had servants. But a month after I
was married they told me to do the outside work too. . . . And
when you don't know the work, then you feel like crying. . . . If I
had learned the work from my childhood, then it would have been
easy for me. I have not done that kind of work since we separated. . . .

When your mother-in-law is a *dusta* [bad person, scoundrel],
then what can you do? Moreover, I had to respect her day and night
and do her every wish. But even then they would not be happy
with me. Moreover, even my children would have been mistreated.
And since my husband's parents treated us with such contempt I am
glad that we live separately from them.

It is clear that such tales have many sides. I would have
liked to hear the story of my informant's brother's illness again
from her sister-in-law's point of view. This example suggests that
some of my observations about the harsh lot of the daughter-in-
law need qualification, not only because of the great complexity of joint family relationships (which we have only begun to

penetrate here), but also because, like any human relationships, they are greatly influenced by the individuals who enter them. Although I have presented in-laws as overly suspicious of affinal women, the passage above demonstrates that sometimes these suspicions are justified. Likewise, the mother-in-law/daughter-in-law relationship which I have described as so full of tension and rivalry can sometimes be one of harmony and cooperation. One woman I knew spoke of her mother-in-law as a second mother and recalled scheming with her to prevent her husband from taking another wife and gambling away the family money.

Being the wife of the senior male in the family is the greatest source of prestige available for a woman in Brahman-Chetri society—just as for men the highest prestige is to be the senior male. However, the degree of prestige involved depends to a large extent on the size of the family and hence the number of sons and daughters-in-law for whom the senior couple are the focus of patrifocal veneration and authority. And it is here that we find the major source of tension between the generations and one of the main reasons for the fragility of the joint family. The patrifocal values of duty and obedience to elders are designed to maintain the joint family unit for as long as possible under the authority of the senior couple—ideally until their death or senility. There is implicit in the values of the patrifocal system a bargain with the men and women in junior positions; accept control that you may eventually have control over others. But the fact is that patrifocal obedience (for men at least) is voluntary. Sons may ask for partition of the joint family estate at any time under Nepali law. For the senior couple partition means loss of control over economic resources and labor as well as considerable loss of prestige in the community. Those seeking partition also forfeit the economic security of the joint family and gain a certain notoriety for having failed to uphold the patrifocal values of duty and obedience. But the point is that every young married couple—and again especially the men who must make the final decision—face a choice of strategies. They may accept the patrifocal ideal and wait to succeed their elders after a prolonged period of dependency. Or they may reject patrifocal authority and establish their own separate household. It is this choice which lies at the root of the proverbial tension between mothers and daughters-in-law and the similar but less admissible tension between fathers and sons.

Relations with a Co-wife

Of all the relationships a woman has in her husband's house, the most openly and bitterly antagonistic is that with her co-wife (*sauta*)—if she is unfortunate enough to have one. There is, in fact, a good chance that she will. Polygamy is socially and religiously sanctioned among the high-caste Hindus of Nepal. Of the 88 high-caste men I surveyed in Narikot, 17 (nearly one-fifth) had more than one legal wife at the same time. Several had three wives, and one man had five. Polygamy however, is clearly related to economic factors, and in a more remote and less well off hill village (from which several Chetri women had married into Narikot) the rate of polygamous marriages was only 4.3 percent (Bennett 1981).

The bringing in of another wife is a constant threat that the husband and his family hold over the new wife. Although recent government laws forbid polygamous marriage (except under certain circumstances including the wife's insanity, leprosy, or her inability to bear a child after ten years of marriage) the laws have had little impact in the village setting. Custom holds polygamy to be a man's right—especially when the first wife has produced no male children after several years—and only a woman with a wealthy and influential maita behind her could hope to win legal redress in the courts.[10]

No matter how strained a woman's relations with her mother-in-law may be, the two women at least share the common desire for healthy male offspring. Her mother-in-law is genuinely pleased when a woman becomes pregnant and has a safe delivery. Also, for the daughter-in-law, there is the knowledge that the dominance of the mother-in-law will lessen in the natural course of events, giving the daughter-in-law more and more responsibility and power in the household. For example, it is a significant footnote to the previous narrative that shortly after the recovery of the bewitched man and the return of his wife, the management of household affairs was turned over to them by the aging parents. But with a co-wife, neither time nor the shared desire for offspring serve to relieve the stress. Co-wives are in direct competition to produce male children and eventually to rule the household when age, death, or separation of the joint family removes the mother-in-law's dominance. Since both their fertility and their influence in the household are so dependent on the husband, co-wives are almost inevitably engaged in a bitter struggle for his support and affection.

I mentioned earlier the importance that women attached to sex as a means of gaining influence over their husbands. This is most startlingly evident in the narrative below, in which a woman recalls more than fifteen years of fierce, no-holds-barred rivalry with her co-wife. Here also a clear connection emerges between the husband's sexual attentions to the wife and her power in the household. Yet, for a woman, physical and emotional pleasure in sex remains somewhat improper—something our narrator imputes to her voracious co-wife and her errant husband but shies away from admitting for herself.

I am including this long narrative, however, not merely because it illustrates points I have been making about the role relations of women in the joint family structure. The narrative also moves us from the consideration of women's roles toward an understanding of their lives in a broader sense. Instead of viewing the joint family as a set of static structural relations, I wish to look at it as a social process—"the way in which individuals actually handle their structural relationships and exploit the element of choice between alternative norms according to the requirements of any particular situation" (Van Velsen 1967:148).

After the lengthy discussion of the "patrilineal ideal" and how it structures the role of women in the joint family, and after all the abstract kinship charts and diagrams, it is, I think, essential that we immerse ourselves now in the day-to-day reality of an actual joint family as it is perceived by one very resourceful and articulate female member.

The narrative will give a sense of what leeway there is within the system for individual influences and manipulations. Certainly this narrative should dispel any impression of women as the helpless, categorical victims of the social structure which more generalized descriptions and abstract analyses tend to create. It is true that the dominant patrifocal model would seem to be "against" the sixteen-year-old bride Devi as she enters the household of a man more than twice her age. In the household are his two other wives and their children, his mother and father, his brothers, their wives, and their children—all of whom have authority over the new bride. But, as Devi—and particularly the case history which follows her narrative—will reveal, the patrifocal model has its own internal stresses, and she is not without the means to capitalize on them. Indeed, though none of the three main characters emerges in a very flattering light, the two co-wives seem a good deal more resourceful than the man they are fighting over:

After my husband had come to ask for me [in marriage] my father talked it over with his sister, who lived near my husband's village and knew his family.

"Well elder sister," said my father, "I'd give her. But over a co-wife? She's an orphan girl. Her mother's dead. What to do if she's mistreated afterward? I won't be able to take her back and look after her."

"She won't have any trouble," replied his sister. "Even if she is mistreated, he has said that he'll register land in her name. If she's mistreated she can take care of herself when she has the land and the fields as a life-portion (juni bhag). If we give her to a young man, then he might marry another woman afterward. Much better that she goes as the youngest wife right now."

So my father said, "All right then. Get him to prepare the necessary papers which say how much rice land she gets and then I will give him Devi."

. . . Later my cousin Sano Maya (who had already been married into my husband's village to one of his nephews) took me to a private place and said, "Listen Devi, if you marry a bachelor or one who isn't married, he will surely bring another co-wife over you. So even if you have to marry one who is already married, what harm is there? You will become the youngest wife. He will love you. An elderly person like this will love you more than a young blade. Don't refuse! You can see that he is very handsome and fair-skinned. He has a strong, healthy body. He is wearing a ring here and a watch there. And when he gets on a cycle and goes along you feel like watching him only. He's not an old man." This is what Sano Maya said to me about one whom she was supposed to treat like her father-in-law!

"Oh Sani!" I said. "I don't want to marry him—whether he is elderly or young. You can marry him yourself!"

She laughed and said, "Do you think a daughter-in-law can do it with her father-in-law?"

. . . . A month later, when they had agreed on the property that was to be set aside for me in my husband's family, I was married. I was so worried. I had heard that there were two co-wives. I didn't know whether they would fight and quarrel with me or whether they would both come to pull out my hair! That's why I was so anxious and scared. I felt like weeping.

And then he came on Friday with the wedding party. At first he seemed tall and frightening to me. . . . I was preparing for worship at the family altar that morning and when I heard he had come I hid myself in the inner room. . . .

[None of the wedding could be performed at my husband's house because] the children of his other wives were not supposed to see their father dressed up as a bridegroom. One's sons and daughters are not supposed to see. When one gets angry one says "I shall show you your father's marriage!" So my husband stayed in the house of a Newar not far from my maita. That Newar had two younger daughters, and my husband began to flirt with one of the daughters of that Newar. She went to fetch water and my husband followed her. One of the wedding party came and joked about it so I could hear. I looked out the window. I felt like weeping because I thought that a man who had come to get married was running after another girl and that he would probably only give me sorrow. I kept on looking to see whether he would splash water on that girl and tease her. She filled her water pot, and instead of washing his face, my groom followed her!

Later one of the wedding party said that my husband had torn open the mouth of that girl and had poured oil into it and "killed" her that evening. Actually they were only teasing me. But I didn't know. I felt great anxiety in my mind. My uncle also became very angry and created an uproar. He began to scold my father, "Why did you give your daughter over a co-wife? Over two co-wives? And with children already there from the other wives! You give your daughter—a daughter who is an orphan, without a mother! There is no need to give her in such a marriage! That man is like one who goes around tasting the curry. He takes one wife, sleeps with her and just tastes her. He is like one who goes around tasting all the curries. He marries a lot of wives. Why are you giving her to him? Our Devi will be unhappy!"

Thus he scolded my father, and there was talk of not giving me. They were calling my groom fickle (*tihun cakhuwa*). I was so worried. But in spite of all this, I made the garland of sacred dubo grass [traditionally given to the groom]. My father and others decided that if they didn't give me now they would appear to be deceivers, and so they gave me in marriage.

My elder sister decorated me. They put cream and powder and ornaments on me—a golden headband, bangles of gold, and ankle bracelets on my feet. Then they put a beautiful sari on me and a veil over my head. . . . And then they took me outside for the swayambar ritual. The Damai musicians were playing and I was trembling. They gave me the garland and I walked round my husband three times and placed the garland on him. I wanted to knot it at the back as my elder sister had told me to do, because it was a bad omen if it fell. But my hands were trembling so! He was the husband of three wives, so I made three knots.

. . . Then the next evening he came as the groom [for the kanyadan ceremony]. When our feet were to be washed he and I sat on the bed which my father had given. As they prepared to wash our feet my husband would slide over and touch me as if it had been accidental. He would nudge me with his elbows and my whole body would seem to swell up with fear. Father and the others didn't see any of this. He pretended not to know what he was doing and he pushed me. Then he even pinched me. I was frightened, my heart was thumping with fear. . . .

Then he gave me the red marriage beads and the shawl and saris and blouses and everything else. My old nurse took them, and then they brought me upstairs. . . . [When it was time] for the fire ceremony they took off the clothes and ornaments from my maita which I had worn for the kanyadan and put on those from my ghar. When they had finished decorating and making me up they brought me to the sacred enclosure and set me down. My father's sister began to tease me, "Well Devi—the *mawali* [maternal uncle's side, family] has to win. You have to give birth to a son. The mawali has to win!" Then she joked with her new son-in-law. "Sir, you mustn't win. Devi has to win. Don't fool around with her. She must give birth to a son!" My father's sister kept on shouting this. My husband replied that he would not fool around with me. That is what he said. Then he took hold of the sacred wedding knot tied around my waist and we went round and round the sacred enclosure. My brother gave me the puffed rice and I offered it up. . . . Then the priest said that the groom had to touch the bride's breast and so my husband touched mine. He was supposed to touch there with a handkerchief but he touched me with his hands—right there in the sacred enclosure itself! I have not seen this in other marriages but that is what they say—that he should touch it.

Then the priest told us that the groom and the bride should exchange places, but I just sat there like a deaf-mute. So my husband told the priest that I had already obeyed in my mind, so he moved from his place. Then the priest told me to catch hold of the edge of my husband's tunic and ask him where his house was and pull him down to sit beside me. Again I was speechless, and my husband said I had already followed the instructions in my mind and he sat down by himself. Then it was time to eat curd. My husband didn't touch it and I just took a little and sprinkled it on his lips. Then the ceremonies were over and I went upstairs. But I didn't feel sleepy. I lay down but I couldn't sleep. My heart was thumping away. I was so frightened. "They say he has two co-wives at home. I wonder what they are like? If my husband is like this, I wonder what the rest of the household is like and what the co-wives are like?" Thus I was thinking and thinking unable to go to sleep.

. . . The next day after the feast it was time for the farewell

ritual. I combed my hair and my elder sister put my clothes on me
and decorated me. . . . Then after worshiping at the family hearth,
my father carried me and placed me in the sedan chair. I was taken
to the Newar's house where the other ceremonies had to be
done. . . .

They twisted my hair with the *amaju's* [the Newari woman
who was playing the role of Devi's mother-in-law] and poured oil
over the knot. They they looked on my face. . . . I just sat there
without saying a word. . . . Then my amaju went upstairs to her
room to sleep. . . . And in a room like this there was only my
husband and myself. I am sitting there and my heart is pounding
away. I am so scared. Then he called me over to sleep. I didn't go.
My whole body seemed to have swollen up. I felt as if there were
thorns on my whole body [goose pimples]. I kept quiet and didn't
say a word. And then he stretched out his legs and put his feet in
my lap! He began to pull at my thighs with his feet. My body seemed
to swell up even more and I felt even more frightened. He began
to call me to him but I wouldn't go.

Then he said, "What! Are you going to sit there shivering
through the whole night with cold?" And he carried me like this
and took me. I lay down near the wall and he lay by the outside
edge of the bed.

Then he asked me, "Why are you afraid? Why are you wor-
rying?"

I had wept before the marriage party came, and Sano Maya
had told him about this. So now he asked me, "Why did you weep
before? There is so much paddy in the field which I have given you.
. . . I will not mistreat you. I will not do anything to you or say
anything to you. Why do you weep?"

But all the while I was keeping silent. What could I say? I
was so scared! He swore that if he ever mistreated me, then may it
be as big a sin as if he had killed something or other. . . . He told
me not to worry because I had no mother but that he would be like
a mother and father to me. He talked and talked. He was actually
coaxing me so that I would sleep with him.

"After I had seen you," he said, "I dreamed of you and you
were always in my mind. Did you see me in your dreams or not?"
I told him I hadn't, but he said he had dreamed of sleeping with me
and making love to me. Such things he said! "You do not have to
wonder about what you will wear and what you will eat. I shall
make whatever ornaments you would like to wear. . . . I shall never
give you trouble but only love you. If there were others for me then
why should I love you? If my other wives would do for me then
why should I marry you? They talk back to me and their looks do
not complement me, so that is why I married you. You do not have
a mother—so whatever you take me as, your mother or anyone

else, I am that person!" He talked a great deal. But I told him that there were a lot of people sitting outside our room and that he shouldn't talk so much.

How could I not worry? He had two co-wives for me and they had four or five children. I didn't know what they would do to me.

"Sir," I said, "You will mistreat me afterward. Now I am young and you will love me. But later, you will mistreat me. Who has ever been able to know what is going on inside the mind of a man? I have seen many who have been treated badly."

"I shall not give you any pain. Why should we fight and quarrel?" he replied. But he was actually meaning something else. . . . But I told him I wouldn't sleep with him then because there were people sleeping outside.

"So what if there are people outside?" he said. "You will run away to your maita tomorrow and there you will sleep in your own room. You won't sleep with me here? Why can't you do it here?"

There was a wound right here where he bit me. There was a bruise on my cheek. Everyone made fun of me. They said that my *poi* [husband, lover] had bitten me and that he had already slept with me because they saw that bruise on my cheek. So that act was done. It was very painful. It was like having pains during childbirth. The first time. It was like having labor pains. That was what it was like. I felt as if there was a very hot chili-pepper there—and then there was water. That day it burned a little and there wasn't much of a discharge. It takes some time.

. . . Early next morning they said the red powder which the groom had placed in the parting of my hair during the wedding had to be washed. So I washed the vermilion off and then bathed myself. Then I put on my clothes and makeup and decorated myself. I again sat in the sedan chair and returned to my maita. . . . My sisters saw the bruise and teased me. "Last time there wasn't anything on your cheeks. And now there is a bruise. He has banged you. He has finished you. He has finished you!" When we had our food my sisters would tease me until 8–9 o'clock. And then they left me. . . . But in the night they lifted Sano Maya up, and she peeked into the room where my husband and I were staying. I knew about it. I was sitting there massaging my husband's feet and there would be snickering outside. So I told my husband they had come to peep at us. So he took a huge glass filled with drinking water and flung it out of the window! Sano Maya, who was peeping, was hit right in the face with that water!

[When it was time for me to actually go to my ghar] I felt like crying. My father accompanied me a little of the way, and when he left me he said, "Well daughter, go without sorrow or any anxiety in your heart. Come again soon to see us." My friends also said goodbye and again I felt like crying. . . .

They carried me in the sedan chair bumping me all over the place until my whole body was full of aches and pains. [When we arrived at my husband's house] my father and mother-in-law brought the rice grains and red powder for giving the tika. . . . My mother-in-law put tika on her son first. "Look after your family and house properly. May you prosper. May all your wives be treated properly." This was her blessing as she put tika on him. Then she put tika on me and I placed a rupee before her and touched her feet. . . . The eldest wife who was the mother of Bhagwati was happy. She had had seven sons and now only that one daughter, Bhagwati, was alive. She had suffered a lot with her first co-wife, and she used to feel that if her husband married another then she would have some ease and happiness. She had been to several places looking for a girl [for her husband to marry] but hadn't been able to find one. . . . But Hom Nath's mother [the middle wife] was sulking. She had a belly this big—she was due in the next month. She was angry with me because I had come as her co-wife and she wouldn't speak with me. . . . She was furious with her husband's eldest brother because he had arranged for a girl for his younger brother and so now she had another co-wife.

I did not touch the feet of my co-wives. My father's sister had told the co-wives before, "You can do whatever you like with her but you cannot tell her to touch your feet. If you had given birth to her then it would have been one thing. But who will touch the feet of a co-wife?" So I offered my greeting like this by bowing down with my hands folded. But Hom Nath's mother went away angry. "When she is new and strange she doesn't touch our feet!" she said. "I wonder what she'll do to us later!"

Later, when my husband had finished eating he told me to go and eat. So I went to eat rice. . . . And, taking an opportunity while I was eating, he went to the room of Hom Nath's mother. That is what men are like! They are sinners and they are selfish. He gave her the mattress and quilt that had been sent with me. And by the time I had finished eating he was already in my room stretched out and sleeping! Bhagwati's mother told me all this. "While you were eating he visited his middle wife. This is what men are like. Be careful," she said.

[Very soon I found out why my husband had taken a third wife]. It seems that in the past when Hom Nath's mother had been the youngest wife he had gone around loving many young girls. Mainly there was a Bhoteni [Tibeto-Burman-speaking woman of middle-ranking Matwali caste]. He had kept her outside in a room in the bazaar, but she was just like his wife. She had been pregnant but then she died. My husband was very sad when she died and even wore a white cap [a sign of mourning] as if she'd been his own wife. But Hom Nath's mother is the jealous type. And after that Bhoteni died she said to her husband, "You thought your Bhoteni was everything. When you had her you wouldn't even look at me. Now when she is dead you have your face up your ass, and you have come to me!"

And because Hom Nath's mother had said this, he vowed he would bring a co-wife over her. He wouldn't rest until he had done so because she had cursed him like that. And so my husband had set out to search for a girl. A person will never set out to beg for something until there is a pain in him.

So now Hom Nath's mother was cursing her elder brother-in-law because he had helped arrange my marriage. "May the one who has given me a co-wife be destroyed. May he die. May the one who has brought a co-wife over me die." . . . And my father's sister had also asked for me [and so she was cursed too].

"My life has been disrupted. May their lives be disrupted!" The second wife said this out loud so that I could hear it. . . . For my benefit she said that someone had come to steal another's husband. I felt like weeping. So I went and told my husband what she had said. "Sir," I said, "You have married me. Now it seems that I have come to your house because I couldn't find a husband for myself anywhere else." I wept.

And then my husband bawled out Hom Nath's mother. "Your mouth!" he said. "Your mouth is responsible! . . . You do whatever you like and you go around! What else is there to do except to bring a co-wife over you? If you had behaved properly, then who would have brought a co-wife! And you dare to say things to Devi! Do you think that she came here because she wanted to? I have married her and brought her here. Why did you have to say such things and curse her?"

. . . [After that] he took all his clothes from the room of Hom Nath's mother where they had been kept in her trunk. He brought them all to my room. Because he was going to sleep in one room, so why should he keep all that in another room? Hom Nath's mother wept a lot. "He has taken all his clothes. Now he will no longer come into my room. Now he won't love me anymore. Now he won't sleep with me anymore."

. . . My husband did "sleep" with her—but she didn't give birth to any more children. When I would go to bathe after my menstruation, my husband would eat his meal in a hurry and take his tobacco and go to sleep after closing the door. He was afraid she would come to him.

One day my mother-in-law said to him. "Look son, Hom Nath's mother is also your wife. She is also young." At this time Hom Nath's mother was thirty; now she must be in her late forties.

"You shouldn't do this," said my mother-in-law, "Let her also come into your room." Thus she scolded her son. But my husband refused to let Hom Nath's mother come to him. Later Hom Nath's mother got up very early in the morning and went to her husband's room. She sat at his feet and said, "If I am not your wife then say so. Don't you think that I should sleep with you? Don't you think that I also need my husband?"

"I have taken some medicine from the doctor," he replied, "so don't shout at me here!" But she asked whether he would be so ill when I was around, and then she said, "Then cut away and give me what is my share [of your penis] and just keep Devi's share!" This is what he told me she had said!

Later she went to Sano Maya and cursed my husband, "*Eski ma cikne* [mother-fucker]! He thinks his youngest wife is the best! He has brought together other people's daughters and now he doesn't come to us!" She was very angry. But that evening she went and prepared tobacco for her husband. He had left the door open and she came into his room and prepared it. And later she pulled him by the arm and slept with him. And then when I had gone to my maita she also slept with him. . . . She would lock herself in the room with him and giggle and laugh. In my room! They were trying to behave like teenagers. They would laugh and tease each other and do all sorts of things. And the next day she would go around and tell people in our village, "Although he married a younger wife he still comes to me. He comes to sleep with me. He is still my lover. He is my lover! So what if he married a younger wife!"

When I came back later the people of the village came and told me. So I said to my husband, "You told me before that the other wives were not good enough to you, that you would make me your youngest wife and that you would love me. Now you go off and sleep with Hom Nath's mother! She has been going around telling everyone in the village!" Then I snatched the sheet he had been covering himself with and threw it off. He just sat there. He used to be afraid of me in those days. He used to love me a lot. Whenever we were alone then we would sleep together. My husband needs it a lot. I don't need it so much. But *she* also needed it a lot and so they got along. . . . Since she wanted sex he showed more love for her.

. . . After my mother-in-law died and the brothers separated . . . I used to look after the storeroom. My husband used to consult me [about household matters]. He trusted whatever I said. He told my father's sister, "Although Devi is young she says things which can be trusted. She says what I find comforting. She doesn't say anything which is flippant or unnecessary. When I ask her what is to be done about anything, then she does it without any loose ends."

. . . He listens to me. He doesn't listen to what others tell him. When his daughter tells him there isn't any salt or oil then he brings them. But if Hom Nath's mother says that she doesn't have a blouse, he won't bring it for her until I confirm it and say that she doesn't have one.

. . . My husband used to have a lot of fights because of us co-wives. He used to have a lot of love for Hom Nath's mother. She had done some *tuna* [black magic] and turned his heart toward her only. *Tuna* means that which is done by the *gubaju* [Newar practitioner of traditional medicine and sorcery]. She had turned her husband's heart and mind toward herself only. He didn't have any love for me. It was not my husband's mind that did this. It was because his mind had been bewitched. He used to show more love toward that side, and so there would be fights. "You married me saying that I was your favorite youngest wife," I said, "and you said you'd do this for me and that for me. You had love for me as long as I was a young thing and had thick buttocks. And now you're mistreating me. Now that I have given birth to a son you think that I'm old, and that's why you treat me so carelessly. It's enough! Go to her!!"

We also fought over household matters whenever he brought clothes. And when I was recovering from childbirth he didn't give me good food because he was attracted to her. If he had brought meat, then he would give most of it to her son, Hom Nath, to eat. He'd only give me two pieces to eat. The rice which had been cooked for me to eat between meals—Hom Nath's mother would eat it herself. Bhagwati's mother used to treat me very well. But the other is a jealous person. If she saw someone wearing something good she would be jealous. She has no love for me. If clarified butter had been brought for me then she would eat that also. . . . After I gave birth to my son I became very weak and ill. Maybe she did some black magic to me also.

That year my mother-in-law died, so my husband used to go to his father's room at night to sleep as a companion for the old man. When night had fallen he would take his pillow and quilt and go. One night the oil in the lamp ran out, so I went downstairs to get some more. I put my baby son to sleep and went downstairs for oil. And there I saw that, instead of going to sleep with his father, he was lying on the bed of Hom Nath's mother! And she was massaging his legs. She was rubbing them right up to his thighs. That is a custom among us Nepalese. I came upstairs pretending not to see. He used to go and sleep with her like that—he used to sneak off.

Of course, later, he would tell me that she had caught him by the arm and pulled him to her to "sleep" with him. She used to make him blow out the light. . . . And she was very strong. She can "sleep" a lot and she does too! She can "sleep" seven times a

day! Ask her—she'll say that it's true. My husband would say that
he had enough, but she would say she hadn't had enough and she
would hold him with her legs round his waist! My husband told me
this. "She's not like you," he said. "She needs a lot of it. When I've
had enough and I begin to take it out, then she says, "It's not enough
for me. I need more. . . . This itch of mine hasn't even been
scratched!" . . . She would even "sleep" like that. He wants a lot.
After all he is a man—all that matters for men is that they should be
able to "sleep" with a woman. If you allow them to "sleep" with
you then they love you; otherwise they don't.

       . . . One time we had a quarrel that lasted for three–four
months. I was menstruating and it was my fourth day. I bathed and
washed my hair and drank the water off my husband's feet. But he
didn't speak to me. He just sulked. I didn't talk with him either. He
knew that I had known about it [that he had slept with Hom Nath's
mother] when he saw my downcast face.

       After that Hom Nath's mother brought ripe guavas from the
village and gave them to him. He ate them too. I was very hurt. He
had done this many times. Now, when I was having my period then
it was all right for him to go to her. He couldn't sleep with me then.
But other times also he would go to her—in the mornings, eve-
nings, and during the day. Those times I was very hurt. My husband
and I didn't talk for three–four months. All I did was cook and serve
the rice to him. He would eat whatever amount was given to him.
No matter how much I gave him he wouldn't even say it was
enough. So I used to remain silent and give him his food.

       He only talked with her. I used to find it very lonely. . . .
No matter how much I wept during the night, he never asked why
I was weeping. Sometimes I used to stay up half the night weeping
in the attic—but he never asked why. Sometimes I felt like throwing
myself from somewhere and killing myself. I felt that if I hung myself
then there would be peace. My husband didn't love me in my ghar,
and even in my maita I didn't have a mother. But then I would
remember my son. "This son is small now," I would say to myself.
"Afterward he will grow up and then his tears will make me suffer
and I won't get salvation. Even if my husband mistreats me now, if
I can bear it and stay, then afterward when this son grows up, then
he'll look after me and take care of me. If my husband and all the
others treat me badly, then this is a result of my karma. But no
matter what happens, Bhagwan has given me a son." Thus I used to
console myself. I never went out but used to stay in my room and
love my baby. . . .

       Four months passed in this manner. Afterward the people of
the village began to tell me that I shouldn't stay like that. They told
me someone had bewitched my husband's mind. So I went to a
practitioner in Dilli Bazaar . . . and consulted him and he said,

"They have oppressed you. There is one man and a woman. One has cast a spell. If you give me the money then I shall reverse that spell. Then he will love you only—otherwise he will leave you like an alley dog."

When I asked how much, I was told that it would cost ten rupees—but I didn't have a single penny. Whatever I was given in my maita—we sometimes went there to receive tika—all that I had put into my husband's pocket. [So I took a loan] and brought the money to the practitioner.

"Don't put a spell on him from my side," I told him. "Only take him away from that side." Because if I have a spell put on him and turn him toward me, then he will go mad. Because he will be attracted to me and towards Hom Nath's mother also. The love spell (mohini) will affect him from both sides and he will go mad. Just get him out from under her spell."

After I had told him this, he blew a spell on some ashes and gave them to me. He packed them in a piece of paper and gave it to me. . . . When I asked him what to do with the ashes, he said that I should place some under my husband's pillow and mix a little with tea or water or anything and feed it to him. I couldn't do it, so I told the field hand who worked and lived with us to do it. He had also been suffering from my husband's bad treatment. . . . So he put a little of those ashes into some tea and gave it to my husband after the ashes had disappeared.

My husband took the tea in the morning, and that evening when it was time to sleep I again felt like weeping. I cried very hard thinking what a karma the goddess of fate had written for me. Here I had no mother, an old man for a husband, and such a co-wife!

But my husband's heart had undergone a change—he had become like he was before. Ten–fifteen days before when I wept, he had never come to me. But on the day we gave him the ashes in the tea he came and asked what the matter was. And then he himself wept also. "I have not treated you properly," he said, "I don't know what happened to me. I won't mistreat you ever again. If I were to mistreat you, then how could I show my face to my brothers who asked for your hand for me? It will be as if I had cut off my own nose and thrown it away. My honor will be lost. I shall not be able to hold my head high. I shall not mistreat you anymore. Don't be anxious—I won't give you any more sorrow. It was my fault, and I'll never do it again. I won't even look upon her face. She did something to me." My husband said this and began to weep. He was weeping on one side and I was weeping on the other. The two of us were weeping in that room in the night. And then my husband loved me.

That is the kind of person she is. A bad person. Her maita is

also bad like that. They don't have any mercy in them, only sin.
. . . Even if she does feel jealous, then what of it? He doesn't go
to her these days. First she had some sores on her buttocks. For four
years she used to fan it saying that it was hot. When that was slightly
better, then her throat began to ache. When that was cured, then
some other sores came out. I don't know what disease it is. But my
husband says that when you "sleep" with someone then both become one, so he might catch her disease so he doesn't go there
nowadays. He says, "I don't like that wife. I cannot make a home
with her. She's unsuitable for me no matter where I take her. . . .
I don't need that wife." When he says this, then what can she do
about it? But when he marries me with all those promises and then
goes back to her, then who would not feel angry? Isn't it so? . . .
When they say that men are sinners, then that is why they say it. It
is very difficult to bear with a co-wife!

Women and Conflict in the Joint Family

After this intimate, intensely personal look into the life of one
member of a joint family, it may be useful to stand back and
view the dynamics of that family as a whole over a period of
time. An extended case study approach is basic to what Van
Velsen (1967) and others have called situational or processual
analysis, in contrast to classical structural analysis. While the
structuralist approach conceives of society as homogeneous and
stable and prefers abstractions to particulars, situational analysis
assumes the ubiquity of conflict and is committed to attending
to the endless individual variation of social reality.

The first premise of situational analysis, then, is that society is invariably based on inconsistent and sometimes contradictory norms and principles of organization. Conflict, such as
the breaking up of the joint family, is an integral part of society
viewed as process. From this perspective the Hindu joint family
brings to mind Van Velsen's (1967:147) comment on the Yao
village of Africa:

The many instances of quarrels, bitter accusations and other symptoms of disunity do not lead to the conclusion that we are confronted by "disintegrating society" (e.g. the result of the British oc-
cupation). Instead [they] show that such periods of bitter and frequent
quarreling are not symptoms of "social pathology" but inherent in

the life cycle of the Yao village from foundation to growth to dispersal.

Partition of the joint family is almost always a painful and contentious process. I mentioned earlier, in the discussion of the worship of the lineage gods, the great pride and security which villagers said they felt as members of a large kul. The same is true, more emphatically, of the *parivar* or family. For, whatever the tensions beneath the surface, the parivar is perceived as a cooperative unit whose members can rely upon each other for support in times of trouble. To break up that unit means considerable loss of efficiency, security, and prestige. This is especially true when—as in the case under study—the split comes not between brothers after the death of the father, but between father and son while the father is still in his prime.

Since it represents a failure of the dominant patrilineal ideal, and since it often involves bitter quarrels and unusual emotional violence, villagers tend to view partition as an aberration. Gould (1968) suggests that sociologists and anthropologists have often added to this impression by talking about Hindu family structure in terms of "static categorizations"—such as joint and nuclear—rather than in terms of a "developmental cycle" based on the continually changing balance between lineal and conjugal ties. We have already encountered these opposing loyalties at work within the joint family—for example, the strict control placed on the conjugal relationship in an attempt to subordinate it to agnatic ties binding the patrilineal unit together.

The conflict between lineal and conjugal relationships is strongly in evidence in the case study that follows. In fact, because of the polygamous situation the conflict is further complicated by the fact that in one instance the conjugal relationship between husband and wife is reinforced by uterine ties between mother and son. *Both* conjugal and uterine ties are pitted against the ideal of patrilineal solidarity. Nevertheless, it is important to emphasize that this case history does not intimate the weakening of the joint family as an ideal model of agnatic solidarity. On the contrary, each of the two new nuclear units created by the partition looks toward becoming a joint family itself and thus a new locus of patrilineal solidarity. What the case history does record is particular individuals tapping the power of alternative, and to some extent contradictory, sets of values present in Hindu culture to meet their own ends in a particular situation.

This brings us to the second premise of situational analysis: the general structural principles of a society must continually be related to the actual observed behavior of particular members of that society. As Van Velsen (1967:136) put it: "Culture is not merely a system of formal practices and beliefs. It is made up essentially of individual reactions to and variations from a traditionally standardized pattern; and indeed, no culture can be understood unless special attention is paid to this range of individual manifestation."

Structural analysis merely provides us with part—albeit an essential part—of the context for understanding the behavior of individuals. This is, I believe, what Geertz (1973:14) means when he writes that "understanding a people's culture exposes their normalness without reducing their particularity." Seeing the "normalness" of individual behavior in an actual conflict situation means that we are able to understand that behavior as articulating (or being justified by) one or another of the conflicting organizational principles that structure the society in question. Seeing the "particularity" of this same behavior depends on our ability to relate the individual's *choice* between these conflicting structural principles to what we have observed of that person's private goals, emotions, and temperament.

The strategies of Devi and Hom Nath's mother and the other acts of individual rebellion and disloyalty lead to the segmentation of the joint family. These strategies are structurally significant—that is, they reflect conflict of shared norms and principles of organization. But at the same time, this behavior remains as unique and exceptional as the human beings from whom it originates.

The family into which Devi was married nearly twenty years ago was a large, fairly prosperous Jaisi Brahman household of more than twenty-five people (see figure 15). Devi's husband, Agni Prasad, was the middle of three brothers. Both the other brothers were married and had numerous children. Agni, however, had had difficulties. Jethi, the girl his parents had found for him when he was thirteen, seemed unable to bear healthy children. After she had borne five sons in succession and seen them all die in infancy, Jethi submitted to her husband's and his parent's joint decision to bring in another wife.

The second wife, whom we shall call Maili, eventually bore a healthy son, Hom Nath, and enjoyed nearly fifteen years as her husband's favored younger wife. During this period, Jethi,

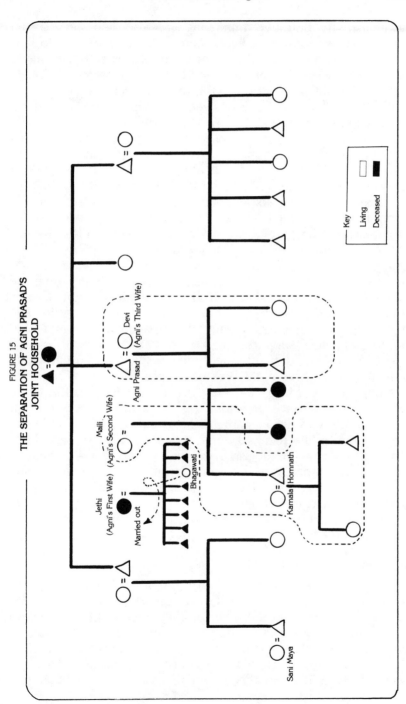

FIGURE 15
THE SEPARATION OF AGNI PRASAD'S
JOINT HOUSEHOLD

his eldest wife, bore two more sons who also died and a daughter named Bhagwati who lived. Agni, however, appears to have had little affection for either Jethi or his daughter Bhagwati, for he sent them both to an adjoining house to care for his invalid father. The old man was irascible and increasingly senile, and could not walk, bathe, eat, or even take care of his bodily functions without Jethi's help.

During his twenties and thirties, Agni seems to have had a reputation for his fondness for women. Maili was not a beautiful woman, and despite the healthy son she bore him, his attentions still wandered. Perhaps Maili's father wished to help his daughter by gaining some control over Agni. At any rate, he offered to give Agni a share of his property and make him a "house son-in-law" (*ghar juwai*) if Agni would settle in Maili's maita. Agni, however, was insulted at the idea that he, the son of a prominent family, could be bought in this way. He continued his wandering and, as we recall from Devi's narrative, became seriously involved with a Gurung woman whom he kept in a rented room in a nearby bazaar town. Shortly after his mistress died, Agni decided—against his parent's advice and without their financial support—to take a third wife.

Agni had a difficult time finding a suitable girl, but finally, with the help of his elder brother (whose son had married Devi's cousin Sano Maya), he found Devi. But Devi's father would agree to the marriage only after Agni had promised to put part of his property in Devi's name as life-portion (*juni bhag*), a portion of joint estate retained by an individual—usually an elderly man or woman—to support him during his lifetime, which reverts to the joint estate at his/her death. Most families cannot bargain this way for a life-portion at their daughter's marriage and must place their hopes for their daughter's security in the fairness of her husband's family and in her ability to have sons. But because of Agni's reputation, and the fact that he was older and already had two wives, he had to offer something more concrete.

Several years after Devi came, Agni's father died, and the three brothers split up the patrilineal estate. Agni was given the big family house, and the other brothers received extra property to pay for the building of their own new houses. Agni and his elder brother sided together against the youngest brother in a dispute over the division of the father's life-portion. Both elder brothers, who had not been formally educated, felt that they should get a larger share of the father's portion since family money had gone to educate the youngest son, who now held a salaried government post. The youngest brother would not give in, and Agni's family still does not speak to the younger brother, who lives next door.

The underlying tension between the women in the household during the next fifteen years is well documented in Devi's account. Jethi felt that she and her daughter Bhagwati had been neglected because of Maili, the second wife, so Jethi formed an alliance with Devi. Despite Maili's best attempts to win Agni over, Devi seems to have gained an increasing hold on Agni's affections. Maili must have realized her declining influence more than a decade ago because, when her son Hom Nath was only twelve, she attempted to get his share of the joint estate and set up a separate household alone with her son. Agni and his eldest brother (along with general village opinion) persuaded her to wait until Hom Nath was older and could be married so she would have a daughter-in-law to help her. Maili gave in and the crisis passed.

Six years later, Maili succeeded in getting her son married. Devi, however, had convinced her husband to marry Hom Nath to a girl from her own maiti area to whom she was distantly related. Probably Devi hoped that this would make the new daughter-in-law, Kamala, her ally rather than Maili's.

Not long after Hom Nath's wedding, and about a year and a half before I met the family, the eldest wife, Jethi, died after a long illness. Villagers speak of her with a combination of pity—that she lost all her sons, had two co-wives, and died a painful lingering death—and respect, because she was very religious and suffered her karma without complaint. In fact, she has been favorably compared more than once in my presence with Agni's other wives, whose squabbling and mutual backbiting the village has watched for nearly two decades.

Jethi's unmarried daughter, Bhagwati, continued as Devi's ally after her mother's death. Devi did less and less of the difficult and less prestigious "outside work," claiming that she was frail and had never really regained her strength after the birth of her second child three years earlier. Agni spent a good deal of money calling in local shamans and buying mysterious "tonics," but nothing seemed to cure Devi's vague complaints (which she confided to me she suspected to be the result of yet another spell cast by Maili) and restore her to what she remembered as her former strength and plumpness. She and Bhagwati (who, as a daughter, was not expected to do the hardest work in her maita) did the cooking, daily worship of the family gods, laundry, and the lighter chores around the house, while Maili (whose persistent cough and infected sores were ignored) and Kamala, the new daughter-in-law, were sent to the fields. Both mother-in-law and daughter-in-law resented Devi, and the traditional enemies became allies.

Despite all these underlying tensions, day-to-day interactions in the household were quite harmonious when I first became acquainted with the family. The women worked cooperatively, showed affection for each other's children, and (except for Kamala, who as a new daughter-in-law was very quiet and withdrawn) they talked and joked freely with one another. Devi's domination of the household seemed natural at first because of her greater energy and intelligence. Agni was obviously more attached to his vivacious, attractive younger wife and hardly even talked with Maili. In contrast to Devi, whose long black hair was neatly combed and oiled, and whose smooth forehead was always adorned with a carefully made red tika mark, Maili seemed old and unkempt and much less sure of herself. At first I had thought she was a servant and had no idea she was Agni's wife. Yet, there were signs of some lingering affection: sometimes Agni would give Maili his unfinished cigarette (Devi doesn't smoke); and once he even praised Maili to me as a hard worker.

Devi was much more actively concerned with dharma than Maili, and she was rather ostentatiously fastidious about maintaining the rules of ritual purity in her kitchen and observing every possible religious fast. Though Devi actually came from much further in the hills than Maili, she considered herself more sophisticated than her co-wife. It was she who criticized Maili's slovenly habits to me in the other woman's absence and gave me the first clues of the mutual animosity beneath the surface.

The first open quarrel, however, did not break out between the co-wives but between Devi and her "daughter-in-law," Kamala. Ostensibly, the argument was over a fight between their two young daughters. Actually, it arose out of Kamala's resentment that Devi—her classifactory mother-in-law, but only seven or eight years her senior—did so little of the hard work. For five days Kamala locked herself in her room and wouldn't eat or work. (Villagers described it as "not eating" because she didn't eat a boiled rice meal, but actually she ate some pounded rice and other foods in her room.) Following this five-day seclusion, she took her daughter and went, without permission, for a long stay in her maita.

During this period Maili and her son Hom Nath took Kamala's side in the quarrel and refused to speak to the rest of the family. In fact, Hom Nath did not return from his city job to visit his parents' home on his holidays but went instead to his wife's maita to visit her. There were rumors that he was going to rent a room for his wife in town and move out of his father's house altogether. Agni Prasad was pained by his son's behavior, and embarrassed to have his household situation discussed all over the village, but he continued to support Devi's view of the situation.

Then it was discovered, beyond a doubt, that before her quarrel with Devi, Kamala had stolen (with the aid of a young neighbor who confessed to the crime) sixty rupees' worth of grain from the family stores. Apparently Kamala didn't feel that she and her fifteen-month-old daughter had been given proper new clothes at Dasai, and she felt she deserved something after all the labor she had contributed to the family. I saw Hom Nath's visible shock when he heard that his wife had stolen from the family. He said he could not leave his father's house for one who stole his father's grain.

By the time Kamala returned from her maita, the balance of sympathy had swung against her. Even Hom Nath and Maili, who had originally sided with her, now refused to speak to her. Hom Nath even talked of bringing in another wife and sending Kamala back to her maita for good. People remarked on the new flannel outfit that Kamala's little daughter had supposedly been given by her mother's brothers, but that had probably been bought for her with the stolen money. For weeks Devi's and Maili's favorite game was to ask Kamala's daughter (who was just learning to speak) if her mother was a thief, and then if she was a thief's daughter. When the little girl innocently answered yes, everyone would laugh and praise her cleverness. The child loved it until suddenly one day she realized they were making fun of her in some way.

For about four months Kamala was generally ostracized by all the family, though there were those in the village who sympathized with her because she had to put up with the harsh demands of Devi. Then Kamala's maiti humbled themselves to intervene on her behalf. Kamala's brother came and mediated

the situation. Kamala wept and apologized and begged forgiveness—from everyone except Devi.

After this, Maili's attitude toward Kamala, her former ally
against Devi, began to soften. Kamala began to do conspicuous
service for her mother-in-law, massaging her feet with oil at
night, etc. One night Kamala, who was scrubbing the pots with
Maili after the evening rice meal, openly asked Devi why she
never helped. "Why do the mother-in-law and daughter-in-law
have to do all the work?" she asked. After that Devi angrily
cleaned her own plates for a few weeks.

Before long Hom Nath's attitude toward his wife also began to change. He had refused to sleep with her after the dis-
covery of the theft, but the family members now reported that
they had begun to "talk sweetly" with each other at night again.
Still he publicly disowned her and refused to leave his father's
house, which (so the other members of the family said) was
what his wife wanted him to do.

This state of uneasy truce lasted nearly a year, during
which time Bhagwati, daughter of the deceased eldest wife, was
married and went away to live with her husband's family. This
left Devi without a female friend in the household, since Kamala and her mother-in-law had reasserted their alliance.

Several months after Bhagwati's wedding, Hom Nath and
Maili asked for their share of the family property. Agni Prasad
tried to dissuade his son, but the combination of Kamala's encouragement and Hom Nath's long-suppressed resentment of his
father's favoritism toward his stepmother Devi overrode his sense
of loyalty to his father. In a nonpolygamous situation, Hom Nath's
uterine ties to his mother would have supported his sense of
obligation to his father and helped maintain the solidarity of the
joint family. Instead, Hom Nath's affection for his mother only
reinforced his conjugal ties to his wife, since both women perceived a separation as a way to escape Devi's domination and
improve their own positions.

Both Agni Prasad and Devi blamed the daughter-in-law,
Kamala, more than Maili for the split. Devi predicted that as
soon as the separation had taken place, Kamala would cease
serving her mother-in-law and begin to quarrel with her. As protection for Maili, Agni even insisted on registering the land in
her name, because he said he did not trust Hom Nath to continue to support her properly as Kamala's influence over him
increased.

Agni lost considerable prestige in the village, since the split revealed that he was not really in command of his wives or his eldest son. The village was divided in their opinion about which of the women was most to blame. Some thought Maili was in the wrong because she was essentially divorcing her husband, and such open defiance flouted all ideals of proper wifely subservience. Others thought Devi was finally reaping the rewards of her arrogance and laziness. Still others thought the blame lay with Kamala for putting a barrier between son and father. Interestingly, Agni's younger brother (with whom he had quarreled over the father's land) sided with Hom Nath, got him a higher paying job in town, and began inviting Hom Nath's little family for festival meals, etc.

The division of the property was a long, acrimonious process. In principle, the estate was to be divided into three portions; one for Hom Nath and his mother; one for Devi and her son; and one as Agni Prasad's life-portion. But these were not to be equal portions, because the expenses of Hom Nath's initiation and wedding had already come out of the joint estate, so some property had to be added to Agni's share to meet these same expenses for Devi's son. Likewise, the future wedding expenses for Devi's little daughter also had to be added to Agni's portion. Since Agni had taken a loan from the Agricultural Bank to help pay for Hom Nath's wedding, the division of the remaining loan repayments also had to be decided. Hom Nath offered to take up the entire remaining debt in return for the share of land that was being added to Agni's portion to pay the wedding expenses of Devi's son. But this was not acceptable to Agni.

The most violent disagreement, however, arose over the house itself. Hom Nath wanted to physically partition the handsome four-story baked-brick structure by erecting a dividing wall and constructing a separate stairwell and door. One sees many village houses divided in this manner—physical symbols of the failure of the ideal of agnatic solidarity. Agni, however, refused to disfigure his house. Instead, he gave his son the brick-paved courtyard and a small two-story mud-brick house overlooking it which adjoined the big house. Hom Nath and his mother were furious. At one point they threatened to tear down the big house brick by brick unless they got half of it. Maili went to her maita and returned with her brother, who threatened to bring suit against Agni Prasad. Devi maintained that they could not divide the house because half of it had been included in her own life-portion (which she mentioned in her narrative). Since she had borne a son and felt secure in her husband's household, her father had never officially registered the life-portion papers. Nevertheless, she felt they gave her the right to claim the big house as part of her son's share. Her brothers firmly supported this view when they visited their sister.

The crisis of partition of the joint estate is only one instance where a woman's support from her filiafocal relationships in her maita can be important in establishing and securing her position in her ghar. There is a shared belief that a married daughter has been completely "turned over" to the mercy of her husband's house,[11] and there is the exaggerated respect which the maiti must show to the wife-taking affines. Nevertheless, a woman's consanguineal relatives—especially her brothers—are often drawn through the ties of affection that mark the filiafocal relationship into her domestic problems in her husband's house. In this instance, the filafocal relatives of both the co-wives and the daughter-in-law were all involved, each supporting the positions and demands of their respective kinswomen.

In addition to his demands for the big house, Hom Nath also complained that the original division of land and movable goods had not been fair because it had been supervised by Agni Prasad's elder brother, who, he claimed, was biased in favor of Agni Prasad. While no one took Maili's brother's threat of legal action very seriously, a second accounting of the share was undertaken. An elderly respected Brahman, who serves as priest for many village families and heads a large joint family household, was called in to arbitrate a new division of the property. It was decided that Hom Nath was to be given a larger share of the land, but that the big house was to remain with Agni and Devi. Disputes continued about the allotment of household articles, such as metal vessels, the family radio, and even a clock. Doors were kept firmly locked after Maili walked into Agni Prasad's kitchen one day and removed a large copper vessel that she said had been part of her dowry.

Maili accused her husband of having several years earlier given money for the wedding of Devi's brother that should have gone to her son Hom Nath. Agni was also rumored to have hidden joint estate monies in a bank account. The fact that he was still working hard to pay off the debt from Hom Nath's wedding, however, made most people skeptical of this tale. In retaliation for these perceived injustices, Hom Nath refused to pay his father back for the wages of the laborers who had worked what was now his land planting the rice crop which he would now harvest.

I was present on the day when an official (*amini*) came to measure and formally record the division of the land. The old Brahman who had arbitrated the second property division went out to the fields with them, and father and son spoke to each other only indirectly through the old man. Both Agni and Hom Nath were extremely uncomfortable. They seemed embarrassed and avoided looking at each other. The women involved sat directly behind their respective men. Once, when Agni seemed to be weakening on a disputed point—who was going to get the cattle shed—Devi plucked a piece of barley and threw it squarely at his back. It was both a signal to him and a gesture of her disgust with his weakness. Agni Prasad held out for the cattle shed.

When the official had gone, one of the fiercest open quarrels I observed during my fieldwork broke out in the courtyard between the two houses. Devi berated Hom Nath for treating her so badly after she had "cleaned up his shit for him when he was a child—just like his own mother." Hom Nath retorted that Devi had always treated his mother Maili like her personal servant. Then the women began to yell at each other and exchange insulting epithets. Agni, looking miserable and ashamed, turned his back and went into the big house to wait for the commotion to cease.

After this, Agni's household stopped using what had been the joint courtyard and cleared a piece of land on the far side of the big house to use for drying their grain. The back door became the main entrance to Agni Prasad's house. Agni said that the large kitchen on the top floor where the family used to eat seemed lonely now, so the kitchen was moved to a smaller room on the second floor.

At Dasai, to everyone's relief, Hom Nath and his mother came to receive tika from Agni Prasad. Kamala, however, did not appear, and Hom Nath and Maili did not stay to eat the traditional meal of meat and curd. They explained proudly that they had slaughtered their own goat (sent from Kamala's maita along with a milch cow). Hom Nath also came at Tihar to receive tika from his two half-sisters, but he pointedly avoided speaking to Devi.

Thus the crisis of partition passed. More than a year later relations between the two families were still cool, though ironically, Maili now speaks with Agni and Devi and visits their house. Kamala has had a son and (as Devi predicted) ceased being so solicitous of her mother-in-law. Kamala, who used to be so withdrawn in the big house, now talks and jokes openly with her husband.

Devi continues, despite her obvious vigor and still youthful looks, to complain of her frailness and her inability to gain weight. She brought in an old woman from near her maita to help around the house (in exchange for food, shelter, and some clothing). But the old woman left after less than ten days in Devi's employ. Then Devi began trying to convince Agni Prasad that it was time to get their fourteen-year-old son married. Agni was reluctant, not only because of the expense, which he had expected to postpone for another six or seven years, but because he considers himself a modern educated man. Nowadays most boys in Narikot who can afford to go to school, like Agni's son, are not married off until their education is complete. In the end, however, Devi's will prevailed. A girl was found and the marriage took place. Now Devi, whose story began with her own entry into Agni's household as a new bride, is herself a stern mother-in-law. On a recent visit, as the daughter-in-law was preparing tea downstairs, Devi began to tell me how girls these days were only interested in wearing lipstick and carrying fancy umbrellas rather than doing field work and making themselves useful.

This case history, coupled with Devi's own narrative, forcefully demonstrates that conflict is an integral part of the fabric of Brahman-Chetri kinship and family organization. That, however, was only one reason for presenting this material. It was equally important to get to know Devi and at least something of the choices and limitations of her particular life situation. This is not a matter of "emotional empathy"—though perhaps that is an element which should be admitted as well—but rather, of immersion to the greatest extent possible in the observable complexities of Devi's situation. It represents an attempt to move from an analysis of women's *roles* to an understanding of their *lives*—from the abstractions of social structure to the particulars of social process.

Notes

1. I mentioned earlier that marriage entails strict gotra exogamy and preferably village exogamy.

2. If a daughter is married, only her male paternal cousins observe the five days; female paternal cousins don't observe any mourning.

3. As much as a month before the Rala Rali festival, unmarried girls gather together and construct clay or mud images of Siva and Parvati. On the first day of the celebrations, the images are solemnly married to each other by the girls. One party acts as Siva's family and the other as Parvati's, and none of the marriage rituals are omitted. Then the next day the girls, singing funeral songs, carry the images to the nearest river or tank, where they are thrown in and washed away.

4. The one exception in the daughter-in-law's constricted relations with affinal men is her relationship with her husband's younger brother (devar). With him, she may have a more relaxed, joking relationship and some emotional outlet in her husband's family. Potentially, a woman's relations with her younger brother-in-law have the same affectional quality as her relations within her maita, especially if he is much younger. In one family I observed, there had been a quarrel and the daughter-in-law and her husband's family had not spoken for a year (though living under the same roof). But she was still friendly with her twelve-year-old brother-in-law and even invited him to come with her on a visit to her maita. (The boy's family did not allow him to go.)

5. Edward Harper (1964:181) calls this "respect pollution."

6. It is considered disrespectful to stop massaging before one is told to. One woman told how when she was a new bride her husband had fallen asleep when she was rubbing his legs and she had been afraid to stop in case he was just teasing her by pretending to fall asleep!

7. I observed the same reaction among women to fights among their children. Women would enter these fights only when they were already angry at the mother of the child who harmed their own. Otherwise, children's battles, however bloody, were largely ignored.

8. If her husband's father had more than one wife, she will have several mothers-in-law, and if his paternal grandmother is still alive she will have a grandmother-in-law as well!

9. Interestingly, the bride is instructed to tend to her mother-in-law (v. 27) before she goes to her husband to serve him (v. 28).

10. One woman whose husband took a second wife during the course of my fieldwork did try legal action, but with no success. Her problems have been increased now; the husband's family refuses to take her back because of their loss of face in the courts, and so she (with her four-year-old daughter) will probably have to live in her maita as a kind of indigent "maiden aunt" for the rest of her life. For further discussion of the laws concerning polygamy in the Nepalese National Code see Bennett 1979.

11. Recall the traditional farewell statement made by the girl's mother to the groom: "If you take care of her the merit is yours; if you kill her then the sin is yours."

CHAPTER 6

Female Sexuality
and the Patrifocal /
Filiafocal Opposition

The basic outlines of the Hindu perception of women are already clear from our investigation of their place in the kinship and family structures. Women are problematic—partly because of their association with sexuality and fertility and partly because they are perceived as destructive to agnatic solidarity. But what gives this ambivalent view of women such power in society is the fact that it is reinforced by and reflected in so many of the conceptual and symbolic structures of Hinduism. Throughout our discussion of religion and kinship in Narikot we have been dealing with these symbolic structures, though we have not focused on them as such. I will turn now, in the final chapters of this study, to a more intentional investigation of the myths and rituals that deal specifically with women and that express on the symbolic level some of the contradictory meanings attached to the female sex in Hindu culture.

One of the most powerful and pervasive symbolic structures concerning women is the set of meanings attached to the female body. The body, with its reproductive processes, is a vehicle through which both positive and negative feelings about women—and about sexuality itself—are expressed, the ambivalence about one reinforcing the ambivalence about the other. The negative view of sex in ascetic ideology combines with the patriline's mistrust of affinal women to produce a deep mistrust of the sexual and seductive aspect of women. This is perhaps most strikingly evident in the Hindu attitude toward menstrual blood—the central physiological symbol of female sexuality.

The Symbolism of Menstrual Blood

In Brahman-Chetri culture menstrual blood is a strong source of pollution—particularly to initiated males. During the first three days of every menses, women become polluted and untouchable. As one woman explained, "We become like female Damai (damini). We become like female dogs."[1] For these three days a woman must not enter the kitchen, touch food or water that others will eat or drink, or even worship the gods or the ancestor spirits. She may not comb her hair or oil it, and she sleeps separately in a downstairs room.[2] Also she may not touch an adult man. Some very orthodox women also avoid touching other women or children (except their own nursing infants), but most women touch each other freely. Thus, high-caste initiated males are singled out as the group specifically endangered by menstruation, and by extension, the female sexuality of which menstruation is a prime symbol.

The segregation of women during their menstrual periods is strictly observed, as the terms used by villagers for menstruation indicate. The more idiomatic term used is na chune, which literally means "not touching," and the slightly more polite word is para sarne, which means "moving away." Older informants told me that in the time of their mothers-in-law (i.e., "the old days") women were hidden in a dark room away from the sun (a symbol of male purity associated with asceticism) and out of the sight of all males for the first three days of their periods. Food, water, and a brass pan for bodily eliminations were brought to them, and they could not stir out or even speak to others until the early dawn of the fourth day, when they had to bathe and purify themselves before sunrise. Each step they took beyond the dark room brought them the sin equivalent to having killed a cow. Nowadays such strict seclusion of women during their periods occurs only at menarche, in the rituals which will be described subsequently. Nevertheless, it is clear that among contemporary rural Brahmans and Chetris, the ritual impurity of menstruation and menstrual blood remains strong.

A Nepali ritual text, The Story of the Rishi Pancami Fast (Rsi Pancami Vrata Katha, Sharma 2022a)[3] describes how menstrual blood came to be polluting. According to the myth, Indra, the king of the gods, sought help from Brahma to purify himself from the heinous sin of killing a Brahman (Brahman-hatya) which he had committed. Brahma helped Indra by dividing the sin into four parts and throwing them in four different places.

The first fell into the flames of the fire, the second into the river, the third on the mountain, and the fourth into the menstrual blood. And that is why these women have to be set aside with great care. They should not touch anything at all. They should set themselves apart, and this is the command of Brahma. . . ! All four varnas should, first and foremost, forsake the woman during her menstruation, because on the first day she is like a *candalini* [accursed and damned woman]; on the second day she is as sinful as one who has killed a Brahman. On the third day she is equal to a *rajhki* or *dhobini* [untouchable washerwoman]; and on the fourth day she is purified. During those three days a most grievous sin is committed. And in order to destroy that sin, to destroy all sin and all kinds of defects, it is necessary to undertake the fast of Rishi Pancami [Sharma 2022a:10–13, my trans. with Prithivi Raj Chettri]

Village women do not feel the sense of personal sin that the text imputes to them. On the contrary, women cite the myth to explain that they are not individually responsible for menstrual pollution unless they disobey the restrictions. Nevertheless, there seems to be a vague sense of sin attached to the female sex as a whole on account of menstruation. Women often mentioned it as the reason they were "lower" and less ritually pure than men, even though many women feel they are actually more religious than men. When I asked one informant why women menstruate, she explained with her version of the myth:

They say that this is a curse given by Bhagwan [God] to women. . . . Bhagwan has distributed sin between the Ganga [holy river goddess], women, and firewood. Just as when wood is set on fire, some foam (*phij*) comes—that foam is sin. They say that when there is foam in the Ganges, then the Ganges is menstruating (*na chune*). They say our menstruation is also a sin, and if our sin is not secluded then it becomes a great sin. . . . Women must have sinned, I don't know. It may be that the sin which was committed long ago has been distributed to all. . . . We must have done something in the last life so He distributed the sin and sent us menstruation.

Then I asked her, "Didn't the men commit any sin at all?" Her reply expressed her skepticism: "No, they didn't. But as far as I can see, it's the men who commit more sin than the women!"

Despite its strongly felt and strictly observed negative import, menstrual blood also has some positive connotations through its connection with fertility. For even though Hindu villagers emulate the ascetic ideal, they still place a high value on the production of offspring, and according to village beliefs about the physiology of conception, menstrual blood is the material out of which much-desired children are formed in the womb. Informants explain that during pregnancy the blood which does not appear in the menses is collecting or solidifying to form the child—"a baby is born after the blood of ten months has solidified" (Das mahina ko ragat jamera nani paucha).

The ambivalence toward menstrual blood is expressed in the myth given above. For, although menstrual blood is connected with the grave sin of Brahman murder, the connection is arbitrary. Furthermore, the other three things which each receive a fourth part of the sin—the fire, the river, and the mountain—are all considered sources of purity in the Hindu tradition. The structural message of the myth is that menstrual blood too is basically a good thing, but owing to human weakness (i.e., Indra's violent crime), it must be regulated.

This positive aspect of menstrual blood is reiterated in the traditional concept of the ritu dan (ritu, season or period of fertility; dan, religious gift), which decrees that it is the husband's religious duty to sleep with his wife on the fourth day of her menstrual period after her purificatory bath. One informant explained: "If a man doesn't sleep with his wife on the fourth day he gets the sin of murderer, because at that time there is a child in the womb—a little menstrual blood is still coming."

Village women have no knowledge of ovulation and its connection with their period of fertility. Instead, they associate the fertile period directly with menstrual blood.[4] The blood which comes during the first three days of menstruation is "bad," and women are believed to be infertile during this period. Yet sex on the fourth day after ritual purification "while a little blood is still coming" is believed most favorable for conception. In one woman's words, "The blood is the same. But the blood which is impure or spoilt comes out when we are menstruating (na chune). When the bad blood (na-ramro) has come out, then the baby is formed out of the good blood (ramro)."

My observations of village women's reactions to the ritu dan rule further adds to the complexity. Although all my informants knew about the ritu dan requirement on the fourth day, quite a few women could not overcome their negative feelings about menstrual blood in order to observe it. They said they did not always do ritu dan because often they were still discharging on the fourth day and either felt ashamed (laj lagyo) to go to their husband when they were called or disgusted (ghin lagyo) at the idea of intercourse while they were still discharging. These women said they would pray for forgiveness in their neglect of ritu dan and wait until their menstrual flow ceased.

This ambivalence is but another expression of the conflicting Hindu attitude toward sexuality. A woman's menstrual period is when she is most blatantly sexual, and thus strict segregation for the first three days represents control imposed on the potentially unruly and destructive forces of female sexuality. Through the rituals of bathing, washing their hair and clothes, and the drinking of cow urine (gaut) with ritually purifying powers on the fourth day, women cleanse their sexuality each month and direct it toward its legitimate end: the production of offspring to carry on the lineage.

Besides this monthly purification, there are two other major rituals in Brahman-Chetri culture directed at the purification of menstrual pollution and, on a deeper level, the channeling of female sexuality. They are the Tij–Rishi Pancami complex and the menarche rites (gupha basne or "sitting in a cave"). These two rituals focus on the problem of female sexuality with respect to affinal and consanguineal women, respectively. Through the symbolic forms used in the rituals, it becomes possible to understand some of the broader meanings underlying the patrifocal/filafocal opposition.

Tij and Rishi Pancami—Channeling the Sexuality of Women

The Tij–Rishi Pancami complex consists of two closely related festivals of fasting and ritual purification in which a woman ensures long life to her husband and purifies herself of the possible sin of having touched a man during her menstrual period. It is particularly concerned with affinal women, women in their patrifocal and specifically sexual role as wife. To the patrilineal unit, affinal women, like menstrual blood, are at once necessary and dangerous. They must be brought in to produce children if the lineage is to continue. At the same time, they are a threat to the joint family as a unit and their own husbands individually.

We are already familiar with the divisiveness caused by women within the patrilineal joint family. Since the status of the daughter-in-law is extremely low in her ghar, her goals are likely to be counter in many respects to those of the agnatic group— aimed at the prosperity of herself, her husband, and their children rather than that of the patrilineal joint-family unit as a whole. Furthermore, her only influence in the joint family (until she has a grown son) is through her husband. To gain power she must use her sexuality to win him away from his ingrained loyalties to his parents and brothers. Often, of course, these lineal ties are already frayed by her husband's restlessness under parental control and the strong sense of competition between brothers. However, since agnatic rivalry is contrary to the dominant patrifocal ideology, affinal women—their devious and contentious nature and, above all, their seductive wiles—are usually the focus of blame for the constant household quarrels and ultimately for the inevitable segmentation of the joint family. Although it tends to be exaggerated by the patrilineal bias, this characterization of women as the divisive members of the group is, as we have seen, not entirely inaccurate.

But besides the threat which affinal women present to agnatic solidarity, there is a strong belief that women are somehow responsible for their husband's long life. In fact for the first part of the festival each woman must do a strict fast meant to ensure the long life of her husband.[5] There is as well a definite sense of sin attached to widowhood which is expressed at Tij. Women who have been widowed during the past year may participate in the purifying fast at Tij and the bathing which follows on Rishi Pancami as a kind of penitence for their husband's death, but they may not on either occasion participate in the auspicious worship of Siva or the rishis that follows these austerities.

Villagers often explain the wife's responsibility for her husband's long life in terms of her karma: some sin in a previous life causes a woman to become a widow in this one. In myth, the connection is often made between the wife's chastity and her husband's lifespan. For example, the demon Jalander loses his life the moment his wife Brinda is seduced by Visnu, even though Visnu disguised himself as her husband. It is perhaps this idea which finds expression in the colloquial word randi, which means both widow and prostitute (Turner 1931).

Carstairs (1967:156) has pointed out a more direct threat

to the husband in the form of the Hindu wife's sexual demands on her husband: "Sexual love is considered the keenest pleasure known to the senses. But it is felt to be destructive to a man's physical and spiritual well being. Women are powerful, demanding, seductive—and ultimately destructive."[6]

The dangers women represent both to the individual male and to his patrilineal unit are well expressed in the mythology surrounding the seven rishis and their notorious wives. We first encountered them in our discussion of gotra organization and then again in the analysis of Janai Purni, a male purification ritual that is structurally very similar to the Tij–Rishi Pancami purification festival for women. We recall that the rishis are worshiped on Janai Purni and invoked into the new sacred thread (*janai*) which the men put on that day after their elaborate bathing (chapter 4).

The rishis, in their role as gotra founders, represent the continuity of the patriline as an institution and the claim of each individual lineage to purity of descent. They also embody the ascetic/householder contradiction. They are ascetic forest dwellers; but they are also householders because they have wives. The wives of the rishis, with their distracting sexuality, their own unsated sexual demands, and eventual unfaithfulness, delude the rishis and hinder them in their spiritual pursuits. "The virtue of the wife is often the crucial point in the forest dweller's dilemma" (O'Flaherty 1973:81)—the flaw that upsets the tenuous balance of the householder/ascetic opposition.

Although the rishis' wives are supposed to be, like their husbands, paragons of virtue and restraint, "the ascetic tradition, based as it is upon a profound misogyny, is quick to challenge the chastity of any woman and is, therefore, suspicious of the wife of the forest dweller" (O'Flaherty 1973:80). O'Flaherty cites many myths (1973:80–81, 98–106) wherein the loss of chastity—even in thought or by accident—on the part of the sages' wives cause the sages to lose the power (spiritual and physical) they have gained through their long, arduous austerities.

The Brahmans and Chetris of Nepal have their own version of this story. It appears in the *Swasthani Vrata Katha* (The Story of the Fast to the Goddess Swasthani) and is here woven into the story of Siva's madness after the death of his beloved wife Sati Devi. Most villagers are well acquainted with this short text of approximately 300 pages. It is read, a chapter a night, in the homes of those who are literate during the holy month of

Magh (January–February). Below, then, is the Nepali version of what O'Flaherty calls the "Pine Forest Story." It forms part of the mythic backdrop for the worship of the rishis on Janai Purni and Tij–Rishi Pancami:

After Sri Mahadev [Siva] had brought his mind under control, he realized that Sati Devi's body was gone. He felt disconcerted and decided to go north to perform austerities. But by mistake he took the route to the South and arrived at Karnatak forest. There was a village there called Brahmapur. The rishis of the village had gone to bathe in the holy river. The wives of the rishis saw Siva. One of them pointed at him and said, "Look, there goes Mahadev! He is roaming about like a madman because of Sati Devi's death. Our rishis are weak of body because they eat only once in twenty-four hours. They are incapable of giving us sexual satisfaction, so let us follow Mahadev!"

So the one hundred wives of the rishis followed him. But the rishis who had gone to take their bath at the river came to know of it and they went in search of their wives. After some distance, they caught up with them. The rishis charged Mahadev with enticing their wives away. Mahadev replied that he was not guilty of such a crime. Then the rishis pointed out the throng of women following him and asked Mahadev who and what they were. Mahadev looked around and was surprised to find a crowd of women behind him. He was amazed to see the wives of the rishis, and he flatly denied having seduced them.

"I don't know why they have followed me," he said. "It must be your phallus which is responsible!" replied the rishis. So they cursed his phallus to fall from his body. Because of the rishis' curse, Mahadev's phallus fell off from his body. Out of it another phallus of flames (jyotirling) appeared, and it continued growing until it covered the entire world. At this terrible calamity the entire host of gods led by Brahma, the rishis, yaksas, gandarvas, kinnaras, and daityas went in a group to Visnu and said, "Oh Baikuntha Nath! Mahadev's flame phallus has grown until it covers the whole creation. We have come to inform you!"

Visnu acted immediately and covered it [the flame phallus] with his body. At this the phallus became small at once. Seeing this all the gods, yaksas, gandarvas, kinnaras, and daityas thanked Visnu and went back home. Sri Mahadev issued out of the flame phallus and addressed the rishis and cursed them. "When I was without fault you cursed me," he said. So he counter-cursed them for their crime saying, "Let your words be not truthful and thus without force, and let your wives be unfaithful to you." After delivering this curse he went north and practiced meditation and devout austerities [Sharma 2022b:142–45, my trans.]

Despite this mythic lapse (i.e., the rishis lost their detachment and became jealous of their wives' sexual attraction toward Siva), the rishis in their role as gotra founders continue to represent the ideal of male ascetic purity to Hindu villagers of Nepal. After all, it was their wives, not they, who caused the trouble. We recall that each lineage traces its symbolic descent from one of the rishis (though not necessarily one of the seven) through its gotra affiliation. As T. N. Madan (1962) has pointed out, gotra does not represent an actual kinship grouping, its only social function being the regulation of marriage. Nevertheless, the *fiction* of patrilineal descent from the ancestral rishi is conceptually important in validating the Hindu patrilineal ideology. The ascetic rishis provide a kind of spiritual pedigree for lineages which by their very nature must be deeply involved with the worldly concerns and distractions of the householder's path. In this sense then, the rishis represent both the individual high-caste male householder and the collective patriline to which he belongs. Both are endangered by affinal women—the lusty and now eternally unfaithful wives of the rishis.

The Tij–Rishi Pancami complex expresses this dangerous and potentially divisive power of women and their sexuality. It also attempts, through myth and ritual, to reintegrate that power into the structures of family and kinship which it threatens.

Tij–Rishi Pancami is actually comprised of two separate festivals, on the third (*tij*) and fifth day (*pancami*) of the bright half of Bhadau (August–September).[7] As mentioned earlier, Tij is meant to ensure the long life of one's husband, while Rishi Pancami is meant to purify women from the possible sin of having touched a man during their menstrual period. But as Bista (1969:7–18) noted, Nepalis think of the two as a single event, because they are both exclusively for women. In my view, this also comes about because the express purposes of the two are conceptually related. Women invariably blended the two goals together when they explained the activities of either of these two days.

The festival, which consists of purificatory fasting (on Tij) and rigorous ritual bathing (on Rishi Pancami), begins paradoxically with extreme indulgence in rich, expensive foods which the women eat at a late-night feast on the eve of Tij (*dar khane*). Women explained that the purpose of their gorge is to "keep a fire burning in the stomach" during the strict fast on Tij. But we should perhaps also keep in mind the romantic overtones associated with gifts of special food. The men of the family, if they possibly can, must provide whatever foods their wives demand for the feast. As Bista (1969:10–11) pointed out, the unreasonable nature of women's requests and the great trouble and expense that men must endure to satisfy them is a common theme of jokes during Tij.

Tij is also the occasion for a lavish gift of food and clothes to one's daughter's mother-in-law during the first year after marriage. Rather like the *samdhini bhet* gifts mentioned earlier, it is an attempt on the part of the bride's maita to make her life in the ghar easier by appeasing her mother-in-law. During the first year the bride usually stays in her ghar for Tij, but in subsequent years there is always a subtle tug-o'-war between maita and ghar during this period of heavy agricultural work. Younger daughters-in-law expect to be allowed to return to their maita to celebrate Tij and have a few days' vacation from the demands of their ghar. A daughter-in-law who is kept in her ghar during Tij because there is work to be done is very likely to sulk quite openly and to receive the sympathy of her neighbors when she complains.

On the day of Tij itself, women reenact the famous fast of the goddess Parvati, who performed austerities to obtain Siva as her husband. This story is part of the traditional Puranic corpus of the Saivite mythology. The Nepali version with which village women are most familiar appears in the *Swasthani Vrata Katha*.

In this story, Parvati (or Uma), the daughter of King Himalaya, learns from her girlfriends that her father has arranged her marriage to Visnu. Parvati is distraught, because she had always wanted to marry Siva. (He was her husband in one of her previous incarnations as Sati Devi.) On her friends' advice, she runs away to a hidden spot by the banks of the river where she makes a sand phallus, Siva's symbol, and worships it. Siva notices her devotion and, pleased, grants her a boon. She asks for Siva as her husband, and her wish is granted.[8]

In some Indian versions of the myth, Parvati undergoes extreme austerities before her wish comes true. For 3600 years she spends the hot season in the midst of four fires, with the sun as a fifth, and the cold season immersed neck deep in an icy mountain stream. She reduces her diet to water, then dry wind-blown leaves, and finally to nothing at all. Parvati, who is usually portrayed in Hindu art as a beautiful, sensual young woman, is sometimes depicted as an emaciated asexual hag at the end of her austerities. This extreme austerity (tapas) is one mythic solution to the Hindu conflict between asceticism and fertility. Parvati's body has been so purified that there is nothing left of her sexuality to threaten or contaminate her beloved ascetic Siva!

Parvati's austerities as they are depicted in the *Swasthani Vrata Katha*, however, are far less violent and much more within the reach of village women themselves. Parvati's good deeds, her attention to the details of the ritual, her distribution of alms, and above all, her religious devotion (*bhakti*) are stressed along with her asceticism.

As it is actually enacted by village women at Tij, Parvati's mythical fast undergoes yet another subtle transformation. The romantic and erotic elements of the myth (i.e., the fact that Parvati fasted to win the man she loved rather than the man her father chose for her) come into much greater prominence. Of course, the underlying theme of purification through asceticism remains. The women observe a strict fast (*Tij ko barta*) for more than twenty-four hours, from the feast late in the night before Tij until the morning of the day after. Most will not even take water, and say that to do so is "like drinking your husband's blood." Some even spit out their own saliva to make the purification more complete.

On the morning of Tij the women go to bathe in the river as part of their purification. After their bath they, like Parvati, make and worship a sand phallus. Later during the night of Tij they also set out offerings and a votive light for Siva.[9] But the main event of the day is when the women, giddy with their fast, dance and sing throughout the afternoon at a local Siva temple. Here the mood of the festival changes from passive worship to virtual seduction of Siva.

After their bath in the late morning, the women spend hours combing their hair, putting on makeup bought in the bazaar, and adorning themselves with all their jewelry and best clothes. Red is by far the preferred color, and by afternoon the village paths to the temple are overflowing with chattering crowds of women dressed in their blood-red wedding saris carrying trays of offerings for Siva. After worship the women linger around the temple talking and admiring each other until usually one of the older women begins to clap and sing and urge the younger girls to dance. Some of the young men of the village may loiter on the outskirts of the temple grounds hoping to see the dancing, and one or two may be allowed nearer if they are playing the drums. There is a great deal of coy reluctance and genuine embarrassment among the women, because dancing is considered highly suggestive and erotic in Brahman-Chetri culture. Respectable women simply don't dance.[10] But at Tij most women will allow themselves to be coaxed into a few graceful steps before they collapse into giggles and run to hide among their friends. If there is a new bride who has married into the village that year, the older women will not let her rest until she has shown her skill at dancing—a skill which, if displayed on any other occasion, would brand her as a shameless prostitute.

The laughing, singing, and dancing at Tij, then, represents a complete reversal of the Hindu ideal of womanly behavior. To say that a girl is shy, embarrassed (laj manne) is to praise her highly. On Tij the high spirits, the flirtatiousness, the sexuality which women must ordinarily suppress are released en masse at Siva's temple. However, this display of the erotic side of female nature is only permissible because, on Tij, it is held in check by the strict purifying fast which the women are undergoing for the welfare of their husbands.[11] On the morning after Tij, women must perform a puja and make offerings to a Brahman priest dedicating the merit of their fast to their husband (present, future, or in the next life) before they can break the fast. The dangers of female sexuality are thus firmly bracketed by the mutually reinforcing ascetic and patrilineal ideals.

But it is not until the rituals of Rishi Pancami are complete that the female sexuality which emerged in the Tij dancing is truly brought under control and integrated into the ideology of the patriline. On Rishi Pancami female sexuality is represented, not by throngs of dancing women in red saris but by the abstract concept of menstrual blood with all its contradictory connotations.[12]

Women explain that Rishi Pancami is "like the fourth day of menstruation" for all women and that only after bathing are they pure enough to touch men. In the morning the women gather in groups of friends to walk down to the river where other women of the village may already have begun bathing. Each woman has prepared the items she will need to purify herself, including 360 stems of the datiun plant, and 360 datiun leaves all tied into neat bundles of twenty each. After removing her sari and drawing her petticoat up over her breasts, she squats in a long row of women beside the river and begins her ablutions.

First she must rub red mud (rato mato) on her genitals 360

times and then splash river water to wash away the mud. She keeps track of the numbers with a small pile of stones from which one is removed after every twenty washings. She continues rubbing mud and sprinkling water 360 times each on her feet, knees, elbows, mouth, shoulders (or armpits), and forehead. The whole process is then repeated with "white" mud (seto mato)[13] or oilseed husk (pina) and then cowdung (gobar). Next she washes her hair with either mud or oilseed husk. She cannot use soap for any of her bathing as it is considered ritually impure (bitulo). Then she puts a piece of holy kus grass around her waist and begins to brush her teeth by chewing on the bundles of datiun stems and spitting them out into the river. After that she dips the bundles of datiun leaves into the water and sprinkles them over her head. Then, borrowing a flat basket sieve from a neighbor, she pours water over her head with it several times. Since each tiny stream of water counts as one bath she can quickly ensure that she has taken the required 360 baths. Then she takes a quick plunge into the river (being held by her friends, since the river is swift and she may not be able to swim). Finally, she recites her mantra and swallows a sip of purifying pancamrit (five purifying substances—milk, curds, ghee, cow urine, and honey). Then she cuts the kus grass from around her waist and her bath is complete.

In some villages the women return to their own households after bathing to do worship that follows. In others, a group of twenty to thirty neighbor women, all Brahman-Chetri, may meet together at the river and do a joint puja under the direction of a single priest.

The women form a circle in the middle of which is placed a large tray of paddy which has been contributed by each household. On top of this is the central water vessel (kalas) into which the gods will be invoked and which the women will worship together. All the women have brought long pieces of white-tipped sama grass which, when extended, give them contact with the central vessel during the worship. The Brahman also gives each woman a ring of holy kus grass to purify the right hand for making the offerings.

On the edge of the circle before each household group (i.e., coresident women who share the same thar and gotra) are baskets full of offerings and the implements for worshiping their own separate votive light, sacred vessel, and Ganes.[14] The ceremony begins with each group individually performing this stan-

On the morning of Rishi Panchami women gather by the river's edge to purify
themselves with 360 ritual baths. *Photo by Linda Stone*

dard puja under the common direction of the priest, who tells each woman to remember her own gotra as she makes the offerings. This is followed by a *godan* ("gift of a cow" represented by coins on a leaf plate full of rice), which each woman must offer to the priest in order to purify herself for the subsequent rituals. Then, there is joint worship of the central vessel, which the priest has decorated with red and yellow powders and into which he has invoked a host of Hindu gods. Holding their long wands of sama grass in contact with the vessel the women worship the gods by throwing flowers, rice, water, and other offerings as the priest directs.

After these preliminaries comes the main ceremony, the rishi puja. The Brahman places a tray on top of the central vessel. The tray contains eight kus grass figures stuck into eight piles of rice. The kus figure in the middle represents Arundhati—the one among all the wives of the rishis who remained faithful to her husband even in the face of Siva's charms. The surrounding seven figures represent the seven rishis.

Arundhati is really the focus of the entire ritual. She is the epitome of the chaste and faithful wife (*pativrat*), and myths of her virtues abound in the Puranas. Those cited by O'Flaherty bring out two points which help clarify the Rishi Pancami rituals. First, O'Flaherty (1973:100) suggests that the vulnerability of the other rishis' wives, who are not faithful to their husbands, is related to menstruation. According to one interpretation of the myth of the birth of Siva's son, Skanda, the rishis' wives had been bathing in the river at the end of their monthly periods when all but Arundhati went to warm themselves by a fire that was actually Siva's burning seed. Here they became impregnated.[15] It is hard to see the rishis' wives' innocent act of warming themselves by the fire as culpable, but symbolically it represents their sexual looseness in contrast with Arundhati's restraint.[16] It echoes the pine forest story recounted earlier where the rishis' wives tried to seduce Siva. On Rishi Pancami, village women, ritually considered to be "in their fourth day" as were the rishis' wives, are particularly anxious to associate themselves with Arundhati. She represents control of the erotic side of female nature which surfaces so dangerously during menstruation. As one village woman explained: "Arundhati can take away the sin of having touched a man during menstruation because she was faithful to her husband."

O'Flaherty discusses another Arundhati myth that reinforces the connection between the wife's faithfulness and the husband's long life. Because Arundhati resists his attempts to seduce her, Siva gives her the boon of immortality and virility for her husband (O'Flaherty 1973:102). This stands in marked contrast to Siva's curse on the rishis to be "without force" and have "unfaithful wives" after their wives had tried to seduce him in the pine forest story quoted earlier from the *Swasthani Vrata Katha.*

Before worshiping Arundhati, the women make their offerings to the rishis. The items offered in this elaborate puja include milk, clarified butter, curds, water, honey, strips of cloth, vermilion, incense, sandalwood powder, betel nuts, and leaf plates full of fried breads. Other plates contain fruits and coins which the priest collects and places in the center. But the most important of the items presented to the rishis are sacred thread, banana, and leaf plates containing the "counted things." Each woman, prior to the puja, must count out exactly 360 grains each of barley, unbroken rice, and sesame and 360 wicks soaked in clarified butter. When the sacred thread and all the "counted things" have been offered to the rishis, the women then offer to Arundhati all the accessories of the married woman whose husband is still alive (*saubhagya saman*).[17] They consist of the following: a small box, containing vermilion powder for making the red tika mark, a hair braid, a comb, a mirror, a strip of cloth representing clothes, glass bangles, a bead necklace, and black eyeliner. These items come in a small preassembled packet that the husband purchases before Tij. No married woman will ever, if she can possibly help it, be without these signs of her auspicious state—especially the red hair braid, beads, bangles, and vermilion mark. These adornments and the privilege of wearing red clothes are at once an enhancement of her beauty and a sign of her virtue. Good women are believed to die before their husbands and have the honor of being cremated in a red shroud (instead of yellow or white) with the accessories of wifehood laid on their chest. Once again, the indirect connection is made between the husband's long life and his wife's virtue. The accessories of a married woman, then, symbolize female sexuality (since they increase a woman's powers of seduction by making her more attractive) and the control of that sexuality (since she may only wear them while her husband is alive and presumably her marital chastity is intact). By dedicating to the chaste Arundhati the adornments which they wore on Tij to

dance seductively before the temple of Siva, women are purifying their own sexuality. They are channeling it in the only direction acceptable to Hindu patrilineal ideology—toward their
own husbands.

This interpretation is reinforced by the final part of the
ritual. After lighting her 360 ghee wicks, each woman purifies
herself by moving her hands from the fire to her face three times.
Then the plates of burning wicks are placed outside the circle,
and the women walk around the central vessel eight times—
once for each rishi and once for Arundhati. The women move
very slowly for, as they explained to me, the whole efficacy of
the puja is lost if they do not keep their knees together as they
walk, or if any space is left between heel and toe as they place
one foot in front of another. The meaning of this restrained gait
in the context of Arundhati's faithfulness is clear enough. When
they have completed the circumambulation, the women are
seated in a circle again and they make their final offerings to the
rishis—either a banana or a cucumber—while the priest instructs
them once again to remember their gotra. Each woman must
bring this final offering home and give it to her husband.[18]

The rishi puja itself is now complete, and the women
may return home for their morning meal.[19] Usually, however,
some women in the village sponsor a priest to recite the *Rsi
Pancami Vrata Katha* in their own home, and other neighboring
women come to hear it. The central myth of the text adds an
important dimension to our understanding of the Tij–Rishi Pancami complex. I have excerpted here the main part of the story
from the Nepali text:

> There was once a Brahman named Sumitra who had become
> an expert in all the Vedas and rites and rituals. He was the kind
> who worked in his fields and cared for his family with love and
> kindness toward all. He had a very devoted wife, a Brahmani named
> Jaisri. She was completely devoted to serving her husband, and she
> had sons and daughters and servants. All she worried about was
> what was happening in the fields.
>
> "The field workers have come," she would say to herself.
> "It is getting late and food has to be prepared for them and taken.
> If I don't go, then they will cheat us. There's no manure. There are
> seeds, and it is time to sow them. The clods have to be broken.
> The mustard has to be threshed, and there is millet which has yet
> to be harvested. The wheat has to be sown. The corn has to be
> weeded. Everyone else has weeded their rice, and we haven't."

These and many other problems of daily household work used to keep her occupied.

One day she saw that she was having her menstrual period, but she did not care about what utensils she touched and, out of contempt, she touched everything. When she became old, then death claimed her and the Brahmani named Jaisri died. And her husband Sumitra Brahman also died. And when both husband and wife had died thus, the Brahmani who had deliberately touched and defiled things was born again as a bitch. And because of the sin committed by his wife, Sumitra Brahman was born as a bull. And both of them happened to go and live in the same house which they had owned in their past life. Because of her deliberate defilement during her period of menstruation, both of them had to go and be born of such miserable wombs.

The son of Sumitra was one who served his ancestors. His name was Sumati and he was very religious. . . . Although Sumati's parents had been conceived in the wombs of animals, both of them were fully aware of what they had been in their past lives and the reason for their present condition. The Brahmani used to remember the deeds of her past life (purwa karma). But what could she do? She used to go from house to house and eat what was thrown away. And her husband Sumitra who had become a bull had to go and plough every day.

Then one day the date for the yearly memorial (ekodhista sraddha) to Sumati's father arrived. And he, who was devoted to the service of his ancestors, was filled with a sense of duty. So Sumati said to his wife Chandrawati, "You with the beautiful smile, today is my father's sraddha. I shall have to feed Brahmans, so prepare a rich feast."

Hearing the command of her husband, Chandrawati prepared different and various kinds of rich food. But at that time a snake came and dropped its venom into the dish of rice pudding (khir). The bitch, who had been waiting outside, saw the venom being dropped and was afraid that if the Brahmans ate the rice pudding, then they would surely die. So the bitch went and touched the food. Then Chandrawati hit the bitch with a flaming stick and it ran yelping out. Then Chandrawati again cooked other food and the sraddha was performed according to the ritual and the Brahmans were fed.

The bitch sat outside. But Chandrawati, angry because it had touched the food, did not give that bitch the food that was left over from the ceremony. So that day the bitch went hungry. Where was it to go? What was it to do? Where it used to be fed every day there was nothing to eat that day. It spent the whole day thus, and then when night fell the bitch who was suffering terribly with hunger went to where the bull, its husband, was and said:

"O lord, O husband! Today they did not give me even a mouthful. I was unable to lick even the dirty plates, and I am sorely troubled with hunger. Before, my son used to give me food every day. Today they did not even give me the leftovers. . . ."

And after that the bitch's husband said to her: "O auspicious one! You have suffered because you touched the rice pudding. What am I to do? I am helpless. I can do nothing. I myself go around with a load upon my back—this you have seen. Look, I also went to my son's field today and ploughed the whole day. While I was ploughing he tied my mouth. Say—what is it that he would give me to eat? I am also suffering from hunger. It is useless for that son to perform my sraddha because today I have to suffer so!"

Hearing his mother and father talk among themselves about their sorrow, Sumati came to know that night that these [animals] were his mother and father. So Sumati took food that was rich and delicious and fed it to them.

And then when Sumati saw this condition of his mother and father he went into the forest, because he wanted to know the reason for this condition and this sorrow of his parents. There he saw the seven rishis, the enlightened ones who always lived in the forests. And there Sumati prostrated himself at the feet of the seven rishis and, for the good of his parents, asked them with great deference:

"O Brahman rishis! Please deign to answer my question. O masters of meditation! By the fruit of what karma did my mother and father take birth in this state? Now what should I do so that they will be liberated from that sin?"

When the rishis heard Sumati's question they replied: "O Brahman! Out of stupidity your mother was careless during her menstrual period. And because of this act she became a bitch. And because of her defilement, your father also has become a bull. And now in order to liberate them from this womb, your wife has to undertake the fast/vow of Rishi Pancami. She has to worship the rishis in the proper manner according to the rites and rituals. O Brahman! You should undertake this fast for seven years. [Here follows the rishis' instructions as to how Sumati's wife Chandrawati was to perform the penitential fast and rituals of the Rishi Pancami described above]. . . . And because of the efficacy of the fast, when it is performed all the sins committed when one touches and defiles during the period of menstruation will be cleansed and destroyed. Your mother and father will also be redeemed. There is no doubt about this." [The rishis then explain the rituals and requirements of the fast in detail.]

. . . Because of the virtues of this fast the mother of Sumati was liberated from the womb of that bitch. Sitting in the best flying chariot (viman) and wearing ornaments which defied description, she went to heaven. And his father was also liberated from the animal womb at his death. Because of the effects of this fast, [Sumati's parents] entered heaven. [Sharma 2022a:16–60, abridged; my trans. with Prithivi Raj Chettri]

The myth immediately relates the ascetic/householder opposition to the opposition between male and female. Initially, the opposition is balanced. The husband who is an expert in ritual also cares for his family; and the wife who is concerned about the prosperity of the fields is devoted to her husband. When Jaisri's worldly concerns overcome this devotion and she touches her husband's food during her menstruation, that balance is destroyed. It is restored at the end of the myth by the ascetic rishis who prescribe the strict fasting and the bathing rituals of Rishi Pancami to rid the couple of the effects of Jaisri's sin. The rishis' instructions about what food may be eaten during the penance also carry a distinct antihouseholder import. "You should eat only that which grows wild, like green leaves, sama grass, and the like. Eat only that which you do not have to sow and reap" (Sharma 2022a:51). This is a sharp contrast to Jaisri's initial overinvolvement in sowing and reaping which caused all the trouble.

Two other recurring themes of the Tij–Rishi Pancami complex find expression in the myth: the idea that a woman's virtue affects her husband's long life, and that women present a threat to patrilineal solidarity. In the myth Jaisri's lack of fastidiousness about menstrual taboos (i.e., her sexual looseness) does not directly cause her husband's death. They both die in old age. It does, however, cause him—and her—to be born in miserable and very impure reincarnations. She is reborn as a bitch—an animal who eats polluted leftovers of others. (We also recall that women during their periods are likened to female dogs.) The husband is reborn as a bull who must plow the land—an act that the pure Brahman caste is forbidden to perform. Instead of enjoying a peaceful and contented existence as ancestor spirits, they become animals on the earth. Because of their lowly rebirth the sraddha ceremony for them (which represents the spiritual continuity of the patriline) is rendered ineffective. The son's attempt to honor and feed his dead parents is unsuccessful, and both the animal-parents go hungry that night. The rishis appear, not in their role as the irascible, cuckolded husbands of the Swasthani myth, but as the promulgators of patrilineal continuity through obedience to the rules of ritual purity. By following their instructions, Sumati, with his wife's help, is able to release his parents and send them to heaven, where his sraddha ceremonies for them will be effective. Thus, the rishis reestablish the patrilineal continuity that had been broken by a temporary lapse of control over the sexuality of an affinal female. In this role the rishis provide the link between the men's festival at Janai Purni where the sacred thread is purified and the women's Tij–Rishi Pancami festival where the married women's accessories (their equivalent of the sacred thread) are purified.

In the myth, Jaisri demonstrates her repentance by reversing her former sin. Instead of polluting others in secret for her own benefit, she publicly pollutes the rice pudding. Thus she ensures that the Brahmans will not be killed by the snake's venom, even though she knows she will go hungry as a result. The firebrand with which she is struck represents the beginning of her purification from her initial sin.

The one who threw the brand—Jaisri's daughter-in-law, Chandrawati—ultimately plays the main role in destroying her mother-in-law's sin through her performance of the Rishi Pancami rituals. Chandrawati, with her fastidiousness about pollution, stands in contrast to her mother-in-law. She went to the trouble and expense of recooking the rice pudding after it had been defiled by the dog. If Chandrawati had been careless, as Jaisri was during her menstrual period, the Brahmans would have been killed by the poisoned rice pudding. Thus, Chandrawati's ritual purity is structurally equivalent to Arundhati's sexual purity. She is opposed to the ritual laxity of Jaisri just as Arundhati is opposed to the sexual looseness of the other rishis' wives. Both are virtuous women. Like the village women who have just undergone the Tij–Rishi Pancami rituals, they have accepted the restrictions placed on them by the dominant ascetic and patrilineal ideology of Hinduism.

The "Cave" of Menarche (*Gupha Basne*) and Consanguineal Women

The final ritual to be considered in our discussion of menstrual pollution is actually the first one a woman undergoes, the *gupha basne* or "staying in a cave" ceremony which occurs at menarche. *Gupha basne* is a rite of passage that marks the transition of a girl from a presexual to a sexual being. As such it reiterates some of the negative ideas about the dangers of female sexuality with which we are already familiar. But beyond that, I believe it also reveals the conceptual basis for the Hindu belief in the sacredness of consanguineal women. Careful analysis of the gupha basne ritual will help is to understand the somewhat paradoxical logic of the filiafocal dimension of Brahman-Chetri kinship.

Among traditional orthodox hill Brahmans—and to a lesser extent among the Chetris—every effort is made to get daughters married before their menarche. This is, in fact, implied by the term *kanyadan* which is used for the orthodox, meritorious form of marriage. While *kanya* means generally "maiden" or "virgin," it is also used specifically to denote prepubescent girls. *Kanya keti* or prepubescent unmarried girls are considered especially pure (*cokho*), and many rituals require the worship of a given number of kanya as incarnations of the goddess Durga. Kumari worship among the Newars is a more fully articulated expression of the same belief (Allen 1975). The goddess ceases to inhabit young girls when menstruation (or some flaw like a bleeding cut, loss of teeth, or a serious disease) renders them no longer pure enough to be her vehicle.

Since we are already familiar with the general suspicion of affinal women and the heavy stress placed on maintaining their purity, there is nothing surprising in the fact that the "guaranteed" purity—and the greater emotional malleability—of prepubescent girls should make them preferred as brides. Yet, in the span of one generation, Narikot has undergone a profound change in this regard. More and more families now prefer the prestige of an educated bride (even though she may get little chance to use her education in her ghar) over the guaranteed purity of a prepubescent one. In turn, more and more girls are being sent to school—some to eighth and even tenth class—rather than being married off.

A survey in Narikot[20] revealed that of the twenty-five women aged 35 and over, the average age of marriage was 13. Among the twenty-two married women in the under-35 age group, the average marriage age was 17. Since the average age of menarche for this sample was 15.4, the shift is clearly away from the ideal of the prepubescent bride.

Even before this recent change, however, many girls—

especially among the Chetris—reached menarche before marriage. For these unmarried girls the gupha basne ceremony has always been, and continues to be, much more strict than it is for girls who have their first period after they are safely married and living in their husband's household. The most important feature of the ceremony is the seclusion of the girl in a dark room where absolutely no light is allowed to enter. This is the *gupha* or "cave" which gives the ritual its name. If the girl is already married, the gupha may be in the attic or cattle shed of her own ghar. But if she is still unmarried and living in her maita, she must be immediately taken to another house, preferably that of an old high-caste widow in some other village—but it must definitely be far enough away from the girl's maita so that she cannot possibly catch sight of the roof of her own home.

The main reason for whisking the unmarried girl away from her maita is the very strict prohibition on "seeing the face" of either her father or her brothers during her first menstruation. "It is forbidden to see the face of one's father or one's brothers" (Ba ko muk ra daju-bhaiko mukh hernu hudaina). She should not even hear their voices; nor should they hear hers. If possible, the sight of all men is avoided. As soon as the girl discovers her condition and announces it to her mother or elder sister, she is covered with a big shawl—so that neither males nor Surya,[21] the sun deity, may see her—and bundled off by the back way to some appropriate place of seclusion. She must stay concealed there for either twelve or twenty-two days.[22] If she is already married, the period of seclusion may be even shorter than twelve days. In one case I observed in Narikot the gupha basne of a married girl lasted only four days—the length of normal menstrual seclusion—and was done in her husband's family's own animal shed. There was some criticism of this laxity, but the general feeling was that, since she was married, the ritual was not so important.

For the first four days the girl may not take any salt with her food, and she may have only one rice meal a day. She may not stir out of the darkened room while the sun is up, and a brass pan is provided in the room for her bodily eliminations. After the fourth day, she may go outside early in the morning before sunrise and bathe. After that she may resume eating normal food. Except for their friends' visits, most women I interviewed remembered their gupha basne ceremony as a lonely and somewhat frightening experience—especially if they were unmarried and had been sent away to a stranger's house.

For all the women I interviewed in depth, the gupha basne ceremony was among the most vivid and significant early memories. They all associated the sexual maturation of their bodies and the awakening of romantic and narcissistic interests indirectly with the onset of menstruation. For those who were not already married it signaled the rapid approach of that ominous event.

With menstruation begins the *taruni* period of a woman's life when she is expected to be healthy, sexually attractive, and desirous of admiration, despite her shyness. The word *taruni* means sexually mature young girl—something close to "nubile," perhaps, in English. A taruni may be an unmarried virgin or a newly married woman who has not borne children. But to get a better understanding of the Nepali concept and how it relates to menarche, I will quote one informant's memories of her gupha basne ceremony:

When one becomes na-chune [menstruates] the *taruni* period begins. During this time [menstruation] you are not supposed to touch the children,[23] and then you become a taruni. A lot of blood accumulates and so this blood comes out. The breasts grow. First they are small—about this big. After the first menstruation they begin to grow bigger. And you begin to feel that if you could wear pretty clothes and do makeup, then you would become pretty too. When you are small you have no desires for that sort of thing. If you get something to eat, then that is enough for you when you are small. But when you grow up, then you want good things to wear. You feel that you would like to be better than all the others—to put on a lot of makeup, cream, powder, and eyeliner—to become a taruni. You think about what others will say—whether they will say you are a taruni or not and whether they will say you are pretty or not. These are the new feelings that you have when you are a taruni.

I was fourteen for my gupha basne. Mother was at the spring washing clothes. . . . I had taken rice to the footmill to pound it to make parched rice for my friend's wedding. After pounding four measures I took it from the footmill and went. On the way I felt like urinating. So I put the rice aside and squatted down—but as I was urinating I felt something cold. When I looked to see what had happened I saw something red. And something black like the excrement of insects. I thought that there had been some insect excrement under that tree. Then when I had gone a little ways I began to think: May be this is what they call *na chune hune* [menstruation]. . . . I didn't know anything about all that. A few days earlier there had been pains . . . Now there were red marks on my dhoti. I didn't know whether I had become na chune or not. I left the rice right there. I didn't go on. I didn't touch the rice. I called out to mother and told her I didn't know but maybe I had become na chune. And then I began to weep. Now I had to stay in the gupha. I would not be able to look upon anyone. I would have to stay all alone. And mother also began to weep.

"Now my daughter has grown up. She'll become bigger day by day and she'll have to be married off to another person's house."

Mother also wept at the thought that she would be all alone and she would have to do everything in the house by herself. . . . When you become na chune, then you feel embarrassed with your father. They begin to think about where to hide you and in whose house you should stay.

Mother said that I would have to be taken to the house of a Jaisi on the ridge above our house. When one becomes na chune, then if a witch (boski) sees one evil will befall one. One becomes ill. If the witch sees the blood or the person taking a bath, then she casts the evil eye upon that person. We would become barren. The witch ruins the womb, and that is why one has to be kept at a place where there are no witches. The first time one can come to harm.[24]

Moreover, a child will do unseemly things because she doesn't know what it is all about. Grandmother scolded and said that a mere child might go around and show her bleeding. And so I went away. . . . I was not supposed to look upon the sun. Nor are you supposed to look at the road straight ahead. So I went with my head bowed and the nurse (dhai ama) put a shawl over my head. My cousin who had already been married was home in her maita for a visit at the time and she came along and teased me.

"Oh, Ambika has become na chune? It is time to get her married. She has become a taruni." She teased me all along. She took me to that Jaisi woman, who had a deaf-mute daughter. And that deaf-mute, who simply used to say "Wah wah," teased me [in sign language]. She made a penis like a man's.

"Your father will play the drum—piti, piti, piti, piti! [Onomatapoeic sound of drums, accompanied by drumming gestures with the forefingers—a common deaf-mute expression for sexual intercourse after the wedding.] He will play the drum and send you away and your husband will do it to you!" She kept on at it. That deaf-mute! I felt so angry. I scolded her and told her to drop dead. But what to say to a deaf-mute like that? So I wept and stayed there. . . .

At that time you are not supposed to eat salt for four days— that is the custom this side. But they gave it to me. They cooked rice and curry and put salt into it. Then I made my bed and slept. . . . I used to sleep through the whole day. Even a small hole which would let the sunlight in would have to be covered up. On the fourth day I bathed once. I would get up early in the morning at about 3–4 o'clock. That old woman used to take me to the place where I was to bathe. . . . When the sun set, then I would come out and go to the bathroom in the fields. During the day I would do it in a brass pan and throw it away.

And then on the twelfth day, I took a bath during the day and prayed to Surya. After the twelfth day you are permitted to look upon the sun. . . . On the fifteenth day I washed my hair and took a bath and returned home. My brother tossed out my new dhoti and blouse to me and I put them on. And then father performed the puja for Surya [25] and put tika on me and gave me money, and then he looked on my face [mukh herne]. You are not supposed to look on your father's face until he has put tika, so I bowed down my head and father put on the tika wihout looking at my face. You can look at your mother. But you must not look at your father or your brothers. You are not even supposed to look at the rooftop of your father's house! It is so bad. If they see our face then ill fortune will follow them. And that is why it is only when Surya Puja has been performed and only after they have given us red hair braid, vermilion, bangles, red clothes, and everything that they can look upon our face.

There are several variations in the rituals of purification after gupha basne. They can take place on the twelfth, the fifteenth (as in the narrative above), or the twenty-second day after menstruation. Besides doing a puja to the sun deity, the girl must also make several godan offerings to the family priest in order to purify herself. These are done with a shawl held up between the Brahman and the girl so he does not catch sight of her face as she gives him the leaf plate of coins and they exchange tika.

But one ritual act is essential to her purification: the girl must receive from her father and brothers a red dhoti and blouse, the accessories of a married woman (saubhagya saman), and daksina before she can be seen by them or enter her own house again.[26] Even if she is married, these items of clothing and decoration must be sent to her in her ghar by consanguineal males.[27]

In the discussion of Tij–Rishi Pancami, a parallel emerged between the sacred thread and the accessories of a married woman. Both are symbols of controlled sexuality, ascetic restraint, and the personal and lineage purity which the householders—male and female, respectively—try to maintain. The sacred thread, as we know, is first given to the male at the bartaman ceremony which initiates him into full caste and lineage status as an adult and prepares him for marriage. Girls, however, receive the red clothes and accessories of initiation twice: once

from a consanguineal male (her father) at the gupha basne and
once from an affinal male (her husband) at marriage. This situation—especially the receipt of the woman's accessories, which
are so strongly connected with marriage, from consanguineal
males—at first seems not only puzzling, but even shocking in a
culture where so much care is taken through gotra exogamy and
various other rules to avoid the possibility of incestuous unions
between any kinsmen. In fact, if the gift of accessories is examined in the context of the gupha basne rite, it quite clearly
signifies the exact opposite of incest: a complete transference
of the daughter's nascent sexuality away from her natal group
and to another patriline.

    Like everything connected with female sexuality, female
initiation in Brahman-Chetri society has certain problematic aspects. For one thing, the signs of physical maturity in a female
are abrupt and unmistakable. As soon as a girl has menstruated
she is considered a taruni. Yet, this sexual maturity which she
achieves at menarche does not coincide with social and religious adulthood, which she achieves only at marriage. If marriage is performed according to the Brahmanical ideal, before
the onset of puberty, there is no problem with the appearance
of sexuality. The girl has already been transferred by her kinsmen to her husband's patriline, where she has assumed full caste
and ritual status. She has already received an earlier gift of the
woman's accessories from her husband, and her emerging sexuality has been properly channeled and controlled.

    But if, as is often the case, menarche occurs before mar-
riage, both the purity of the girl and the reputation of her maiti
become extremely vulnerable. Her nascent unattached sexuality
is an anomaly which endangers herself and her male consanguineal relatives. She has changed from a female child into a
nubile girl, but she has not yet been transferred to the affinal
group that will channel her sexuality forward its own legitimate
continuity.

    Here we have reached the crux of the strong contrast
between affinal and consanguineal women in Brahman-Chetri
kinship and social organization. The sexual and procreative roles
which are felt to endanger the purity of the patrilineal group are
exclusively associated with affinal women. Hence the bride, so
strongly identified with her procreative role, must be protected
by the strictest social and ritual means in her ghar. The daughter,
on the other hand, is categorically shielded from any association

with sexual roles. To her maiti a woman is always perceived as the pure, virgin kanya. There is no need for the harsh restrictions of the ghar because, from the point of view of her maiti, a daughter has no sexuality to be controlled. This is, in fact, the conceptual basis of filiafocal relationships and of the high ritual status of consanguineal women: daughters and sisters can be "sacred" to their consanguineal kin only because they are not structural members of their natal patriline. Once she is married, a woman's purity does not concern her maiti; it has been established by her acceptance into an affinal group of the appropriate ritual status.

There is, however, great concern about the purity of kinswomen who have reached pubescence but have not yet been transferred to another patriline. For, as the name kanyadan suggests, a girl must be pure in order to be given away as a religious gift, and until her marriage, her actions reflect directly upon the prestige of her maita. Any "loose" behavior on her part (and this might include such things as talking with boys on the village path, laughing too much, or lack of proper shyness in front of men) makes her father's job of finding a suitable groom that much more difficult. For the whole village is the custodian of her reputation, and the prospective groom's family will doubtless sound out her neighbors before finalizing the engagement.

In the unlikely event that she should disgrace her family by becoming pregnant, they may be forced to expel her to save their own caste standing. There is great urgency to disclose the caste status of such an unmarried girl's lover, since this man will determine the future status of the girl and her child. If the gentle questioning of the girl's own family does not succeed, she is subjected to the harsh interrogation of a gathering of male lineage members. Even if the lover was a Chetri or a Brahman, the girl's chances of marriage almost disappear unless her family can bring pressure on her lover to marry her.

But if the girl will not identify her lover, then her family must assume the worst—that the lover was lower caste or even untouchable. On the eleventh day after the birth, when no father can be produced to give his gotra and thar names to the child in the name-giving ceremony, both the child and the mother become untouchable. From then on the girl may not enter her father's house and must fend for herself. In practice a bastard child may be adopted by another family[28] and the maita of an unmarried mother does attempt to secure her future,[29] but if the father cannot be identified they must treat her as an outcaste.

By separating the girl from her consanguineal kin before the emergence of her sexuality, the Brahmanic ideal of prepubescent marriage avoids the possibility of such heartbreaking scandal. It also provides the ideological basis for the entire filiafocal dimension of kinship: the sacredness of consanguineal women and the special relaxed and affectionate treatment of daughters and sisters. The menarche of an unmarried girl presents her family with a grave threat to the categorical purity on which her sacred status is based. Gupha basne is a ritual attempt to protect that purity by establishing a symbolic barrier between the girl's sexuality and her consanguineal male relatives. The girl's seclusion is, of course, meant to protect her from *all* men (and conversely to protect all men from her menstrual pollution)—but there is a strong emphasis on avoidance of the father and brothers in particular. The fact that an unmarried girl is specifically forbidden to stay in her maita or even "see the roof of her father's house" during this period, while married girls may undergo seclusion in their husband's house, further indicates that it is the filiafocal relationship which is especially endangered by her menarche.

The father's puzzling gift of the woman's accessories instead of symbolizing a sexual claim on the girl, is, on the contrary, an acknowledgment that her sexuality and fertility are transferable and, indeed must soon be transferred. Her potential for fertility serves as the basis for the marriage and the ensuing linkage between the group that gives her and the group that receives her. If she is already married, the father's gift of accessories at menarche is a ritual recognition of his responsibility to provide the affines with not just a virgin but a sexual/fertile being. If the girl is unmarried, the father's gift is an acknowledgment that she has reached marriageable age and must soon be sent away. The response to menarche quoted in the passage above was typical: "Now your father must marry you off!" After the physical separation of her seclusion, the girl's father must present her with the signs of her impending marriage before he can "look upon her face."

Two individual items which the groom has to give the bride in the marriage rituals are the red marriage beads and the vermilion mark in the parting of her hair. The latter carries strong connotations of the groom's impending sexual possession of the bride. Significantly, these two items are *not* included in the gifts which the father gives at the conclusion of his daughter's gupha basne ceremony.[30] The other items which he does give (i.e., the red clothes, bangles, hairbraid, mirror, comb, etc.) may be worn and used by both married and unmarried women (though not by widows), but only married women may wear the red marriage beads and vermilion mark in the hair.

This interpretation of gupha basne as symbolic of the filiafocal necessity of separating male lineage members from the sexuality of consanguineal women is reinforced by the other prescribed ritual separations between them. A woman may not "look upon the face" of her father and brothers for ten days after she has given birth and for a full year after the death of her husband. Both are situations, like menarche, which emphasize the sexual aspect of consanguineal women. All three events are potentially dangerous "oubreaks"[31] of female sexuality which can only be controlled within the patrifocal structures of kinship.

Until the name-giving ceremony on the eleventh day after birth when the child's father claims it as a member of his lineage, neither the child nor its mother may be seen by the mother's consanguineal male relatives. Other men may see both mother and child, but her brothers and father may not. This period of seclusion, called literally "sitting in a corner" (*sutkeri* or *kona ma basne*), is likened by villagers to the gupha basne period and would, once again, seem to shield the woman's sexuality from men of her maita until her affines reassert their patrifocal control and responsibilities at the naming ceremony.

At childbirth a woman's sexuality is responsible for the giving of life; when her husband dies, her sexuality is associated in a vague way with the destruction of life. In the discussion of Tij, we encountered the idea that a woman's sexual looseness, or even her sexual demands on her own husband, weaken him and may be responsible for his death. This is not to say, of course, that individual widows are actually thought to be guilty of such crimes in the minds of their fellow villagers. The sense of sin connected with widowhood is far too diffuse and inarticulate in most cases to provoke such accusations.

Nevertheless, a widow's sexuality—like that of an unmarried pubescent girl—is a social anomaly. Since she is no longer under the control of her husband, she presents a potential problem to both her affinal and her consanguineal kin. Most important, her affinal group can never make fully legitimate use of her fertility again. There is also the problem of responsibility for supporting her. Since she was transferred at marriage to her husband's thar and gotra, her affines have an obligation to support her and her children for the rest of her life. In some families, however, this responsibility for a deceased kinsman's wife may be resented—especially if she and her children are young, or even worse, if she is childless. The period immediately following her husband's death is a time when her children's rights to a share of the patrilineal land must be established.

Before the barakhi ceremony which marks the end of the year of mourning, the maita must send a set of clothes to their widowed daughter. For a year she has worn only the plain white clothes of widowhood, in which her father and brothers may never see her. But after the barakhi, for her husband, she can put on clothes with designs and colors (any color but red) and go to visit her maita. One widow informant remembered that even though her father became seriously ill and eventually died during the year of enforced separation, she was not allowed to go to visit him:

> We are not supposed to go to our maita wearing white clothes. My father wept and wept when my husband died. And within six months he also died, but I was not able to go to him. We couldn't meet until a year had passed. He sat there—at the pipal tree—with his grandchildren and he wept his heart out and went away. He couldn't meet me or see me, so he sat there and wept and went away. In those days we didn't have paper money. But he sent coins worth twenty, twenty-five rupees to his two grandchildren. And for me he sent a lump of crystalized sugar (*misri*) this big and a coconut. And then, when six months had passed, my father also died. He told my brothers that they should give this and that to his daughter. He had made a bangle of gold and a necklace with coral and gold nuggets and told them to give it to me. But when father died, who would give that to me? No one gave it. They brought a set of clothes with designs on them because this has to be given when the maiti is putting on the tika [after the year of mourning]. They brought shoes and clothes and shawls and I put them on and went to my maita.

The proscription against seeing her father and brothers during the year of mourning means that a woman cannot follow what is probably her natural inclination to escape to the comfort and support of her maita. It places the responsibility for her and her children squarely on the shoulders of her affinal kin where, in terms of patrilineal kinship structure, it belongs.

Behind the ban on seeing consanguineal men during the year of mourning is the idea that the maita should never become the permanent home of an adult woman. Of course, women given away in kanyadan always retain the right to return to their maita permanently if the situation in their ghar is absolutely unbearable. But, while short visits to the maita are a cherished delight to both the woman and her natal kin, prolonged or permanent stays can place severe strains on the filiafocal relationship.

Just as the filiafocal dimension of kinship reverses the major patrifocal status relations, so a daughter's behavioral standards in her maita are to a large extent the reverse of what they are in her ghar. A daughter visiting her maita is given the lightest, most enjoyable of the household work—cooking, doing puja, weaving straw mats, or looking after children. Here, she may complain freely to sympathetic ears about the treatment she receives from her mother-in-law or her co-wife. She will be allowed to sleep when she feels tired during the day, and she will be expected to avail herself of her mother's hair oil, eyeliner, and even city-bought cream and powder to do her toilet. Special rich foods will be prepared for her if the family can afford it, and, if possible, they will try to send her back with a new blouse or sari for herself as well as a load of gifts for her in-laws. The general laxity of the maita extends even to a woman's relations with men. No one will criticize a married daughter if she talks and laughs a little with men she meets on the paths of her natal village.[32]

Obviously, this indulgent situation in the maita is not meant to be a permanent one for women, and if it becomes so, serious structural problems and deep mutual resentment can result. The most open resentment comes from a woman's brother's wife (bhauju). As a junior affinal woman in the household, the brother's wife does the hardest work and has the lowest status. Since she will be similarly pampered on visits to her own maita, the brother's wife is usually willing to defer to her husband's sister—but only on a temporary basis. In the case I mentioned earlier of the woman who returned permanently to her maita after her husband brought in a co-wife, the two brothers' wives complained bitterly to me of the hard field work they were forced to do in the hot sun which dried them out and darkened their skin, while their husbands' sister sat in the cool house doing the easy chores and maintaining her fair complexion. From this it is easy to see how resentment spreads to the woman's own brothers. Not only do they have to listen to the complaints of their own hard-working wives, but they are forced to support a relatively unproductive household member and her children. As long as the woman's parents are alive and the extended family intact, her place and at least her food and clothes are assured. But when the joint estate is broken up after the father's death, the question of which brother takes on the support of the sister can be a problem—especially if the sister's relations with her brother's wives have been acrimonious and the family lands are already insufficient.

Women are, as I mentioned at the outset, well aware of their ultimately tenuous position in the maita. Many women informants expressed the feeling that only while their mother was alive did they have a firm right to remain in their maita. In fact, the nature of woman's principal link to her natal home is expressed in the word maita itself which is derived from the word *ma* or *ama,* which means "mother." Recall Devi's lament when she was worried about the insecurity of her marital situation: "My husband didn't love me in my ghar and even in my maita I didn't have a mother." She also remembered her father as expressing the same idea when he was trying to find her a suitable husband: "Her mother is dead. What to do if she is mistreated after [her marriage]? I won't be able to take her back and look after her." This attitude would seem to reinforce my interpretation of the ritual separations imposed at menarche, childbirth, and widowhood between a woman and her consanguineal kinsmen. In all three cases, the mothers and sisters may visit the sequestered woman freely. Her sexuality is no threat to them or to their filiafocal relationships with her. But for men, the sacredness and ideal purity of the filiafocal relationship can only, it seems, be maintained at a distance.

Bhai Tika and the Sacred Status of Sisters

There is one more major ritual celebrating the filiafocal dimension of kinship: the calendrical festival of Bhai Tika (brother-tika) which takes place several weeks after the Dasai festival usually in early November. Here sisters worship their brothers and vice versa. The brother/sister relationship that emerges in Bhai Tika is, both structurally and emotionally, the paradigm for opposite-sex filiafocal relations.

Bhai Tika is the fifth and culminating day of the five days of the death-god Yama, which are together called Tihar. On the first day (Kak Tihar) the crow is worshiped; on the second day the dog (Kukur Tihar); on the third day, both the sacred cow (Gai Tihar) and the goddess Laksmi are worshiped. The fourth day is devoted to the bull (Goru Tihar) and to the worship of farming implements. And finally on the fifth day, brothers are honored at Bhai Tika. Several themes relating to purity and pollution, long life and prosperity recur throughout the Tihar cycle and are important to the meaning of Bhai Tika.

In the Tihar festivals the purity/pollution opposition is emphasized by the movement from worship of the inauspicious crow and lowly scavenger dog on the first two days to the worship on the third day of the cow and Laksmi, the auspicious goddess of wealth. The cow, which is probably the strongest symbol of purity in Hinduism, is closely associated with Laksmi. In Hindu mythology both the goddess and the famous wish-granting cow (Kamadhenu Gai) were extracted from the purest part of the ocean when it was churned by the gods and demons to produce the sacred elixir. A popular religious poster of this mythic event pictures the beautiful smiling goddess Laksmi standing to the left of Mt. Meru (which was used as the churning pole) with a shower of gold coins falling from her hands. On the right, emerging from the ocean's froth, is the mythical wish-granting cow. She has the head of a lovely smiling woman, with cow's horns jutting from her elaborate hairdo, a peacock's tail and wings, and the body of a white cow. Milk streams from her pink-tinted udder onto a holy stone representing the phallus of Siva (Sivalingam). Certainly, Laksmi and the cow, both of whom are worshiped on the third day of Tihar, form a powerful composite image of the auspicious and pure side of female nature— the perfect symbolic context for the sister's return home to worship and be worshiped by her brother.

The cow is worshiped on the morning of the third day, while Laksmi is honored that night with scores of tiny mustard oil lamps set in the doors and windows of village homes. The goddess is supposed to come to earth on the dark new moon night of Gai Tihar. Since she is attracted to purity and light, village families will thoroughly clean their homes and courtyards and set out lights so that the goddess will come and bring them prosperity for the following year. At nightfall the women of the house light the lamp and perform an elaborate puja to Laksmi in the family storeroom. During the day they will have cooked special sweets and fried breads. Some of these are offered to Laksmi; others are kept in readiness, along with small coins, for the groups of young girls who will come signing and begging from house to house (a tradition called *bhailo khelne*). The simple four-line song which they sing over and over announces to everyone that "Fresh gobar has been spread and the Laksmi puja performed" on the new moon night of Gai Tihar.[33]

The next morning is Goru Puja—the worship of bulls. That night it is the boys' and young men's turn to go out singing and begging for sweets and money. Their songs have much more variety than the girls'. Indeed, it seems that the lead singer can sing any tale, or even nonsense phrases, so long as his chorus backs him up at the end of each line with a rousing *"deusi reh!"* Most of the improvisations start out with a story about a brave king and end up praising the generosity (or the niggardliness) of the inhabitants of the house the boys have just begged from.

The climax of Tihar comes on the fifth day when sisters ensure the long life of their brothers by worshiping them. Yama is the god of death, and many aspects of the Tihar cycle involve either escaping his dreaded call for the next year or ensuring that, when the call does come, one's soul will be able to avoid the many perils which will beset it on the year-long journey to Yama's kingdom. Thus, the inauspicious crows that are worshiped on the morning of the first day are thought to foretell death with their crowing. Similarly, dogs are fed and honored with tika on the second day so that the fierce dogs which are said to guard the gates of Yama's kingdom will let the soul pass through. Likewise, on the third day the protective yellow string which the family priest tied on each family member's wrist several months earlier at Janai Purni[34] is removed and tied to the tail of the worshiped cow. Villagers say this is done so that the soul will be able to grab the tail of a cow and so cross the terrifying Bhaitari river that bars the way to Yama's kingdom.

But the most important insurance of long life is the protection from Yama that a sister gives on Bhai Tika. In a myth explaining the origin of the ceremony, Yama is said to have come to take the life of a young man, whose sister begged Yama to wait until she had finished worshiping her brother. Yama agreed, and the girl did a long meticulous puja to both her brother and the god of death. Pleased with the girl's devotion, Yama granted her brother a stay of execution for as long as the puja flowers remained fresh. After she had kept up her worship with continually fresh flowers for an entire year, Yama relented and let the boy live.

There is a certain light-heartedness in the villagers' explanations about the rituals involving the dog and cow and how they help the soul after death. But Bhai Tihar is taken very seriously. A man who has no sister will ask even a distant female cousin or the sister of a ritual brother to give him tika. Also, no woman's ghar will keep her from going to her maita to give tika to her brothers, no matter how much work remains to be done.[35]

The ceremony takes place in the morning before anyone has eaten. A space on the mud floor of the house is purified with gobar and a straw mat and cushions or woolen rugs are placed in the center, where the brother will sit. A betel nut in a leaf cup of rice is set out to represent Ganes. There are a brass vessel filled with water that has a piece of holy kus grass in the spout, a wick soaked in clarified butter placed in a leaf plate, and other plates containing fruits, flowers, and items needed for worship. On the edge of the gobar circle are a walnut and a stone.

The brother (or brothers) must sit in the center of the circle while the sister worships Ganes and all the other gods and finally the walnut which represents Yama. Then she lights the votive lamp in the circle and, taking the spouted vessel in hand, walks three times around the edge of the circle evenly spilling out a little of the water as she goes. Next she makes another triple circumambulation of her brother, this time dripping a steady line of oil from a sprig of kus grass. She then sprinkles oil seven times on her brother's head and once in each ear. Then she puts flowers on his head, shoulders, knees, and hands and garlands him with a necklace of Amaranth flowers. These special purple flowers retain their color and shape as they dry and are virtually everlasting; so like the boy in the myth, the brother will be safe from Yama as long as these flowers look fresh. As a sign of her blessing and protection, she now gives the special tika mark on his forehead which only a sister can give on Bhai Tihar. With her little finger she makes a long vertical line of yellow. On this she carefully places dots of red, green, blue, and white. Then she must go to the edge of the ceremonial circle and with one

To protect her brother from the god of death during the coming year a sister places a special garland of everlasting flowers around her brother's neck at Bhai Tika. *Photo by author*

blow smash the walnut with the stone, thus vanquishing Yama. Finally, she gives her brother his *bhag* or "share"—a gift of food which must contain curds, mustard greens, dried fish, and *sel roti* (a doughnut-like fried bread), along with as many other sweets and delicacies as she can afford.[36] The brother must eat some of the yogurt and sel roti, after which his sister washes his hands. Then the brother gives tika[37] to his sister, touches his forehead to her foot, and presents her with daksina. The daksina which grown men give to their sisters can be quite substantial, including gifts of clothes and sometimes even a cow along with considerable amounts of cash.[38]

     To understand the meaning of Bhai Tika it is helpful to look again at the symbolic connections between long life and female purity which we encounter in the Tij–Rishi Pancami complex. In my view, the same logic governs Bhai Tika. As a consanguineal woman, the sister has an absolute purity which even the faithful wife, Arundhati, cannot match. No matter how "pure" an affinal woman may be—in terms of her own caste pedigree, her virginity at the time of marriage, or her subsequent faithfulness to her husband—she still cannot have the ideal categorical purity which a sister has to her consanguineal kin. This purity is the basis of her sacred filiafocal status and of her power to bless her brother with long life. In the Tij festival discussed earlier, the wife merely prevents herself from shortening the life of her husband. Moreover, unlike the sister in Bhai Tika, the wife must undergo a severe fast and take multiple baths before she attains sufficient purity to ensure her husband's normal life-span.

There is an illuminating similarity here between the brother/sister relation (or filiafocal relationships in general) and the patron/priest relation. Men have political and economic power within their natal patriline. While women lack this power, they have, instead, ritual superiority over consanguineal men. This is structurally parallel to the historical relation which Dumont (1970:66–72, 215) has pointed to between the royal Ksatriyas who held political powers and the priestly Brahmans who by virtue of their ritual purity held the powers of religious legitimation. In both situations "worldly" and "spiritual" powers complement each other.[39]

The similarity between Brahman priests and consanguineal women is further attested by the fact that both are the recipients of daksina.[40] Because of their sacred status in the maita, women (like Brahmans) can confer spiritual benefits on their consanguineal kinsmen—notably, the protection given by a sister to her brother and the spiritual merit that parents gain from giving their daughter in marriage. In contrast, the men in filiafocal relationships contribute concrete worldly support to their sisters and daughters. This is symbolized by the daksina gifts which, as we have seen, are given at any auspicious religious ceremony where consanguineal women are present. The gifts to the bride at the wedding foot-washing ceremony and the subsequent flow of gifts from the girl's parents to the girl and her in-laws are all part of this pattern. Although these prestations are based on the ritual superiority of wife-takers, most families are much more concerned with boosting their daughter's status in her own ghar than with actually honoring her in-laws. Moreover, in crisis situations with her affines, a woman's father and brothers are crucial sources of emotional, legal, and sometimes even monetary support. In the case history given in the last chapter involving the segmentation of a joint family, it will be recalled, the maitis of all three women involved came to their aid. Maili's brother threatened to take Agni Prasad to court over the land distribution; Kamala's maiti sent her a milch cow and gave other economic aid in setting up her new household; and

Devi's brothers supported her and reminded Agni Prasad of the life-portion which had been promised to Devi.

There are, as we have seen, limits on the long-term help a woman can expect from her consanguineal kinsmen. Generally, however, men feel a genuine affection as well as a strong sense of duty toward consanguineal women. The fact that married daughters and sisters do not inherit ancestral property and are not involved in the inevitable partition of the joint family estate means that they are removed from the tensions that often affect relations between a man and his father, his brothers, and even his wife. While interactions with these relations tend to be conceived primarily in terms of "duty," relations with consanguineal women are viewed as enjoyable and much more a matter of personal choice. Men appear to derive considerable pride and emotional satisfaction from being generous and supportive of their sisters and daughters. In fact, one could even say that if there is anything that could be called chivalry in the rural Hindu tradition, it is the filiafocal relationship.

The Symbolism of Mother's Milk

There is one striking exception to the ambiguous and largely negative meanings attached to the physical signs of female reproductive powers: mother's milk. Like menstrual blood, mother's milk is undeniably connected with female sexuality— not, however, its destructive threatening aspect, but its creative, nurturing side. Mother's milk represents, in fact, the justification—and purification—of female sexuality through motherhood.

Mother's milk is the obvious link in the strong Hindu association between the cow and the woman in her role as mother. Both are symbols of purity and objects of veneration. In his article on female purity Yalman discusses the connection:

> And again it is most appropriate that the "cow," the supreme symbol of the Hindu mother, should also be the most potent symbol (as well as the main source) of purity. The cow is sacred. Its five gifts—the milk, the ghee, the curd, the urine, the faeces (cowdung)—are all sacred. They are referred to as *pañcagauyon* (or *pañcagauya*) and are the most directly effective purificatory agents. . . .

Small doses of this substance are often taken internally to purify internal pollution. It may be recalled that the sacred ash which Hindus put on themselves is made from burnt cowdung. Thus, "the cow is *kāmā dhenu,* the giver of all things, and hence whenever a cow is approached, it is touched with the hand in token of veneration which is then raised to the head." . . .

The association between the cow and women (especially the mother) is, of course, freely made. . . . Sinhalese villagers, who also hold similar opinions, would often remark that the cow is sacred because it is like the mother. It can, they would say, be substituted for the mother: it provides milk for the babies left motherless. [Yalman 1963:43]

Hindu villagers in Nepal hold views similar to those Yalman reports, and, as we have seen, they make identical use of the purifying powers of the cow and its products, as evidenced by the many ritual contexts that require cow's milk—or some of the other products of the cow—either as purifying agents or as pure offerings to the gods and ancestors.

Mother's milk also seems to have certain purifying powers in that the nursing infant is, by and large, immune from either being polluted or causing pollution. In my discussion of the rituals of childhood I noted that newborn infants are not considered to be full social and ritual beings. They have not yet entered into samsara, which is characterized by constant fluctuation between states of purity and pollution. Unlike the purity of the religious mendicant, who has transcended samsara through his own renunciation and mighty discipline, infants exude the passive purity of one who has not yet fully entered the world. It is an ascribed purity closely connected with their dependence on the mother and her milk. Even among the most orthodox, menstruating women may freely touch their nursing children; the pollution of menstrual blood is neutralized by the purity of mother's milk. Likewise, many women informants explained (often as they were calmly cleaning up a child's "accident") that infant urine and feces are not considered so polluting as that of adults because the infant's only food is its mother's milk.

The nursing link between mother and child symbolizes the infant's immunity. As this immunity weakens—first with the rice feeding ceremony and then with the sacred thread ceremony and marriage rituals—the child moves from dependence toward religious and social responsibility and adulthood. In the process of separation from the mother and her milk the child

becomes more and more vulnerable to pollution and, conse-
quently, more and more involved in the ritual means of purification. The end of the nursing relationship between mother and
son is ritualized when the mother feeds her son curds (called
sagun) before he sets off with the marriage party to bring back
the bride. Among other Hindu groups, including the Brahmans
and Chetris of the Jumla region the groom actually sucks his
mother's breast at this ceremony.[41] Symbolically, the groom is
not only expressing his gratitude to his mother (for which he
will repay her by bringing in a daughter-in-law to help her). He
is also completing the move from purity and dependence on his
mother to the inevitable pollution of his householder's role and
his impending sexual relations with a wife.

Motherhood as the Mediation of Patrifocal and Filiafocal Views

Thus far, I have not discussed the symbolic dimensions of the
mother in Brahman-Chetri kinship organization, partly because
the mother has high ritual status that cannot be explained fully
by either patrifocal or filiafocal principles. The mother cannot
be classed with the wife as a low-status (sexually threatening)
affinal woman. Nor, despite her strong association with purity,
is the mother in the same category as other female consanguineal kin like the sister and the daughter.

　　The mother, in fact, is the diachronic synthesis of the opposing affinal and consanguineal categories of female kin. With
respect to ego's father and his elders—and to the patriline as a
group—ego's mother is an affinal woman. But she is also a permanent member of her son's patriline, as his sisters and daughters cannot be.[42] And although she is obviously related consan-
guineally to her son, her high ritual status with respect to him is
not due to filiafocal reversal. It is part of the patrifocal structure.
She receives bheti rather than daksina from her sons at Dasai
(see no. 15 on chart 4.1). Mothers—and by extension, all senior
women who married into ego's lineage—are the only females
who have high status *in the patrifocal model*.

　　The mother is as powerful, if not more powerful, than
the sister or the daughter as a representation of female purity.

Like them, she stands in symbolic opposition to the wife. Swami Nikhilananda, a devotee of Ramakrishna, expresses the common Hindu view of the distinction: "A mother's love and sacrifice qualify her spiritually to stand above all other relations. A wife's love may fluctuate with the sweetness bestowed upon her. But the mother's affection by its very nature grows deeper as the need grows . . ." (1962:81–82). He goes on to express the more extreme Hindu idealization of motherhood, betraying his underlying ascetic commitment to renunciation:

By seeing God in a woman [man] gradually sublimates his carnal desires. Carnality, which seeks fulfilment through physical union with a member of the opposite sex, is one of the deadly enemies with which spiritual seekers, both men and women, have to wrestle. A woman can easily conquer it by regarding a man as her child. She is, in essence, the mother of all men, no matter what other relationships society may sanction or speak of. A man, too, easily subdues his lust by seeing in a woman the symbol of motherhood. But alas, an ignorant person regards woman as an object to satisfy his physical appetite. He craves her body and pushes away the Divinity in her. Thus he becomes entangled in the coils of the world. If he worships the Divinity in her, he is blessed with the nectar of immortality. [1962:82]

The village householder has, of course, no intention of transforming *his* wife into his mother as the ascetic Ramakrishna did with his wife, Sarda Devi. After all, the villager's first concerns are to have children and perhaps even physical enjoyment, rather than the attainment of spiritual release. The householder is, however, nonetheless sensitive to the symbolic opposition between mother and wife. The mother is associated with purity, breast milk, constancy, and selfless asexual love; the wife with pollution, menstrual blood, potential unfaithfulness, and sexual demands. Yet (Nikhilananda aside) the mother's purity is actually less remote and static than that of other female consanguineal kin. In the village setting, female sexuality is not denied in the mother as it is symbolically in the sister and the daughter; it has been transformed and legitimated by its manifest service to the patriline. This is perhaps the reason that newly delivered women are permitted to sun themselves with their beasts and legs exposed. Motherhood purifies the affinal women—the dangerous wives—of one generation and transforms them into consanguineal women of the next. Even to the lineage members of her own and senior generations, motherhood makes the affinal woman seem like less of an outsider in her ghar. It gives her a common cause with her fellow lineage members. Her status increases, and she has less need to escape to her maita for solace. By middle age a woman with children is usually deeply identified with her affinal group. Her threatening and highly sexual identity as a wife is increasingly overlaid and neutralized by her role as a mother. Thus, the synchronic reversal of female status that occurs between ghar and maita is diachronically achieved within the ghar itself. Woman in her role as mother mediates the opposing views of women reflected in the filiafocal and patrifocal dimensions.

The mediating powers of motherhood are demonstrated in the story of the foundation of the Bisankhu Bista lineage in the Kathmandu Valley. Bista (1972:77, my trans.) records this story as follows:

There was once a Bista who married a girl from Bisankhu (probably a Khatri). One day she had gone to see her parents in Bisankhu and afterwards she returned carried in a sedan chair (doli). On the road the porters who were carrying the sedan chair stopped for a moment to rest, and the young girl took the opportunity to glance outside her sedan chair. She saw then that there were some greens for sale, and when the porters returned, she asked them to buy the greens. That evening in her husband's house she gave the greens to her parents-in-law along with the koseli gifts from her parents. Her father-in-law was at first very happy at the sight of the greens, but he became angry when he learned she had bought them herself on the journey. It was scandalous that the daughter-in-law of a family of his rank should be exposed to the eyes of the public in a wayside establishment. He said then that he would no longer accept water from the hands of his daughter-in-law and refused to allow her to enter the house. She passed the night outside, and returned to her parents' house the next morning. The young woman's husband (that is to say the Bista) was in the service of one of the Malla kings of the valley, and this permitted the couple to meet often in Bisankhu. After several such meetings the woman became pregnant, and when the time for her delivery grew close, she left her parents' house. They built a little house on a piece of land which the woman's parents had given her, and after the baby was born, the husband went to live there openly. Meanwhile, the young Bista had received a land grant (birta). The Bista of Bisankhu are descendants of this Bista, who was without doubt called Dasarath.

The affines' fear of her sexual betrayal (i.e., her glance from the sedan chair, which is "scandalous" and makes her too impure for her in-laws to take water from her hands) and her own parents' inability to deal with even her legitimate sexuality (i.e., she cannot stay in her father's house for the delivery of a child fathered by her own husband) forces the woman first from her ghar and then from her maita. So she and her husband must move to a third place, the "little house" given by her maita, and with the birth of their child they found a new lineage. Motherhood thus forces a compromise between the patrifocal view of woman as impure and sexually loose and the filiafocal view of woman as the perpetual, asexual virgin.

Notes

1. In Nepal dogs are scavengers, eating not only leftover foods but human excrement. Thus, they are considered very low and impure animals.

2. As I mentioned earlier, among the Brahman-Chetri of Jumla women may not enter the house at all for three days and so they must sleep in a cattle shed or outside with a fire. Linda Stone reports that this rule holds also for the Brahman-Chetri women of Nuwakot.

3. This text is read at the end of the Tij–Rishi Pancami festival described later in the chapter.

4. Women's fertile period is believed to occur between the fourth and the fourteenth day after menstruation begins. Intercourse thereafter is for pleasure rather than procreation. For further discussion of Brahman-Chetri ideas about conception and reproduction see Bennett 1976.

5. Unmarried girls fast to find a good husband, and widows fast so that they may not be widows again in the next life.

6. Had Carstairs been able to interview Rajasthani women, he might have found that, like Narikot women, they also viewed their husbands' sexual demands on them as debilitating.

7. Usually the two are separated by a day in between, but since the dates for the festivals are determined independently by astrological calculations they sometimes fall back to back—even though *tij* means the third day of the lunar fortnight and *pancami* means the fifth day.

8. The whole *Swasthani Vrata Katha* is dedicated to extolling the powers of the goddess Swasthani and the efficacy of the Swasthani *vrata* or *barta*—a religious vow to the goddess with power to grant any desire. Thus, Parvati's fast is used by the text as an occasion to demonstrate the power of the vow. Siva appears to Parvati in response to her worship of the sand phallus. But, instead of directly granting her boon, Siva directs her to follow Visnu's advice. Visnu then tells Parvati to perform the Swasthani vrata and describes the procedures for it in meticulous detail. Only after she performs the vow to Swasthani does the goddess grant Parvati her wish to have Siva as a bridegroom. Village women usually perform the arduous Swasthani vrata at least once during their lives—but as the vow can only be performed during the month of Magh (January–February) and requires a month of fasting and worship, it is not performed on Tij. Instead, at Tij village women reenact the first and more traditional part of Parvati's austerities in which she worships the sand phallus.

9. Although my informants reported that the offerings were to Siva, Bista (1969:12)

reports that women in his area, near Godavari on the edge of the Kathmandu Valley, made offerings to Krsna on the night of Tij.

10. As mentioned earlier, the only occasion besides Tij when it is proper for a woman to dance is at her son's or brother's wedding during the *ratauli* celebrations.

11. However, even this pious, patrilineally acceptable goal can be subverted, because some women told me that if a woman didn't like her husband she should dedicate her fast to finding a new one to run away with (*poila janu*). Even though women and even widows who marry a second time lose ritual status and a certain amount of respect in Brahman-Chetri culture, a recent study of one Parbatiya community (Bennett 1981:116) showed that 5.6 percent of the ever-married high-caste women had been married more than once.

12. Women past menopause do not need to bathe on Rishi Pancami, although they gain extra merit if they do so.

13. In Bista's very thorough account of the bathing ritual the more orthodox seven types of pure earth (*sapta mrtika*) are mentioned.

14. Ganes is simply a betel nut set in a plate of uncooked rice representing the elephant-headed god. According to some informants a married daughter in her *maita* could worship the votive lamp, Ganes, and sacred vessel with her mother, but she had to do her own godan and make her own offerings to the rishis and Arundhati. Other informants maintained that a married daughter also had to do a separate *kalas puja*.

15. This myth is also briefly recounted in chapter 15 of the *Swasthani Vrata Katha*, though Arundhati is not mentioned by name (see Sharma 2022b: chap. 7).

16. The myth is echoed in the traditional belief mentioned earlier that the husband must sleep with his wife on the fourth day after menstruation because women begin their fertile period then and are particularly desirous of sex—though village women themselves usually deny that they are.

17. Turner's (1931) Nepali dictionary glosses *saubhagya* as "happiness, good fortune, prosperity—the possession of a living husband."

18. Although no explicit association was made to me in this context, women often joked about the phallic nature of these fruits at other times.

19. This meal is cooked and served by the husbands and the women eat first, reversing the normal procedure. Because they are considered ritually to be in the same state as if they had just bathed on the fourth day of menstruation, the women returning from their Rishi Pancami observances are pure enough to touch men but not pure enough to cook food or carry water (this they may do only on the fifth day). The meal of rice, *piralu* (a white potato-like root) and *karkalo* (the dried edible stalk of the piralu) must be served on a banana leaf which the women must bury themselves when the meal is finished because it is highly polluted. The karkalo which the men must serve is interesting, as it is believed to arouse sexual desires when eaten. Women in the late stages of pregnancy are advised not to eat karkalo since "it will make their buttocks itch"—i.e., it will make them want intercourse. Informants themselves, however, never mentioned this aspect of karkalo in connection with the Rishi Pancami meal.

20. I conducted a survey on marriage and fertility for all the Brahman-Chetri women past menarche who were presently members of the local patrilineal kin groups of one hamlet in Narikot. Specifically, this group of 59 women includes 12 unmarried daughters who are still members of their father's thar and gotra and 47 married women who have become members of their husband's thar and gotra. Married daughters who have become members of their husband's thar and gotra in other villages are not included.

21. Surya is a male deity worshiped by Brahman and Chetri women in many different contexts as a symbol of purity.

22. Nowadays the twelve-day period of seclusion even for unmarried girls is much more common. But many of my older informants recalled a twenty-two day seclusion.

23. This informant was fastidious in her observation of all rules for maintaining ritual purity. She was among those women who believed menstruating women should

not touch *anyone* except a nursing child. Many other women avoided only adult men during their periods.

24. This is a reference to the common belief that the witches can cause harm—especially fertility problems—if they are allowed to see the menstrual blood of a victim. It is part of this same belief which requires the bride to cover the vermilion line on the parting of her hair after the groom has first put it there. Female sexuality, then, is not only dangerous to men. Women themselves are vulnerable if their sexuality is not carefully shielded.

25. According to other informants and my own observations, the girl herself performs the Surya puja.

26. The gift of a red blouse and dhoti here is actually preceded by several years by the gift of the first dhoti and blouse (*guniu colo*) which are also red, given to daughters sometime after their seventh year for Brahman and eleventh year for Chetris on the eighth day of Dasai. In traditional hill families this would signal the girl's approach to marriageable age.

27. The ritual seclusion and purification are repeated for a period of seven days following the girl's second and third menses.

28. Often such children are abandoned before the name-giving. If the child's umbilical cord is uncut when it is abandoned, it will assume the caste of whomever finds it and claims it by cutting the cord.

29. In all the cases of unmarried motherhood which I encountered, the lovers were known and were acceptable (i.e., marriageable) caste status. In one instance, the disgraced girl was taken in as a youngest wife (*kanchi*)—causing his indignant elder wife to leave him and go to live in her maita. In another case, the girl's family managed to marry her off to an Indian in the distant plains where the fairness of hill women cancels out many other defects. In the third case, the boy—though of proper caste background—refused to marry the girl. She is still unmarried and expects to remain so, but her family had the resources to train her for a profession. She now supports herself as a schoolteacher (her child died soon after birth).

None of these cases occurred in Narikot itself. Rather, they happened to more urbanized relatives of Narikot villagers and, in the eyes of the villagers, they reflect the dangers of the greater freedom (in terms of later marriage, education, even office jobs) allowed to "modern" middle-class girls.

Nevertheless, a fourth case, which did occur in the village (nearly two decades ago), seems to have been accepted with surprisingly little permanent damage to the woman's place in the community. The unmarried sister of a village woman came to help her during her birth-pollution period after childbirth and was impregnated by the woman's husband. They were informally married (with the *diyo kalas puja* ceremony), and now the two sisters have separate households in Narikot. The offspring of the second sister are of thimbu rather than jharra status because of the irregularity of her marriage, but otherwise the two women are treated as equal co-wives by the village.

30. Vermilion powder is included in the father's gift, but informants stated emphatically that it was to be used only to make the red tika mark (which can be worn by unmarried girls) and not to decorate the parting of the hair (which only married woman may do).

31. One vivid symbolic expression of this temporary loss of control over female sexuality in all three instances is the unoiled, uncombed hair which menstruating women, new mothers, and new widows must all maintain.

32. In the Jumla region of far western Nepal the relaxation of behavioral standards in the maita is carried to an extreme. A married woman in her maita may go to all-night singing parties with eligible men (i.e., potential partners for a second or third marriage) from neighboring villages. Such behavior in the ghar would be a disgrace warranting at least a severe beating and perhaps permanent expulsion from her husband's house (Campbell 1978).

33. The Nepali words are: *Hariyo gobar le lipeko, Laksmi puja gareko; He ausi baro, gai tihar bhailo.*

34. Interestingly, on the same lunar date that Janai Purni is observed in Nepal, the Raksabandhan festival is celebrated in India in which sisters (as well as Brahmans) tie protective threads around their brothers' wrists to wish them long life. Although there is no Bhai Tika celebration in India, the Raksabandhan festival expresses the same sacred and mutually protective brother/sister relationship.

35. If an older woman is already the head of her own household and has many children of her own who will be celebrating Bhai Tika, she may well remain in her ghar, where her brother will visit her to receive her blessings.

36. One typical share I observed contained along with the traditional yogurt, greens, and fishes: raisins, pieces of coconut, a waternut called *makan*, betel nut, cashew nuts, fried breads, doughnut-like sel roti, almonds, cardamom, cloves, cinnamon, an orange, banana, guava, and various sweets. These are expensive luxuries which are rarely consumed in village homes.

37. In some families the brothers give their sister the same elaborate multicolored tika they receive; in others brothers give *daiacheta tika* with curds, red powder, and rice grains to their sisters.

38. For poorer farmers with several sisters, daksina might be only ten or twenty rupees, but I encountered cases where unmarried brothers gave their sisters a hundred rupees and an expensive sari at Bhai Tika.

39. Though many Brahmans become economically and politically powerful, my observation in Nepal has been that when they do, Brahmans tend to give up their priestly work. They expressed the view that accepting dan and daksina was somehow demeaning, like accepting charity.

40. Villagers also say that it is a sin to accept anything (even a sister's gift of food at Bhai Tika) from a daughter, sister, or Brahman without giving a greater gift in return.

41. James Gabriel Campbell, personal communication.

42. Even if she should subsequently elope with another man, a woman is still considered a member of her first husband's gotra for ritual purposes in the sraddha ceremonies for her which any sons from that union must perform. Sons by the second marriage, however, will also offer sraddha to her as if she were a member of their gotra. This potential unfaithfulness symbolized by the switching of gotra is perhaps another reason why women must always remain peripheral members of their affinal lineage.

CHAPTER 7

The Goddess: Mythic Resolutions to the Problem of Women and Women's Problems

Oppositions Within the Nature of the Devi

With the Hindu view of women so strongly characterized by contradiction, it is not surprising that the nature of the Hindu goddess Devi should also be contradictory.[1]
There are hundreds of forms of the Devi in village Hinduism,
but to the villager they are all one no matter what their differences in appearance or attributes. There are, however, two major categories into which the myriad manifestations of the Devi
fall: the terrifying, destructive forms and the gentle, nurturing
forms.

The terrible side of the Devi is represented by the bloodthirsty virgin warrior Durga and her hosts. Also in this category
are Kali, Camunda, Mahisamardini, Yogi Nidra, and Ambika, all
epithets or emanations of Durga; Sansari Devi, a local Narikot
goddess who receives a community sacrifice at the onset of the
hot season to invoke her protection against illness for women
and children; Sitala, the smallpox goddess; the five virgins (*panca
kumari*), to whom there are several well-kept shrines in Narikot;
the seven matrkas (mothers);[2] the sixty-four yogini—and perhaps
even local *boksi* or human witches.[3] These forms of the Devi
share a wrathful nature which is potentially dangerous, but which
can be protective if the Devi is properly appeased with blood
sacrifice (*bhog*).

The gentle side of the goddess is perhaps best represented by Uma Parvati, the devoted wife of Siva, whom we encountered in our discussion of Tij–Rishi Pancami. In addition, Sati Devi (Parvati in a previous incarnation), Laksmi (wife of Visnu and goddess of wealth), Annapurna (another form of Parvati), Sita (Ram's faithful wife), and many other lesser goddesses as well fall into this category. We might characterize the gentle aspect of the Devi as the pure (yet alluring), devoted wife and the gentle, nurturing mother.

Both aspects of the Devi, however, are fraught with contradiction, and therein lies the Devi's power as a symbol. For Parvati, though she is the epitome of purity and though she is associated with asceticism through her famous fast, is above all, known as a *wife*—what is more, a particularly erotic and enticing one. In the popular religious posters she is almost always pictured with her husband Siva—sometimes flirting seductively with him, sometimes in a more sedate family portrait of the handsome couple and their two children, Ganes and Kumar, atop the bull Nandi. Despite her extreme purity, Parvati is not exclusively associated with the perpetually "virginal" and "asexual" consanguineal woman. In fact, Parvati seems to contain within her the same extremes of asceticism and eroticism which O'Flaherty (1973) has so thoroughly documented for her husband Siva.

Durga/Kali presents similar problems in such an analysis. She is strongly associated with blood and potential destructiveness. The common bazaar poster of Kali shows a beautiful woman with a lolling red tongue and loose streaming hair who stands astride the prone body of her husband Siva. She holds the bloody severed head of a man in one of her four hands and wears a garland of human heads around her neck and a girdle of human hands around her waist. In the background there are pools of blood and dismembered limbs—carnage from the battle that rages around her. Yet, despite this threatening image and the strong associations with blood, Durga is not directly connected with affinal women, nor with pollution or eroticism. Instead, she is the chaste warrior-virgin closely linked with purity and asceticism.

Both aspects of the Devi, then, are linked with pollution and affinal women on the one hand (e.g., Parvati's erotic nature and her status as a wife; Durga's association with blood and destruction) and with purity and consanguineal women on the other (e.g., Parvati's ascetic austerities before her marriage; Durga's virginity and her birth from ascetic heat generated by the austerities of the gods). In both cases the contradictions have been mediated by the myths surrounding each aspect of the Devi. Such myths, of course, are legion. The Puranas abound with them, and it is far beyond the scope of this book to trace or analyze their many variations. I will confine myself here to the versions of the two major mythic complexes which appear in Narikot. Both myths form part of the background for two important calendrical festivals concerning the Devi, one in her terrible aspect and one in her gentle aspect.

Dasai: Village Men and the Goddess Durga

The Myth

In my earlier discussion of Dasai, I mentioned that in most families a text called the *Candi Path* is used in the worship of the Devi. The *Candi* (sometimes called the *Durga Saptasati*) as I found it in the village appears to be a version of the famous sixth-century Sakta devotional work, the *Devi Mahatmya*.[4] In the village copies I examined, the Sanskrit text of the *Devi Mahatmya* was rendered in Nepali at the bottom of each page. During ceremonies the priest could thus chant the Sanskrit version for its ritual efficacy, and then repeat it in Nepali as he went along, allowing the villagers to follow the story.

The *Candi* is essentially the story of three different occasions when the Devi in her terrible aspect intervened to save the gods—and, by extension, mankind as well—by defeating various demons who had usurped the gods' powers and were terrorizing the universe. Interspersed between these heroic episodes are hymns of praise to the goddess (*stotra*) in which the gods beseech her protection. The local texts differ from the original *Devi Mahatmya* in that they begin with a short invocation called the "The Armor of Durga" or *Durga Kabac* which does not appear in the original work. It calls on the nine forms of Durga by name to protect the devotees: "Those [devotees] who are being burnt by fire, those who are being encircled by enemies in the battlefield: those who are terrified and afflicted with great difficulties, if they take shelter under the Durgas, will

not suffer, nor will they have any difficulties in battlefields"
(*Durgasaptasati* 1974:17, my trans.). The text then proceeds to
invoke a different form of the goddess to protect each part and
specific function of the devotee's body. Some Brahman and
Chetri men know the *Durga Kabac* by heart and recite it every
day. Others who are illiterate may keep a copy of it—or the
whole *Candi*—as an object of worship. The literate and devout
may read a portion or all of the text on each of the first nine
days of Dasai in their altar room. But in every household the
Candi, or at least part of it, is read by the family priest before
blood sacrifice is offered to the goddess on the eighth day of
Dasai. One striking feature of the *Candi* is the fact that it is read
and heard almost exclusively by men. Villagers do not recall
anyone ever sponsoring a pandit to do a public reading of the
Candi in the village (as is sometimes done for other Puranic
works), though a few families have paid for it to be read by a
priest in the Gujeswari temple. One informant told me that
women are specifically forbidden to recite the *Durga Kabac* because of its power as a mantra. Women might mispronounce
the long Sanskrit words and inadvertantly cause harm to themselves or others. Most women had never heard the text read
and knew the myths only vaguely—though quite a few could
give the name of Durga's most famous demon foe, Mahisa, and
all expressed great respect for Durga's powers. Yet it was my
impression that men are much more involved in the worship
and mythology of Durga than are women.

The basic plot of the three myths recounted in the *Candi
Path* follows the familiar form of conflict between gods and demons. The first, brief story is not very well known to the villagers, as its import is mainly philosophical and sectarian.[5] But
the second story, of Durga's victory over the buffalo demon
Mahisa, is known to all and is an important part of the meaning
of Devi and her worship at Dasai. In the myth, Indra and the
gods were defeated by the powerful demon king Mahisa, who
expelled them from heaven. The gods went to Visnu, Siva, and
Brahma to ask for help. When the three great gods heard of
Mahisa's deeds they were so angry that a brilliant heat (*tejas*)
radiated from their bodies. A similar brilliance issued from the
other gods, until

all this light became unified into one. The Devas [gods] saw in front
of them a pile of light blazing like a mountain whose flames filled
the whole space. Then that matchless light born from the bodies of

all gods gathered into a single corpus and turned into a woman
enveloping the three worlds by her lustre. [Agrawala (trans.) 1963:47]

After her birth from the ascetic heat of the gods, the Devi was
given each god's most potent weapon, and she set forth on her
vehicle, the lion, to fight Mahisa's army. She defeated the en-
emy army and Mahisa himself in his buffalo form. She left utter
destruction in her wake: "The tidal blood from the bodies of
elephants, demons and horses of that Asura [demon] army
gushed forth like mighty rivers in the field of battle" (Agrawala
1963:55).

The next episode is more complicated. The story begins
like the Mahisa myth with the gods beseeching Devi's protection (which she had promised at the end of the last episode to
give them in times of need). This time the gods sought protection from the two demons Simbha and Nisimbha, who had
gained control of the universe. But this time Durga, who had
been born earlier from the radiance of the male gods, issued
from the body of the gentle Parvati:

> while the gods were thus engaged in invoking the goddess through
> praises and in other ways, Pārvati came there to bathe in the waters
> of the Gangā. She, of the lovely brows, said to the gods, "Who is
> being praised by you here?" Then sprang forth from her physical
> sheath Śiva Kausiki [Durga] who replied, "This hymn is being ad-
> dressed to me by the assembled gods vanquished by the Asura Sim-
> bha and routed in battle by Nisimbha." [Agrawala 1963:85]

Because the goddess Kausiki was so beautiful, Simbha
decided that either he or his brother Nisimbha should add her
to their collection of the great treasures of the universe which
they had won from the gods. The demons' marriage proposal
was, however, rebuffed by the Devi. She explained that she had
taken a vow to marry only a man who could conquer her in
battle. The two demon kings were furious at this haughty reply
and began sending their generals to bring Devi, "dragging her
by the hair or binding her" if necessary.

When the first two demon generals, Chanda and Munda,
were sent to fetch her, the goddess brought forth Kali as an em-
anation of herself. "From the broad forehead of curved eyebrows suddenly sprang forth Kali of terrible countenance, armed
with a sword and a noose" (Agrawala, 1963:98). Kali quickly
killed Chanda and Munda and devoured their army.

After this, Simbha and Nisimbha sent their own army

against the Devi. But she caused the seven matrkas (the vital female power or *sakti* of the seven major male gods) to join her and Kali in the fight. The matrkas were no match for the demon Raktabij who was now sent to battle by Simbha and Nisimbha. This demon was almost invincible because "whenever from his body a drop of blood fell on the ground, instantaneously sprang up from the earth an Asura of the same size" (Argrawala 1963:109). The more wounds the matrkas inflicted on Raktabij, the more demons were produced, until "from his flowing blood were born thousands of great Asura of his stature [which] filled the world all over" (Agrawala 1963:11). Then the Devi commanded Kali to drink Raktabij's blood before it could fall to the ground and produce more demons. This time when the Devi attacked Raktabij,

> from his stricken body blood flowed profusely; Cāmuṇḍā [Kali] also swallowed the great Asuras, born from the flow of his blood, who came in her mouth; and at the same time (she) drank the blood which flowed from his body.
>   The Devi smote Raktabij with her dart, thunderbolt arrow, sword and spear, while Cāmuṇḍā went on drinking the blood.
>   Thus stricken with a multitude of weapons and rendered bloodless, the great Asura Raktabij fell on the ground, O King.
>   Thereupon the gods attained great joy, O King. The Mātṛkā born from the bodies of the gods danced, being intoxicated with blood. [Agrawala 1963:113]

Following this there was another gory battle scene in which the Devi and her hosts slew Nisimbha, one of the demon kings. The remaining brother Simbha taunted the Devi to fight him alone, and so she commanded Kali and the seven matrkas to withdraw back into her body saying, "through my power I stood here in many forms; all that has been withdrawn by me, and now I stand alone. Be you steadfast in combat" (Agrawala 1963:123). With that, she killed Simbha, and the universe returned to normal.

The Devi's heroic exploits in the *Devi Mahatmya*, for the most part, follow the standard Puranic formula for the battles between gods and demons. Some of the details of the myth, however, are important to the symbolic meanings of the terrible forms of the goddess. For example, Durga's birth from the heat of the gods means that she begins with the kind of ascetic purity which Parvati only obtains after rigorous austerities and fasting. The specifically antierotic nature of Durga's purity is further em-

A common bazaar poster of Kali, one of the more bloodthirsty forms of the goddess in her terrible aspect. *Photo by David Sasoon*

phasized in the episode in which she declares her vow to remain unmarried until she is defeated in battle by her suitor. These story elements serve to neutralize the goddess's strong negative association with blood and death, both sources of impurity. Symbolically the Devi transcends the categories of purity and pollution and of life and death. In the *Devi Mahatmya*, Durga is depicted as enjoying wine and blood sacrifice. For Parvati—and the high-caste women in Narikot—drinking wine or performing sacrifice would be polluting. Brahman-Chetri women may not perform sacrifices themselves, and if possible, should not even watch them. Although they may (except for a few who are very strict) eat certain kinds of meat, they may not take any intoxicating liquor without losing caste status. Like Parvati, adult villar women must attain and guard their purity through fasting abstention. Durga, however, is so pure that these things cannot pollute her, and she may enjoy them freely, in rather the way very young high-caste girls may drink liquor and even eat at a Damai's house (before their adult teeth come in).

The Raktabij episode connects the Devi with fertility—specifically with controlled fertility—which is one of her most important powers. Raktabij's blood is structurally similar to menstrual blood, in that both are sources of fertility. But the demon's blood is even more dangerous because it is overproductive—it circumvents the long process of human conception and birth, and the myriad offspring it produces are destructive demons. When Kali devours Raktabij's blood, she is doing more than simply indulging her famed voracious bloodlust. She is imposing control on the dangerous forces of fertility by absorbing them all into herself.

This brings us to another important point made in the Simbha-Nisimbha episode: the many forms of the Devi are all one. Before the battle, Durga produces first Kali and then the fierce matrkas, but she withdraws them all into herself for the final struggle with Simbha. The text points out the ultimate unity of the fierce and gentle aspects of the Devi when Durga, responding to the plea of the defeated gods, emerges from Parvati's body. From the point of view of the text, the goddess's terrible form is definitely ascendant. Parvati is unaware of her powerful warlike alter ego. When she hears the gods praising the goddess, she asks, "Who is being praised by you here?" And after Durga's appearance, Parvati withdraws and has no part in the ensuing battle scenes. Nevertheless, the Devi clearly encompasses both aspects in all their many forms. If the myths leave any doubt of this, we have only to look at the three major hymns of praise in the text, where the different forms and epithets of the Devi number in the hundreds.

The Ritual

The basic elements of the Dasai Durga worship were described earlier in some detail (chapter 4). I return to the Navaratri rituals here because they form an important link between Brahman-Chetri kinship structures and the meaning of the goddess Durga to ordinary villagers.

One aspect of the Navaratri rituals that was found significant in terms of kinship is also crucial to the understanding of

Durga. That is the fact that Durga puja is performed only by initiated males. We recall that only adult men can enter the darkened Dasai ghar where Durga in her nine forms is worshiped during the nine nights of Navaratri. Women are not considered pure enough to approach Durga's shrine, and menstruating women are not even allowed on the same story of the house where the Dasai ghar has been erected. Earlier I interpreted this exclusion of women as an indication of their peripheral membership in the institution of the patriline, coinciding with their low status in what I called the patrifocal dimension of kinship. Later, the low status of women in the dominant patrifocal model was in turn found to be linked with the fundamental Hindu conflict between asceticism and sexuality as well as with certain structural tensions inherent in the patrilineal joint family. Women were perceived as a threat to the ideals of ascetic purity and agnatic solidarity, and yet, because of their procreative role, they were also perceived as necessary for the continuation of society. This ambivalence about women applied with particular force to *affinal* women—who generally had the lowest status—because they were most closely associated with sexuality and because they were also perceived as the major source of divisiveness within the joint family.

All this suggests that there are deeper reasons, closely connected with the fundamentally anomalous position of women in Hindu patrilineal society, that explain why the Navaratri sacrifice to Durga is an exclusively male affair, and why Brahman-Chetri men are far more involved with Durga than women are. It appears to me that in some respects Durga embodies a predominantly *male* perception of women (or at least a part of the male perception) that women themselves only partially share. To the agnatically related males who gather to worship her in the dark chamber of the Dasai ghar, Durga perhaps represents the dangerous aspect of women, particularly the affinal women who threaten the purity and the cohesiveness of the patriline even as they produce its next generation.

There are certain definite structural similarities between Durga and affinal women. Just as affinal women must be controlled through rules about menstrual pollution and by other behavioral restrictions, so Durga must be appeased with praise and blood sacrifices. Both Durga and affinal women are powerful but uncertain and potentially destructive sources of fertility. We are already well acquainted with this aspect of affinal women.

The hymns of praise in the *Devi Mahatmya* are very explicit about Durga's potential destructiveness, threatening human beings as well as demons. The goddess is said to "forthwith destroy whole families when enraged" (Agrawala 1963:69). And in another section she is thus described:

In times of prosperity she indeed becomes Laksmī who bestows prosperity on men in their homes; and in times of misfortune, she herself becomes the goddess of misfortune and brings about ruin. When praised and worshipped with flowers, incense, perfumes, etc., she bestows wealth and sons and a mind devoted to dharma and an auspicious life. [Agrawala 1963:149]

In the text Devi also gives very definite instructions on how her protective rather than wrathful aspect is to be brought forth by the householder:

Where this poem is duly recited always in my special shrine, I will never forsake that place and there my presence is certain.

At the offering of the sacrifice during worship, in the cere- monies with fire, and at great festivals, all this story of my exploits should be chanted and heard.

I will accept with love the sacrifice and worship that is done to me as well as the Agnihotra [fire sacrifice] that is offered either with knowledge or without understanding.

During the autumn season when the great annual worship is performed for me, the man who listens with devotion to this glori- fication of mine,

Shall assuredly through my grace be delivered from all trou- bles, and be blessed with riches, grains and children. [Agrawala 1963:145]

The basic outlines of the worship suggested in the text— i.e., sacrifice, fire ceremony (*hom*), and reading or hearing the *Devi Mahatmya*—are all very similar to the Kalratri sacrifice, the climax of the Dasai rituals which I described earlier.[6] Even the timing of the Devi's great festival in autumn is consistent with the present-day timing of Dasai.

But perhaps the most striking and significant similarity be- tween the text and the Brahman-Chetri Dasai rituals is that in both there is strong emphasis on the Devi's control over fertility. Besides her metaphoric victory over Raktabij, the text also ex- plicitly and repeatedly mentions Durga's power to give or de- stroy her devotee's offspring at pleasure.

The Dasai rituals are equally expressive of Durga's asso- ciation with fertility. For example, the Devi is said to be present in the water-filled pot which is smeared with cowdung and barley seeds on the first day of Navaratri. By the tenth day, the seeds have sprouted and are cut and dispersed among the members of the household and other relatives. When questioned, villagers say these yellow barley sprouts, like the tika mark itself with which they are given, are simply "auspicious," or "good luck" or "necessary on Dasai." But in the context of this symbolic analysis, I would suggest that the barley sprouts clearly signify the fertility and prosperity—the "riches, grains and children"—which Durga bestows on her devotees when she is pleased.

Even the tika mark contains symbolic associations with prosperity and fertility. Concerning prosperity, there is a structural parallel between tika, which is made of unbroken rice grains, curd, and red powder, and special Dasai foods: pounded rice, curd, and meat. As for expressions of fertility, there is another possible symbolic link between the tika ingredients of curd and red powder and the body fluids associated with the positive and negative aspects of reproduction in the human female: mother's milk and menstrual blood. This rather speculative interpretation is supported by the kinds of blessings (asik) which are given by superiors along with tika and barley at Dasai. Usually prosperity in the form of monetary or (these days) academic success is wished for young men, while senior women bless a younger married woman with the wish that she may bear a son in the coming year.

There is also the explicitly stated efficacy of the "neck blood" (gardan ragat) from the goat sacrifice to Durga as a remedy for women's menstrual irregularities and fertility problems. Coupled with the fact that Durga will only accept the sacrifice of uncastrated male animals, this would seem to further strengthen Durga's association with fertility and with the reproductive aspect of menstrual blood—and thus indirectly with affinal women.

Of course, the goddess Durga has many meanings to the villagers who worship her. I have chosen to focus on that symbolic aspect which helps to explain why Durga is of special concern to men at Dasai. In so doing, I have attempted to suggest that Durga is a symbolic expression of the patrilineal group's vulnerability to and dependence on its affinal women, who like Durga may or may not use their power for the good of the patrilineal group. Despite all the ritual and social controls imposed on them, affinal women are still perceived as a threat. Thus, Dasai can be interpreted as yet another ritual attempt to neutralize the negative and dangerous aspects of the female sex. Through their secret worship and blood sacrifice, men seek to appease the destructive side of the goddess and gain control over the powers of fertility that she represents.[7] Perhaps, on some level, the men of each household are also seeking through the Dasai sacrifice to symbolically direct the formidable but uncertain powers of affinal women away from the disruption of the lineage toward its economic prosperity and reproductive fertility—both areas where the participation of the women is crucial.

In our earlier discussions of Dasai we found that an important part of the festival's meaning lay in the reaffirmation of those principles and ideals that bind agnatic kindred together. Although filiafocal principles also emerge in the Dasai tika exchange, the values of patrilineal ideology predominate. I suggest that the bloodthirsty goddess Durga—as a symbolic representation of the patriline's ultimate but inadmissible dependence on affinal women—is an important part of that ideology. However, while the goddess must be appeased for the good of the patriline, women must be controlled. Thus, every woman with a living husband must first receive her tika and barley from him when she enters the heretofore forbidden Dasai ghar where Durga is installed. As she touches her forehead to her husband's feet, she is ritually acknowledging not only her submission to him as an individual but also her acceptance of the patrilineal ideology he represents.

Magh Swasthani Barta: Parvati and Village Women

The Magh Swasthani Barta is a ritual celebration of the gentle aspect of the Devi. We have, of course, already encountered this aspect in the discussion of Tij–Rishi Pancami and the Laksmi puja during Tihar. In those rituals the goddess embodied the beautiful, but above all pure and faithful wife, and the selfless, nurturing mother—in short, the ideal Hindu woman. By now the many contradictory elements which go into the Devi's role as perfect wife and mother are apparent: she must be both sensual and ascetic; flirtatious and faithful; fertile and yet utterly pure. In

the myths about her gentle aspects—most notably as Parvati—
the goddess is all these things. She represents an ideal, a blend-
ing of opposing qualities which actual village women can never
fully achieve. O'Flaherty (1973:38) in her discussion of Siva's
mythic role has, I think, pointed out why such unattainable
mythological models remain so compelling:

> The myth makes the Hindu aware of the struggle and its futility.
> They show him that his society demands of him two roles which he
> cannot possibly satisfy fully—that he becomes householder and be-
> get sons and that he renounces life and seek union with god. The
> myth shows the untenable answer arrived at by compromise—the
> forest-dweller and his wife—and suggests a solution finally in the
> re-examination of the nature of the two roles, of the presence of
> each in the other so that a balance may be sought without any of
> the unsatisfactory accommodations necessary in real life. The myth
> makes it possible to admit that the ideal is not attainable.

This is exactly what Parvati does in Hindu mythology. She
is the impossibly perfect model, embodying the contradictory
values of Hinduism particularly as they affect women in Hindu
patrilineal social structure. This, I maintain, is why the gentle
side of the goddess is especially important to village women.

Like Durga, of course, Parvati is worshiped and greatly
revered by both men and women. But, just as men are largely
responsible for the worship of Durga and more conversant than
women with the texts about her, women are more involved
with the rituals and texts concerning Parvati and the other gentle
forms of the goddess.[8] Tij–Rishi Pancami, which celebrates Parvati's fast, is almost exclusively a woman's festival. Laksmi puja
is also usually performed by the women of the house. And the
third major festival concerning the Devi's gentle aspect, the
Swasthani Barta that we will presently consider, is also predominantly a women's festival.

One reason for women's greater involvement with the
gentle rather than the terrible side of the goddess could be the
fact that women are barred from performing the blood sacrifices
of which Durga and her hosts are so fond. But more important,
I think, is the fact that Parvati especially, among the gentle forms,
presents mythic solutions to the kinds of problems which face
village women in real life. Though perhaps she is a less overtly
powerful protectress than Durga, Parvati is closer to village
women.

Nevertheless, on the level of symbolic analysis, Parvati's paradoxical domestic life and Durga's bloody battles can be seen as structurally equivalent attempts to mediate certain fundamental ideological and sociostructural conflicts within the Hindu world view. Since, as we have already noted, both aspects of the Devi contain opposing elements in their natures, both have the power to mythically transcend the contradictions they embody. On the ideological level, both forms of the goddess are dealing with the anomaly of female sexuality in an essentially puritan patrilineal society. At the level of social structure, both express the fundamental contradiction between the ideal of unbroken agnatic solidarity embodied by the patrilineal joint family and the inherent instability of that unit—due in no small part to the fact that affinal women are essential to its creation but have the least stake in its continued existence. The difference between the two aspects of the goddess is not in their symbolic meaning but in the *perspective* from which that meaning is articulated. Durga reflects a predominantly male view, focused on the problematic woman, while Parvati presents Hindu women's own idealized perceptions of themselves and the problems they experience.

Swasthani—Text and Ritual

This ideal image of Hindu women has symbolic ramifications as well as social and emotional implications for the lives of actual village women. The extended meanings of the ideal are explored at great depth in a text called the *Swasthani Vrata Katha* (Sharma 2022b). This text is the basis for the *barta*—the ritual fast or vow which women undertake to honor and win assistance from the goddess Swasthani. Nearly every Brahman or Chetri home in Narikot contains a copy of *Swasthani Vrata Katha* (or *Swasthani Puran,* as it is more often called). These copies are all in the Nepali language, though the text also exists in a Newari version and may even have originated in that language. Brahman and Chetri villagers, however, believe that the work is of Parbatiya origin, that it originated with Hindu immigrants into Nepal rather than native Newari Hindus. In support of this they claim the text is most revered and read in Parbatiya homes, and they further believe one of the major myths (the Goma story) is about a Parbatiya Brahman girl.

Linguistic and textual research into the actual origins of the *Swasthani* clearly remains to be done, though it seems safe to say that the text probably originated in Nepal. Although roughly two-thirds of it consists of reworked versions of familiar Puranic episodes about Siva and Sati Devi/Parvati, mixed in with other classic stories, the last section appears to be a local story found only in the *Swasthani*. Throughout the work, familiar place names from the Kathmandu Valley are mentioned.[9] There is also an interesting story about Parvati disguised as a Kirati girl (though it is not, I believe, unique to the *Swasthani* and does not necessarily refer to the Rai and Limbu peoples of eastern Nepal known as Kirati). However, it is in the last section of the *Swasthani,* when the scene of the narrative moves from the "world of the gods" (*swarga*) to the "mortal world" (*martya mandal*) that the sense of Nepal is the strongest. For, although only one place name is recognizable (the Sali Nadi river), the mountainous landscape and the social background clearly reflect the life of village Hindus in Nepal.

Swasthani is the name of the supreme and transcendent form of the Devi to whom the text is ultimately dedicated. However, she remains a remote figure, important mainly as the effective power behind the Swasthani Barta rituals which are the main concern of the text. This epithet of the goddess does not appear among the many in the *Devi Mahatmya,* nor, to my knowledge, is it found as such in any other Sanskrit texts about the Devi. The name Swasthani is derived from the Sanskrit *swasthana,* which means "one's own place" or "one's own home." Thus, two interpretations seem possible: that the Swasthani Devi is the "goddess of one's own place" in the sense of country or locality (which would probably be Nepal), or that she is the "goddess of one's own home" in the narrower sense of home and family.

The frequent occurrence of Nepali place names, etc. would seem to support the first interpretation—that the *Swasthani Vrata Katha* is meant to link the supreme pan-Hindu goddess and her mythical exploits as Parvati, Sati Devi, etc. with the geography and social patterns of Nepal. However, there is also much that supports the second interpretation of Swasthani Devi as the goddess of the house, because the text is particularly concerned with domestic problems. The wrong marriage partners,

problems with in-laws, marital strife and the separation of husband and wife, barrenness, and poverty; these problems beset
all the characters in the *Swasthani* text, whether they are gods,
demons, or human beings. And always, it is the goddess Swasthani, invoked through rigorous fasting and worship, who inter-
venes to bring about a miraculous solution. In fact, it is the self-
proclaimed purpose of the text to solve just such problems as
they affect village women by instructing them on how to perform the same religious vow or fast (*barta, vrata*) undertaken
with such success by the characters in the myths. The preface to
the text (at least in the modern copies I have seen) gives detailed instructions to women who wish to take the arduous
month-long vow to the goddess Swasthani. These same instructions are repeated (in varying amounts of detail) on numerous
occasions in the text itself. Visnu teaches the Swasthani Barta
rituals to Parvati, who performs them to obtain Siva as her chosen husband. The seven rishis explain the rituals to another major character, Goma; and finally a band of heavenly maidens
(*apsara*) tells Chandravati, the third principal character, once
again how to perform the rituals.

The characters who perform the Swasthani fast in the text
are all female, and in the village only women undertake it.
Women usually do the full Swasthani fast only when they have
a specific problem or goal in mind—though a few reported doing
it simply for merit. To have a son, get a good husband, alleviate
family money problems, bring back an absent husband are some
of the reasons women have for doing the fast and its accompanying rituals.[10] Almost every adult Brahman-Chetri woman in
Narikot had done the full Swasthani fast several times in her life,
though no one reported doing the rigorous, time-consuming, and
fairly costly ritual regularly every year.

Instead, during most years women participate with the
rest of the family (or sometimes with a larger group in the house
of a neighbor who has called in a priest) in nightly readings of
the *Swasthani* text during the month of Magh (January–February). The text is conveniently divided into thirty-one chapters,
and usually one chapter is read each night, after which those
who have listened worship the book with flowers, coins, rice
grains, red powder, etc., before it is carefully wrapped up again
in a cloth and placed somewhere safe from accidental ritual defilement. Obviously, the participation of the men in this part of
the Magh Swasthani celebrations is crucial, since until recently

only men could read the text. Nevertheless, village men say that the *Swasthani* text is mainly for women.[11]

When women decide to undertake the Swasthani fast, the rituals they perform are almost identical to those described in several places in the text itself. Below is an excerpt containing the heavenly maiden's instructions to the wretched Chandravati when she asked how to do the vow:

Hearing this Apsara said: "Oh sinful woman! Today is the full moon of Pus [December–January]. From today you must cut your fingernails and toenails and bathe every day. And after you are pure you must worship Sri Mahadev [Siva] with singleminded devotion and concentration every day at noon for a full month. If possible you must listen to the story of Swasthani, and you must tell it to others. On the full moon day of Magh you must prepare 108 pieces of bread, 108 grains of unbroken rice, 108 *beli puspa* flowers, 108 sacred threads, 108 bundles of pan, 108 pieces of betel nut, 108 different kinds of flowers, and all the other articles necessary for worship. Then, in a copper tray you must write the letter *Om* and bathe it in water from the river. Then you must decorate [the tray] with vermilion, sandalwood paste, red sandalwood powder, and a garland of flowers. Then offer incense, a votive light, fried sweets, flowers, musk, delicious things to eat, cloth, and money. With singleminded concentration, you must worship Sri Swasthani, chant verses of praise, meditate, offer libations, and then, calling on the goddess, ask her for a boon. Then take the prasad. Take out eight of each of the counted items and give them to your husband. If you have no husband, give them to your son, and if you have no son, then give them to the son of your ritual friend. And if you don't have a friend's son, then say in your mind 'Let my wish be accomplished' and take the prasad to the river and let it float away. The remaining 100 pieces of bread should be eaten by you. When you have done this your sin will be destroyed along with your suffering and anxiety. Your wish will come true. Do not believe otherwise. Now we must go." So saying, the Apsara went to heaven. [Sharma 2022b: chap. 28, my trans.]

There are several variations in the way village women actually carry out these instructions. Some of the most devout make a pilgrimage to a holy spot beside the Sali Nadi river, where certain events recounted in the *Swasthani* text are supposed to have taken place. I visited this place one year and saw about forty women who were performing the Swasthani fast together under the direction of Brahman priests. They had brought with them supplies for their single daily meal and were living in an open-sided shelter for religious travelers surrounding the temple courtyard. Many of the women were dressed in red with new red flannel shawls to shield them against the winter cold. All had large red tika on their foreheads and sat on special woven mats made from kus grass. The majority were older women, but there were some unmarried girls as well. Their routine was a daily bath in the nearby Sali Nadi, worship of Siva at noon, and a single meal after which they listened to the priests read from the *Swasthani* text. They then worshiped the book and an image of the goddess Swasthani in the temple courtyard.

Most village women who wish to undertake the fast cannot afford the luxury of a month's retreat from their domestic responsibilities. So they observe the fast as best they can in their own homes. They bathe every day in the river and worship Siva by making a sand phallus similar to the one worshiped at Tij, eat only one meal, and join the family at night for reading and worship of the *Swasthani* text. On the full moon day marking the end of their month of fasting, some women go to the Gauri Ghat (where Parvati is supposed to have done the fast) in the Pasupati temple complex to perform the final worship of Swasthani with the "counted items" mentioned in the text. Most women, however, perform the Swasthani Puja in their own home where they offer the 108 breads, etc., to the goddess. Unlike the ceremony described in the text, these domestic rituals include the service of the family priest. In one instance, a woman's husband read the final chapter of the *Swasthani* text in Nepali, while the priest alternately chanted in Sanskrit and directed the woman's worship in Nepali. After all the "counted items" had been offered to Swasthani Devi and the book had been worshiped with red and yellow powders, the woman touched her husband's feet and, just as the text directs, gave him eight of every item. As soon as the Brahman had blessed the family and given them tika, the husband ate his share of the offerings. The woman, however, kept her share of a hundred of each item for her only meal later that day. The only offerings I observed which were not mentioned in the text were a blouse and a set of accessories of a married woman, which were given as dan to the priest for his wife.

The Swasthani fast is both thematically and structurally related to the fast which women observe at Tij–Rishi Pancami. Both are imitations of Parvati's fast to win Siva. Both are dedicated to the husband—though in the Swasthani fast, other male relatives or a river may be substituted. Most important, both fasts represent that particular combination of religious devotion (bhakti) and austerity (tapas) which is so characteristic of contemporary village Hinduism—especially as it is practiced by the women.

The Swasthani Myth

The Swasthani text teems with traditional mythic characters and episodes from the Hindu Puranas. To give a sense of the richness and variety of the text, I present here just a bare outline of episodes by chapter:

Chapter 1	Cosmology
Chapter 2	"
Chapter 3	Daksa Prajapati refuses to give his eldest daughter, Sati Devi, to Siva in marriage.
Chapter 4	Siva marries Sati Devi by tricking her father.
Chapter 5	Siva destroys the demons of the three cities.
Chapter 6	Daksa insults his son-in-law and Sati Devi commits suicide.
Chapter 7	Destruction of Daksa's sacrifice.
Chapter 8	Daksa is beheaded and given a goat's head.
Chapter 9	Siva, mad with grief, scatters Sati Devi's body at the fifty holy spots.
Chapter 10	"
Chapter 11	The demon Taraka takes over the universe while Siva is distracted with grief.
Chapter 12	Siva is cursed falsely by the rishis; flame phallus; rebirth of Sati Devi as Parvati; Parvati refuses to marry Visnu; Visnu explains Swasthani Barta to Parvati as a means to win Siva.
Chapter 13	Siva destroys the love-god Kama; Parvati's fast (Swasthani Barta); marriage of Siva and Parvati.
Chapter 14	Siva and Parvati in Kirati disguise.
Chapter 15	Creation of Parvati's son Ganes; interrup-

tion of Siva and Parvati and birth of Kumar; competition of Ganes and Kumar; Kumar defeats Taraka.

Chapter 16 Siva as one-horned golden deer; Ravana wins a fake Parvati; Jalandar tries and fails to deceive Parvati.

Chapter 17 Visnu tries to deceive Jalandar's wife, Brinda, and is tricked; Visnu released through handsome ascetic created by Siva; Visnu seduces Brinda by deception and makes Jalandar vulnerable to Siva in battle.

Chapter 18 Brinda curses Visnu with *patibrata* curse; rishi Aswathama sent to netherworld to tell of Swasthani Barta; reunites the Nagini (female snake spirits) with their husbands by teaching them the Swasthani Barta.

Chapters 19 to 31 Goma-Chandravati story.

Clearly, an analysis of the full text would carry us far beyond the scope of the present work. Besides, except for the Goma-Chandravati story, most of the episodes and themes have been rather thoroughly dealt with elsewhere with a structural approach that focuses on the householder/ascetic opposition.[12] In fact, we have already encountered the erotic/ascetic conflict in those episodes from the Swasthani text considered earlier— i.e., Parvati's fast and the rishis' false accusation of Siva. This familiar theme plays throughout the Swasthani and is an important part of its meaning.

What I am mainly interested in here, however, is the way in which certain central Hindu problems arising from women's position is the kinship system are expressed and, on the symbolic level, solved in the Swasthani myths. Of course, very often these problems are closely related to the ascetic/erotic conflict. As we have seen, the Hindu attitude toward women and the high value placed on asceticism are almost reflexes of each other. But since the Swasthani text is supposed to be especially for women, I will focus here on what the text reveals about women's place in society and what role models it presents to them.

Two major stress points in Hindu kinship emerge repeatedly in the Swasthani myths. One centers around the difficulty of producing the male heir required to continue the patriline. In several episodes sonless parents cause conflict by trying to substitute daughters for sons. In another sequence Siva and Parvati become parents of anomalous sons by unorthodox means of procreation. The second recurring problem involves the difficulties women face in adjusting to marriage and the move from maita to ghar. Both the need for sons and women's trauma at marriage seem to generate tension between the young couple and their in-laws, which is a prominent theme throughout the *Swasthani* text. In the myths there are several sets of dissatisfied parents-in-law, a series of inadequate sons-in-law, and a particularly reprehensible daughter-in-law. These problems are expressed and explored in the four principal episodes of the text, each of which centers on the marriage of a different woman.

The World of the Gods—Sati Devi and Parvati
        The first two major episodes are played out on the divine level and involve Sati Devi and Parvati, two forms of the Devi in her gentle aspect. The first episode begins with Daksa Prajapati and his wife Virani (or Baruni), who had 33 billion daughters. The couple decided to give all their daughters to the 33 billion gods in kanyadan marriage—except for the eldest daughter, Sati Devi. Daksa did not want to give Sati Devi away because he had no son and he needed someone to be his heir.
        All the gods received Daksa's other daughters as brides except for Siva, who was annoyed to be the only bachelor left. So he went to ask Daksa for the hand of Sati Devi. But Daksa was horrified at the idea of a naked, hashish-eating ascetic as a husband for his favorite daughter. He not only refused Siva but insulted him and showed him to the door.
        The reasons for Daksa's hostility to Siva are complex. In part, his is the reaction of a doting father who expects something better for his favorite daughter. Siva as homeless, irresponsible ascetic is considered a poor match. O'Flaherty (1973:129) interprets the enmity between the two men as "the traditional conflict between ascetic and erotic creation. . . . personified in the Dakṣa myth as the conflict between Śiva the ascetic and Dakṣa Prajāpati the creator." In O'Flaherty's work the origin of Siva's somewhat paradoxical anti-erotic role in his own wedding is traced back to one of the Vedic antecedents of the Daksa myth wherein the creator god (Prajapati/Brahma) is punished by

Rudra (an earlier form of Siva) for committing incest with his own daughter.

The incest theme is never overtly mentioned in the *Swasthani* version of the Daksa myth.[13] Instead, it is Daksa's lack of sons that causes him to go against the rules of patrifocal society and try to keep Sati Devi unmarried. He wants her to remain at home "to protect his inheritance." But in Brahman-Chetri kinship the imperative to *transfer* daughters out of their natal patriline and into another is the essential condition for the high status and ritual purity daughters enjoy in the maita. In that context Daksa's attempt to keep Sati Devi unmarried is the structural equivalent of incest. By not giving her away in kanyadan (and thereby separating himself from her sexuality), he destroys the basis of her ritual purity as a daughter in her maita.

In the next episode, Siva, consistent with the anti-erotic side of his character, is actually protecting Sati Devi's purity when he marries her and takes her away from her father.

Siva went to his friend Visnu to ask for his help in securing Sati Devi as his bride. Visnu agreed and suggested a plan. Visnu was to go and, by trickery, get Daksa to promise to marry Sati Devi to *him*. Then Siva would come to Daksa's house at the time of the kanyadan disguised as an old *sanyasi* or wandering mendicant. He was to threaten to curse the marriage party unless he received alms. Visnu would then pretend to appease him by saying that the auspicious moment for the marriage was about to pass. He would ask the old sanyasi to sit nearby and wait for his alms. Then, when Daksa was giving his daughter's hand over to Visnu in kanyadan Visnu was to distract Daksa's attention so that Siva could take Sati Devi's hand at the auspicious moment of the ritual and irrevocably become her husband.

Visnu succeeded in tricking Daksa into promising him Sati Devi as a wife. But on the day of the wedding, Siva was almost late because he had taken so much hashish. He arrived in time, however, and, just as Visnu had planned, Daksa was distracted at the crucial moment. Mistakenly Daksa gave Sati Devi away to Siva in his sanyasi disguise. When the trick was discovered, Daksa was deeply distraught at losing his favorite daughter to a worthless ascetic. Sati Devi was unhappy too, but she resigned herself to her fate and bravely prepared to depart with her new husband.

"Recalling my younger sisters, all married to gods, I see that this is my karma. Clearly I am accursed!" Thus Sati lamented and began to weep bitterly. Again she spoke: "My karma is written thus, I see. All this has been caused by fate. Now I must not weep and cry. Whatever is done is done. Whatever [my husband] may be, my father and mother have given me. He will be my Lord." Having said this she accepted all. Then Mahadev [Siva] in his sanyasi form spoke to Sati Devi. "O wife! How long do you intend to linger here? You cannot stay in your maiti. You must go to your ghar also. You must go to your own husband's house. Now let us take leave of your father and mother!" Having heard her lord speak thus Sati Devi said, "So be it," and went to Daksa Prajapati and Baruni and said, "O Father, Mother! I will go now with your leave."

Daksa Prajapati and Baruni, holding back their tears, gave their daughter various words of advice. "Don't forget us! Come frequently!" they said and gave their leave. Sati Devi made obeisance [to her parents] and left with Mahadev in his sanyasi form.

On the road Mahadev in his sanyasi form said, "O beautiful one! Never having crossed the threshold of your courtyard, you have grown up like a flower in your parents' hands. You might get tired, so walk slowly." Hearing this, Sati Devi said, "O Lord, I am of age. I can walk. Rather it is my Lord's old age and [he] will become tired. Please walk slowly." In her mind she was thinking to herself, "My own Lord is old. I am young like this. Anyone might give us any kind of trouble!" Thus, very worried in her mind, she followed [Siva], never leaving him for even a minute.

After arriving at Mount Kailas, Mahadev in his sanyasi form, in order to see Sati Devi's [true] disposition, created a grass shack on top of the mountain. "Hey beloved! This is our house. We have finally arrived!" Sighing, he pointed it out. When they arrived at the courtyard he said, "Go inside. You are probably hungry. Eat something. I am tired and I will sleep for a moment." Having said this, he ate some dhatura, hashish, and wild thornapple and lay down outside.

Sati Devi, seeing that straw shack, remembered her own father Daksa Prajapati's sparkling golden house. "I see I am cursed. After living in such a luxurious home, fate has delivered me today to such a straw hut." Then she worried and many, many tears fell from her eyes. Then she said, "This has been brought about by my karma. What to do? Whatever has happened, if I don't make the best of it, I will never find happiness."

Having accepted [her fate], she dried her tears with her headcloth and went inside to see the house. And finding only spider webs and rubbish lying everywhere, she cleaned out the spider webs with her broom and swept out the dirt. Then she said, "When my

Lord has awakened what will I give him to eat?" She went to look for something to eat. But she found nothing, and with an uneasy mind she came to where Mahadev in his sanyasi form was sleeping and sat down at his feet.

After four days had passed, Mahadev woke up and looked at Sati Devi's face. "O loving wife! While I have slept alone outside, you have slept inside. But even so you will have to eat. Have you eaten or not?" Seeing [her husband] begin to get angry, Sati Devi said with a smiling face, "O Lord! Your lordship was so fast asleep I could not wake you up. Until now I have not even slept. I came and have been sitting here. I see that there is much food in the storeroom. I have eaten my fill. What will you eat?"

Sati Devi's disposition was very good. Always grooming herself beautifully and keeping a bright face through anger and pleasure alike, she attended her lord with devotion.

After Sati Devi had spoken [Siva] said, "What was here that you might have eaten?" Great pity arose in Mahadev in his sanyasi form, and he who has the form of compassion said, "Oh beloved! You have been deceived. This is not our house. Tear this grass wall aside and look inside."

Sati Devi said, "O Lord! But when even this our existing house is destroyed, where shall we find another nonexistent one! If we must build it again, how will we do it? My Lord is old and I am a woman. Who will build it for us?"

Having heard Sati Devi's words, Mahadev in his sanyasi form got up, and striking the straw wall with his leg, [he] threw it away and showed her the vision of [his heavenly abode] Kailas.

Seeing such a house, set with many jewels and wonderfully built, Sati Devi was overjoyed. "This house is even more beautiful than my father Daksa Prajapati's house. What kind of house might this be?"

Then Mahadev in his sanyasi form called Sati Devi into the courtyard in order to show her his true form. "O beloved, spread the middle of the courtyard with a circle of cowdung."

Sati Devi said, "So be it," and spread the floor with cowdung, and Siva in his sanyasi form went to the place spread with cowdung and gave her the vision as clear as crystal of his all-pervading divine form. And then Sati Devi, relieved in her mind, let tears of happiness come from her eyes. "Lord of all the world! I see I am blessed! I have received Mahadev as my Lord!" Having said this and put a flower garland around his neck, she circled him three times, and then those two became the true image of Siva Sakti.[14] [Sharma 2022b:chap. 4, my trans.]

This episode beautifully expresses some of the main difficulties women face in adjusting to marriage and the change from maita to ghar. Interestingly, two different forms of marriage are presented, each with its contrasting ideology. First, there is the kanyadan where Sati Devi is handed over to a complete stranger by her father. No matter how ugly, old, and impoverished he is, she must accept him as part of her fate. Out of duty to her parents she must obediently accept the husband they have chosen for her. This stands in sharp contrast to the last scene, where Sati Devi herself spontaneously garlands Siva and circles him in what is essentially the swayambar or "self-choice" ceremony. As I noted earlier, the ideology behind the swayambar is a romantic one in which the bride is recognized as an active and emotionally involved participant rather than a passive piece of transferable property. The swayambar is concerned with love and the kanyadan with duty. The fact that in the myth the swayambar comes after the kanyadan is significant. For although in actual ritual practice the swayambar (if it is done) comes before the kanyadan ceremony, most village marriages are founded on duty rather than love,[15] and love, if it comes at all, comes well after the marriage ceremonies when the couple have had a chance to get to know each other.

Sati Devi's feelings about marriage are movingly similar to those I saw expressed by village women. She is not at all attracted to the man whose wife she has just become; she is loath to leave her parents; and her husband's house seems inferior in every way to her beloved maita. All that Sati Devi's situation lacks to make it comparable to the trauma facing a village bride is a set of inquisitive and demanding in-laws waiting to greet her in Siva's straw shack.

Sati Devi's reactions to her disappointment are those of the ideal Hindu wife. Uncomplaining, self-effacing, she accepts her unhappy situation as the result of her own fate. This means that she takes the blame for her suffering, rather than seeing it as an injustice externally imposed. Even though Sati Devi's reactions are saintly in the extreme and inhumanly perfect, they were, nevertheless strangely familiar to me when I first read the *Swasthani* text after two years of fieldwork. I recognized in Sati Devi (and later in the text in Goma) an obvious model upon which the behavior of actual village women in similar situations must have been, at least to some extent, based. Even the sighing phrase that Sati Devi speaks and that echoes throughout the *Swasthani*—"I see that my fate is such"—I had heard from the lips of my village friends as they told me of thoughtless unloving husbands and critical, penny-pinching mothers-in-law. Of course, there was a great deal of variation in the manner in which these familiar words are uttered. Some women spoke with real acceptance or at least resignation; others with a good deal of irony and even bitterness. It will be recalled that even the resourceful Devi in the narrative of her struggle with her co-wife spoke of her situation this way, though she certainly never accepted it passively as her due in the way that Sati Devi did.

The next scene in the domestic life of Siva and Sati Devi begins with Daksa's decision to hold a great sacrifice and invite all his daughters, their husbands, the gods, and all the inhabitants of heaven and the netherworlds. Only Sati Devi and Siva have been excluded because of Daksa's intense dislike and contempt for his son-in-law.

The couple was happily engaged in a romantic game of dice when the celestial busybody, Narad, came to ask why Sati Devi and Siva were the only ones not attending Daksa's sacrifice. Sati Devi was deeply hurt and began to weep when she heard that she and Siva had not been invited. Siva consoled her and tried to dissuade her from going. But she was stubborn and insisted on going to her maita for the sacrifice.

On arriving home, Sati Devi greeted her parents respectfully and then, in tears, she asked why she and Siva had been excluded from the ceremony. She told her father that his sacrifice would be incomplete and fruitless unless Siva, the Lord of the Universe, was included. Daksa replied that his exclusion of Sati Devi was not out of lack of love for her but from his reluctance to see the splendid company of the gods insulted by the presence of the drunken, half-clad Siva. He laughed at his daughter's idea that his sacrifice would bring no merit without Siva's presence, saying that Siva was not even a god.

Sati Devi was so angry and insulted by what her father had said about her beloved husband that she jumped into her father's sacrificial fire. She died in the flames even though the fire god Agni would not touch her body out of fear of Siva's wrath.

When Siva heard of Sati Devi's suicide, he went mad with grief, and the demons Mahakali and Virbhadra issued from his topknot. After Siva instructed them to wreak vengeance, the two demons descended on Daksa with Siva's army. They destroyed Daksa's sacrifice and beheaded him. When Baruni, Daksa's wife, begged Virbhadra to restore the life of her foolish husband, Virbhadra agreed. But since Daksa's head had already been burnt up by the fire, it could only be replaced with that of a sacrificial goat.

After Mahakali and Virbhadra were reabsorbed into his body, Siva visited the scene of the sacrificial fire, where Sati Devi's body lay untouched by the flames. He was deeply distraught at her loss, and embracing her corpse, he lifted it onto his back. He began to roam the world carrying Sati Devi's body, which remained undecayed as if she were in a deep sleep. The gods began to worry that in his grief Siva would not be able to protect and rule them. They beseeched Visnu, who sent houseflies that caused Sati Devi's body to decay and fall in pieces from Siva's back. As each piece of the body fell a holy place (*pitha*) arose. The *Swasthani* text mentions fifty such places altogether,[16] each with a Siva linga, a form of the Devi as *yogini* (female ascetic), and a form of the Devi and Siva joined together as Siva Sakti. At each of the fifty holy places some heavenly being came to worship the goddess and was granted a boon.

Besides the Vedic theme of the creator god's incest with his daughter, O'Flaherty (1973:116) has also traced the origins of the Sati Devi myth back to the theme of Siva's destruction of Daksa's sacrifices. Both the sacrificial fire and the daughter are means of creation and productivity. Evidence of the mingling of these symbols—even to the point of interchangeability—appears in the *Rig Veda:* "The hunter shot him [the great father, heaven] as he embraced his own daughter. Heaven laid the bright seed aside and Agni brought forth a youth. The father, heaven, impregnated his own daughter. The sacrificer into the fire committed incest with his own daughter" (O'Flaherty 1964:9) In the Vedas the hunter Rudra destroys the sacrificial fire (from which he had been excluded) by piercing it with his arrows, and also punishes the incestuous father-creator. Later, Siva, becoming identified with Rudra, took up both these roles as Siva Sudanvan, the hunter.

In the figure of Sati Devi, the symbolism of the daughter and the sacrificial fire merge with and intensify each other (L. B. Campbell 1971:23–27). Siva's exclusion from Daksa's great sacrifice can be seen as a reinforcement of Daksa's earlier attempt to bar Siva from his daughter. Furthermore, in the context of the incest theme, Sati Devi's self-immolation in her father's sacrificial fire becomes an act of purification—an extreme form of asceticism to balance the erotic theme of incest.

This is even clearer in another Puranic version of the Sati Devi myth which appears in the *Devi Bhagvatam* (Vijanananda, trans., 1922). There, the rishi Durvasa, through his austerities, received a vision of the goddess and a beautiful garland as her prasad. It smelled so sweet that a swarm of bees (a common erotic motif in Hindu literature) was about to attack it. But the rishi quickly placed it on his head. He then went to see Sati Devi. Her father, Prajapati Daksa, asked for the garland and the sage gave it to him thinking the king a devotee of the goddess. Daksa took the garland, and he too placed it upon his head to honor it. But when he transferred it to "the bed that was pre-pared in the bedroom of the couple," Daksa became excited by the smell of the garland and had sexual intercourse. The text does not say with whom Daksa had intercourse, but immedi-ately afterward he became suddenly jealous of his son-in-law Siva and his own daughter. He abused Siva, and Sati Devi was so offended that she "resolved to quit her body that was born of Daksa to preserve the prestige of the *sanatanā dharma* [ortho-dox religious practice] of devotion to her husband and she burnt her body in the fire arising out of *yoga*," (Vijanananda 1922:698).

Even without the incest theme as background, Sati Devi's self-immolation can be interpreted as a kind of austerity—an ex-treme form of Parvati's ascetic fast—through which the impurity of female sexuality is transcended. Thus in the *Swasthani* text's version of the myth, Sati Devi's body is so pure that it does not decay when Siva removes it untouched from the fire. And yet, the power of Sati Devi's fertility, which her father had first tried to block by preventing her marriage and then caused her to de-stroy through suicide, remains. It has been transmuted, how-ever, to another level of reality. Thus, when Visnu finally causes Sati Devi's body to decay, each of her falling limbs produces a holy spot on the earth where "the Devi and Mahadev remained in a joint body as Siva Sakti."

In Nepal the most famous of these holy spots is Gujes-wari temple, where Sati Devi's *yoni* or vagina is said to have fallen. Like the forms of the goddess at the other holy spots men-tioned in the *Swasthani* text, Gujeswari Devi is known to grant offspring to those who come to her temple to worship. Her pra-sad is believed to be a particularly powerful cure for barrenness. Thus, Sati Devi, though thwarted by her sonless father from pro-ducing a son for her own husband, is able to help others per-petuate their lineages. Through her great austerities she is able to grant her own unfilfilled and purified fertility to others.

At this point, a paradoxical characteristic of Siva's sexual relation with the Devi begins to emerge: this famous erotic couple do not themselves produce offspring together through normal human means. Once again, we encounter the ubiquitous householder/ascetic opposition. In order that Siva might fulfill both his contradictory roles as a loving husband and as a stern ascetic, the myths about his marriage mediate the clash between these roles. One way, which emerges in both the Sati Devi and Parvati episodes, is to so purify the body of Siva's wife so that the normal danger of pollution through connubial contact is symbolically removed. Another device, which we have seen at work in the Sati Devi myth, is to substitute indirect or supernatural fertility for the direct fertility of normal human intercourse. This pattern becomes even clearer in the next section of the myth, which deals with the marriage of Siva and Parvati.

While Siva was distracted by his grief over Sati Devi's death, the demon Taraka took over and tyrannized the universe. Taraka was the demon to whom Brahma had given the boon that he could only be defeated by a child under five. Finally, after a century of aimless wandering, Siva regained control over his emotions and decided to go north to perform austerities. On the way he was falsely accused of seducing the wives of the rishis. The angry rishis cursed Siva's phallus to fall off, but instead Siva's flame phallus arose and threatened to engulf the universe until Visnu covered it with his body and put out the fire. Siva then counter-cursed the rishis and proceeded north.

Meanwhile, King Himalaya's wife became pregnant and gave birth to a beautiful girl, a reincarnation of Sati Devi, whom they named Parvati. The astrologers predicted that Parvati would marry Siva, and as she grew up her favorite game was doing Siva puja. But Narad, the heavenly messenger, convinced Visnu that Visnu should marry Parvati instead. King Himalaya was also pleased with the match, and the wedding arrangements were made. When Parvati's friends informed her of this, she was distraught and threatened suicide if she could not marry Siva. Her friends helped her run away and hid her in a secret spot. When King Himalaya sent for his daughter on the wedding day, she could not be found. So the auspicious moment for the kanyadan passed, and Visnu and his wedding party returned home without a bride.

Parvati in her hiding spot beside the river made a sand phallus and worshiped it, beseeching Siva to marry her. Siva appeared but explained that he could not marry her unless her parents gave her to him as kanyadan. He advised her that Visnu would help her in her quest and she should follow his advice.

When Parvati returned home, her father was angry, but relented when he recalled the astrologer's predictions that Parvati would marry Siva. Parvati began doing religious fasts and giving alms. Visnu was pleased with these acts of piety and offered her a boon. She asked that she might obtain Siva as a husband. Visnu then told her about the vow to the goddess Swasthani whose power would enable her to win Siva. He explained the rituals of the Swasthani fast, and Parvati began carefully following his instructions during the month of Magh–(January–February).

The gods were pleased, because now Siva would be drawn out of his deep meditation and, from his marriage with Parvati, a son would be born strong enough to destroy the demon Taraka. But the gods were impatient to awaken Siva from his ascetic trance in the North, and they sent Kama, the god of love, to shoot an arrow at Siva and arouse his passion for Parvati. Siva, however, was angered by this interruption of his meditation and burned Kama with his fiery third eye. Kama's wife, Rati, begged to have her husband revived, and Siva agreed to do so in another world cycle.

Through his power of contemplation, Siva learned that Sati Devi had been reborn as Parvati and was performing the Swasthani fast to obtain him as a husband. Disguised as Indra, he went to test Parvati, just as she was finishing her fast. "Indra" tried to get Parvati to marry him by insulting Siva. Parvati became angry and was about to curse Siva in his Indra disguise. So Siva quickly took his own form and explained that he had come only to test Parvati's devotion.

Parvati and Siva were married quickly, so that she might give Siva the 8 of the 108 counted items which, according to the Swasthani fast ritual, should be given to one's husband. But during the kanyadan ceremony, there was an embarrassing moment when King Himalaya asked for Siva's gotra name. Narad intervened and explained that, as Lord and Creator of the Universe, Siva could not be expected to have "dynasty and parentage." King Himalaya respected this and yielded Parvati, who then garlanded Siva and fell at his feet.

Siva's lack of a gotra is significant in light of the *Swasthani's* pervasive concern with lineage maintenance. On first sight this seems to make Siva unfit to participate in the patrilineal

Parvati, a form of the gentle aspect of the goddess, with her ascetic husband Siva and one of their sons, Ganes. The simultaneous presence of the goddess in her terrible aspect is also suggested by the lion, the vehicle of the fierce warrior goddess Durga. *Photo by David Sasoon*

system as an ordinary householder. But, Siva, as the lord of the universe, is the descendant of no one, and as an immortal has no need of the patrilineal institution of gotra. Thus the myth places the Hindu preoccupation with descent and the struggle to maintain the patrilineage firmly in the context of human mortality.

After their marriage, Siva and Parvati led a happy life, amusing themselves and teasing each other with various disguises. Two very unusual sons were born to the divine couple. One day Parvati made a son, Ganes, out of the impurities she removed from herself while bathing. She then placed him at her gate to guard her until she completed her bath. When Siva returned, Ganes did not permit him to enter. Siva, angry at being obstructed at his own gate, cut off Ganes's head and went in to see his wife. But when Parvati discovered what he had done, she wept piteously and explained that the guard was her own son. Siva promised to revive Ganes and, lacking human material, replaced his head with that of a white male elephant.

After this, Siva spent all his time making love to Parvati, and the gods became restive. The demon Taraka still terrorized the world. So Indra sent Agni to summon Siva to the city of Kasi, where the gods were gathered. Agni could not get past the gatekeeper guarding Siva and Parvati's chambers, so he slipped in through the keyhole. Taking the form of a mendicant, he disturbed the privacy of the divine couple while they were making love. Siva was angered and he made Agni take his fiery hot semen into his mouth. The semen was so hot it burned Agni's mouth. He quickly ran to the Ganges and vomited it out on the bank of the river into a kus plant. The semen was burning there on the bank when the wives of the seven rishis walked by and decided to warm themselves at the fire. One (unnamed in the text) disliked the idea of warming herself at someone else's fire and went straight home. The other six stayed by the fire, and afterward they conceived. The rishis suspected their wives of infidelity. When the women refused to confess, the rishis cursed them. Upon this, the wives went to the Ganges, vomited the seed, and flew to the skies, where they remained as the Pleiades constellation. Out of the semen they left behind in the Ganges a six-headed baby boy was born. The boy, named Kumar, was known as the son of the river goddess, Ganga. Kumar, while still a child and living with his father Siva, led the battle against the tyrant demon Taraka. Since Kumar was still under five years old, Brahma's boon did not protect Taraka against the child warrior. With Ganes's help, Kumar slew Taraka and restored the gods to their rightful places in the universe.

Neither Ganes nor Kumar were born by normal means. There was no intercourse involved in the "birth" of Ganes. For Kumar, the sexual union of Siva and Parvati is "interrupted." The conception is then symbolically mediated first by Agni, who receives the seed; then by the six rishis' wives, who incubate it; and finally by Ganga, who gives birth. Parvati herself has nothing to do with Kumar's birth beyond the initial erotic stimulation of Siva. Although at some places in the *Swasthani* text, Kumar is called Parvati's son, he is also called the son of Ganga, and in other versions of the myth (as an explanation for his six heads) he is said to be born of the six "unfaithful" wives of the rishis. The unusual conception and gestation of Siva and Parvati's "family" is, then, another instance where normal direct fertility is replaced by miraculous indirect fertility in the attempt to buffer some of the contradictions inherent in the phenomenon of ascetic marriage.

The remaining scenes in this section of the *Swasthani* center around the theme of the chaste and devoted wife (*pativrata*). In fact, at this point the text becomes almost a sermon on the virtues of marital fidelity. As I noted in the discussions of Tij, a man's physical well-being is believed to depend on the purity of his wife.[17] Not surprisingly, the virtuous Parvati is invulnerable to any adulterous advances, and so Siva also remains invincible in his battle with the demon Jalandar. But, when Jalandar's innocent wife Brinda is seduced by Visnu (disguised as Jalandar), Jalandar is immediately defeated by Siva. When Brinda found out what happened, she turned to Visnu and cursed him.

"Because of your trickery you have destroyed my vow to be faithful to my husband [*pativrata dharma*] and thus you have caused his death! Now I curse you to exist as grass, tree, stone, and weed!"

After saying this she fell down dead. The curse of the faithful wife (*pativrata*) is terrible. Even great gods are not immune to it. So Visnu had to take the form of the tulsi plant, kus grass, pipal tree and saligram stone. Therefore, Hindus worship all the above mentioned things as forms of Narayan [Visnu]. Chastity in a woman is a great vow and exercise. Even a great god like Visnu had to suffer for violating a chaste woman. [Sharma 2022b:chap. 18, my trans.]

The World of Mortals—Goma and Chandravati
    Now the text turns from the world of gods to the world
of mortals. In this section are the related stories of the marriages
of Goma and Chandravati, the two other heroines of the *Swasthani* text. In many ways this part of the text is the most interesting; although the problems and themes remain the same, the
people and their situations are much closer to the lives of Nepalese villagers. In fact, when the four heroines—Sati Devi, Parvati, Goma, and Chandravati—are considered together, this difference in the two sections of the text becomes clear. Both Sati
Devi and Parvati, as incarnations of the Devi, are divine beings,
while Chandravati is an ordinary woman. Goma is the transitional figure between the human and the divine. Although Goma
too is born into the world of mortals, her birth is miraculous;
although she never knows it, her husband is actually Siva in another of his many disguises. Both Sati Devi and Parvati are paragons of virtue and purity. Their behavior in all their many trials
is always that of the ideal Hindu woman: self-effacing, obedient, and passionately devoted to her husband. As we shall see,
Goma's reactions to similar problems on the human plane are
just as saintly as those of Sati Devi or Parvati. Chandravati, on
the other hand, has not only human problems (really very mild
ones), but very human reactions to these problems. She is chiefly
concerned with her own comfort and convenience rather than
her duty. The *Swasthani* text, then, recognizes the discrepancy
between ideal and actual behavior which we have frequently
witnessed in the course of the book. Let us now look at how
the myth deals with this discrepancy.
    A poor but virtuous Brahman couple, Siva Bhatta and his
wife Sati, obtained great wealth by worshiping Ganes. Still they
were worried because they had no children and felt insecure as
old age approached. So they worshiped Ganes again. Although
he could not give them a son, Ganes granted them a daughter,
who would be born from the cowdung that they were to collect
and keep in a cooking pot for four days.
    After four days, a beautiful baby girl appeared in the
cooking pot where the dung had been. Siva Bhatta and Sati were
very pleased, but they worried because Sati had no mother's
milk to feed her daughter. Ganes then brought milk to Sati's
breasts. The couple named their little daughter Goma, since she
was born of *gobar* or cowdung.
    The child grew up to be a beautiful five-year-old. Then

one day her parents went to bathe in the river, leaving Goma to husk rice to make unbroken rice grains (acheta) for the family's worship ceremonies. While she was husking, Siva came to the house disguised as a sanyasi. He had come because the great religious virtue of Goma's parents had made them so powerful that they threatened Indra, the king of the gods, and made his kingdom shake. So Siva had determined to reduce the religious power of the couple by bringing them some misfortune.

Goma refused to give the unbroken rice as alms to the ascetic, saying she had to save it for the worship ceremonies that her parents were going to perform. Siva became angry at Goma's refusal and cursed her to marry a seventy-year-old Brahman in her seventh year, and cursed her father to lose his wealth and die. He also cursed Goma to have great troubles in her life. Goma's parents returned and found her crying because of the curse. They told her not to worry—that it was just a beggar whose curse would have no effect.

But when Goma entered her seventh year and her father began to search for a groom, he could only find an ugly old Brahman of seventy years. This Brahman, named Siva Sarma, had been seeking a bride since he was sixteen. He told Goma's father that he would kill himself unless Goma was given to him. So then Goma's father had the horrible choice of giving his beloved seven-year-old daughter to the old man or being responsible for the murder of a Brahman. He realized that the ascetic who had cursed his daughter had indeed been Siva. Goma's mother Sati did not want to give their daughter to the Brahman, but her husband was afraid of Siva and insisted on giving Goma as kanyadan to Siva Sarma.

Goma's parents began to treat Siva Sarma with the respect due a son-in-law, touching his feet and feeding him. Goma accepted her fate bravely. The marriage was performed with great lavishness, and Goma began to serve her husband with love.

Goma and Siva Sarma spent the first eight to ten years of married life in comfort and happiness in the house of Goma's parents. But finally, Siva Sarma grew restless to see his own house. Despite the pleading of Goma's parents, he insisted on going for a visit. But he told Goma she could remain in her maita, since the journey was long and difficult. Goma, however, said that it was her duty to go with her husband. Her parents pleaded with her,

"O daughter Goma! Please don't you also say you are going. It is our old age. Whether you are son or daughter you are young. If you begin to talk like this who will cook for us? Who will even give us water? When you are not here it is like a moonless night to us. Just as [in the *Ramayana*] King Dasarath died without Ramchandra and Sita, so our life will go if you are not here. Therefore, stay here and care for the two of us husband and wife and look after our wealth. Let your husband go. He will return in two months!"

Hearing her parents' words, Goma replied, "O mother and father! For a woman all pilgrimages, fasts, religious gifts, and dharma are her husband. As long as she has her husband, she need not do any other pilgrimage, fast, religious gifts, or dharma. You have seen all the *Smriti* and Puranas. If a woman gets angry at her husband, she will be squint-eyed [in her next rebirth]; if she scolds him she will stutter; if she answers back, she will be dumb; if she hides from her husband and eats [on the sly], she will be a dog; if she fights, she will be spiteful. Therefore, please don't prevent me. Please let me go. Also my husband is an old man. If I am not there, who will care for him on the road? Besides, nowhere in the world can a full-grown daughter remain in her maita! And I will return quickly!" [Sharma 2022b:chap. 21, my trans.]

Goma's parents relented, and, their eyes full of tears, they sent her off with her husband. They climbed a tree to watch her slow departure for as long as they could, but they both fell from the tree and died. They instantly ascended to heaven, where Siva gave them divine bodies.

Meanwhile, the first night out on their journey, Goma and Siva Sarma were robbed of the lavish dowry that Goma's parents had given them. They sent their porters back to Goma's parents and set out in search of fruits—for Goma was hungry and weak because she had just become pregnant. They wandered through mountain forests, and Siva Sarma fed her fruit and water. Finally, they arrived at a straw shack on the outskirts of a town. This was Siva Sarma's house.

Goma, having gone inside to look at it, saw only spider webs and dirt. Remembering her father's house, she was unable to control herself and began to cry. Then she said to herself, "My karma has brought this about. What is the use of crying?"

And with a contented mind, she swept away the cobwebs and cleaned out the dirt and, eating whatever there was in the house, she began to serve Sarma. [Sharma 2022b:chap. 22, my trans.]

The parallels between this part of the Goma story and the first episode in the Sati Devi myth are striking. Both deal with the same problems: the parents' lack of a son, the unsuitable son-in-law, and the woman's difficulty in moving from maita to ghar.

Goma's parents' solution to their sonless condition is far less drastic than the one attempted by Daksa. They do not seek to keep their daughter unmarried. They are far too scrupulous about maintaining the "Brahman dharma" to commit such an obvious sin. Instead, they attempt the same solution I observed in several Narikot families who had daughters but no sons. They bring the bridegroom to live uxorilocally with them, as a "house son-in-law" (ghar juwai).

Given the strong patrilineal bias of Brahman-Chetri society, it is not surprising that this solution is not entirely satisfactory either in real life or in the myth. Although keeping one's daughter and son-in-law at home does ensure that one will be cared for in old age, there are other drawbacks. One's property passes to the son-in-law's lineage (though the daughter may be given control of it during her lifetime) and the full ekodista sraddha is performed only for one generation instead of three. Furthermore, in such a strongly patrilineal and patrilocal society, the status of the "house son-in-law" is low. In a strange village, cut off from the support of his family and lineage, he is deprived of the full authority which a man should have over his wife. The worshipful respect which most sons-in-law receive from their wife's kin on their infrequent visits to their in-laws' house can hardly be maintained day in and day out. There is, then, considerable loss of honor in living with one's wife's parents. A proverb I heard in Narikot reflects the general attitude of most villagers towards such men: "The chicken is worthless as a winged creature; millet is worthless food; and the house son-in-law is a worthless man" (Ku-pakchi kukhura; ku-anna kodo; ku-manche ghar juwai). Hence, usually only a poor, landless man with no other prospects will consent to become a house son-in-law.

Siva Sarma was such a man. He was poor, old, and extremely unattractive. The text describes him as "bent over, deaf, cross-eyed. . . . with gray eyes, and eyebrows that joined in a single line across his forehead. His hair was white and spittle dribbled from his dark face" (Sharma 2022b:chap. 20). He was obviously happy to find a wife under any conditions, and for eight years or so he enjoyed the comforts of his wealthy in-laws' home.

But eventually his patrilineal conditioning surfaced; he remembered his own ghar and wished to return if only for a visit. Goma too suddenly felt it inappropriate to remain in her maita as a grown-up daughter (especially without her husband), so she insisted on accompanying him. It is, I think, symbolically important that Goma became pregnant the moment she finally did leave her maita. This is consistent with what we know of the categorical asexuality of daughters which is the condition of their sacred status in the maita. Even though Goma's parents did not attempt to actually block her fertility the way Daksa tried to block Sati Devi's, they had effectively done so by subverting the normal patrilocal structure of marriage. Goma could not become a full sexual being, able to produce offspring for her husband's lineage, until the transfer from maita to the ghar (and the accompanying transformation from daughter to wife) was complete.

The transfer was as traumatic for Goma as it was for Sati Devi. She too found herself with an old man for a husband who had nothing but a dirty straw hut to offer her. She responded with the same cheerful saintly strength which Sati Devi displayed. The difference is, however, that Siva did not take pity on her and rip aside the shack to reveal a palace. It appears that Goma's troubles have only begun.

Siva Sarma decided that he must go out and beg money for the coming expenses of Goma's delivery and the subsequent birth ceremonies. Goma pleaded with him not to leave her alone, but he insisted and departed from their straw shack. On his journey he was killed when he fell from a tree he had climbed to pick some fruit as an offering for his daily worship. He then assumed his true form as Siva and ascended immediately to heaven, where Parvati scolded him for having left Goma pregnant and alone. Siva promised Parvati that his earthly wife Goma would eventually be happy.

Goma, alone in her little hut, gave birth to a son. When she had his naming ceremony performed, the priests said his name should be Navaraj because he would be king one day.

Goma, unaware that her husband was dead, supported herself and her son by spinning, husking rice, and grinding wheat for others. Her son was good and obedient to his mother and, with the aid of her employers, she was able to have his initiation rites performed. Then her employers offered to do the boy's wedding, and Navaraj was married to a Brahman girl named Chandravati.

But Navaraj's friends began to taunt him, saying he was

fatherless. So Navaraj set out to seek his lost father. On his journey in a far country, he learned that his father had died. He gathered his father's bones and performed the proper funeral ceremonies for him. He decided, however, that he could not return to his mother with this bad news until he had earned some money. So he went to seek service with the king.

Meanwhile, no sooner had Navaraj left to seek his father than his wife, Chandravati, left her mother-in-law and returned to her maiti to wait there in greater comfort until her husband returned. Goma thus found herself utterly alone, without husband, son, or daughter-in-law. She prayed to Siva for help, and Parvati took pity on her. Parvati told Siva that he should help Goma because she was also his wife. So Siva sent the seven rishis to teach Goma how to perform the Swasthani fast as a means of relieving her suffering.

When the seven rishis arrived at Goma's house she did obeisance to them, and they explained how she could destroy her troubles by performing the same vow to the goddess Swasthani that had once enabled Parvati to win Siva. After hearing, in detail, the technique for the Swasthani ritual from the rishis, Goma thanked them and begged them not to leave until she had at least offered them some hospitality. But when she left the house to buy them some pan with a skein of cotton she had just spun, the rishis departed, each leaving a golden seashell in his place.

When Goma tried to exchange her thread for pan to give to the rishis, the storekeeper's depleted *pan* supplies were suddenly replenished. Seeing this miracle, he refused to take the thread and made Goma a gift of the pan. She was disappointed when she returned home and found that the rishis had gone. She worried that she might have insulted them until she discovered the golden seashells they had left her.

Goma began the Swasthani rituals as the rishis had instructed. Since she was all alone, she set her spinning wheel, bedding, etc. in front of her and told them about the glory of the Swasthani Devi. The cowherd children heard her talking to herself and they thought she had gone mad, but they stayed to listen and left food for her. By the power of the Swasthani Devi, their cows found grass nearby and didn't wander. At the completion of her month-long vow, Goma beseeched the goddess to bring her son back and to remove the curse Siva had set upon her.

Just then, Navaraj returned. He told Goma of his father's death, and comforted her as she lamented. Then he went to bathe in the river and worship Siva and Visnu. The two gods appeared to him in a vision and told him that, because of the vow his mother had performed, he would be crowned king if he traveled to the country of Lavanya.

So Navaraj set out for the country of Lavanya. There the king had died, leaving a daughter but no male heir. An elephant had thus been sent out to choose a new king. Siva and Visnu entered the elephant and caused it to garland and anoint Navaraj. At first the people were puzzled that the elephant chose a Brahman rather than a Ksatriya to be king, but they relied on the elephant's divine inspiration and accepted Navaraj. Navaraj married the king's daughter and became king. Then he sent for his mother Goma to come and crown him. To the amazement of her female neighbors, the impoverished Goma was carried away from her straw hut as a queen, dressed in jewels and fine clothes and seated in a palanquin.

In this section the motif of the fatherless son is played against the already familiar *Swasthani* motif of the sonless father. Both conditions are anomalous, especially in the context of a patrilineal society, where so much of a man's social and ritual identity depends upon the father-son link. Just as Daksa and Goma's father found it difficult to either assure their security in old age or to keep their estate intact without sons, so Navaraj found himself ostracized by his childhood friends because he had no father:

> Then one day Navaraj was going outside to play, and his friends said: "O Brahman. Until today we have called you Navaraj. Now that can no longer be. You are a son of no father, so your name should be "Fatherless" [bina babu]. If you have a father what is his name? Whose son are you? Tell us."
>
> Hearing his own friends say such things, Navaraj was unable to answer. He went to Goma, told her about the whole incident, and asked [about his father]. Hearing this, a stream of tears fell from her eyes like rain from a monsoon cloud.
>
> "O son! Your father's name is Siva Sarma. When you were in the womb he went to another country saying he would beg alms to do your birth ceremonies and up to now he has not returned! Perhaps he has stayed in a job there or something—that is to say, he certainly is not here."
>
> Then Navaraj said, "O mother! In that case tell me where my father is. I will go search for him and bring him back."

Goma said, "O son! Seeing your face, I have forgotten your father. Now if you also leave me and go, who will support me? If you go, my daughter-in-law will not stay. She will go to her maita. Therefore, please do not say you will go!"

Hearing this Navaraj said, "O mother! Listen to the saying of the *Dharma Sastra,* which is that the son's greatest religious duty is to work for the salvation of his father. The son who, paying no attention to his father's salvation, goes after his own happiness and pleasure anywhere under the moon and sun, anywhere on earth, he will be caught in a terrible hell. O mother! My father who left when I was still in the womb, shouldn't he have returned by now when I have reached this age? Shouldn't we search for news of him? If he is alive, I will bring him back with me. If he is dead, I will do the funeral services for him and return. If I can't even do this, then what is the use of my having been born? Whatever trouble it causes me, I must go. Mother, your daughter-in-law is always here to serve you. Please give me leave." [Sharma 2022b:chap. 22, my trans.]

In order to be accepted in Hindu society, Navaraj must establish his patrilineal descent and also carry out his patrilineal obligations toward his father by performing the proper funeral rites. Navaraj's journey to reestablish himself in the patrilineal system by finding and honoring his father sets off a series of events that lead his real father, the god Siva, to intercede and grant Navaraj what is in effect his missing patrimony, the kingship of Lavanya. Navaraj's departure, followed soon after by that of his wife Chandravati, leaves Goma without husband, son, or daughter-in-law. Thus, because of Siva's irresponsibility in the role of a householder, the relationships upon which the Hindu family are built have disintegrated, leaving Goma as the victim. Her plea for help finally forces Siva to send the rishis to her aid. And they, as embodiments of the ideal patrilineal continuity, play a role similar to the one they played in the Rishi Pancami myth. They mediate the broken patrilineal link between father and son. In both myths the rishis work *indirectly through women* to restore patrilineal continuity. In each case they teach a powerful ascetic fast (the Tij–Rishi Pancami fast and the Swasthani fast, respectively) which, when performed by a virtuous woman, brings about a solution to the problem.[18] Thus Goma's performance of the Swasthani fast causes Siva and Visnu to make Navaraj the king of Lavanya.

With the deceased king of Lavanya we encounter the *Swasthani* text's third instance of the sonless father. This time, however, the situation is balanced by Navaraj, the fatherless son. Unlike Siva—who is also "fatherless" in that he is uncreated and immortal, independent of the whole patrilineal institution—Navaraj's need for a patrimony and the king of Lavanya's need for an heir coincide. In this case the solution of bringing in a "house son-in-law" works.

In this episode, then, one of the main problems with which the *Swasthani* text deals—the difficulty of producing a male heir—is, on the mythic level, resolved. However, the other area of recurring conflict remains, one deriving specifically from women's perspective: the problems women have in adjusting to marriage, in integrating their roles as daughter and wife. Unlike Sati Devi and Goma, who "accepted their karma" and put up with whatever conditions they found in their ghar, Chandravati is more of a fallible human being and decides to return to her maita and wait there until times are better in her ghar. In the final episode of the myth, Chandravati pays dearly for her selfishness but in the end is transformed through the mediation of the rituals of the *Swasthani* fast into the ideal wife and daughter-in-law.

The new king Navaraj, with Goma's advice, decided to perform dharma by feasting all the Brahmans in the kingdom—even his old childhood friends who had called him "fatherless." At his mother's suggestion, he also sent for his first wife, Chandravati, who was still living in her maita. Chandravati and her parents were pleased at their good fortune, though the other women in Chandravati's natal village shook their heads that such a selfish and disobedient girl had been so lucky: "Lord! That Chandravati who left her mother-in-law in such difficult circumstances when her husband went to a foreign country, and went off to live in her maita! Despite it all she gets to be queen!" [Sharma 2022b:chap. 25, my trans.]

Chandravati dressed herself in the jewels and fine clothes that had been sent for her and set off for her husband's kingdom. On the way, Chandravati's porters saw some heavenly maidens doing the Swasthani ritual in the forest. The porters approached them reverently and joined them in the worship. The maidens blessed the porters and gave them prasad from the goddess Swasthani.

Chandravati, who had been left alone in the woods while her porters went to worship, was furious with them when they returned. She was impatient to arrive at her husband's palace and couldn't understand the delay. She took the prasad which they offered her and, spitting on it, threw it to the ground and stamped on it with her feet.

Because of Chandravati's contempt for her, the goddess Swasthani became angry and caused the bridge over the Sali Nadi river to break as Chandravati was crossing. A great storm and a flood arose, and Chandravati and her porters were washed away in the river. The porters died immediately and went to Siva's heaven. But Chandravati remained half dead in the river. So sinful and impure was Chandravati that even the river stopped flowing.

The fishermen were alarmed at this and went to their king Navaraj for help. He came and fished out Chandravati with a net. But no one could even recognize her as a human being; her body had become leprous and she was covered with mud. They threw her up on the bank of the river and went on searching for the cause of the river's sudden cessation. Finally, Navaraj made an offering of purifying cow's milk to the river, and it began to flow again.

After that, Chandravati remained by the river, delirious with hunger and thirst and yet unable to find any food. At last, in desperation, she tried to eat mud, but the mud became stone; when she tried to eat the stone it turned to ashes and a wind blew it away before she could eat it.

Meanwhile, Navaraj had declared a feast at the palace for all the Brahmans. So the starving Chandravati begged two Brahmans who passed her on their way to the feast to bring something back for her. They promised to try. After the feast these two Brahmans lingered around the palace, and Goma asked them what they wished. When they explained, she sent her steward to get something for them to take to the poor hungry creature they had met on the road. But the moment the steward entered the storeroom, all the food disappeared. So Goma gave them the food that had been prepared for herself. As soon as they had left, all the food returned to the storeroom.

The Brahmans brought the food to Chandravati and told her how the food in Goma's storeroom had dried up the moment they asked for it. They were shocked when Chandravati went to eat the food they had brought without even washing her hands and face. They told her she should perform the rituals of the Swasthani fast to remove whatever great sin she must have committed to find herself in such a miserable condition.

Chandravati struggled to the river on her leprous hands and knees, but the river dried up the moment she touched it. Then she tried to eat the food, but it turned to ashes and blew away. She spent the next five years in a trance of hunger and misery by the banks of the Sali Nadi.

Then, on the full moon day of the month of Pus (December–January), some heavenly maidens came to the banks of the Sali Nadi to begin their vow to Swasthani Devi. Chandravati saw them and asked for help in undoing the results of her great sin, for she realized now her arrogance and conceit in spitting and stepping on the prasad of the great goddess. They told her that she should do the Swasthani fast, so with great repentance she undertook the vow. The maidens directed her worship, and day by day as she fasted and prayed, her leprosy disappeared and she became more and more beautiful. On the last day of the fast, Chandravati asked the maidens how she could complete the offerings, since she had nothing to give. They told her to make the items out of sand. As she did this, the articles became real. When the maidens saw this miracle, they said she had been transformed from a sinful woman to a virtuous one. That night she completed her vow with a vigil meditating on the glories of the Swasthani Devi. Then, in the morning, since her husband was absent, she offered eight of the 108 fried breads to the river and asked for the boon that she might see her husband soon.

A snake goddess (nagini) found four of the eight breads Chandravati had thrown into the river. The snake goddess decided she must share these with her snake husband, even though he had been gone for twelve years. At this same time her husband, wandering in another part of the ocean, found the other four of Chandravati's breads and went in search of his wife to give her some. The two met at the confluence of the ocean and the Sali Nadi river and, overjoyed to be together again, they gave their blessing to whomever had thrown the bread into the river.

Then, some citizens of Lavanya discovered Chandravati on the banks of the river. She was so beautiful they asked if she were a heavenly maiden or a human being. She told them that she was the wife of Navaraj. When the citizens reported this to their king, he remembered his first wife and told them to bring her to the palace in a palanquin. Chandravati thanked Swasthani Devi for her compassion and went to meet her husband.

On arriving at the palace, Chandravati touched the feet

of her mother-in-law, Goma, and those of her husband and then gave her blessing to her junior co-wife Lavanyawati. When Navaraj asked Chandravati why her arrival had been so delayed, she told the story of her arrogant contempt toward Swasthani Devi, the punishment she received, and how she destroyed her sin through the rituals of the Swasthani fast. Goma then told her daughter-in-law of the hardships she had undergone when Chandravati had left her to go to her maiti and how the seven rishis had taught her the Swasthani fast which resulted in their present happiness and comfort. Then she addresses Chandravati:

> O Chandravati, just as the day cannot be light without the sun, as the night cannot be bright without the moon, so among men there is no home without a woman of excellent character. It is now my old age. You two must get along like sisters. You must manage the affairs of the kingdom and serve my son Navaraj."
>
> With this command to Chandravati, she handed over all the business [of the house] to her eldest daughter-in-law. Queen Lavanyawati said, "Oh mother! By your austerities our husband has become king and we are queens. You are blessed!" They fell at the feet of their mother-in-law Goma. From then on, they lived always faithfully, increasing their devotion to Sri Swasthani. [Sharma 2022b: chap. 31, my trans.]

Thus the myth ends with Chandravati perfectly integrated into her ghar and her roles as affinal wife and daughter-in-law. The dynamic of this final episode is very simple. The arrogance and immature selfishness that caused Chandravati to leave her mother-in-law and go to her maita also caused her to show contempt for Swasthani Devi. As punishment, the goddess transforms her into a subhuman creature whose impurity is so great that she even dries up the Sali Nadi until the river is purified with an offering of milk. She exists in an anomalous condition in which she is tortured by hunger and thirst but unable to eat or drink. In short, she suffers the privations she avoided earlier by retreating to her maita—only these privations are multiplied a thousandfold.

It is Chandravati's story that demonstrates the purifying powers of the Swasthani rituals for mortal women. Because they were either divine like Parvati or semidivine like Goma, the other characters who performed the rituals were already pure and virtuous, while Chandravati was neither. In the idiom of village religion, Chandravati's physical impurity—the fact that she doesn't even observe the bare ritual minimum of washing her hands before eating—is symbolic of her moral weakness and her unwillingness to accept the duties and restrictions of a high-caste Hindu woman. We are witness to Chandravati's transformation. As the Swasthani fast proceeds, Chandravati is changed from a leprous, starving creature whom the heavenly maidens address as "sinful woman" (papini) to a beautiful creature that other humans mistake for a heavenly maiden. The most important transformation is not in Chandravati's appearance, however, but in her behavior as a wife and daughter-in-law in her husband's house. The fast and austerities which she undergoes during her observance of the Swasthani barta symbolize her submission to patrifocal control. The dangerous and disruptive potential inherent in every incoming affinal woman has been tamed, and in a sense purified, by Chandravati's belated acceptance of the patrifocal values of duty and obedience.

The Swasthani text's "solution" to the trauma of moving from maita to ghar at marriage is already very clear: on the model of Sati Devi and Goma, women must accept their karma and submit uncomplainingly to this radical change in their freedom, workload, and status. Unlike Sati Devi and Goma, however, Chandravati and the village women who listen to her story must bear with a mother-in-law and often a co-wife along with other physical and emotional difficulties of marriage. Chandravati's final submission to her mother-in-law and cheerful acceptance of her co-wife is the real message of this section of the myth. Some of the harsh implications of the message for actual village women are softened in the myth by the royal comforts in which the three women live, by their saintly good natures and, above all, by the fact that the mother-in-law has handed over the storeroom key (and, thus, the control over household affairs) to Chandravati. My copy of the text carries an illustration of this important event. The act clearly reveals that the long period of suspicion and mistrust of the new affinal woman is finally over for Chandravati. She has completed the most difficult adjustment that a Hindu woman faces in her lifetime: the transfer from maita to ghar.

Notes

1. It would perhaps be more accurate to say simply that it is part of the character of the goddess to oscillate between certain extremes of human behavior (i.e., the nurturing and the punitive), which are conceptually opposed in Hindu and Western perception.

2. Sapta Matrka alone among the fierce forms do not take blood sacrifice. I have placed them with the fierce forms because of villagers' beliefs about their potential destructiveness when they are not appeased and because their connection with the fertility and prosperity of the patrilineal unit (see chapter 3).

3. Witches, of course, are human, but symbolically they are like extensions of the violent and dangerous aspect of the goddess in the human world. These spiteful, envious individuals, who are almost always female, are said to become devotees of the goddess so that they can send her out to attack others with illness or barrenness, etc. The boksi represents a kind of underground reverse image of the ideal, self-effacing, and nurturing Hindu woman—a fact which is vividly symbolized by the belief that, in order to gain their boksi powers, they must sacrifice either their own husband or their own son to the goddess. Interestingly, every one of the many witchcraft accusations I encountered during my fieldwork was directed at an affinal woman.

4. For English translations see Agrawala 1963; Pargiter 1904:chaps. 80–94.

5. In the myth Brahma, seated on the lotus growing from the navel of the sleeping Visnu, is about to be slain by two demons, Madhu and Kaitaba. Brahma beseeches the Devi, who is dwelling in Visnu's eyes in the form of sleep, to leave the god and cause him to waken so he can protect Brahma. The Devi, here called Yogi Nidra, grants Brahma's plea, and Visnu awakes to slay the demons. The myth demonstrates the Sakta sectarian belief that the other Hindu gods (here Visnu and Brahma but also Siva etc.) are dependent on the supreme Devi, who is their *sakti* or power. Narikot villagers do not themselves belong to specific sects. They worship all the gods in the orthodox traditional (*sanatana*) manner and are not really concerned with issues of ultimate supremacy.

6. Interestingly, however, no mention is made in the *Devi Mahatmya* text of the exclusion of females.

7. The eighth-day sacrifice perhaps could even be interpreted as the patrilineal group's attempt to "restore" the menstrual blood which its affinal women have lost during the last year. Through sacrifice men are thus contributing to the mysterious reproductive powers of the female sex.

8. This is only an observed preference, not a hard and fast rule. Women will travel long distances to worship at the shrine of Daksin Kali, who is perhaps one of the most bloodthirsty of all the Devi's incarnations. And men may well worship one of the gentle forms of the goddess occasionally either in temples or in the home.

9. For example, the Bagmati and Sali Nadi rivers, Slesmantak forest, the Kirateswar Siva Linga, Gauri Ghat, and the Gokarna, Pasupati, and Guyeswari temples. Of course, other place names outside Nepal (some real and some mythical) are mentioned as well—especially in chapters 9 and 10, which describe the creation of the fifty *Devipitha*—holy places which arose where parts of the Sati Devi's body fell from the back of her grief-crazed husband Siva. Nevertheless, Nepali names predominate.

10. Interestingly, these are all publicly acceptable goals—unlike the reasons women have for going to practitioners of witchcraft or those who know magic spells, such as the Gubaju, or Newari healer, described by Devi in her narrative.

11. One incident with an educated Brahman in Kathmandu illustrates an extreme of the general male attitude toward the *Swasthani Vrata Katha*. I once asked the gentleman a question concerning the *Swasthani* and he replied disdainfully that the work was "just a collection of stories for women." The implication was clear. Since *he* was a Sanskrit scholar, interested in Hindu metaphysics, etc., the *Swasthani* could hold no

possible interest for him. When I talked to his wife (an uneducated traditional woman), however, I found that she knew the stories by heart and kept a copy of the text which she worshiped reverently during the month of Magh.

In the village the attitudinal gap between men and women in such matters is much less severe, though it still exists; many men consider themselves to be more intellectual in their approach to religion and women to be more devotional.

12. See O'Flaherty 1973; L. B. Campbell 1971.

13. It is present, however, in other Puranic versions. See O'Flaherty 1973:111–30; also Vijanananda 1922:book 7, chap. 30.

14. As I mentioned in note 5 above, Sakti is both the consort and in Sakta sectarian belief the active power or strength of Siva. In tantric imagery Siva Sakti is often conceived as a couple joined in intercourse, but the reference here may simply be to a divine couple.

15. That is, first marriages arranged by parents. If a woman goes into a second marriage on her own, she is said to "run off with a lover" (poila janu), and duty has been superseded by concern for personal security and/or love.

16. Other texts, such as the Devi Bhagvatam, list 100 different pitha.

17. Sinclair Stevenson (1971:137) reports an interesting belief among Brahmans she studied more than fifty years ago in India which is clearly related to this idea: "Another sign that tells a man death is at most six months off is, that when he looks at the sky at night, though to others it is plain, yet he himself cannot distinguish Arundhati (one of the seven stars of the Great Bear, and the wife of the great sage Vasista)." In other words, a man's loss of visual contact with Arundhati, the epitome of the chaste wife, is a sign of his impending death.

18. A significant difference between the Rishi Pancami myth and this episode of the Swasthani is that in the former an impure woman brings about the problem, while in the latter the cause of the trouble is, at least partially, Siva himself, who has abandoned his duties as a householder after having indulged in the pleasures.

CHAPTER 8

Symbolic Mediation
and Individual Choice

The Hindu perception of women as it has emerged in this book can be at least partially expressed as a series of oppositions that echo and reinforce one another to reveal a deep ambivalence toward women and what they represent in the dominant patrifocal ideology. In chart 8.1 I have presented a schematic representation of some of these contrasting social roles, attributes, powers and mythic images which together help define the Hindu concept of female.[1] Implicit in the chart are a number of interrelated themes, with which we are now familiar: the problem of sexuality in an essentially puritan culture; the inadmissible dependence of the patriline on the fertility of affinal women for its own continuation; the fact that the patriline must send its beloved kinswomen away; the contradiction between the ideal of agnatic solidarity and the unstable nature of the patrilineal extended family which embodies that ideal. Although women figure in all these problems, the problems are not solely or even always primarily to do with women, but rather with the certain fundamental structural tensions in Hindu society. From this perspective the pervasive ambivalence toward women and its many levels of expression can be seen as both a result of these inherent tensions and a powerful metaphor for them.

In the area of kinship we encountered the extreme status difference between woman in her role as wife and daughter-in-law on the one hand and as sister and daughter on the other, vividly expressed in the contrast between ghar and maita. We found this difference to be based on opposed but complemen-

Chart 8.1 Symbolic Oppositions in the Hindu Perception of Women

Positive Extremes A	Mediations B	Negative Extremes C
consanguineal women	senior affinal women	junior affinal women
sister/daughter	mother	wife/daughter-in-law
high filiafocal status (receives *daksina*)	high patrifocal status (receives *bheti*)	low patrifocal status (gives *bheti*)
no material benefit to natal patriline; but confers spiritual merit when given away and offers spiritual protection to her kinsmen	contributes to prosperity and continuity of affinal patriline by her labor and by producing offspring	destructive to solidarity of affinal patriline by luring husband to separate from joint family
maita (natal home)		*ghar* (married home)
sacred		dangerous
purity		pollution
cow's milk (esp. *sagun* or curd mixture given to males by consanguineal women)	mother's milk	menstrual blood
selflessness/control		selfishness/lack of control
asceticism	reproduction	eroticism
denied sexuality	controlled procreative sexuality	dangerous/self-indulgent sexuality
kanya (prepubescent girl, virgin)	*buri* (old woman, no longer sexual)	*taruni* (nubile pubescent girl)
Arundhati (the faithful wife of the rishi Gautam)		the six unfaithful wives of the other rishis
Parvati and the gentle, nurturing forms of the goddess	Devi (the goddess)	Durga and the terrible, destructive forms of the goddess, including human witches

tary sets of values—patrifocal and filiafocal respectively—each entailing its own principles governing kin relations. The principles of the dominant patrifocal model reflect a basic distrust of and an attempt to exert control over women—particularly affinal women, whose status relations they determine. By contrast, filiafocal principles are based on reverence and affection for women—extended, however, only to relations with kinswomen.

The salient values of the dominant patrifocal model are duty and obedience to one's superiors, with rank precisely determined by the twin principles described earlier: age and male superiority. These values are in support of the cherished ideal of agnatic solidarity—an ideal which finds its social embodiment in the patrilineal joint family. However, although the ideal is strongly held, we have seen that its embodiment is in fact highly unstable. Much of the distrust of affinal women and consequent attempts to control their behavior stem from the fact that they are perceived as the major reason for this instability. But a deeper look at the dynamics of the joint family suggests that it is not only women who have motive to rebel against the patrifocal values of duty and obedience.

The joint family requires prolonged dependency on the part of *both* grown sons and their wives. As long as the extended family persists, only the senior male and his wife are considered fully mature adults. Only they enjoy unquestioned authority in their respective spheres of the family, and the consequent prestige outside it. And the larger the family—the more sons and their nuclear families it encompasses, the more coparcenary assets it keeps intact—the more prestige attaches to the senior couple. For its junior members the joint family offers a high degree of security as well as the prestige of being part of a unit embodying central patrifocal values. To belong to a harmonious joint family marks both men and women as unselfish, cooperative, and concerned with the good of the wider group. To precipitate a separation may be a shortcut to adult status as household head, but it also betrays a selfish, contentious, and undisciplined character.

Accepting the authority of one's patrifocal superior is in a sense the householder's parallel to the austerities of the ascetic path. Like the high-caste restrictions on marriage and food, obedience to one's elders (and for women to one's in-laws) is a kind of discipline that imposes control on the dangerous, self-indulgent tendencies of the individual. The difference between these disciplines and that of the ascetic is that they are directed toward the maintenance of a given social order—in particular the institutions of caste and the patrilineal extended family—while the ascetic seeks to transcend these institutions in pursuit of release from samsara and ultimate spiritual salvation. Of course, as we have already seen, the patriline itself, as a vehicle for the performance of funeral and commemorative ceremonies, offers a parallel though less radical form of spiritual salvation: existence as an ancestor spirit and continued respect and support from one's descendants after death.

Beyond whatever spiritual rewards may attend the individual's submission to patrifocal authority, there is also the promise of very real political and economic power and prestige in one's lifetime. For by obeying one's elders, one gains the right and presumably the wisdom to exert control over one's juniors and thus eventually to become the focus of patrifocal veneration as head or wife of the head of household. However, this is a demanding ideal, which requires married men and their wives to defer their own full social adulthood and economic autonomy for sometimes as long as thirty or even forty years after they achieve ritual adulthood at marriage. For men, as we have seen, this entails down playing their own fatherhood, and for both women and men, a public suppression of the husband-wife relationship.

But perhaps even more onerous than postponed maturity are the distrust and constant competition for limited common resources among joint family members, attested to by the emphasis on locking away grains and valuables, the frequency of intrahousehold theft, and the patterns of witchcraft accusation. This competitive distrust seems much more intense between members of the same generation; recalling the uneasiness which brothers expressed about the exchange of formal greetings among themselves, it appears that patrifocal seniority on the basis of birth order within the same generation is much more problematic than generational seniority.

In addition to these structural strains, there are the inevitable irregularities of the particular joint family which intensify the stress. Examples of such irregularities abound in the case history of Agni Prasad and Devi: polygamy leading to more intense rivalry between sons of different mothers and a weakening of the father/son bond; insecurity on the part of the less favored wife, who then casts her lot with her son rather than her husband at partition; a young third wife who soon becomes a mother-in-law with patrifocal authority over a woman only a few years her junior. These are the realities against which individuals must judge the feasibility of maintaining agnatic solidarity and continuing to uphold the values of duty and obedience.

The case study of Agni Prasad's family is not unusual, and as I have noted, few joint families do actually remain intact until the death of the senior male. Nevertheless, the strength of the ideal is attested to by the other case study, where an adult man nearly succumbed to complete mental collapse brought on at least to some extent by the conflicting pull of conjugal ties and loyalty to the agnatic group. What I would like to suggest is that the preoccupation with affinal women and *their* defiance of duty as the cause for the frequent premature dissolution of the joint family is in a sense a smoke screen to cover the similar but less admissible rebellion of male agnates. This is not to say that affinal women do not indeed pose a real threat to the maintenance of the joint family. The behavioral restrictions on them are much more severe than those faced by junior males, and for inmarrying women the commands of patrifocal seniors are not softened by the affection and pride of parents for their own children. By the same token, women are not defying their own parents if they push for partition. They have considerably less at stake, ideologically and emotionally, in preserving the joint family unit. Nevertheless, junior males also have a motive for defiance, and such defiance is a far more serious challenge to patrifocal ideology. Hence it tends to be submerged while women's rebellion becomes the focus of concern, and the already negative views of women are vindicated and intensified.

It is in this context that Brahman-Chetri women's specific responsibility for and frequent personal preoccupation with dharma—with the honoring of household gods, the maintenance of strict ritual purity in the kitchen, and the observance of frequent fasts and religious vows—becomes so understandable. As we have seen, part of being a good woman (or a good man for that matter) is being respectful of one's elders and submitting to their control. Patrifocal deference is in fact part of dharma, and is even couched in the same idiom. The same verb (*mannu*) is used to describe the worship of the gods, observance of a religious fast, observance of caste rules, and obedience to in-laws.

In terms of patrifocal values then, chart 8.1 can be further elaborated into the following behavioral choices which confront the individual:

obedience	*defiance*
duty	self-indulgence
harmony	contentiousness
the good of the joint family and wider group	the good of oneself and one's nuclear family
↓	↓
purity	pollution
strict observance of dharma	laxness
↓	↓
sexual restraint	sexual indulgence
the faithful wife	the Rishi's wives

The negative consequences set out in the two lower sets of oppositions do not of course necessarily follow from the collapse of the joint family (any more than the positive consequences follow from its maintenance). But there is a strong belief that they are connected and that especially for women, one type of defiance or looseness leads to another. Even women who have rebelled against the restrictions of the patrifocal model by pushing for partition continue to share its values and seek to define themselves as dutiful and obedient. Thus while men and patrifocal elders may see women's religious observances as a way to instill and reinforce habits of obedience in a potentially rebellious category, women who *have* rebelled may see these observances as a kind of substitute submission to control. For them a fastidious kitchen, or strict observance of the Tij fast or menstrual taboos, may be important as proof that they are still good women; that despite their refusal to obey their mothers-in-law they have not broken all restraints and rushed off like the Rishi's wives in lusty pursuit of Siva.

Part of the deep attraction of filiafocal relationships for both men and women is the fact that they celebrate the values of affection and personal choice as opposed to the more somber patrifocal values of duty and obedience. Yet, unlike the negative side of the oppositions discussed above, these relationships are not perceived as self-indulgent or as in any way impure. They are in fact considered more noble and selfless than patrifocal relationships. Much of this is due to the social and economic powerlessness of kinswomen within their natal patriline. While fathers and brothers feel a strong moral obligation to support their married kinswomen in times of trouble, there is no *legal* obligation which binds them. Once their marriage expenses have been paid, these women have no further claim to the ancestral property of their natal lineage. And this is, I think, part of the reason that kinswomen are sacred. Unlike gods and patrifocal superiors, daughters and sisters are worshiped not out of duty or fear of their power, but out of choice and compassion for the difficulties they must face in establishing themselves in another lineage.

As we have learned, however, the major reason for women's high status in their filiofocal relationships (and the low status of affinal women in the patrifocal model) is the Hindu attitude toward sexuality. On the model of the householder/ascetic conflict, involvement in procreation is seen as polluting and celibacy as pure. Thus the affinal woman, involved as she is in her reproductive role, is linked with sexuality and pollution. The behavioral restrictions placed on a woman in her ghar are considered necessary not only to enforce patrifocal obedience, but also to control her sexuality and maintain her purity. By contrast, the sexuality of daughters and sisters, is as we have seen, ritually shielded from consanguineal males. Kinswomen, even after marriage and childbirth, remain categorical "virgins," ever pure and worthy of both their sacred status and the freedom allowed them in their maita.

There is another reason why the sexuality of affinal women is negatively viewed. It relates to the earlier discussion of the vulnerability of the joint family. For it is the sexuality of affinal women which is perceived to create new bonds of conjugal affection, and it is their fertility which creates the nuclear family unit within the joint family. Again we are confronted with one of the central structural conflicts in the Hindu kinship system: without affinal women the joint family cannot exist, and yet they carry the seeds of its dissolution.

The pervasive ambivalence about women is further articulated in the symbolic physiology of female reproductive processes, the pure aspect of the female sex being associated with mother's milk and the impure aspect with menstrual blood. But like many of the other linked oppositions set out in the chart, this association of static pairs hides a much more dynamic symbolic articulation of the complex meanings attached to women in Hindu society. We have discovered, for example, that blood and milk, though clearly opposed to each other on the symbolic level, each contain their own ambiguities that do not permit a perfect linkage with the other sets of oppositions lined up in columns A and C in chart 8.1. Instead, this ambiguity allows symbolic mediation of the opposed extremes. For instance, while milk is strongly associated with purity and thus with consanguineal women, it is also manifestly linked with motherhood and fertility and thus with affinal women as well. Not surprisingly, the symbolism of mother's milk echoes that of motherhood itself; both transcend the fundamental conceptual opposition between the pure, asexual kinswoman and the impure, erotic affinal woman. Both motherhood and mother's milk appear in column B of the chart, along with perhaps the most powerful mediating symbol we have encountered in the study, the goddess. We are familiar now with the great complexity—or one could say the divine paradox—of the Devi's nature which enables her to express so effectively the Hindu ambivalence about the female sex. Through her opposing gentle and threatening forms (each of which in turn contains its own divinely mediated contradictions) she subsumes both the nurturing and the punitive, the pure and the impure, the sacred and the dangerous aspects of women.

Perhaps the most important message of the chart—and of this book as a whole—is that the social and symbolic structures of Hinduism largely interpenetrate each other. With reference to women this has meant that the social roles of women in patrilineal Hindu kinship and family structures are reinforced by their symbolic roles in ritual and myth, and that these, in turn, gain much of their conceptual impact and emotional force from the fact that they are so firmly grounded in the social structure.

It is well to bear in mind, however, that like the title of this book itself, the chart distills what is essentially the Hindu male's perspective on women—women from the standpoint of the dominant patrifocal ideology. From this perspective woman is the "other." Each individual woman can be categorized as either kinswoman or affine, pure or polluting, sacred or dangerous. But for women both these opposing categories and sets of attributes are "self." Women must somehow integrate and internalize two different roles and valuations of the self. As members of what Shirley Ardener (1977) has described as a "muted group," they must transform the world view presented by the dominant group in order to express their own perceptions—and sometimes to justify their own actions, which may be counter to the dominant ideology. This does not mean that the sets of symbolic oppositions and the problems they express are not understood and shared by Hindu women. I do not believe, as Edwin Ardener at some points seems to imply (Ardener 1977), that women have a separate or "autonomous" model of reality and that they categorize and bound things differently from men. Rather I think that dominant and muted groups can be said to have radically different *perspectives* on a shared world view.

This difference in perspectives we have already encountered in the contrast between Durga and the heroines of the *Swasthani.* Durga can be seen as embodying the male perception of women and the *problems women present to the patrifocal system.* She is a symbol of the patrilineal group's vulnerability and dependence on affinal women who, like Durga, may or may not use their power for the good of the patriline. Parvati, Goma, and Chandravati, on the other hand, seem to embody the female perspective, and their stories enact the *problems which the patrifocal system presents to women:* the problem of integrating the roles of wife and daughter and adjusting to the transfer from maita to ghar.

Of course the problems women present and the problems they face are bound together, and from a structural point of view they are one and the same—both the result of inherent contradictions or stress points in the system. But experientially they are very different. And it is women's experience that the structural oppositions set out in the chart fail to convey but that is captured in the *Swasthani*. In the *Swasthani* we get a sense of woman not as object or symbol but as subject and actor. There is recognition that actualization of the negative or positive potentials of these oppositions is a choice to be made by the individual woman. Every woman's life involves transit through a series of categories from presexual child to sexual woman and finally to asexual old age. No woman can remain, as Goma tried to, forever sacred, presexual kanya in her maita. The transition to sexuality and wifehood must be made. She must leave one lineage and establish her position in another. But there are, as we have seen in the case histories and in the *Swasthani,* alternative strategies for dealing with this transition. From the point of view of the patrifocal system, the potential of a woman's sexuality can be used positively to produce offspring for the patriline or negatively to lure her husband from the agnatic group. It may even lead her to abandon him for another or to allow pollution into the lineage by sleeping secretly with another man of lower caste. These are the powers and choices a woman has. To what degree she will submit these powers to patrifocal control is the question which lies unanswered in the chart and which is at the root of the pervasive ambivalence toward women it reveals.

Note

1. In fact none of these oppositions are as rigid or "neat" as such a chart makes them appear. Often in ritual contexts the entire meaning of an item in one column or

another is transformed—or mediated—by its association in the course of the ritual with concepts normally opposed to it. For example, as we have seen in the Tij–Rishi Pancami rituals, "wife" (normally associated with impurity and erotic sexuality) is associated with "purity" and "Arundhati."

Glossary

abhyudāyikā śrāddha	Offering to the ancestors performed at the beginning of the initiation and wedding ceremonies and other auspicious meritorious rituals as a way of including the ancestor spirits in the family celebration and invoking their blessings.
achetā	Unbroken rice grains used in *pujā* offerings.
ādyabdika śrāddha	The first of the monthly commemorative offerings to the deceased performed during the first year after death.
Agni	The fire god.
agni hotra	The worship of Agni by tending the sacred fire and making fire sacrifices.
ainā herne	"Looking in the mirror": ritual indulgence of bride and groom's vanity by having them each view themselves in a mirror during the wedding festivities.
āmā	Mother.
āmāju	Respectful form of address for "mother" also used by a woman to address her mother-in-law.
Ambikā	A destructive emanation of the goddess Devi.
annaprāsána	"Giving food to eat": ceremony during which a child is fed its first boiled rice.
ansa	Lit. share, division: ancestral property.
ārti syāuli	"The shadow or reflection of the lamp": wedding ritual where the sisters of the groom welcome the wedding party and the new bride by waving a lighted lamp before the sacred water vessel and worshiping it with flowers, rice, and *dubo* grass.
Arundhatī	Wife of the rishi Vasistha; the epitome of the chaste and faithful wife.
āsik	Blessing given by a superior to an inferior.
astu	A piece of bone left over from a corpse after cremation.

asura	A demon.
ātman	The individual's self or soul, which in Hindu philosophy is believed to be part of the Universal Soul.
āyu baras	Ritual during marriage ceremonies to ensure long life of the husband.
āyurda	Life, longevity (*āyurveda:* medical science of the Hindus).
bāhuni	Woman of the Brahman caste.
baṁsāwali	Family record or genealogy.
bāpati pitṛ	Patrilineal ancestors.
Baṛa Dasaī	"Great Dasaī." The major fall festival in honor of the warrior goddess Durga. Durga is also worshiped again in the spring during the month of Cait (February–April) in a minor festival called Cait Dasaī.
barakhi śrāddha	Ceremony performed on the first anniversary of a death, marking the end of the year of mourning.
barani	Procession of the bride and groom to their house on the day of their marriage. Welcoming of the groom and his party by the bride's father in the wedding ceremony (Turner: 1931).
barta	A religious vow or fast.
bartaman	The initiation ceremony of high-caste males during which they are invested with the sacred thread.
bāun bhojan	"Brāhman feast" where twelve Brāhmans are fed following the Sapiṇḍa Śrāddha.
bewārisi	Without claimant or heir.
Bhagwān	God.
Bhairav	A fierce and terrifying form of the god Śiva.
Bhaitarṇi Nadi	The terrifying river which bars the way to the kingdom of Yama, the god of death.
Bhāi Ṭikā	Festival during Tihār when sisters worship their brothers and vice versa.
bhakti	Devotion or religious faith.
bhandār; bhāṛār	A locked storeroom.
bhānij	Sister's son.
bhaṛār dekhāune	"Showing the storeroom": part of the wedding rituals when a bride and her new mother-in-law put paddy from the *pāthi bharne* ceremony into the household storeroom.
bhār bandan	The first of the preliminary rituals for the *bartaman* and wedding ceremonies. Bhār bãdhnu: to tie up a bundle of auspicious items, which is then placed in the altar room during the ceremony.
bhāt-mārā	Lit. one who cares only about eating: people who work as occasional laborers or servants in return for rice (*bhāt*), lodging, and clothing.

bhāuju	Elder brother's wife.
bheṭi	A gift of money made to a superior. Also a bribe.
bhikṣā māgne	Begging for alms. Part of the bartaman ceremony where the initiate takes the role of a mendicant and begs from his own relatives.
bhikṣā pātra	Plate for collecting alms.
bhog	Blood sacrifice.
Bhumi	Earth god.
Bhuswāmi	Lit. Lord of the Earth. Used by informants in reference to the late father of King Birendra.
bhut	Ghost or malevolent spirit.
biāite	Marriage sanctified by a *bihā* or wedding with full *kanyādān* rituals; a woman married with such rituals.
bihā	Marriage (also *biyā*).
binā bābu	Without a father.
birtā	A grant of land.
biśrāmsthān	Resting places (where funeral procession rests on way to cremation ground).
biśwadevā	The entire pantheon.
biṭulo	Polluted or defiled.
boko	Uncastrated male goat.
boksi	Witch.
Brahmā	The god of creation; the ultimate reality.
brahmacārin	A chaste student; used with reference to a boy or young man undergoing the first of the four stages (*brahmacarya*) in the life of a high-caste Hindu male.
brāhman	Member of the highest of the four *varnas* in the Hindu caste hierarchy, traditionally filling the role of priest. Brāhmans are also called bāun, bāwan, bāhun and bāman in rural Nepal.
buḍi sāsu or *buṛi sāsu*	Husband's paternal grandmother (*buṛi:* old woman; *sāsu:* mother-in-law).
buhāri	Son's wife.
buṛi	An old woman. Used colloquially to refer to one's wife.
Cāmuṇḍā	A destructive emanation of the goddess Devi.
caṇḍālini.	Accursed or damned woman.
Caṇḍī	An epithet of the goddess Durgā; also name of an epic hymn in praise of the goddess. (See *Caṇḍi Pāṭh*)
Caṇḍī Pāṭh	Lit. Durgā lessons. A hymn of praise to the goddess Durgā, telling of three occasions when the Devi, in her terrible aspect, intervened to save the gods from various demons who had usurped the gods' powers. (Also known as *Durgā Saptasati, Caṇḍī*.)
caūsaṭṭhi yogini	The sixty-four female ascetics who accompany Śiva; emanations of the goddess Durgā.

chāk-khalko	Death pollution ritual of bathing and abstaining from one meal on the death of a distant relative.
chekā rākhne	"Putting up an obstacle": ritual separation of the groom and the bride's father in the marriage ceremony.
Chetrī	Sanskrit: Kṣatriya. Name of the second ranking twice-born Parbatiya caste who in the traditional varna system held the position of warriors or kings just below the Brahman priests.
chetrinī	Woman of the Chetri caste.
chewar	Hair-cutting ritual, performed as part of the initiation ceremony.
chiṭo kāṭne	Purification rite where a polluted person is sprinkled with pure water.
citā	Funeral pyre.
citā piṇḍa	Rice-balls offered to the deceased by the chief mourner after the cremation.
cokho	Clean or pure.
cokho māṭo korne	"Digging pure earth," one of the preliminary ceremonies for the bartaman and wedding rituals in which two unmarried Brahman girls bring in dirt from the field that will be used in the construction of the ceremonial enclosure.
culo	Hearth, cooking place.
culṭho jorne	"Joining the hairbraids": marriage ritual where the hairbraids of the bride and her new mother-in-law (and co-wives if they exist) are entwined and annointed with ghee.
cup lāgera basne	"Sitting and saying nothing": a phrase often used to compliment a woman's behavior.
dai achetā ṭikā	Special *ṭikā* (or auspicious mark on the forehead) of curds, red powder and rice grains.
dāijo	Dowry.
daītya	Demon.
dāju-bhāi	Elder and younger brothers.
dākh ko piṇḍa	Raisins pressed into a ball, used for offerings to the ancestor spirits on auspicious occasions such as weddings and bartaman rites.
dakṣiṇā	Gift or offering made to an officiating priest. Also given to daughters of the house on ceremonial occasions.
dāl bhāt	Lentil curry and boiled rice—the staple food of Nepal.
damāi	The untouchable tailor-musician caste belonging to the Parbatiya group.
damini	Woman of the damāi caste.
dān	Religious gifts made to a priest.

dar khāne	Feast of rich food eaten by women on the eve of the Tij festival when women fast to ensure the long life of their husband. The men of the family must, if possible, provide whatever foods their wives demand for the feast.
Dasaī	A major festival held in the light fortnight of the month of Asauj (September–October) in honor of the goddess Durgā (see Barā Dasaī).
Dasaī ghar	Altar established for worship of the goddess Durgā in each household during the Dasaī festival.
devāli	Celebration in honor of the lineage gods.
devatā	A god; personified form of Bhagwān.
Devī	The goddess or female divinity, who manifests in the forms of many different goddesses.
Devi Bhāgavatam	A *Purāṇa*. Containing version of the Sati Devi myth along with many other stories about the goddess in her various forms.
Devi Māhātmya	Famous sixth-century Śakta devotional work in praise of the goddess.
dewar	Husband's younger brother.
dhāi āmā	Nurse.
dhāmī	Man who becomes possessed by a god and thus able to serve as an oracle or healer.
dharma	Religious duty; caste duty; religion. Used in a wide range of meanings from the performance of specified rites to general ethical behaviour, righteousness, goodness, etc.
ḍhiki	Footmill, device for husking rice. "A machine for husking rice [which] consists of two upright posts holding between them a long pole, the head of which is weighted. The worker stands on the other end, thus raising the head which is then allowed to descend sharply into a hole in the ground in which is the rice" (Turner: 1931).
ḍhikuro śrāddha	Nine-day period following the *kṣetrabās* when the chief mourner feeds the spirit of the dead in its ghost form. *Ḍhikuro* = a mound of dirt where the spirit of the deceased comes as a ghost to be fed.
ḍhokā	Door or gate.
ḍhokā chekne	"Barring the door": light-hearted ritual where groom's sisters prevent the bride from entering the husband's house until she has promised each a new blouse.
ḍhok dine	Bowing down in salutation and touching the forehead to a respected person's feet.
dhotī	For males a loincloth or long piece of thin cotton, wrapped to cover the lower half of the body. In colloquial use in Nepal it is also used to refer to a cotton

dhotī (continued)	sari worn by women. Often in the rural areas the end piece of the sari is not thrown over the shoulder as in India but tucked into the waist, thus resembling the male dhoti.
dibya pitṛ	Servants or messengers of the ancestors; alternatively the kings of the realm of the ancestors. Also called *kābyabat.*
diyo or *diyo batti*	Small earthenware votive lamp.
diyo kalas pujā	Ritual of worshiping the kalas or sacred vessel with lighted lamps; used to perform *liāite* marriages.
dubo	Grass, *Cynodon dactylon,* with purifying powers.
dulāhā dulahi	"Groom-and-bride": game played with dolls in which wedding rituals are acted out.
dulai anmāune	A ceremony in which the bride's parents bid her farewell after the *kanyādān* ceremony before the bride is sent to her husband's house.
dulan pharkāune	The bride's return to visit her natal home after she has been married and taken to her husband's house.
Durgā	The bloodthirsty virgin warrior goddess, a destructive form of the Devi.
Durgā Kabac	"The armor of Durgā": a short invocation in the *Caṇḍī* epic which calls on the nine forms of Durgā for protection.
Durgā Saptasati	See *Caṇḍī.*
duṣta	A scoundrel or rogue.
eghāraũ śram	Rites performed on the eleventh day after a death to help release the soul from its worldly sins so that it may reach heaven rather than hell (*śram:* work, effort; *eghāra:* eleven).
ekodhiṣṭa śrāddha	Commemorative offering ceremony performed on the lunar anniversary of a death by the deceased's male descendants for three generations.
Gairu	The god of cowherds, guardian deity of cattle.
Gāi Tihār	The third day of Tihār when the sacred cow and the goddess Lakṣmī are worshiped.
Gandharva	A celestial musician; a class of divine being.
Gaṇeś	God of prosperity with the head of an elephant.
Gaṅgā	The river Ganges and the River goddess.
gaũt	Cow's urine, which has ritually purifying powers.
gāyatrī mantra	A sacred verse from the *Ṛgveda,* in gāyatrī meter, recited mentally by Brāhmans at morning and evening devotions.
ghar-juwai	House or home; specifically for a woman, her husband's home and her family of marriage.
ghar-juwãi	"House son-in-law": man who lives with his wife's parents.

ghāṭasthāpanā	"Establishing the slaughter": the beginning of *Nauratha,* the nine nights of Durgā, of the Dasaī festival.
gobar	Fresh cowdung or a purifying paste of cowdung and mud.
godān	A ceremonial gift consisting of a cow, usually represented by a leaf plate with money on it.
goṛā ḍhoknu	To bow down and touch the feet of a highly respected person.
goṛā dhune	"Foot-washing" ceremony where the bride's family wash her feet before she is given to the groom in marriage.
goṛā pāni khāne	Second foot-washing ceremony following the giving away of the bride, when she washes her husband's feet and drinks some of the water. Subsequently high-caste women repeat the ritual before every rice meal when their husband is present.
goṛdhuwāi	Gifts to the bride made by her relatives at the foot-washing ceremony.
gotra	Clan; an exogamous agnatic unit whose members claim to be descendants of one of seven mythical sages or rishis.
gotrājā	Agnatic relatives between eight and ten generations removed.
graha śānti pujā	Marriage ritual to placate and pacify the nine planets and the gods they represent before beginning the main ceremonies.
grihastha dharma	The duty or path of the householder, the second of the four stages of a Hindu's life, during which emphasis is placed on following the rules and rituals of conventional Hinduism and producing male offspring.
gubhāju	Newar priest and practitioner of medicine.
guphā basne	"Staying in the cave": menarche rite wherein the girl on her first menstruation must stay for a number of days in a dark room out of sight of her father and brothers and undergo a purification ceremony before she may see them again.
gupti āhuti	"Secret oblation": the touching of the bride's feet by the groom during the marriage ceremony.
guru	Teacher or spiritual master.
hā̃ga	Lit. "branch": a *kul* unit or offshoot of a larger patrilineage.
hāt ḍhok	Gesture of deference in which the inferior bends over as it to touch the honored person's foot, but is stopped by the other's hand extended to his forehead in the *āsik* or blessing gesture.

havasya basne or *havisyak basne*	A purifying fast accompanied by a number of temporary ascetic restrictions, observed before religious ceremonies when the worshiper must reach a state of great purity.
Himālaya	Lit. abode of snow; King Himālaya was father of Pārvati.
Indra	The king of the gods and god of war.
hom	Fire ceremony where grain and butter are offered to the sacred fire with the assistance of a Brāhman priest.
jagge	Sacred enclosure or pavilion set up for a wedding, bartaman, or other auspicious ceremony.
Jaisī Brāhman	Offspring of a Brāhman widow or divorcee who has remarried with another Brāhman man. Lower status than full Upādhyāya Brāhmans, Jaisis are not allowed to be priests and thus have often taken up the profession of astrologer.
jajamāni	See *kamāune*.
jajmān	The client of a priest or the one who offers sacrifice to the gods.
jamarā	Yellow barley sprouts planted on the first day of Dasaī and distributed to relatives on the 10th day when *ṭika* is given.
janai	Sacred thread worn by the twice-born castes.
janai purne or *janai purṇimā*	Annual festival when Brāhman and Chetri men receive new sacred threads.
jāt	Caste, race.
je pani bhanche jahā̃ pani hiṛche	Woman who "says what she likes, goes where she likes"; a contentious and immodest woman (slightly disrespectful form).
jharrā	"Pure"; having full caste status; the offspring of orthodox Hindu marriage between members of the same caste, or between a Brāhman man and a Chetri woman.
jholi ko devta	"God in a bag"—term of respect and affection for sister's son or daughter's son.
juni bhāg	"Life portion": The share of ancestral property retained by a widow, an old man, or a couple after their sons have separated and the joint family property has been divided.
juṭho	Impure, defiled.
juṭho khāne	Ritual eating of polluted food during marriage, when bride must show her subservient status by finishing some food from which her husband has eaten.
juwā̃i	Son-in-law.
juwā̃i-celi	Daughter, son-in-law, and their children (celi = daughter); also celi-beṭi.

jyotirliṅg	Śiva's penis of flames.
jyotiṣ	Astrologer.
Kailāś	Sacred mountain where the gods dwell; home of Śiva.
kalas	Copper water pot used in the performance of religious rites.
Kāli	A destructive emanation of the goddess Devi.
Kāl rātri	"Black night": night ritual worshiping the nine forms of Durgā with blood sacrifice on the ninth evening of Dasaī.
Kāma	The god of love and passion.
kāmadhenu gāi	The cow of Hindu myth which grants all wishes.
kamāune	"Working for hire": system whereby artisan-caste families perform a specialized service for patron families in return for set annual grain payments (equivalent to the Indian *jajamani*).
kāmi	Untouchable Parbatiya blacksmith caste.
kām kuro chinne	Simple ceremony signifying that the bride's and groom's family both have agreed to the match.
kānchi	Youngest wife or daughter.
kanyā	Prepubescent girl or virgin.
kanyādān	Lit. "Gift of a virgin"—orthodox Hindu marriage.
karma	The moral law of cause and effect whereby the transmigrating soul is accompanied by the results of its previous actions.
karma caleko	"Activated karma": the state of full adult responsibility—especially with reference to observance of caste restrictions; full caste status.
karuwā	Brass water vessel with a spout.
kasār	Sweet made of molasses, water, and powdered rice rolled into a ball.
Kāśī	The city of Vārāṇasi.
kāśiv	A "catch-all" gotrā for members of middle and lower castes who are not twice born and do not belong to any particular gotrā.
khatri chetri or *K.C.*	Offspring of a Brāhman man and a Chetri or a Matwāli woman.
khir	Rice and milk pudding.
khocā	Small cup made of a single leaf, often used to hold offerings during rituals.
khukuri	Long, curved Nepalese knife.
kinnārā	Kinnar, a mythical being with the body of a man and head of a horse (Turner: 1931).
kiriyā basne	Thirteen days of death pollution immediately following a death—a time of austerity and social isolation for the bereaved.
kiriyā putra	The chief mourner—normally the son.

konā mā basne	"Sitting in a corner": the eleven-day period following the birth of a child during which the mother is considered to be polluted and remains apart from the rest of the family. See also *sutak* and *sutkero*.
koseli	Presents or bribes to an honored person.
Kṛṣṇa/Krishna	Cowherd god and romantic hero, the eighth avatar of Viṣṇu.
Kṣatriya	Sanskrit name of the second-ranking warrior caste, or varna, which includes the Chetris.
kṣetrabās	"Staying in a field of purity": period of mourning and isolation for the chief mourner immediately after the cremation. (Also called *korā bārne*.)
kul	Lineage or agnatic descent group.
kul devtā	Lineage gods.
kul ghar	Ancestral home.
Kumār	A grass, *Poa cynosuroides,* used for purification in religious ceremonies and worshiped as a form of Viṣṇu.
lacchiṇ	Auspiciousness or good luck.
lagan	Astrologically determined auspicious moment for commencing a ritual.
lagan gāṭho	The marriage knot tied between two pieces of cloth from the bride's and the groom's side to symbolize the union.
lāj	Shame, embarrassment, or modesty; hence, *lāj lāgyo* and *lāj mānne*: ashamed, embarrassed, shy.
Lakṣmī	The goddess of wealth and fortune: a gentle emanation of the Devi, wife of Viṣṇu.
liāite	A form of marriage (in contrast to *biāite* marriage performed with full *kanyādān* rituals) where the man simply "brings" the woman into his household. This form of marriage, while recognized, confers lower status on the woman and her offspring. Many inter-caste marriages are *liāite* as are all second marriages for women. Also used to describe a woman married in such a manner.
liṅga	Phallus, a symbol of Śiva.
lugā pherne	"Changing clothes": ceremony during the marriage procedure when the bride puts on a new set of clothes given to her by her husband. For *liāite* marriage this may be the ceremony performed.
mā	Mother.
Māgh Swasthāni Barta	A ritual celebration during the month of Māgh (January–February) in which a form of the goddess called Swasthāni is worshiped and nightly readings are made from the *Swasthāni* text and women often perform a fast.

Mahādeo	(Also *Māhādev*). Lit. the great god; Śiva.
Māhākali	Demon who, with Virbhandra, issued from Śiva's topknot on the death of Sati Devi. A name for the goddess Durgā (Māhākāli).
mahātmā	A "great-souled" or spiritually enlightened person.
māhātmya śrāddha	A rite performed on the final day of the 16 days of *sora śrāddha* for ego's mother's father.
Mahiṣa or Mahiṣāsura	A buffalo bull: the buffalo demon overcome by Durgā in the Caṇḍī epic.
māiti or maita	A woman's natal home and her own consanguineal relatives.
māmā	Mother's brother.
māmāpati pitṛ	Ancestors on the mother's brother's side.
maṅgal kalas	An auspicious water pot.
mānnu	To obey or respect.
mantra	A mystic formula of Sanskrit syllables, words or phrases; it is made effective by repetition and meditation.
māsik śrāddha	Monthly rituals performed during the first year after a death.
mātṛkā	Mother goddesses; hence, the Seven Mātṛkās: destructive form of the Devi. (Also *mātṛ* or *mātri*.)
matwāli	"Those who drink liquor": the middle-ranking castes in Nepal. These castes are considered clean or *cokho* and water and certain types of food can be accepted from them.
māwali	Mother's brother's home. (Also *māmāli*.)
māyā	Love or infatuation.
mit	For a man a male friend with whom a special ritual has been enacted to solemnize the friendship. For a woman, the husband of her *mitini*.
mitini	Female friend (of another woman) with whom a special ritual has been enacted to solemnize the friendship. For a man, the wife of his *mit*.
mohani	Charm or love spell.
mukh herne	"Seeing the face": when the women of the groom's family lift the bride's veil during the wedding ceremonies to look at her face.
mukti	Salvation or release from the cycle of rebirth.
Munda	A demon killed by Kāli in the Caṇḍī epic.
na chune	"Not touching": term denoting the segregation of women during their menstrual periods. Also used to describe a woman who is menstruating.
namaste	"Honour to thee": common form of greeting with the hands folded.
Nandī	The name of the bull on which Śiva rides.
narka	Hell.

nātādār   Akin or related.
Nau Durgā   The nine forms of Durgā.
Nauratha   The nine nights of Durgā, during the Dasaĩ festival.
                            (Also Navarātra; Navarātri.)
navāhā   A special ceremony wherein Brāhmans are engaged
                            to read from the sacred text for nine days.
Newār   A Tibeto-Burman speaking people, the original in-
                            habitants of the Kathmandu Valley.
niskarmarā   "First outing": when a newborn baby is brought out-
                            side for its first view of the sun on the eleventh day
                            after birth.
nitya pujā   Obligatory daily worship of the household gods.
nuwāran   The ceremony of naming a child, performed when
                            he or she is eleven days old. The mother of the child
                            also bathes and is purified of birth pollution on this
                            day.
pān   The leaf of the betel nut, eaten with areca nut and
                            lime.
pañcagabya   A purifying drink made of the five sacred items (ur-
                            ine, dung, milk, and curds from the cow, and kus grass)
                            mixed with water.
pañcagavya   "The five elements": the sacred and purifying gifts of
                            the cow: milk, clarified butter (ghee), curd, urine and
                            dung. (Fr. Locke, personal communication.)
pañcāmrt   "The five nectars": a purifying mixture of ghee, curds,
                            sugar, milk, and honey.
pañcāyat   Administrative unit generally encompassing one or
                            more traditional villages; the council or committee
                            of the elected representatives of that unit.
Pañc Kumāri   The five virgin goddesses, destructive emanations of
                            the Devi.
paṇḍit   A learned Brāhman man who is a teacher or scholar
                            especially of Sanskrit.
pāni na calne   Those from whom water is not accepted, i.e., un-
                            touchables.
pāp   Sin or vice.
para sarne   "Moving away": a polite term for the isolation of
                            women during their menstrual periods.
Parbatiyā   "A hill or mountain person": used with reference to
                            the Indo-Aryan Hindu peoples—both high caste and
                            untouchables—who have migrated from India up into
                            the hills of Nepal at various periods and who formed
                            the bulk of the conquering army of Prithivi Nārāyan
                            Shāh when he invaded the Kathmandu Valley in the
                            eighteenth century.
pardā   Lit. veil: among Hindus this refers to various forms of

	respect avoidance observed by women in the presence of senior affinal relatives. In the Nepal hills actual veiling of the face is not practiced.
parivār	Family or household, ideally consisting of a man, his wife or wives, his brothers, their wives, all their unmarried daughters, sons, son's wives and their children who share a common hearth and own property as a unit.
parmā	Mutual exchange of labor.
Pārvati	Wife of Śiva, a gentle emanation of the Devi.
pāsni	The ceremony of giving a child its first rice, performed at 5 months for a girl and 6 months for a boy.
pāt	Lit. leaf or feather—one with a slim body.
pāthi	A measure of capacity of grain, equal approximately to 8 pints.
pāthi bharne	"Filling a grain measure": wedding ritual in which the groom's mother fills a measure with grain and hides in it money, a sacred thread and betel nuts. The contents are then put in a winnowing tray and the bride and her new mother-in-law compete to find the objects.
pativratā	A chaste and faithful wife.
phuki bhāi	A patrilineal relative for whom at least minimal mourning rituals must be observed.
phupu	Father's sister.
phuri	One who is looking for trouble.
piṇḍa	A ceremonial rice-ball used in offerings to the ancestors.
pipal	A kind of fig tree, *Ficus religiosa,* worshiped as a form of Viṣṇu.
pīṭha	A tantric center or holy place; hence *Devi pīṭha:* the 108 holy places which were created where parts of Sati Devi's body fell from Śiva's back as he danced with grief at her death.
pitṛ	Ancestor spirits.
pitṛadhan	"Wealth of the ancestors": patrimony.
pitṛlok	The abode of the ancestors.
poi	Husband or lover.
poila jānu	To run off with a man—a union other than *kanyādān.*
Prajāpati	See Dakṣa Prajāpati.
prasād	Lit. a favor—an offering (usually consisting of fruit, flowers, rice, red and yellow powders, etc.) made to a deity, and then returned to the giver as a sign of the acceptance of the offering, or to others as a sign of their participation in the *pujā.*
prāyaścitta	Propitiation or expiation. Hence, *prāyaścitta godān:*

prāyaścitta (continued)	a gift of a cow, or coins symbolizing a cow, made for the expiation of sins.
pret	Ghost; unsatisfied and potentially harmful spirit of a deceased person who has not been able to reach the *pitṛlok.*
pujā	Worship or religious ceremony.
pujāri	Priest or officiant at a *pujā, or the keeper of a temple* or shrine.
puṇya	Merit or virtue.
purā hã̄ga	Agnatic relatives up to and including seven generations removed.
Purān or *Purāṇa*	Sacred Sanskrit works containing traditional lore and history.
purbāṅga	Preliminary rituals to the bartaman or a marriage.
purohit	Domestic priest.
putali	A doll; also an image of the deceased used in funeral ceremonies in cases of death when the body cannot be recovered.
Rālā Rāli	Ritual performed in Kangra Valley region of India in which the images of Śiva and Pārvati are married and then destroyed.
Rām Candra or *Rām*	The Hero of the *Rāmāyaṇa;* seventh avatar or incarnation of Viṣṇu.
raṇḍi	A widow or prostitute.
ratauli	(Old *ratyauli*) A night of dancing, male impersonation, and sometimes sexual joking for women only. Ratauli is hosted by the women of the groom's household after the groom and his wedding party have left the village and gone to fetch the bride.
Rati	Lit. love, passion. Wife of Kāma, the god of love.
Rāvaṇa	The name of the Rākṣas king who carried off Sītā, wife of Rām.
rekhi	A ritual diagram drawn with flour; used in religious ceremonies.
rishi (*ṛṣi*)	A sage or saint. The number of rishis usually cited in Hindu mythology is seven: Jamadagmi, Gautama, Bharadvāja, Atri, Viswāmitra, Kasyapa, and Vasista.
ritu dān	Lit. seasonal gift. The husband's obligation to sleep with his wife on the fourth day after menstruation when she has been purified and is believed to be fertile.
roṭi	Unleavened bread.
Ṛṣi Pañcami Vratā Kathā	Nepali text explaining the mythic origin of the Ṛṣi Pancami festival and setting out the manner in which the ritual should be observed.
Rudra	The archer god, whose arrows brought disease. Also guardian of healing herbs; the precursor of Śiva.

runce sāpro	"Tearful leg": a feast in the bride's family of a goat's leg sent by the groom's party.
sabya	Right or proper: the usual auspicious positioning of the sacred thread over the right shoulder.
sādhu	Holy man or ascetic.
sagotra	Of the same *gotra.*
sagun	A gift of curds given on various ceremonial occasions. (*sagun* = omen, portent; *sagune* = a present of fruit and flowers given to a superior on the eve of a journey as a sign of good augury [Turner: 1931]
śākhā	Branch or offshoot: a *kul* unit, offshoot of a larger patrilineage. (Also *hāga.*)
sākhācarna	A recitation in Sanskrit of the bride's and groom's male ancestors for three generations recited during the *kanyādān* ceremony.
Śakta	A Hindu sect whose members worship the goddess Śakti.
śakti	The strength or active power of the deity personified as his wife; the female principle in Hindu tantric philosophy; the goddess.
śāligrām	A black quartz containing ammonite fossils which is worshiped as a representation of Viṣṇu.
sāmā	A white-tipped grass.
samāvartanā	The end of studenthood or the *brahmacarya* stage of life.
samdhi	A son's or daughter's father-in-law.
samdhini	A son's daughter's mother-in-law.
samdhi/samdhini bhet	See *sāsu/sasurā cinne.*
saṁsāra	The phenomenal world; the cycle of birth and death and rebirth.
saṁskāra	Life-cycle ritual.
sanātana	Everlasting or traditional.
sanātana dharma	Orthodox religious practice.
sannyāsi dharma	The ascetic's path or duty.
sannyāsin	An ascetic, one in the fourth and final stage of life wherein worldly concerns and comforts are renounced.
Sansāri Devi	Local goddess, a destructive emanation of the Devi.
sapiṇḍi bhāi	Patrilineal kinsmen connected by the fact that they must offer *piṇḍa* to the same patrilineal ancestor: a patrilineal descent group encompassing five generations including the ego.
sapiṇḍa śrāddha	Death ritual performed on the twelfth day after death, in which the deceased is transformed from an inauspicious ghost to an ancestral spirit.
sapiṇḍiya	A patrilineal descent group encompassing seven generations including ego.

sapta dhānya	Seven kinds of grains used in the marriage ceremony and other rituals.
sārki	The untouchable Parbatiyā caste of leatherworkers.
śāstra	A religious book, especially of the law.
sāsu	Mother-in-law.
sāsu/sasurā cinne	"Meeting the mother and father-in-law": the bride's father travels to his daughter's new home with gifts for her in-laws, to ease the relationship between the two families.
sasurāli	Wife's parents' home.
Sati Devi	The wife of Śiva, whose death caused him to go mad with grief.
satya Nārāyan pujā	Worship of Nārāyan, who is Viṣṇu.
saubhāgya sāmān	Lit. the symbols of happiness or having a living husband—consisting of red bangles, a red hairbraid, a comb, a mirror, a box of red powder, and red beads.
sautā	Co-wife.
śayyā dān	"Gift of a bed": gifts from the bride's family to the new couple; also ceremony on eleventh day after a death, in which furniture such as beds, etc., are given to the priest so he can present them to the dead.
sidhā	Uncooked food; a gift of the ingredients of a meal.
sīdur	Red or vermilion used (in worship, in *ṭikās* and) by married women to decorate the hair parting.
sīdur hālne	"Putting on the vermilion powder," when the groom first applies the red powder to the bride's part during the wedding ceremony.
sikā	The Hindu man's top knot, a lock of hair which must not be cut.
Sītā	Wife of Rām, a gentle form of the Devi.
Sitalā	Smallpox, or the smallpox goddess—a destructive emanation of the Devi.
Śiva	The god of destruction, one of the major gods in the Hindu pantheon.
Śiva Kausiki	A name of the goddess Durgā.
Śiva Śarmā	Name of the husband of Gomā in the Swasthāni myth.
Śiva Sudanvan	Śiva in his hunter form.
smṛti	Lit. memory: traditional doctrine or code of law, as opposed to revelation.
sobath	Decorum (*śobhā*: beauty, splendor; *sobhit*: beautiful, adorned, charming; *sobhāu*: nature, disposition, conduct [Turner: 1931])
sodasi śrāddha	A mourning rite which takes place on the eleventh day after death in which sixteen *piṇḍas* are offered to the deceased.
sora śrāddha	Death rite performed for the collective honoring of

all the ancestors, performed during the fortnight preceding the Dasaī festival.

śrāddha — Ceremony performed in honor of and for the benefit of the deceased ancestors. The ceremony centers on the symbolic offering of food and water to sustain the ancestors in the afterlife.

śramdān — Voluntary labor.

śrī — Lit. happiness and prosperity: a title of respect prefixed to a name or other title.

śrīmān — Lit. one who is fortunate—husband.

strīdhanam — "Woman's wealth": as represented by the gifts which accompany her as a bride to her husband's home.

śuddha śānti — "Pure and peaceful": a series of rituals ending death pollution on the thirteenth day after death.

sulṭo — The correct or auspicious direction.

sunpāni — Water that has been touched with gold, thus acquiring purifying properties.

Sūrya — The sun, or the sun god, a form of Viṣṇu.

sutak — A period of pollution following a birth or death. Most frequently used to denote the observance by a newly delivered mother of the period of birth pollution, ending on the morning of the eleventh day after the birth.

sutkeri — A woman in sutak after the birth of her child; by extension any woman who has recently delivered and is recovering from childbirth. (Also sutkero.)

swarga — Heaven.

Swasthāni — The supreme and transcendent form of the Devi; possibly derived from the Sanskrit svasthāna: one's own place or home. (Also used to refer to the Swasthāni Purān or Swasthāni Vrata Kathā. See below.)

Swasthāni Vrata Kathā (or Swasthāni Purān) — A religious work which tells the story of Pārvati and her marriage to Śiva and then recounts the trials of two mortal women. Repeatedly the fast or vrata in honor of the goddess Swasthāni is extolled as a means of overcoming difficulties.

swayambar — Lit. A girl's free choice of a husband: a ceremony where the bride-to-be places a garland around a man's neck signifying that she has chosen him as her husband.

tāgādhāri — "One who wears the sacred thread": the "twice-born" castes at the top of the hierarchy.

tapas — Lit. heat: austerities practiced by ascetics.

tarpaṇ — Lit. satisfaction, given or received: libations offered to the ancestor spirits.

taruni — A sexually mature girl, ready for marriage.

thakāli	Headman of a kul or lineage.
ṭhakuri	A caste group in the second, *Kṣatriya* varna, which includes the royal Shāh clan.
thar	Clan or surname.
ṭhāu sārne	"Changing place" rite during a wedding, expressing the lowering of the bride's status relative to her husband.
ṭhimbu	Lit. hybrid or mixed: offspring of irregular unions.
ṭhulo mānche	"Big man," who through age, wealth, or personality has attained high status in the community.
Tihār	A five-day festival falling during the dark half of the month of Kārtik (October–November) during which the crow, the dog, the cow, the ox, and finally brothers are worshiped on successive days. The evening of the day on which the cow is worshiped is also *diwāli* or the festival of light in honor of Lakṣmi the goddess of wealth, who is often symbolized by the cow.
tij ko barta	The 36-hour purificatory fast observed by women during the Tij–Ṛṣi Pañcami festival.
Tij–Ṛṣi Pañcami	A complex of two closely related festivals of fasting and ritual purification in which a woman ensures long life for her husband and purifies herself of the possible sin of having touched a man during her menstrual period.
ṭikā	A mark of blessing placed on the forehead.
tulsi	The sacred plant, *Ocimum basilicum,* worshiped as a form of Viṣṇu. (Also *tulasi.*)
tyāgi	A self-denying person or ascetic.
ulṭo	Backwards, in the inauspicious direction, inside out.
Umā	A name of Pārvati.
uparnā	A kind of shawl.
unamāsik	One day less than a month: the beginning of the monthly cycle of rituals performed during the first year after a death.
upanayana	The ceremony in which a young man is invested with the sacred thread.
vaiśya	The third, middle-ranking varna in the classical Hindu caste hierarchy.
vānaprastha	A man who dwells in the forest, with or without his wife—the third *āsrama* or stage of the Hindu's life.
varṇā	The four major divisions in the classical caste system of Hinduism.
vedārambha	The beginning of a four- to twelve-year study of the Vedas.
Vedas	Sacred ancient scriptures of Hinduism.

Virāni or *Baruni*	Mother of Sati Devi and 33 billion daughters; wife of Prajāpati.
Viṣṇu	One of the major Hindu gods; the god of preservation.
Yama	God of the dead.
yogī	An ascetic or religious mendicant.
Yoginidrā	A form of the goddess personified as the deep sleep into which Lord Viṣṇu fell. In this state he was almost slain by two demons Madhu and Kaitabha until the gods beseeched Yoginidrā to withdraw so that Viṣṇu could awake and destroy his attackers.
yoni	Vagina, the female organs of reproduction.

Bibliography

Acharya, Meena, and Lynn Bennett. 1981. *The Rural Women of Nepal: An Aggregate Analysis and Summary of Eight Village Studies.* The Status of Women in Nepal, vol. 2; Field Studies, Part 9. Kathmandu: Centre for Economic Development and Administration (CEDA), Tribhuvan University.

Acharya, Sri Bhanubhakta. 1968. "Badhu Siksa." In *Badhu Bar Siksa,* ed. by Bhimnidhi Tiwari. Kathmandu: Matribhumi Press.

Agrawala, Vasudeva, trans. 1963. *The Glorification of the Great Goddess* (The *Devi Mahatmya*). Banaras: All India Kashiraj Trust.

Allen, Michael. 1950. *The Cult of Kumari: Virgin Worship in Nepal.* Kirtipur: Institute of Nepal and Asian Studies, Tribhuvan University.

Ardener, Shirley, ed. 1977. *Perceiving Women.* New York: John Wiley and Sons.

Bennett, Lynn, 1973. *Two Water Case Studies.* Research-cum-Action Project, no. 5. Kathmandu: Department of Local Development/UNICEF.

—— 1974. *Locally Produced Plays as a Medium of Communication Between Village and Government in Nepal.* Research-cum-Action Project, no. 8. Kathmandu: Department of Local Development/UNICEF.

—— 1976. "Sex and Motherhood among the Brahmans and Chetris of East Central Nepal." *Contributions to Nepalese Studies* (June), no. 3. Special Issue on Anthropology, Health, and Development. Kirtipur: Institute of Nepal and Asian Studies, Tribhuvan University.

—— 1978. "*Maiti-Ghar:* The Dual Role of Women in Northern Hindu Kinship from the Perspective of the Chetris and Brahmans of Nepal." In *Himalayan Anthropology,* ed. by James Fisher. The Hague: Mouton.

—— 1979. *Tradition and Change in the Legal Status of Nepalese Women.* The Status of Women in Nepal, vol. I; Background Report, Part 2. Kathmandu: Center for Economic Development Administration (CEDA), Tribhuvan University.

—— 1981. *The Parbatiya Women of Bakundol.* The Status of Women in Nepal, vol. 2; Field Studies, Part 7. Kathmandu: Centre for Economic Development and Administration (CEDA), Tribhuvan University.

Bista, Khem Bahadur. 1969. "Tij ou la fête des Femmes." *Objets et Monde* (Spring), 5:7–18.

—— 1972. *Le Culte du Kuldevta au Nepal en particular chez certains Ksatri de la valle du Kathmandu.* Paris: Centre National de la Recherche Scientifique (CNRS).

Blustain, Harvey. 1977. "Power and Ideology in a Nepalese Village." Ph.D. diss., Yale University.

Borgström, Bengt-Erik. 1980. *The Patron and the Panca: Village Values and Panchayat Democracy in Nepal.* New Delhi: Vikas Publishing House.

Campbell, J. Gabriel. 1976. *Saints and Householders: A Study of Hindu Ritual and Myth Among the Kangra Rajputs.* Kathmandu: Bibliotheca Himalayica, Ratna Pustak Bhandar.

—— 1978. "Consultations with Himalayan Gods: A Study of Oracular Religion and Alternative Values in Hindu Jumla." Ph.D. diss., Columbia University.

Campbell, Lynn Bennett. 1971. "Śakti: Polarities of Asceticism and Fertility in the Literature and Mythology of the Devi." M.A. thesis, Columbia University.

Carstairs, Morris G. 1967. *The Twice Born.* Bloomington: Indiana University Press.

Doherty, Victor S. 1974. "The Organizing Principles of Brahman-Chetri Kinship." *Contributions to Nepalese Studies,* 2:25–41.

Douglas, Mary. 1970. *Natural Symbols: Explorations in Cosmology.* New York: Vintage.

Dube, S. C. 1967. *Indian Village.* New York: Harper and Row.

Dumont, Louis. 1961, 1964, 1966. "Marriage in India: The Present State of the Question." *Contributions to Indian Sociology,* vols. 5, 7, and 9.

—— 1970. *Homo Hierarchicus: An Essay on the Caste System.* Trans. by Willard R. Sainsbury. Chicago: University of Chicago Press.

Durgasaptasati. 1974. Banaras: Bombay Pustakalaya.

Geertz, Clifford. 1965. "Religion as a Cultural System." In *Reader in Comparative Religion: An Anthropological Approach,* ed. by W. Lessa and E. Vogt, pp. 216–26. New York: Harper and Row.

—— 1973. *The Interpretation of Cultures.* New York: Basic Books.

Ghurye, G. S. 1972. *Two Brahmanical Institutions: Gotra and Charana.* Bombay: Popular Prakashan.

Gould, H. A. 1968. "Time Dimension and Structural Change in Indian Kinship Systems: A Problem of Conceptual Refinement." In *Structure and Change in Indian Society,* ed. by M. Singer and B. Cohn. Chicago: Aldine.

Haimendorf, Christoph von Furer. 1966. "Unity and Diversity in the Chetri Caste of Nepal." In *Caste and Kin in Nepal, India, and Ceylon,* ed. by Christoph von Furer-Haimendorf, pp. 1–63. Bombay: Asia Publishing House.

Harper, Edward. 1964. "Ritual Pollution as an Integrator of Caste and Religion." In *Religion in South Asia,* ed. by Edward Harper. Seattle: University of Washington Press.

Höfer, András. 1979. "The Caste Hierarchy and the State in Nepal: A Study of the Mulki Ain of 1854." In *Kumbu Himal.* Innsbruck: Universitätsverlag Wagner.

Jacobson, Doranne. 1970. "Hindu and Muslim Purdah in a Central Indian Village." Ph.D. diss., Columbia University.

Jacobson, Doranne and Susan S. Wadley. 1977. *Woman in India: Two Perspectives.* New Delhi: Monohar.

Karve, Irawati. 1953. *Kinship Organization in India.* Deccan University Monograph Series. Madras: G. S. Press.

Lewis, Oscar. 1958. *Village Life in Northern India.* New York: Vintage.

Luschinsky, Mildred. 1962. "The Life of Women in a Village in Northern India: A Study of Role and Status." Ph.D. diss., Cornell University.

Madan, T. N. 1962. "Is the Brahmanic Gotra a Grouping of Kin?" *Southwestern Journal of Anthropology* 18: 67.

—— 1965. *Family and Kinship: Study of the Pandits of Rural Kashmir.* New York: Asia Publishing House.

Monier-Williams, Monier. 1959. *A Sanskrit English Dictionary.* Delhi: Oriental Publishers.

Nepal Rastra Bank. n.d. "Rastra Bank Household Economic Survey." Kathmandu. (Mimeographed.)

Nikhilananda, Swami. 1962. *Holy Mother.* New York: Ramakrishna-Vivekananda Center.

O'Flaherty, Wendy. 1964. "Asceticism and Sexuality in the Mythology of Siva, Part II." *History of Religions* (August), vol. 9.

—— 1973. *Asceticism and Eroticism in the Mythology of Siva.* London: Oxford University Press.

Ortner, Sherry B. and Harriet Whitehead. 1981. *Sexual Meanings: The Cultural Construction of Gender and Sexuality.* Cambridge: Cambridge University Press.

Pandey, Raj Bali. 1969. *Hindu Samskaras.* Delhi: Motilal Banarsidass.

Pargiter, Eden F., trans. 1904. *Markandeya Purana.* Bibliotheca Indica. Calcutta: Royal Asiatic Society of Bengal.

Rose, Leo E. and John T. Scholz. 1980. *Nepal: Profile of a Himalayan Kingdom.* New Delhi: Selectbook Service Syndicate (by arrangement with Westview Press).

Sharma, Babu Madhav Prasad, comp. v.s. 2022a (1955). *Rsi Pancami Vrata Katha.* Banaras: Dudhvinayak.

——, comp. v.s. 2022b (1955). *Swasthani Vrata Katha.* Banaras: Dudhvinayak.

——, n.d. *Gorkha Thar Gotra Savai.* Banaras: Dudhvinayak.

Srinivas, M. N. 1966. *Social Change in Modern India.* New Delhi: Allied Publishers.

Stevenson, Sinclair. 1971. *The Rites of the Twice Born.* New Delhi: Oriental Books.

Stone, Linda S. 1975. "Aspects of Education in Nepal." Paper presented at Seminar of Research Division, Tribhuvan University. (Mimeographed.)

—— 1976. "Illness, Hierarchy, and Food Symbolism in Hindu Nepal." Ph.D. diss., Brown University.

Tambiah, S. J., 1973. "Dowry and Bridewealth, and the Property Rights of Women in South Asia." In *Bridewealth and Dowry*, ed. by Jack Goody and S. J. Tambiah. Cambridge Papers in Social Anthropology. Cambridge: Cambridge University Press.

Turner, R. L. 1931. *A Comparative and Etymological Dictionary of the Nepali Language*. London: Routledge and Kegan Paul.

Turner, Victor W. 1969. *The Ritual Process: Structure and Anti-Structure*. Chicago: Aldine.

Van Gennep, A. 1909. *Les rites de passage*. Paris.

Van Velsen, J. 1967. "The Extended-Case Method and Situational Analysis." In *The Craft of Social Anthropology*, ed. by A. L. Epstein. New Brunswick, N.J.: Transaction Books.

Vijananananda, trans. (Hari Prasanna Chatteriji). 1922. *Sri Mad Devi Bhagvatam*. Sacred Books of the Hindus, vol. 16. Allahabad: Panini Office.

Yalman, Nur. 1963. "On the Purity of Women in the Castes of Ceylon and Malabar." *Journal of the Royal Anthropological Institute* 1963), no. 193.

Index

Abhyudayika sraddha, 62, 96, 111
Abyabdika sraddha, 96, 108
Adulthood of female, 240; see also Karma caleko
Acharya, Bhanubhakta, "Instructions for the Bride," 175, 180
Affection, displays of, 91, 176–78
Affinal men, bride's relation to, 173, 213n4
Affinal women, viii, 170–72, 218–19, 240–41, 269, 271–72, 311; ritual purity of, viii–ix, 250–51; and purity of patriline, 125–28; and agnatic solidarity, 169, 179, 214, 219, 274; suspected of witchcraft, 182–85, 197, 199, 307n3; and motherhood, 255–56; and joint families, 312–13; sexuality of, 314–15
Age: at initiation, 120nn7–8; and superior status, 142
Agnatic kin groups, viii, 18–19, 21
Agnatic relatives, death observances for, 112, 113
Agnatic solidarity, 18, 22, 129, 135–36, 142; affinal women and, 169, 179, 214, 219, 274
Agni, 49, 83, 99, 292, 293
Agricultural labor, 23–24
Agriculture, as base of economy, 23
Almsgiving, 47; see also Begging for alms; Gifts, ritual
Ancestor spirits, see Pitr
Animal husbandry, 24
Annaprasana, 121n13
Annapurna, 262
Annual mourning rites, see Ekodhista sraddha

Ardener, Edwin, 316
Ardener, Shirley, 316
"The Armor of Durga," 263–64
Artisan castes, 13
Arundhati, 228–30, 308n17
Asceticism, 39–40, 44, 50, 68, 126–27, 311–12; and ritual purity, 40–41, 43; and life-cycle rituals, 59; and fertility, 61; of death ceremonies, 100–1; of devali ceremony, 133–34; and female sexuality, 218, 224–25, 234; of Siva, 289
Ashes, sacred, 128, 253
Astrological consultations: at birth of child, 54, 120n5; for timing of kanyadan, 81
Atman, 48–49

Bandu Mandal, 7
Bara Dasai, see Dasai
Barakhi sraddha, 96–97, 108, 123n15
Barani, 75, 79–80
Barbers, 14
Barley sprouts, 139, 141, 271
Barrenness, cure for, 288
"Barring the door" ritual, 75, 89
Bartaman, 59–70; age for, 120nn7,8
Baths, purifying, 127–28; for women, 225–28, 258n13
Beads, red, 82, 242–43
Begging for alms: by sadhus, 40; in bartaman ceremony, 67–70
Behavior, proper, for women, 3, 125, 174–75, 225; see also Wife, perfect
Betrothal ceremony, 74
Bhagavata Purana, 45

Bhagwan, 47, 48–50; and menstruation of women, 216
Bhairav, 132
Bhai Tika, 142, 246–54
Bhakti, 50
Bhar, 62, 63, 76–78, 131n23; of groom, 79; of bride, 79, 88
Bhat-mara, 28
Bheti, 69, 151; to mother of groom, 78; exchange of, 151–58
Bhiksa manne, 67–70
Bhumi, 49, 62
Bhut, 49
Birth, position for, 123n55
Birth pollution rituals, 52–54; obligations for, 19, 21
Bista, K. B., 10–11, 14, 21, 131–33, 135, 222, 223, 256
Blessing gesture, 150
Blood, menstrual, 215–18, 315; see also Menarche
Blood, sacrificial, 140; drinking of, 135
Blood sacrifice, 48, 163n11, 264, 267, 271, 307nn2,7; at Dasai, 140; to Devi, 261; women barred from, 273
Brahma, 264, 307n5; sons of, 117
Brahmacarin, 59, 67
Brahmacarya, 60–61
Brahman caste, 10–11, 14–15
Brahman households, Dasai rituals in, 140
Brahmans: ritual gifts to, 104, 107, 111, 121n13; ritual feeding of, 105, 123; at death ceremonies, 112, 116–17, 148–49; ritual greetings of, 164n17; see also Priests, Brahman
Brahman women, purbanga rites by, 64
Bride: ritual status of, 83, 142, 145; subservience to husband, 91; relationship to affinal males, 173, 213n4; services to mother-in-law, 180–81; prepubescent, 235; see also Weddings
Bridegroom: clothes of, 78; festivities at home of, 78; see also Weddings
Bridegroom choice, see Swayambar
Bride's feast, 91
Bride's house, festivities at, 79–88
Bride's pavilion, rituals in, 83–87
Bride's trunk, 78
Brinda, 293
Brotherhood of devali, 135–36

Brother-in-law, relationship with bride: elder, 173; younger, 213n4
Brothers: competition of, 179; younger, 161–62
Brother/sister relationship, 142, 247–54
Budgets, household, 29–30
Burial of dead, 56

Campbell, J. Gabriel, 10, 56, 87, 126, 144–45
Candi Path, 138, 140, 163nn3,9, 263–65
Carpenters, 14
Carstairs, Morris G., 219–20
Caste hierarchy, 8–16
Caste membership, 60–61
"Catching fish" game, 75, 90
Chak khalko, 112, 113
Chandravati, 277, 294–306, 317
"Changing of clothes" marriage, 71
"Changing places" rite, 75, 87
Chastity of wives, 220, 293
Chetri caste, 10–13; bartaman roles, 69
Chetri households, Dasai ritual in, 140–41
Chewar, 65–67
Childbirth, and consanguineal male relatives, 243; see also Birth pollution rituals
Child care, 26–27
Children: agricultural work of, 24; pollution rules for, 42; vulnerability to pollution, 58; of second marriage, 71; fights of, 213n7; ritual purity of, 253–54; see also Infant
Choosing of husband ceremony, see Swayambar
Cito katne, 32n7
Civic groups, 6–7
Clans, see Gotra; Thar
Clothing: unstitched, 15, 41, 42; of bridegroom, 78; of bride, 81; of funeral procession, 98; of chief mourner, 100; of mourners, 107; new, for Dasai, 137; red, given to daughters, 239, 259n26; of widows, 244
Colors, symbolism of, 116, 229
Communitas concept, 142, 144
Community action groups, 6–8
Competitiveness within family group, 179
Conception: rituals of, 120n1; villagers' ideas of, 217–18

Conditional immortality, 37–39, 93; means to, 44–50
Conflict, in joint family, 200–12
Conjugal relationships, and patrilineal solidarity, 177, 201
Consanguineal male relatives, and birth of child, 243
Consanguineal women, viii, 142, 144–45, 235, 315; ritual purity of, ix, 250–51; see also Filiafocal relationships
Consummation of marriage, 91, 122n35
Conversation, 2
Cooking of food, 4, 26; by Brahman women, 15; of dal bhat, 41–42; wedding ritual, 91
Courts, 8
Courtship, 71
Cow: purifying products of, 43; given to bridegroom, 81, 83 (see also Godan); worship of, 247; sacred, 252–53
Cowdung, purifying, 43, 252; in purbanga rites, 62; at wedding, 88; in funeral rites, 100, 102, 117; purifying bath, 127–28; see also Gobar
Co-wife relationships, 187–200
Cow urine, purifying, 43, 104, 105, 117, 218, 252
Crafts, of Narikot women, 27
Cremation, 98–99, 122n41; of child, 57; substitute for lost body, 122n39
Crops in Narikot, 23
Culture, defined, 202
Cyame caste, 13

Daksa, 281–84, 286, 288, 297, 298
Daksina, 11, 15, 43, 55, 70, 128, 149–50; and filiafocal principles, 151; and status, 159; given to sisters, 250, 251, 260nn37,38
Dal bhat, 4, 11, 41–42; and ritual status, 12–13; wedding ritual, 91
Damai caste, 13, 14; and bartaman ceremonies, 64; musicians at wedding, 76–78, 88
Dan, 11, 15, 43, 144–45, 149; at death of infant, 56; see also Daksina; Godan
Dancing of women, 78, 180, 224–25, 258n11
Dasai, 15, 29–30, 136–41, 263–74; tika exchange, 150–62

Dasai Durga ritual, 268–72
Dasai ghar, 138
Datiun leaves, 128, 225, 226
Daughters, see Filiafocal relationships
Daughters-in-law, attitudes to, 170–72; see also Affinal women
Dead people, pitr as, 93
Death, nearness of, 308n17
Death ceremonies, 92–120, 129–31; shared, 18; sequence of, 96–97; in-laws and, 148–49; for woman, 165–66; obligations for married daughter, 213n2
Death pollution, 19–21, 32nn11–15, 98–107; at death of infant, 56; at death of child, 57; of betrothed, 74
Decoration of bride, 81, 88, 190, 191
Defiance, as behavioral choice, 313–14
Demeanor, proper, for women, 3, 225; see also Wife, perfect
Devali, 13, 131–36, 163nn5–7
Devi, ix–x, 48, 49, 132, 272, 307n5; contradictory nature of, 261–68; birth of, 265; worship of, 270; aspects of, 274, 316
Devi Bhagvatam, 288
Devi Mahatmya, 263–67, 270, 275
Devta, 48–49, 93; rituals of worship, 115, 116
Dhami, 134–35
Dharma, 34–40, 44–50, 50n1, 313; and ritual purity, 41; reward for, 94; for women, 175–76
Dhikuro sraddha, 101–4
Dhok, 69, 81, 87
Dhok dine, 90
Dhoti, 41
"Digging pure earth" ceremony, 64
Dishes, washing of, 4
Disputes, local settlement of, 7–8
Divinities, hierarchy of, 48–49
Divorce, 162, 209
Dogs, 257n1
Doherty, Victor S., 133, 179
Dolls, marriage games with, 168–69
Douglas, Mary, 34
Dowry of bride, 80–81, 147, 163n14
Dress, see Clothing
Dube, S. C., 35
Dubo grass, 62, 73, 74, 80, 128, 190
Dumont, Louis, 145, 251

Durga, 137–41, 261–68, 274, 316; worship of, 268–72, 273; destructiveness of, 269–70
Durga Kabac, 263–64
Durga puja, 269
Durga Saptasati, see *Candi Path*
Durvasa, 288
Duty: dharma as, 34; of wife, 174–75; marriage based on, 285

Ear piercing ceremony, 121n13
"Eating of polluted food" ritual, 91
Eating rituals, 41–42, 174
Eating squares, 4, 42
Economic base of parivar, 22
Education of girls, 235
Egharau sram, 104
Ekodhista sraddha, 92, 94, 97, 108–11, 297
Elements, purifying powers of, 43
Endogamy within gotra, 17
Even numbers, symbolism of, 120n6
Exogamy, 17–18
Extended families, 32n16, 311–12; see also Joint family

Family, see Parivar
Family groups, break-up of, 179
Family conflict, 200–12
Farewell of bride, 75, 88
Farm work, 23–24
Fasts, purifying, 123n47, 127; by women, 47, 219, 222–24, 257n5, 276–79, 301; see also *Rsi Pancami Vrata Katha; Swasthani Vrata Katha*
Father, role in bartaman, 67–69
Fatherhood of dependent son, 173
Fatherless son, 300–2
Father of bride, 79, 81; and in-laws, 92, 148
Father/son conflicts, 201
Feasts: wedding, 75, 87, 91; for women on eve of Tij, 222
"Feeding a snack," 75, 92
"Feeding the maur," 86
Feet, touching of, 69–70, 150, 159, 161, 163n17; in wedding ceremony, 73, 81, 84, 87, 90
Feet, washing of, 174, 175; at wedding, 75, 81–82, 91; of mother-in-law, 180
Female body, symbolism of, 214

Female identity, in ghar, 165
Female sexuality, ix, 125–28, 214; purification through motherhood, 252
Fertility: and asceticism, 61; of women, 257n4, 258n16; Devi and, 268; Durga and, 270–72
Fieldwork for this study, x–xii, xiiin3
Filiafocal relationships, viii, 144–50, 251, 314–15; and daksina exchanges, 151; status relations, 152–58, 161; and menarche of daughter, 242
"Filling a grain measure" game, 75, 89–90
Fire ceremonies, 55, 107, 121nn1,13, 140; at bartaman, 65, 70; at wedding, 75, 90
First outing of infant, 55
First rice ceremony, 57–58, 121n13
Five virgins, 261
Food gifts to bride, 79
Food processing, 24–26
Food pollution, 41–43
Food restrictions in mourning, 107
Foods for Dasai, 137
Food treats for wives, 177–78, 223
Fund drives, for community projects, 7, 31n2
Funeral procession, 98; see also Death ceremonies
Funeral pyre, 99
Funeral rites for infant, 56
Furnishings, 5–6

Gai Tihar, 247–48
"Gambling with cowries" game, 84–86
Games: ritual, at weddings, 84–86, 89–91; of marriage, in childhood, 168–69, 213n3
Ganes, 48, 49, 262, 291–93; worshiped at wedding, 74, 80, 86; worship of, 107, 128, 249, 258n14, 294
Ganga, 292, 293
Gayatri mantra, 67, 69, 100
Geertz, Clifford, 35, 202
Gender system, vii
Genealogies, 16–17; of bride, 82
Ghar, 165, 166; status of bride in, 169–72, 223; status of motherhood in, 256
Ghost of deceased, 101–2, 105
Gifts, ritual, 43, 149–50; to bride, 81–82, 92, 145, 147–48; in death rites, 102; at

gupha basne, 239–40; see also Daksina; Dan; Godan; Sidha
Girls, unmarried, 166–69
Goats, sacrificial, 163n11
Gobar, 3, 27, 42, 118; purification with, 99, 249; washing with, 226; see also Cowdung
God, villagers' concept of, 48; see also Bhagwan
Godan, 43, 117, 228; at bartaman, 65, 67, 70
Goddess, the, see Devi; Durga; Kali; Laksmi; Parvati; Sati Devi
Gods, see Devta
Goma, 294–306, 317
Gora pani khane, 174
Gorkha Thar Gotra, 17, 32n10
Goru puja, 248
Gossip, 2
Gotra, 16–18, 20, 126, 222; of bride, 74; Siva's lack of, 290–92
Gotraja, 20, 21; death obligations of, 113
Gotra rishi, 16, 220, 222
Gould, H. A., 201
Grain: processing of, 24–26; storage of, 28; sales of, 32–33n17
Grandfathers, 173
Great-grandfathers, memorial rites for, 111
Greetings, ritual, 150, 159, 161, 163–64n17; touching of feet, 69–70, 150, 159, 161, 163n17
Groom's pavilion, rituals in, 90–91
Gujeswari temple, 138, 288
Gupha basne, 59, 234–46
Guru, at bartaman, 67, 69, 70

Haimendorf, Christoph von Furer, 11, 12, 16, 136, 140, 145, 147, 179
Hair: preparation for tonsure, 64; of mourners, 100; of widows, 107; uncombed, 259n31
Haircutting rite, 65–67
Hath dhok, 164n17
Headmen, ritual, 133, 136
Head of household, 27–28
Heaven, 37, 94
Hinduism, 34–35; of Matwali groups, 13–14; caste ideology, 15; in Narikot, 34, 40, 59–60; samsara/mukti opposition, 35–40; purification rituals, 43–44; and

marriage, 71; contradictions in, 126, 273; perception of women, 214, 309–10; see also Village Hinduism
Höfer, András, 8, 10
Holy places, 287, 288, 307n9
Horoscope of child, 55, 120n5
Housecleaning, 27
Household economy, 22–31
Householder's path, 38–40, 44–50, 68, 94; life-cycle rites, 52–123; and asceticism, 59
Household gods, worship of, 41; see also Lineage gods
House repairs, at Dasai, 137
Houses, in Narikot, 3–5
House son-in-law, 111, 297
Husband: merit of wife transferred to, 47; conflicting loyalties of, 181–85; long life of, 219
Husband/wife relationship, 172–79
Hypergamous hierarchy of marriage, 145–47

Immortality: concepts of, 37–39; means to, 61; of ancestors, 93
Impure castes, 10
Incest, 282, 287, 288
Indra, 215–16, 264, 292
Infant: karma of, 53; name-giving ceremony, 54–56; burial of, 56; ritual purity of, 253–54; of unmarried mothers, 259n28
Inheritance of land, 95, 97, 122n38, 123n52, 129–30
Initiation ceremony, 59–70; age for, 120nn7–8
In-laws: father of bride's visit to, 92; attentions to, 148; see also Mother-in-law
"Instructions for the Bride" (Acharya), 175, 180
Intercaste relations, 13–16
Intermarriage: of ethnic groups, 10; of castes, 11–12
Isolation of menstruating women, 215–16, 218

Jacobson, Doranne, 173–74
Jagge, see Sacred enclosure
Jaisi Brahmans, 11
Jajamani, 14

Jalandar, 293

Janai, see Sacred thread

Janai Purni festival, 127, 220

Janti parsane, 75, 79

Jatakarma, 121n13

Jewelry of bride, 82

Jharra Chetri, 12, 130

Jobs held by villagers, 28

"Joining of the hair-braids" ceremony, 75, 89, 192

Joint family, 22, 136, 188–200, 311–12; tensions of, 186; conflict in, 200–12; affinal woman in, 219; behavior patterns, 314

Jutho, 4, 120n2, 174

Jutho/cokho opposition, 40–44

Jutho khane, 75, 91

Kali, 261, 262, 265–68

Kalratri sacrifice, 140, 270

Kamaune system, 14

Kami caste, 13, 14

Kam kuro chinne ceremony, 73

Kanyadan marriage, 12, 74–75, 80–83, 144–45, 147, 191, 235, 241, 285

Karkalo, 258n19

Karma, 36–37, 48; good, 44–45; of infant, 53; acceptance of, 306

Karma caleko, 53; and pollution, 58; women as, 59, 165; male status, 60; bride as, 74, 91

Karve, Irawati, 169

Kasai/pore caste, 13

Kausiki, 265

Khatri Chetri, 12, 32nn8–9, 130–31

Kinship units, 16–22; and life-cycle rites, 52; complementary structures, 124–64; status relationships in, 137; see also Gotra; Thar

Kinswomen, see Consanguineal women; Filiafocal relationships

Kirya basne, 92, 94–96, 98–107, 129

Kirya putra, 98, 129

Kitchens, 4

Knot, sacred, 82

Koro barne, 99–100

Koseli, 149, 168

Ksatriya caste, 10, 11

Ksetrabas, 99–101

Kul, 18, 20, 21; and death obligations, 112; size of, 131; devali of, 163n6

Kul devta, 18, 49, 131–36

Kul ghar, 19

Kumai Brahmans, 11

Kumar, 48, 49, 262, 292–93

Kus grass, 64, 65, 117, 226; in wedding ceremonies, 74, 76, 78, 80, 83; in funeral rites, 98, 99, 100, 101, 104, 105; in Janai Purni, 128; at Bhai Tihar, 249; at rishi puja, 228

Laborers, 28; agricultural, 23–24

Labor exchange groups, 23, 24

Laksmi, 247–48, 262, 270

Laksmi puja, 273

Land inheritance, 95, 97, 122n38, 123n52, 129–30

Legs, rubbing of, 176, 213n6

Liaite marriage, 71

Life-cycle rites, 50, 52; birth pollution, 52–54; name-giving, 54–56; first rice, 57–58; initiation, 59–70; marriage, 71–92; death ceremonies, 92–120

Life stages, cycle of, 59

Lineage, and asceticism, 61; see also Patriline

Lineage gods, worship of, 18, 49, 131–36

Lineal joint family, 22; see also Joint family

Liquor drinking: by child, 58; by women, 267–68

Liquor-drinking castes, 13

Living expenses, 29–30

Loans, 30

Long life: of husband, 219; of brothers, 249–51

"Looking in the mirror" rite, 75, 86

Love, nature of, 255; see also Sexual love

Madan, T. N., 18, 173, 222

Magh Swasthani Barta, 272–74

Mahadev, 221, 283; see also Siva

Mahakali, 286–87

Mahatma, 39; immortality of, 93

Mahisa, 264–65

Maita, xiiin2, 165; bride's visit to, 75, 91–92; gifts from, 147, 148; tika exchanges in, 159; attitudes to, 166–67, 169; support from, 210, 251–52; return for Tij,

223; woman viewed in, 241; widows and, 244–45; return to, 245–46, 259n32; asexuality of daughters in, 298
Male identity, and patriline, 165
Male offspring, 38, 50, 129, 281; and death rituals, 129–30
Males: kirya rituals by, 95; superiority of, 142
Mangal kalas, 63, 64, 78
Marriage: forbidden within gotra, 17; types of, 71; postponement of, 121n22; irregular, and death rites, 130; socioeconomic parity of, 147; and female status, 165; relationships in, 172–79; adjustment to, 281, 284–86, 302, 306; see also Kanyadan marriage; Remarriage; Weddings
Marriage games, in childhood, 168–69, 213n3
Married woman, accessories of, 79, 82, 229, 239–40, 242–43
Masik sraddha, 92, 94, 96–97, 108
Matrka, 62, 63
Matrka puja, 62, 121n23; room for, 79, 88, 89
Maturity, postponed in joint family, 311–12
Matwali castes, 10, 13
Maya, 39, 177
Mealtime rituals, 41–42, 174, 175
Meat: preparation of, 26; from sacrificial animal, 136, 140–41; goat meat, 163n11
Men: activities of, 2–3, 6; agricultural work of, 24
Menarche, ceremonies of, 59, 234–46
Menstrual blood, 315; symbolism of, 215–18
Menstrual pollution, 122n37, 215–16; sin of, 230–34
Menstruating woman, 163n8; purification from contact, 51n5; and dasai ghar, 138; and children, 253
Merit: earned by rituals, 45–47; nonritual, 47; of woman, transferred to husband, 47
Metals, hierarchy of purity, 44
Midwives, 14
Milk, mother's, 56, 252–54, 315
Money gifts, 150; and status, 151
Monthly mourning rites, 92, 108

Mother: role in bartaman, 69–70; status of, 254
Mother goddesses, see Matrka
Motherhood, 254–57, 315; and status of bride, 181
Mother-in-law: ritual games with, 89–90; as role in children's games, 168; relationship with daughter-in-law, 180–86; gifts from maita of bride, 223
Mother's milk, 56, 252–54, 315
Mourner, chief, 99
Mourning, year of, 107–8; see also Death ceremonies
Mourning enclosure, 99–101
Mukti, 37, 39, 48, 94
Music, 14; for weddings, 76–78, 88
Muslim Curaute caste, 31n4

Namaste, 74, 81, 150, 159, 161, 163–64n17
Name-giving ceremony, 54–56
Narikot, x, 1–16; economy of, 23; Hinduism in, 34, 38–40, 59–60; rituals performed in, 45; women of, 124; socioeconomic hypergamy of, 147; gods worshiped in, 307n5
Natal home of bride, see Maita
Nath cults, 126
National Legal Code of 1854, 8
Nau Durga, 139, 140
Navaha, 45
Navaraj, 298–306
Navaratri, 138, 268–72
Newari Hindus, 10, 11, 13
News exchange, 2
Nikhilananda, Swami, 255
Nine nights of Durga, see Navaratri
Nine planets ceremony, 75, 76
Nisimbha, 265–66
Nitya puja, 41, 123n54
Nuharan, 54–56
Number symbolism, 120n6
Nursing infants, ritual purity of, 56

Obedience, as behavioral choice, 125, 313
Obligations, ritual: shared, 19–21; for death ceremonies, 21, 92–97, 110–11
Odd numbers, symbolism of, 120n6
O'Flaherty, Wendy, 59, 61, 126, 220, 228, 262, 273, 281, 287

Old people, life-style of, 60
Oppositions, symbolic, in perceptions of women, 310
Orthodox marriage, 71–92

Panchayat system in Nepal, 6, 31n1
Pani na calne jat, *see* Untouchable castes
Parbatiya castes, 10
Parents of married couple, 160–61; *see also* In-laws; Mother-in-law
Parivar, 19, 22; as kul, 131; perceptions of, 201
Parma system, 23, 24
Partition of estate, 8, 186, 209–11
Parvati, 223–24, 262–99 passim, 317
Patrifocal kinship, viii, 128–29, 144, 310–11
Patrifocal status, 142, 152–58; and tika exchange, 150–51; of mother, 254–55
Patrifocal values, 186, 313–14
Patriline: ideology of, viii, 38, 128–29, 201, 272; and pitr, 94–97; purity of, and female sexuality, 125–28; male identity and, 165
Patrilinear units, 18–19, 22; organization of, 20; death obligations of, 113; and affinal women, 218–19
Patronage relationships of castes, 14–15
Penis envy, 167
Phuki bhai, 20, 21–22, 32n13, 112, 113
Pinda, 21, 123n48; in funeral rites, 99, 100–3, 105–7, 108, 114, 122n43, 123n50
"Pine Forest Story," 221
Pitr, 37, 49, 93–94, 123n49; and bartaman, 62–64; and patriline, 94–97; transformation of ghost to, 105; obligations to, 108–11; shared by kul, 112; status of, 114–16, 122n37; offerings to, 115, 116–17; categories of, 117, 119
Pitrlok, 37–38, 50, 94, 114; journey to, 104
Planets, propitiation of, 76
Plants, purifying powers of, 43
Polluting processes, 40–44; birth, 52–54; death, 98–107; menstruation of women, 215–16
Pollution rules for rice meals, 41–43
Polygamy, 187; sleeping arrangements, 6; and family conflict, 208; mothers-in-law,

213n8; legal status of, 213n10; problems of, 312
Prasad, 43, 51n6, 136; given at wedding, 80; from Durga, 141
Pregnancy, 53, 120n1
Prenatal rites, 120n1
Prepubescent girls, 235; marriage of, 242
Prestige, 186
Pret, 49, 98, 101; transformation to pitr, 105
Priests, Brahman, 10, 11, 15, 251, 260n39; rituals performed by, 45, 62, 65–68, 128, 227–28, 230; name-giving, 54–55; weddings, 74, 76, 79–83, 89; death ceremonies, 101, 104, 105, 107; Swasthani fast, 277, 278; *see also* Brahmans
Priesthood, 251
Puja, 47, 48
Pujari, 133, 134
Purbanga rites, 62–64; for wedding, 74–76, 120n9
Purbiya Brahmans, 11
Purdah, 173
Purifying agents, 43–44, 252–53
Purifying rituals, 43–44, 50–51n5, 117; of kitchen area, 4; after giving birth, 55; of menstruating women, 218; of women, 224, 225–28
Purity, ritual, viii–ix, 40–44; of child, 56–58; of consanguineal women, 250–51; of Durga, 266–68
"Putting on the vermilion powder," 75, 86–87

Raksabandhan festival, 260n34
Raktabij, 266, 268
Randi, 219
Ratauli, 75, 78, 180
"Reassembling the body," 101–4
Red color, 116, 229
Red marriage beads, 82, 242–43; *see also* Married woman, accessories of
Red powder, 61, 116; not used in mourning, 107
Relatives at wedding, 81–82
Religion, xiin1, 34–35; and marriage, 71; Hindu, *see* Dharma; Hinduism
Religious devotion, 50
Remarriage, 258n11, 260n42, 308n15; and status, 12

Reputation of women, 125; of unmarried girl, 241
Respect-avoidance relationships of bride, 173–74
"Return of the bride," 75, 91–92
Reversals, in death ceremonies, 102, 115, 116
Rice: culture of, 23; processing of, 26; cooked, and ritual purity, 4, 41–42, 53, 57; see also Dal Bhat
Rice balls, ritual, see Pinda
Rice-feeding ceremony for infant, 57–58
Rig Veda, 287
Rishi pancami, 218–34, 258n19
Rishi puja, 228
Rishis, 16, 32n10, 126, 127, 220–22, 233–34, 297, 301; offerings to, 229; wives of, 220, 292, 293
Rituals, organized by women, 45
Ritual status, 12–13
Ritual superiority of consanguineal women, 251
Ritu dan, 217–18
"Roasting the puffed rice" rite, 86
Rsi Pancami Vrata Katha, 215–16, 230–34
Rudra, 282, 287

Sacred enclosure: for bartaman, 64–66; for wedding, 74–76, 77, 88; for death ceremonies, 107, 122nn44–45
Sacred knot, 82
Sacred thread, 127, 163n1, 220, 239; reception of, 61, 67; new, 78, 128; position of, 115–16, 117
Sacred vessel: of groom, 86; of bride, 88
Sacrificial animal, meat of, 135, 140–41; see also Blood sacrifice
Sadhus, 40
Saints, 39, 93; burial of, 56
Sai pata, 75, 79
Salutations, see Greetings, ritual
Samsara, 36–39, 93; purity and, 41; hierarchy of objects in, 43; freedom from, 50; infant and, 53, 56
Samskara, see Life-cycle rites
Sanakadi, 117
Sankar, 132
Sano jat, 13
Sansari Devi, 261
Sanyasi, 60

Sanyasi dharma, 39
Sapinda sraddha, 105–7, 113, 114
Sapindi bhai, 19–21, 112–14
Saptaha, 45
Sarki caste, 13, 14
Sati Devi, 262, 281–89, 294
Satya Narayan puja, 45
Sayya dan, 80–81, 104
School, public, 6–7
Second marriage, see Remarriage
Secular greetings, 161
"Seeing the face": marriage rite, 75, 90; menarche prohibition, 236
Segregation of menstruating women, 215–16, 218
Servants, 28; of bride, 121n29
Service castes, 14–15
Seven matrkas, 261, 266, 307n2
Seven rishis, 49; see also Rishis
Sexual intercourse, 257n4, 258n16; and woman's status, 176–77; obligatory, 217–18
Sexuality: of women, ix, 214, 252; of affinal women, 125–28; and spiritual power, 126; expression of, 177; Hindu attitudes to, 314–15
Sexual love, views of, 176–79, 220, 255
Sexual symbolism of vermilion mark ritual, 87
"Shadow of the lamp" rite, 88–89
Sharecropping, 23
"Showing the storeroom" rite, 75, 90
Sidha, 43, 62, 63, 108, 135; offered to pitr, 114, 116
Simbha, 265–66
Sin, 37, 45; refusal of sexual intercourse, 87; of menstruating women, 215, 216; menstrual blood and, 216–17; and widowhood, 219, 243; of menstrual pollution, 230–34; and gifts, 260n40
Sister/brother relationship, 142, 247–54
Sisters-in-law, 245–46
Sita, 262
Sitala, 56, 261
"Sitting in a corner," 54, 243
"Sitting in mourning," 98
Situational analysis of joint family conflict, 200–2
Siva, 48, 49, 132, 221, 223, 229, 257n8, 262, 264, 281–301 passim

Siva Bhatta, 294
Siva Sakti, 308n14
Siva Sarma, 295–99
Sleeping arrangements, 5–6
Sleeping position, 122–23n46
Smallpox victims, burial of, 56
Soap, 116, 226
Social aspects of Dasai, 137
Socioeconomic hypergamy, 147–48
Sons, 38, 50, 129, 281; and death rites, 122n44, 129–30; patrifocal obedience of, 186
Sora sraddha, 92–93, 96, 111–12, 114–20, 123n53, 137; women and, 166
Spirit world hierarchy, ancestors in, 93–94
Sraddhas, see Death ceremonies
Status: ritual, 12–13; and farm labor, 23–24; reversal at wedding, 83–87; sex-determined, 125; kin group relationships, 137; tika as index of, 150
"Staying in a cave," 59, 234–46
Storage spaces, 4–5
Structural analysis of family conflict, 202
Structure concept, 142–44
Suddha santi, 107
Sudra caste, 10
Sukla Dev, 68
Surya, 49, 258n21
Sutak, 52–54, 98, 120n2
Swarga, 37, 94
Swasthani fast: by Parvati, 290; by Goma, 299–300
Swasthani rituals, 273–79, 304–6
Swasthani Vrata Katha, 220–21, 223–24, 257n8, 274–81, 294, 306, 317; attitudes re, 307–8n11
Swayambar ceremony, 15, 71, 73–75, 121nn19,21, 190, 285

Tagadari, 10
Tailors, 14
Tambiah, S. J., 145–47
Tapas, 61
Taraka, 289–90
Tarpan, 96, 108, 111, 114–15, 117, 123n54
Taruni, 237, 240
Teething of infant, 57
Thakuri caste, 10, 11
Thar, 16, 18, 20
Theft: fear of, 2; within families, 31

Thimbu Chetri, 12, 130
Thread, see Sacred thread
Thulo manche, 7–8
Tihar festival, 7, 247–49, 272
Tij–Rishi Pancami, 218–34, 357–58nn8–10, 272, 273, 278
Tika, giving of, 133, 141; at name-giving ceremony, 55; at bartaman, 70; at wedding, 73, 74, 80, 81; during mourning year, 107; in death ceremonies, 116; ritual exchange of, 150–62, 164n18; from husband, 162; symbolism of, 271
Tonsure, 65, 121n14
Transcendent immortality, 37, 39–40, 48, 94
Transmigration of soul, 36, 38, 39; see also Samsara
Tulsi, 3, 98, 99
Turner, R. L., 36, 149
Turner, Victor, 142–44

Umbilical cord, cutting of, 54
Uncle, maternal, role in bartaman, 69
Unmarried girls, 166–69; prepubescent, 235
Unmarried mothers, 241–42, 259n29
Unstitched garments, 41, 42; worn by Brahman women, 15
Untouchable castes, 10, 13, 14–15; food taken by child from, 58
Upadhaya Brahmans, 11, 24, 130
Upanayana, 67
Uterine ties, and family conflict, 208

Vanaprastha, 59, 60
Van Gennep, A., 104
Van Velsen, J., 200, 202
Varna system, 9, 10, 11
Vedic fire ceremony, see Fire ceremonies
Vedic study ceremony, 70
Vermilion powder, 259n30; mark in hair, 75, 86–87, 242–43, 259n30
Village Hinduism, 35, 37–40, 279; bartaman ceremony, 60; death rituals, 93; forms of Devi, 261; Parvati and, 273
Village perceptions of family conflict, 209
Virani, 281
Virbhadra, 286–87
Virgin gift, bride as, 71–73, 80–83, 144–45; see also Kanyadan marriage

Virtue of woman, 233
Visiting, 1–2, 137, 141
Visnu, 49, 221, 264, 282–93 passim, 307n5

Wages for farm labor, 23
Warrior caste, see Chetri caste; Ksatriya caste
Washing, purification by, 127–28
Washing of dishes, 4
Water libations, ritual, see Tarpan
Water vessels, sacred, 78, 79
Weddings, 71–92, 189–93; Chetri, 15; and bartaman, 60
Welcoming of groom, 75, 79–80
Wheat, culture of, 23
White color, 116
Widower, remarriage of, 107; see also Remarriage
Widows, 219, 243–44; mourning rituals of, 100; mourning restrictions, 107; and consanguineal males, 244–45
Wife: accessories of, 79, 82, 229, 239–40, 242–43; attitude to husband, 91, 172–79; duties of, 174–75; and motherhood, 256; perfect, attributes of, 272–73, 285, 294
Wife-givers, 145–47, 160; status of, 144, 149

Wife-takers, status of, 144, 145, 148, 160
Witchcraft: fear of, 2, 259n24; at meal-times, 50n4; feared at wedding, 86; attributed to wives, 182–85, 197, 199, 307n3; feared at menarche, 238
Wives of rishis, 220, 292, 293
Women: status of, viii–ix, 124–25, 129, 142, 269; activities of, 3; work of, 24–27; rituals performed by, 41, 45–47; merit transferred to husband, 47; initiation of, 59; and kirya rituals, 95; sequence of inheritance, 97; and death rituals, 129; and devali, 133; consanguineal relationships, 144; and patrilinear group, 165; death obligations, 165–66; unmarried, 166–69; sexual strategies of, 176–77; strategies of, 188–200; Hindu perception of, 214, 309–10; and long life of husband, 219; self-view of, 316; see also Affinal women; Bride; Consanguineal women

Yalman, Nur, 252–53
Yama, 248–50
Yellow color, 116
Yellow powder, in funeral rites, 98, 99
Yellow thread, protective, 128, 248
Youth organizations, 7